PRAIRIE CAPITALISM

PRAIRIE CAPITALISM:

Power and Influence in the New West

John Richards and Larry Pratt

Canada in Transition Series
McCLELLAND AND STEWART

The Canadian Publishers
McClelland and Stewart Limited
25 Hollinger Road
Toronto

CANADIAN CATALOGUING IN PUBLICATION DATA

Richards, John.
  Prairie capitalism

(Canada in transition series)

Includes index.
ISBN 0-7710-7179-5 pa.   ISBN 0-7710-7177-9 bd.

1. Alberta – Economic policy.   2. Saskatchewan –
Economic policy.   3.   Petroleum industry and trade –
Alberta.   4. Gas, Natural – Alberta.   5. Potash
industry and trade – Saskatchewan.   I. Pratt,
Lawrence.   II. Title.   III. Series.

HC117.A6R53   338'.09712   C79-094297-6

Printed and bound in Canada by Webcom Limited

Contents

To Christiane
To Tricia, Rebecca, Shaun, and Kate

Preface

Although the actual writing of this book occurred in 1977 and 1978, its origins should be traced to our first meeting – in Edmonton one cold wintry afternoon in early 1974. Much of that initial conversation (and far too many subsequently!) revolved around the international oil crisis – the Arab embargo had not yet been lifted and world oil prices had recently quadrupled – and its impact on Canada. Repeatedly did we return to the effects of the oil crisis on western Canada. Relations between the western oil-producing provinces and Ottawa were tense and embittered because of federal energy policies; there would be further deterioration in those relations as 1974 wore on. It seemed to us the upheavals in energy politics, at a world level and within Canada, would have a lasting influence on the political and economic strategies of the provincial governments of Alberta and Saskatchewan. Their ideological differences notwithstanding, the NDP in Regina and its Conservative counterpart in Edmonton had been so angered in the autumn of 1973 by what they perceived as a fundamental encroachment by Ottawa upon provincial jurisdiction over resources that they overcame accumulated bureaucratic inertia and broke with their tradition of passive entente with the oil industry. Both provincial governments unilaterally terminated long-standing arrangements, formal and informal, with the petroleum industry, and rushed through sweeping new omnibus bills designed to strengthen the capacity of the provinces, first, to withstand further assaults from the federal government and, second, to capture the incremental economic rents from resource price increases.

We set out to analyse these events, but to do so without reference to the history, of which they constitute merely the last chapter, appeared superficial. Inevitably we found ourselves tracing the patterns of development in these two provinces back to the 1930s and beyond. From the morass of primary and secondary sources upon which we relied two themes predominate. The first is the nature of public entrepreneurship generated by the various left and right populist movements of the prairies, and the inability of populist culture and institutions to survive the transition of prairie society from an economy based on wheat to one based on new mineral staples. In both provinces the populist thrust to exert local control over the pattern of prairie development was by 1950 largely spent, and the provincial governments entered into a passive rentier entente with the external and largely foreign companies dominating the burgeoning resource sector. The second theme is the re-emergence during the 1970s of provincial entrepreneurship – under a social democratic guise in Saskatchewan and, in the far more significant case of Alberta, under a form of dirigisme in which the provincial government and an arriviste local bourgeoisie act in tandem.

Another influence on our collaboration deserves mention. In attempting to grasp the broad changes which have overtaken western Canada since the war, we were tangentially engaged in intellectual debate with the "left-nationalist" perspective on Canadian economic and political development – a perspective we had shared, but many of whose assumptions and conclusions we came gradually to reject. The nationalist critique should be grasped in conjunction with the political vehicles articulating it; the two most visible during the last decade were the Committee for an Independent Canada and the Waffle, respectively related (in terms of leading personnel and in terms of incestuous bonds of conflict) to the Liberals and NDP. We both participated in the Waffle, witnessing its brief existence from within. Overtaken by events it slipped within half a decade into political oblivion, but the Waffle has left an intellectual legacy – a certain unqualified dependency theory that views Canada as having suffered an uninterrupted series of exploitative relations with metropolitan powers: France, Britain, and now the United States.

Albeit American capital and culture do play an excessive role in Canada and do currently threaten the integrity of the nation, the left-nationalist version of dependency theory was, we concluded, curiously incomplete and flawed: centralist in its sympathies, it was largely indifferent to the persistent problems of regionalism and the growth of interregional rivalries in Canada in the 1970s; impatient with the legalistic and institutional traditions of federalism and with regionalism (at least outside Quebec), it ignored the complex historical relationship between national economic development and the federal political system, and underestimated the entrepreneurial role, past and present, of the provincial state in English Canada; obsessed (here was the leading dogma) with demonstrating the dependent and moribund nature of Canadian capitalism within North America, it could not account for the emergence in the 1970s of an ambitious arriviste bourgeoisie in a province such as Alberta. It drew unwarranted generalizations that economic specialization upon staple products inevitably implied political dependency of that region upon the "metropolis" to which it exported, and finally, generally underestimated the autonomy of the state in Canada, notably in its relationship to foreign capital. In Marxist terms it committed the fallacy of reductionism, analysing all events as the intended outcome of some dominant class, in this case American capitalists. These were not unimportant deficiencies and it became obvious to us that the left-nationalist critique could not be applied to post-war prairie development without leading us into a swamp of egregious error. *Prairie Capitalism* thus emerged as our attempt to evolve a more satisfactory analysis, at least with respect to two of Canada's provinces. While certain themes are relevant beyond the prairie context, we have not attempted to generalize beyond Saskatchewan and Alberta.

We have received much help and encouragement from friends and colleagues while writing this book.

Our first acknowledgement must be to Ed Dosman and David Bell who invited us to publish our manuscript in the Canada in Transition Series and later provided us with valuable editorial advice and assistance.

We owe a large debt of thanks to Premier Allan Blakeney, former Premier Tommy Douglas, and Mrs. Vicki Lloyd, widow of the late Premier Woodrow Lloyd, for permission to consult government archival material bearing on economic development and politics in Saskatchewan since 1944. Their undefensive attitude on access to historical records was in refreshing contrast to the negative reception our enquiries for analogous access to historical Alberta records provoked from the Alberta government. Senator Ernest Manning was, however, kind enough to tape a lengthy account of Social Credit's policies with our researcher, Barry Wilson.

For invaluable help with research we thank Barry Wilson, who spent the summer of 1976 conducting interviews with approximately fifty Alberta businessmen, politicians, and government officials, and to Laurie Hunter who spent much of the following summer digging for statistics.

Three respected friends, Leo Panitch, Allan Tupper, and Ken Norrie, were good enough to read drafts of large sections of the manuscript; their comments and criticisms were always to the point. John Burton, with his intimate experience of the Saskatchewan government and of the CCF-NDP dating back to the early 1950s, guided us to relevant sources and offered informed criticism. We also received a variety of aid and sustenance from Ed Shaffer, Dave Gillen, Terry Levesque, Pat McDonald, Bob Moncur, Don Ching, Ian McKay, Don Gordon, John McCallum, Tom Gunton, Doug Karvonen, Don Kerr, Michael Fellman, Allan Hustak, Andy Jackson, Mike Lebowitz, Trish Smith, and Christiane Richards.

We interviewed many busy individuals while doing research for the book. We are particularly grateful to Robert Blair, Dianne Narvik, Nick Taylor, David Cargo, ex-governor of New Mexico, Senator Dave Steuart, Hon. Roy Romanow, and Hon. Elwood Cowley. Among the most enjoyable and spirited conversations were with Joe Phelps and his wife, Eva. As minister in the first CCF cabinet, from 1944 to 1948, Joe Phelps played a significant role in establishing precedents for provincial entrepreneurship.

For their assistance we wish to thank the highly competent staffs of the Saskatchewan Archives in Regina, and the Alberta and Saskatchewan legislative libraries. And, finally our warm thanks to Donna Wilson who undertook the gruesome task of retyping the entire manuscript under pressure of a deadline.

This book has been a collaboration in the fullest sense of the word. We are jointly responsible for all the ideas and interpretations put forward in the pages that follow. Those mentioned above may take credit for whatever the book contains of value but, as is traditional, are not held responsible for its failings. That our collaboration finally produced something more than a string of broken New Year's resolutions ("This year, by God, we'll finish the damn thing!") is largely owing to the forbearance of Trish Smith and Christiane Richards.

Edmonton and Vancouver
January 1979

Editors' Foreword

The volumes in this series, *Canada in Transition: Crisis in Political Development*, draw on concepts and theories from the field of political development, in an attempt to place our current national dilemma in historical perspective. As a country embedded from the outset in the political and economic fortunes of powerful neighbours, Canada has encountered unique social, economic, and political obstacles to unity and cohesion. Indeed, the term "crisis" denotes for us the central features of the Canadian experience: a fascinating mix of dangers and opportunities in a rapidly changing international environment.

Prairie Capitalism: Power and Influence in the New West by Professors Richards and Pratt is a path-breaking work from this perspective. The unparallelled prosperity in the 1970s of these two traditionally agricultural, but now also mineral-rich, provinces is well known. The implications, however, are less clearly understood, and they are not confined to the West. Rather we are witnessing a historic shift in the economic centre of gravity away from Central Canada — a development which concerns every province and region of the country.

Immediately many questions arise. Long accustomed to platitudes regarding "the golden horseshoe," scholars have neglected the study of regional political economy in the West. What are Alberta and Saskatchewan really like? What forces have shaped their history, and their sense of alienation from central Canada? What role have the governments of these two provinces, both with rich though different populist legacies, played in creating the conditions for economic growth? How have their societies been changed in the process? What has been the interplay of federal institutions and corporate interests in the determination of Alberta and Saskatchewan to change the rules of the game? Have they been successful?

Professor Richards, an economist, and Professor Pratt, a political scientist, have blended the insights from their respective disciplines to produce an authoritative examination of these central questions. Disrespectful of established orthodoxy, and exhaustively researched, the book is a careful, absorbing interpretation which will be welcomed by all Canadians as the momentum of development in Western Canada gathers strength.

David V.J. Bell
Edgar J.E. Dosman

1

CHAPTER 1
Introduction

It is sometimes argued by Canadian socialists that their opposition to the United States is not based on narrow nationalism, but on the fact that complete American domination would tend to prevent Canada as a community from realizing values good for human beings. In other words they believe that socialism can more easily be achieved in Canada, as a smaller unit, than on the whole North American continent. Surely then they should not underestimate the importance of trying to realize socialism in the even smaller units of the provinces, which have, within the limits of the constitution and particularly of section 92, many of the prerogatives of sovereign states.

> P.E. Trudeau
> "The Practice and Theory of Federalism"
> in M. Oliver (ed.), *Social Purpose for Canada* (Toronto: University of Toronto Press, 1961), 377

Prairie Capitalism is a study in regional political economy. Its focus is on the provincial governments of Alberta and Saskatchewan and their development policies during the rise of the post-war resource industries of oil, natural gas, and potash in western Canada. We trace the impact of the new staples on the economic base, class structure, and political institutions of prairie society, but our central and unifying theme throughout the book is the gradual, if uneven, emergence of the provincial state as an entrepreneurial actor in staple-led economic development. What factors have shaped the nature and role of the province as entrepreneur?

The question is not a familiar one. Neither economists nor political scientists have traditionally evinced much more than a negative interest in the behaviour of the provincial state in the Canadian development process. With a few noteworthy exceptions, such as H.V. Nelles' studies of Ontario's resource policies,[1] students of development in Canada have regarded the provinces as institutional impediments to the growth of national entrepreneurship. At best, the provinces have been tolerated as constraints upon federal decision-making, pulling simultaneously in opposing directions and thereby exercising a conservative veto power over Ottawa; at worst, they have been viewed as backwaters of reaction, the allies or dependencies of business interests (often foreign) determined to neutralize federal intervention through the mobilization of regional opinion.

Certainly few observers have regarded the provinces as competent, relatively autonomous agents of economic development. Bora Laskin exemplifies the critical stance. "Has provincial autonomy been secured?" he asked in 1947. "In terms of positive ability to meet economic and social problems of interprovincial scope, the answer is no. A destructive negative autonomy exists, however, which has as a corollary that the citizens of a province are citizens of the Dominion for certain limited purposes only."[2]

The conventional economic wisdom holds that previous successful nation-building enterprises justify current attempts by Ottawa to enlarge its entrepreneurial leadership role, at the expense of parochial exercises in province-building. Even if their development goals are legitimate, the provinces are allegedly incompetent to pursue them. Summarizing the lessons drawn from the various provincial development fiascos documented by Philip Mathias in *Forced Growth*, Abraham Rotstein commented at the opening of the 1970s that "our provincial governments appear vulnerable, if not helpless, before the magnitude and complexity of these projects." Rotstein fixed the blame for provincial weakness on "the absence of expertise, judgment, experience and reliable advice on which these governments can draw. They are hardly a match for the sophisticated and experienced multinational corporations who are often called upon to be their partners. Given the present level of technical and administrative competence, it seems highly premature to propose that [provincial] governments take over the whole area of regional development on their own."[3]

Implicit in the diagnosis of provincial impotence has been a rather paternalistic faith in the rejuvenating powers of a strong dose of centralization. Kari Levitt, for instance, gloomily predicted in *Silent Surrender* that without determined federal leadership, the provinces would drift further into the orbit of continentalism, reinforcing the trend to balkanization and wholesale Canadian political disintegration. Though she sympathized with Quebec's nationalist evolution, she felt that collectively the provinces had emasculated the nation-building initiative of an already weak federal government. "They opposed the

4

rationalization of the fiscal structure proposed by the Carter Commission and the government White Paper on taxation; they pressured the federal government into begging exemption from the U.S. interest equalization tax. They may be expected to oppose each and every measure devised to control the terms on which foreign capital may enter Canada. In the absence of effective leadership by Ottawa they reinforce the continentalism of big business by dismembering the federal structure of Canada."[4]

These are ancient complaints of Canadian political and economic commentary, and nowhere are they more dogmatically entrenched than on the English-speaking left. Impatience with provincialism and indeed with federalism itself is one of its foremost distinguishing traits. Indeed its dominant tradition, apart from its incorrigible penchant for sectarianism, is one of unabashed centralism, expressed as the belief that only a powerful federal government armed with overriding legislative and financial powers can regulate modern industrial capitalism and set in motion the transition towards a socialist society. The Anglo-Canadian left understands federalism as a pyramid of powers and hierarchies, with Ottawa holding overriding emergency powers as well as all the requisite legal and economic authority necessary for nation-building, and with the provinces relegated to the status of subordinate and purely local units. If few have dared say it aloud, many spokesmen of the English-Canadian left privately agree with that grandest of centralists, John A. Macdonald, who commented in 1864 that, "If this Confederation goes on you ... will see both local governments and all governments absorbed in the General Power."[5] The left has bitterly decried the degree to which Macdonald's centralist aspirations, embodied throughout the British North America Act of 1867, have been thwarted.

In the 1930s, when the inability of the provinces to cope with the devastating effects of the great depression was plain for all to see, all groupings on the Anglophone left demanded political and constitutional centralization and attacked the Judicial Committee of the Privy Council in London for having upheld provincial rights and undermined the centralist doctrines of the Fathers of Confederation. Lords Watson and Haldane and the other villains of the Privy Council had emasculated the federal powers adumbrated in the opening "peace, order and good government" clause of s.91, and "the regulation of trade and commerce" in s.91(2) of the British North America Act. "Canadian federalism has developed continuously away from the original design. Constitutionally we have grown disunited," declared Frank Scott, McGill law professor, a founder of the Fabian-modelled League for Social Reconstruction and prominent figure in the CCF.

"The Dominion Parliament does not play today the full part which the Fathers of Confederation planned for her ... Just at the time when the exigencies of the economic situation called for drastic action, for increased international co-operation and for a planned internal order, we find ourselves with cumbrous legislative machinery and outworn constitutional doctrines."[6] Scott argued that the "large economic interests" who opposed government regulation sided with the provinces in the attempt to weaken Ottawa's reach. This was echoed by Frank Underhill, another prominent CCF-LSR intellectual, who described provincial rights as "largely camouflage put up by our industrial and financial magnates." "The only province which has not been subject to the regular alternation between short periods of comparatively good government and long periods of decay is Quebec," Underhill wrote in 1931. "In Quebec they enjoy bad government all the time."[7]

Nothing, accordingly, could be accomplished through the exercise of power in the provinces. The left must form the government in Ottawa and augment federal power by constitutional change. Without centralization, national economic planning could not go forward, nor could the private centralizing impulse of modern industrial capitalism be constrained. Section 9 of the CCF's 1933 Regina Manifesto demanded amendment of the BNA Act "so as to give the Dominion government adequate powers to deal effectively with urgent economic problems which are essentially national in scope. ... Our constitution must be brought into line with the increasing industrialization of the country and the consequent centralization of economic and financial power." In its 1938 brief to the (Rowell-Sirois) Royal Commission on Dominion-Provincial Relations, the Communist Party of Canada justified its call for "national unification" by portraying Ottawa as representative of that which was progressive about Canadian capitalism and the provinces as remnants of backwardness and reaction: "Confederation represented a compromise of the rising industrial capitalist class, desiring internal free trade and central jurisdiction over external trade, with pre-capitalist and semi-feudal influences, seeking to preserve the powers of landlordism and feudalism in the provinces."[8] Federalism, from this perspective, was but a temporary concession to uneven development, another transitional stage enroute to an era when the "semi-feudal" influences of regionalism and provincialism would be levelled beneath the steamroller of industrialization and the socialization of the the means of production.

Underlying the centralist bias of the Anglophone left is a tactical confusion and naiveté that is sometimes breathtaking. We argue later, in our review of the development policies of the first CCF government in Saskatchewan, that the left's singleminded and largely fruitless pursuit of power at the centre and its impatience with provincial autonomy have limited its contribution to the debate over the prospects for progressive change via the provincial state. The rigidity of the English-speaking left, which persists to this day in the national NDP, has probably on balance retarded the development of socialism in Canada and its regions – a point which has always been understood by the Francophone left.

In a classic essay written in the early 1960s, Pierre Trudeau argued, quite correctly, that a relatively decentralized federal system presented far more alternatives for creative radical politics than did a highly centralized unitary state, but the centralist thrust of Anglophone socialists ignored the possibilities of building regional and provincial socialist bases. Far from welcoming the given federal system "as a valuable tool which permits dynamic parties to plant socialist governments in certain provinces, from which the seeds of radicalism can slowly spread," the English-Canadian left continued to regard the federal division of powers as an unfortunate datum of history. Approvingly citing Mao Tse-tung on strategy and tactics ("Revolution and revolutionary wars proceed from birth to development, from small to large, from lack of power to seizure of power"), Trudeau indicted the tacticians of the national CCF for their inflexibility and insensitivity to the differing circumstances and requirements of particular regions and provinces and their insistence on "speaking with one voice and acting with one purpose" in all parts of the country. "In Quebec alone, where the socialist vote has usually hovered around one per cent of the total, a book could be filled with the frustrations of former members of the CCF who felt or imagined that provincial affairs must always be subordinate to the raison d'état of the national party." Himself soon to be a "former member" of the CCF, Trudeau noted that while party strategists sometimes argued that the road to national power might well lie through the provinces, by denigrating the value of provincial rights they effectively precluded that very option: "Such subservience of the tacticians to the postulates of the 'theory class' is amazing, in spite of the fact that the CCF has become the government or the official opposition in several provinces, whereas it has never come within sight of such successes in the national Parliament."9

Prairie Capitalism is not a celebration of what Premier Lougheed of Alberta calls the "New West," nor is it a polemic in favour of provincial rights and autonomy. But it does take the provinces and "province-building" seriously. We begin from an acceptance of two undeniable facts of Canadian life: that Canada is a country of regions, and that under the political and constitutional system as it has evolved, what can be accomplished through the exercise of power in the provinces is by no means insignificant.

We cannot agree that the provincial state lacks either competence or the capacity for entrepreneurial initiative. Nor can we accept the image of the provinces as the captive dependencies or instruments of international capital. There is no evidence for the argument that big business in Canada has typically resisted centralization and supported provincial autonomy. The only things that capital consistently supports are its own interests, and when these have been threatened by aggressive provincial governments, business has unhesitatingly pushed for a stronger central government. When Ontario moved to nationalize hydro-electric installations in the early years of this century, large capital threw its weight behind centralization in the attempt to nullify provincial initiatives; local business, on the other hand, recognized that its goal of cheap power was most readily attainable through the exercise of provincial authority in a decentralized federation.[10] Capital arrayed itself on the side of Ottawa in the 1930s in its war with Aberhart's Alberta.[11] And if the oil industry used its traditional alliances with the producing provinces to blunt the movement towards federal tax reforms in the late 1960s or to argue for federal concessions for Syncrude, it has also allied itself with Ottawa in its constitutional struggles with Saskatchewan. About all that can be concluded is that big business understands that a federal political system provides interest groups with a number of potential sources of leverage and veto points, and that capital, like perfidious Albion, has no permanent allies or enemies, only permanent interests.

In our study of the development of the oil, natural gas, and potash industries of Alberta and Saskatchewan we find no confirmation of the thesis that provinces heavily dependent on the exploitation and sale of staples are thereby placed in a permanent position of political dependency vis à vis external capital. We reject this view for two reasons. First, it ignores the obvious fact that some of Canada's provinces are far stronger than others. Second, it assumes that relationships of power are constant over time, and that the advantages in bargaining over terms of economic development are heavily weighted in favour of the foreign investor, not merely at the outset but in perpetuity. Our analysis of resource development in post-war Alberta and Saskatchewan suggests this to be a profoundly static view of bargaining, and one whose false political implications should be evident.[12] If the original concession agreements reflect the asymmetries of power in the initial negotiations over the terms of development, the agreements tend to be unstable because of shifts in uncertainty and risk and because provincial governments have a strong incentive gradually to move up a learning curve of skills, information and expertise.

Once the foreign investor has sunk his costs and has fixed assets in place and his monopoly of expertise has been eroded, under certain conditions there occurs a shift in power toward the province. The economic and social character of the region is changed by development of the new export staple. Markets change, profits rise, and provincial pressure groups, including elements within the state bureaucracy, insist upon re-negotiation of the original concession. As the opportunity costs of inertia grow, new administrations come to power determined to utilize resources for ambitious strategies in economic development but are constrained by the dead weight of earlier decisions. Encroachments by the federal government have served as catalysts to provoke the provinces into defensive interventions, which in turn create tensions with the resource industries. Within the context of a changing balance of bargaining power, conflicts arise among the provinces, federal government, and the international firm over the distribution of rents, pricing, and rates of development; or over the regional impact of the investor's operation. What begins as a relatively simple and highly unequal, often exploitative relationship evolves into a much more complex pattern of relations as the provincial government moves up a learning curve of skills and negotiating expertise and the foreign company faces the steady erosion of its monopoly power.

A brief preliminary overview of developments in Alberta and Saskatchewan can serve as illustration. Prior to 1930 the primary goal of prairie politicians was to improve the prairie's terms of trade within an economic environment of agricultural staples established by the National Policy. The economic disasters of the 1930s – combining drought, an end to the prairie agricultural frontier, and depressed international markets for cereals – led in the 1940s to the prairies' first consistent political debates, particularly within the CCF in Saskatchewan, of broad economic development issues. How could the prairie economy diversify to lessen the preponderance of agriculture? What was the appropriate role for private capital as an alternative to public investment by the provincial government? Should priority be attached to import substitution secondary manufacturing or to new non-agricultural mineral staples?

During its first term of office from 1944 to 1948 the CCF in Saskatchewan experimented with crown-owned secondary manufacturing ventures (e.g. woollen mill, shoe factory/tannery) which were in effect an attempt by a regional government to exercise autarkic (i.e. self-contained) development, in the hope that the natural barrier of high transportation costs from eastern Canada would provide adequate protection to permit the growth of a more sizeable indigenous manufacturing sector supplying the provincial market. The hope proved illusory and, despite determined efforts, the government was unable to overcome the basic cost disadvantages of these small manufacturing ventures. The fundamental problem was not the form of ownership, for while failing in manufacturing the CCF succeeded with most of the crown corporations it launched in several non-agricultural staples (e.g. a sodium sulphate mine, the Timber Board). Clearly, in industries in which the province did have a comparative advantage, provincial crown corporations could operate efficiently and negotiate sales successfully in external markets over which the CCF had no control.

By 1946 the Saskatchewan Government Planning Board drew the appropriate conclusion that the potential of manufacturing within the province had been "considerably overrated," and argued "that any substantial diversification of the provincial economy is most likely to arise from the development of our major natural resources."[13] Oil and potash discoveries within the next decades vindicated the Board's prognosis, for both Alberta and Saskatchewan. Henceforth the major arena for provincial entrepreneurship in both provinces would be mineral staples. Although the original CCF cabinet intention was to develop potash under public ownership, and the CCF party – but not the majority of the cabinet – wanted to do the same for oil and gas, neither resource was developed by the crown. Starting in 1945, national business-financed organizations launched major campaigns against socialism in general, and the CCF in particular; the local Saskatchewan business community joined suit. Although this opposition did not electorally defeat the CCF, it did convince party leaders to abandon this significant attempt at regional entrepreneurship by a provincial government. In Alberta much less governmental entrepreneurship was attempted. The ideological limitations of Social Credit's "right populism" foreclosed any serious government initiatives beyond the unsuccessful monetary reforms attempted during the party's first term from 1935 to 1940.

Extensive private development of oil and potash occurred in the two provinces during the quarter century following World War II, although, from the provincial perspective, this development was undertaken in a decidedly suboptimal fashion. The passive nature of provincial government regulation, and the myopic efforts to maximize the rate of mineral development at the price of forgone rents and economic linkages, made credible the dire expectations of certain critics as to the consequences of heavy dependence on staple development. However, the initial imbalance in power and knowledge between indigenous provincial elites and foreign resource companies has proved unstable. In each province an elite has emerged in the 1970s capable of effective entrepreneurship within its respective resource sector. In Saskatchewan this elite is essentially bureaucratic – a revival of the Fabian administrative tradition that accompanied the CCF government. Support for Saskatchewan's exercises in public entrepreneurship comes from what remains of the traditional "left populist" farm-labour constituency. As in the late 1940s, however, the opposition of the local business community may again abort the phenomenon before it reaches fruition.

In Alberta there has emerged in the years since Leduc a more complex phenomenon, a nascent regional bourgeoisie of substance and considerable power. We broadly define it to include the owners and managers of Alberta-based corporations, urban upper-income professionals with a stake in the continued growth of the regional economy, and senior provincial Conservative politicians and government bureaucrats. This new bourgeoisie has not only learned to use the provincial government to capture resource rents and bargain for linked industrial developments, but it is also developing the capacity to compete successfully with major foreign resource companies for large-scale private resource projects. The extent of regional transfer of income from oil-importing provinces to the Alberta treasury and to private indigenous capital is the most telling statistic to suggest the capacity of this new bourgeoisie to capture rent; the ability of the Foothills consortium headed by Calgary-based Alberta Gas Trunk Line to defeat the competing Arctic Gas consortium dominated by Imperial Oil, and thereby win the right to construct the pipeline bringing Alaska gas south, shows the growth of private entrepreneurial capacity in the province.

Our focus in this book is on the new mineral staple industries – oil, gas, and potash – all of which have been characterized by a traditional dominance of American capital, and the attempts by successive provincial governments (Social Credit and Conservative in Alberta; CCF, Liberal, and NDP in Saskatchewan) to stimulate staple-linked regional development and thus to diversify the prairie economy out of its historical dependence on agriculture. Broadly, and with inevitable retreats and fluctuations, we describe a movement away from passive rentier policies in the 1940s and 1950s to entrepreneurial development strategies in the 1970s, reflecting the dynamic of bargaining outlined above. Our studies suggest that under certain conditions the power of international capital can be substantially reduced and the original dependency relationship reversed. Alberta and Saskatchewan have taken the first steps towards the ultimate "provincialization" of their respective resource sectors and, while the process is certainly reversible, the indications are that it will continue. It is a process neither predetermined nor mechanistic, and we advance no claims of universality for our conclusions. We have forsworn any temptation to extend this analysis to the other western provinces, let alone to all ten.

The structure of the book is as follows. Chapter Two situates the politics of development in Alberta and Saskatchewan within the political and intellectual legacy of North American populism. Right and left variants of populism, and their appearance in Social Credit and the CCF respectively, are examined. Chapters Three and Four describe and analyse the early developments of oil and natural gas in Alberta, giving special attention to such problems as the coming of conservation, American influences on Alberta's regulatory system, and the controversies over natural gas exports. Chapters Five and Six discuss the economic development policies of the first Saskatchewan CCF government from 1944 to 1948. Chapter Seven assesses the impact of oil on Alberta's economy and social structure, tracing the roots of the Lougheed era to the rise of new social classes after the oil discoveries at Leduc in 1947. Chapter Eight reviews the early development of the potash industry in Saskatchewan and describes a classic staple "boom and bust" in Ross Thatcher's "New Saskatchewan." Chapter Nine is an analysis of "Empire Alberta." Lougheed's development strategy of petroleum-linked industrialization is discussed against the backdrop of the world oil crisis and conflicts with Ottawa. Chapter Ten describes the renaissance of Fabianism within the Saskatchewan NDP and government bureaucracy, and the partial nationalization of potash. Chapter Eleven summarizes the constitutional bases of authority to which the federal and provincial governments can appeal in the areas of resource management and taxation, and the role of the Supreme Court as arbitrator of the conflicting constitutional claims. As illustration of the significance of the Supreme Court as determinant of the nature of Canadian federalism, and of its current thrust to enhance federal jurisdiction, the chapter analyses the 1977 Supreme Court decision ruling Saskatchewan's oil royalty legislation ultra vires (*CIGOL v. Government of Saskatchewan*), and the 1978 Supreme Court decision on Saskatchewan's potash prorationing (CCP v. Government of Saskatchewan). The last chapter analyses two key concepts employed throughout the text – staple-led economic development and economic rent.

Notes

1. H.V. Nelles, *The Politics of Development: Forests, Mines and Hydro-Electric Power in Ontario 1849-1941* (Toronto: Macmillan, 1974); and Nelles, "Empire Ontario: The Problem of Resource Development," in D. Swainson (ed.), *Oliver Mowat's Ontario* (Toronto: Macmillan, 1972).

2. B. Laskin, "'Peace, Order and Good Government' Re-examined," *Canadian Bar Review*, 25 (1947), 1054.

3. P. Mathias, *Forced Growth* (Toronto: James Lewis and Samuel, 1971), viii-ix.

4. K. Levitt, *Silent Surrender* (Toronto: Macmillan, 1970), 146.

5. Cited in A.C. Cairns, "The Judicial Committee and its Critics," *Canadian Journal of Political Science*, IV, 3 (September 1971), 305, at n.5.

6. Cited in *Ibid*, 309. Writing in the early 1960s, Scott recalled that the founders of the CCF "were agreed that there must be more central authority, for reasons obvious to anyone faced with the conditions in Canada at the time. But this was centralization for planning's sake, not for centralization's sake ... Private centralization had obviously already taken place in the hands of big business — a centralization before which the provinces were powerless. What was needed was a countervailing public power to restore the national interest." (F. Scott, "Social Planning and Canadian Federalism," in M. Oliver (ed.), *Social Purpose for Canada* (Toronto: University of Toronto Press, 1961), 394-5 and 402.)

7. Cited in Cairns, "The Judicial Committee and its Critics," 314 at n.57 and 339-40.

8. The Communist Party's position is discussed in N. Penner, *The Canadian Left: A Critical Analysis* (Toronto: Prentice-Hall, 1977), 114-15. The Regina Manifesto is reprinted in M.S. Cross, *The Decline and Fall of a Good Idea: CCF-NDP Manifestoes 1932 to 1969* (Toronto: New Hogtown Press, 1974), 19-23.

9. P.E. Trudeau, "The Practice and Theory of Federalism," in Oliver, *Social Purpose for Canada*, 371-93.

10. C. Armstrong and H.V. Nelles, "Private Property in Peril: Ontario Businessmen and the Federal System, 1898-1911," in G. Porter and R. Cuff (eds.), *Enterprise and National Development* (Toronto: Hakkert, 1973), 20-38.

11. Cf. J.R. Mallory, *Social Credit and the Federal Power* (Toronto: University of Toronto Press, 1954).

12. See T.H. Moran, *Multinational Corporations and the Politics of Dependence: Copper in Chile* (Princeton: Princeton University Press, 1974), for a brilliant exposition on bargaining in resource industries.

13. "Program Planning: Planning Document No. 1," Economic Advisory and Planning Board, T.C. Douglas Papers, Premier's files 136 [henceforth abbreviated as "TCD Premier 136"], September 9, 1946, 16 and 8.

CHAPTER 2
The Legacy of Alienation

This, the first great labor conference of the United States, and of the world, representing all divisions of urban and rural organized industry, assembled in national congress, invoking upon its action the blessing and protection of Almighty God, puts forth, to and for the producers of the nation, this declaration of union and independence.

The conditions which surround us best justify our cooperation.

We meet in the midst of a nation brought to the verge of moral, political and material ruin. Corruption dominates the ballot box, the legislatures, the Congress, and touches even the ermine of the bench. The people are demoralized. Many of the States have been compelled to isolate the voters at the polling places in order to prevent universal intimidation or bribery. The newspapers are subsidized or muzzled; public opinion silenced; business prostrated, our homes covered with mortgages, labor impoverished, and the land concentrating in the hands of capitalists. The urban workmen are denied the right of organization for self-protection; imported pauperized labor beats down their wages; a hireling standing army, unrecognized by our laws, is established to shoot them down, and they are rapidly degenerating to European conditions. The fruits of the toil of millions are boldly stolen to build up colossal fortunes, unprecedented in the history of the world, while their possessors despise the republic and endanger liberty. From the same prolific womb of governmental injustice we breed two great classes – paupers and millionaires.

> Preamble to the St. Louis
> Platform of the People's
> Party, 1892

The Early West
The Rupert's Land Act of 1868 transferred, from the Hudson's Bay Company to the new Dominion, vast territories – portions of which

became the provinces of Manitoba, Saskatchewan, and Alberta. Rupert's Land comprised the Hudson Bay drainage basin, to which the imperial government in London added the so-called North-Western Territory, most of the unappropriated Crown lands in the Arctic drainage basin. The transfer of Rupert's Land "marked a revolution not only in administration and land policy, but in the very nature of the Canadian federation. It transformed the original Dominion from a federation of equal provinces each by a fundamental section (109 of the British North America Act of 1867) vested with the control of its own lands, into a veritable empire in its own right, with a domain of public lands five times the area of the original Dominion, under direct federal administration."[1]

Within the political framework of the National Policy of John A. Macdonald's Conservative governments, the prairie West was consciously settled and developed as an economic hinterland. This colonialism was no accident of history. It was imposed as an act of policy by the ambitious business-state coalition put together by Macdonald and his associates following confederation. The political motive behind the policy of westward expansion was defensive: to offset the increasing north-south pull of American markets and to strengthen Canada's east-west axis through western settlement and construction of an all-Canadian transcontinental railroad. This policy of defensive expansionism complemented the designs of the business and financial interests in Macdonald's coalition: these interests promoted the establishment of a new investment frontier, "an area where commercial and financial activity could readily expand and where labour and capital might find profitable employment. In terms of the economic competition of the day the requirement was for an agricultural frontier which could attract an adequate population of the annual flow of emigrants from the British Isles and Europe."[2] The transfer of Rupert's Land gave the Dominion control over an immense public domain and the raw materials necessary for the creation of a frontier to rival that of the United States.

Ottawa, it soon became apparent, intended to maintain that control as an instrument essential to the policy of transcontinental expansion and settlement. Under sections 92 and 109 of the BNA Act the original provinces owned and managed public lands and resources within their respective borders. Upon becoming a province in 1871 British Columbia secured title to most but not all of the public land within the province, but when in the previous year Manitoba had achieved provincial status, the public domain was withheld and "vested in the Crown, and administered by the Government of Canada for the purposes of the Dominion."[3] Included in the "purposes of the Dominion"

15

were Ottawa's intention to use land grants to build the Canadian Pacific Railway and to promote immigration and western settlement. Only when these objectives had been attained and most of the arable land alienated in the process (mineral rights were not alienated after 1890), would ownership of the public domain of the prairie West finally revert to the provinces – and then only after decades of protest and opposition.

As settlement of the West proceeded and new western metropolitan centres emerged, the alienation of the public domain became a leading point of contention in the campaign of the old North-West territories for autonomy and provincial status. Western lands, timber, and mineral resources were in the hands of the Dominion; the Territorial government (situated in Regina) furthermore was prohibited from borrowing on its own account. Manitoba and the Territories were thus limited in their ability to charter railroads, build new schools, or invest in public works. Frustrated in their development goals, the merchants, farmers, journalists, and politicians of the West turned their energies to agitation against their anomalous status, demanding control of the public domain "in the West, by the West, for the West" and compensation for lands and resources already alienated by the federal authorities.

The boom in immigration into the prairies at the turn of the century placed an almost intolerable strain on the inadequate and inelastic revenues of the Territorial government and heightened the West's sense of dependency on the annual subsidies of the Dominion. Financial considerations and ownership of the public domain were consequently overriding issues in the movement for provincial status before 1905. The granting of valuable lands and mineral rights to corporations such as the CPR accentuated the settlers' sense of grievance and added additional fuel to the push for autonomy. "The Territories, government and people alike, regarded the development of the West as a national necessity and resented federal control of natural resources. The central government accepted in principle the view that the natural resources should be used to further western development, but its practice, involving the alienation of Crown lands to railways, colonization companies, and cattle barons, seemed to the Westerner a negation of all the word 'National' stood for."[4]

The erosion of this formal structure of colonial power was only partially accomplished by the accession of Alberta and Saskatchewan to provincial status in 1905. The Territorial government had advocated one large province in the Territories but the federal cabinet, fearful that such a province would challenge the political hegemony of Ontario and Quebec interests, created two. Like Manitoba before them,

Alberta and Saskatchewan found that some provinces were more equal than others. Ottawa insisted that retention of the public lands and resources of the West was necessary for implementation of the vigorous immigration and settlement program being pursued by Sir Clifford Sifton, Wilfrid Laurier's Minister of the Interior. Although the 1905 autonomy legislation provided for an annual federal grant to the three prairie provinces as compensation for forgone revenue from public lands and resources (prior to 1882 Manitoba received no such compensation), the provinces were far from being mollified.

The ink had barely dried on the 1905 statutes before federal retention of the public domain and other anomalies in the legislation had come under strong attack from provincial rights enthusiasts in the West. For instance, the new Alberta Conservative party with Calgary lawyer and businessman R.B. Bennett (partner of Senator James Lougheed) at its head, resolved at its first convention in August 1905 that the people of Alberta were "entitled to the lands, mines, minerals, forests, and other natural resources" of the province, together with the right of full benefits and administration, and protested the resources "being unjustly withheld to be exploited by any political party at Ottawa."[5]

Western frontier settlers saw the alienation of their land and its resources as inseparable from their subordinate political situation, and their descendants, with their strong views on provincial autonomy and control of resources, would not disagree. The "quasi-colonial" status of the prairie provinces was not only economic but political, and this "made it a primary requirement of their provincial political systems that they should be able to stand up to the national government, that is, able to make effective demands on it and to resist national legislation which they regarded as exploitive."[6] Many early settlers admittedly expressed faith in Laurier's Liberals as the party that had permitted them to migrate to Canada, and as the sometime advocate of low tariffs. Saskatchewan and Alberta gave overwhelming support, for example, to the Liberals during the 1911 federal election in which the Conservatives defeated Laurier in a campaign fought over the latter's proposal for trade reciprocity with the United States. But Westerners of all classes came to perceive Ottawa as an imperial government, a complex of institutions organized by central Canadian elites for the purpose of dominating and plundering the hinterlands. The provincial administration, whatever its political colouration, became the indispensable agent for attacking political colonialism and bargaining with external economic interests.

Agitation against their second-class status continued in all three prairie provinces until the final transfer of resources in 1930, but in

Alberta the campaign was lent a special sense of urgency by the province's chaotic pattern of economic development. In both Regina and Edmonton provincial politicians invested extensively prior to 1930 in utilities (telephones were the earliest example), but the financial constraint on provincial revenues due to federal retention of public lands and resources was felt more keenly in Alberta where leading businessmen and politicians overinvested in a series of costly schemes to develop the province's fabled resource wealth. With an enthusiasm both irrepressible and reckless, Alberta Liberal administrations of 1905 to 1921 plunged into a series of costly schemes that eventually landed the province deeply in debt.

The North held a special place in the affections of the Alberta Liberals, a party which addressed the aspirations, not of the ranching-CPR elite of the South, but of Clifford Sifton's "men in sheepskin coats" – the new settlers and immigrants of Edmonton, the growing towns along the railways, the farms of the northern parkland, the newly arrived merchants and businessmen of the province. Successive Liberal administrations gave high priority to settlement and exploitation of the north of the province and, to that end, unwisely guaranteed the bonds of proposed northern railroads into the Peace River farming district and the mineral-rich Athabasca area. The agreement to guarantee bonds of the Alberta and Great Waterways Railway (with northern terminal adjacent to Fort McMurray) precipitated in 1909 and 1910 Alberta's worst political scandal. Controversy over the terms of the agreement became sufficiently intense, within the ruling Liberal party as well as the opposition, that Premier Rutherford was forced to resign. The Liberals survived in office, however, until 1921 by which time all these northern railroads had become bankrupt and were reorganized – either under direct provincial government ownership and management, or with running rights granted to the CPR.

The consequences of such grandiose regional development schemes weighed heavily on less prosperous and optimistic generations of Albertans. On one hand, the provision of new communication and transportation links, organized and controlled on a regional basis, had a considerable impact on the integration of Alberta society. State expansion of railroad track and low-cost telephone service helped to break down the isolation of farms and remote towns, stimulated the expansion of business activities and agricultural development in a country of immense distances and short growing seasons, and, by facilitating effective organization and communication, played a role in the growth of the co-operative movement in the West. But these gains were expensive and the province was soon badly in debt. By 1913 Alberta's debt was $33.7 million, while Saskatchewan's stood at $21.3

million; between 1913 and 1921 Alberta's debt grew by $62 million, but Saskatchewan's increased by only half as much. A 1938 study written for the (Rowell-Sirois) Royal Commission on Dominion-Provincial Relations concluded that Alberta's entire financial position after World War I "turned on the growing significance of the debt burden." Even in boom years the debt charges never absorbed less than 38 per cent of net expenditures. "The great significance of the debt burden and the expansion of social and other services that were also difficult to counteract, were creating in the budget a large sector of inflexible expenditures. In such conditions Alberta required a broader and if possible a more elastic revenue system. ... the more a provincial government has relied on extensive capital borrowings to expedite development, especially by the undertaking of risky ventures, the greater is the difficulty of resorting to this medium again."[7]

Such fiscal pressures would play their part in Social Credit's dramatic confrontations with what William Aberhart called the "Money Interests" in the late 1930s, and a desire to retire its large public debt clearly influenced Alberta's decision to promote a rapid exploitation of its oil resources after the Leduc discovery in 1947. Although Alberta's provincial indebtedness was, before 1930, the most acute, growing indebtedness was an important spur in all three prairie provinces to gain provincial ownership of public lands and resources.

Until 1921 in the case of Alberta and 1944 for Saskatchewan, both provinces were ruled by provincial affiliates of a federal party. Over time these provincial parties became more independent of their federal counterparts, but this first phase of provincial government entrepreneurship – in utilities, railroads, and to an extent elevator construction – was led by indigenous prairie elites who assumed they could realize their ambitions within the existing framework of established political parties and prominent external corporations such as the CPR, line elevator companies, and the chartered banks. By contrast the rise of populist parties, most of which evolved out of the cooperative movement, represented a more fundamental, even if essentially "reformist" in spirit, challenge to the status quo.

Typically the prairie farmer was an independent homesteader having title to the family farm (although many were reduced to tenant status) and employing little if any wage labour. The political demands, organizations and culture arising from such a society have been indiscriminately labelled "populism." The term came into widespread use in the United States in the 1890s as applied to the ideas and supporters of the People's Party. It has since come to signify a wide range of agrarian protest movements supported by dirt farmers.[8]

The Strategic Alternative – Left versus Right Populism

The prairie provinces contain the northernmost extension of the great inland plains extending west from the Mississippi River to the Rockies and south from the Peace River to the Gulf of Mexico. Before the white man came, these plains served as the resource base for the hunting and gathering economy of the Indians. But they were far more valuable as agricultural lands – either seeded to grains or devoted to pasture for livestock. Once devoted to agriculture, the plains generated extensive additions to aggregate national income. Who would get the rent component?

Rent (see our discussion in Chapter Twelve) is income from an economic activity in excess of costs of production. The most significant component of "cost" was the net income accruing to farmers. Thus the minimum net income required to induce settlers to farm was the key determinant of the surplus to be appropriated as rent – either by farmers themselves or by those to whom they sold or from whom they bought. The minimum net farm income in turn depended upon the rewards of alternative employment open to settlers – essentially wages from urban employment. Viewed from this vantage, much of the politics on the plains during the previous one hundred years has concerned the struggle between the farmer on the one hand and, on the other, various corporate and financial interests over the distribution of agricultural rents. The Indians, the original owners of this vast and valuable asset, of course received virtually nothing. They were forced to "sell" at a price reflecting the powerlessness of a conquered people. Thereafter came the white (and some black) settlers, and the battle was joined.

Prairie farmers dealt in markets which initially guaranteed the bulk of economic rents would accrue to financial and corporate interests – to banks via high interest rates for mortgages and other credit, to railroads via monopoly freight rates, to Eastern manufacturing trusts selling farm equipment. The farmers' political response, in the United States as in Canada, in the Southern states as well as those of the West, was populism, a complex radical movement that gave birth to a multitude of organizations from the cotton exchange, launched by the Texas Alliance in the late 1880s, to wheat pools in the Canadian prairies during the 1920s. (Farmers' Alliances, organized in numerous states, were concerned with the economic advancement of farmers. But in a fashion quite analogous to farm associations in the three prairie provinces, they provided the organizational foundation for populist political parties.)

The family farmer – from Alberta homesteader to Texas sharecropper, both black and white – has provided one of the important bases of support, along with urban labour, for North American reform politics. There are serious blemishes to the populist record, for example the racism of Georgia's populist leader Tom Watson[9] in his later years or the anti-semitism of Social Credit financial conspiracy theories. However, it would be a mistake to conclude the blemishes have been more serious than those of urban-based labour movements, or of established parties dominated by urban elites.

In both Canada and the United States populist movements brought about the participation in politics of large numbers of "plain people," and contributed substantially – directly via state and provincial governments they controlled, or indirectly via their impact on the programs of established parties – to the realization of the set of reforms that constitute the modern welfare state. The role of the Saskatchewan CCF in pioneering medical care insurance is an obvious example, but there are many others. The People's Party and its successors enacted considerable progressive labour legislation. Farmers were prominent supporters of the social security measures introduced both in Ottawa and Washington between the two world wars.[10]

Populist contributions to the welfare state are substantial; the legacy of their economic policy is far more ambiguous. The first reason for ambiguity is that populism assumed a multitude of organizational guises and goals. By the criteria of the more radical populist organizations the economic legacy is ultimately one of failure. Their programs constituted an explicit attack on contemporary corporate capitalism and linked the economic advancement of farmers to fundamental changes in the entire economy. For these groups Lipset is correct when he concluded in his classic study of the Saskatchewan CCF: "The large measure of 'socialism without doctrine' that can be found in the programs of agrarian political and economic organizations is in many respects more socialistic than the nationalization policies of some explicitly socialist parties."[11] For other populist groups the goals were far more modest – the improvement of the net income of farmers, often by means of monetary reform, with little concern to transform the economic system. By these more modest criteria the economic legacy is arguably one of success.

Social Credit and the CCF were the last of the populist parties of the great plains, and the competition between them for the loyalty of prairie farmers was the final re-enactment of the tension between populism's left and right variants. This tension within populism between alternate strategies was manifested earlier, during the 1890s, in the battle within the People's Party between the midroaders on the left and fusionists on the right. The former wanted to steer their party down the "middle of the road" until it established itself as a national

farm-labour party of reform, avoiding the threat of co-optation existing on both sides – in the form of Republicans in the South and Democrats in the West. The latter's aim was more modest – to "fuse" the
forces in favour of silver coinage as a means of increasing the money
supply and lowering the ability of banks to extract high interest rates.
The climax occurred when the People's Party met in convention in St.
Louis immediately after the capture of the 1896 Democratic nomina-
tion by William Jennings Bryan, a leading "silver Democrat" with
populist inclinations. Opposition between the two camps was bitter,
and at times the convention erupted in near riot. The fusionists succeeded in committing the People's Party to support Bryan for president; the midroaders succeeded in getting the party to nominate its
own vice-presidential candidate – Tom Watson, a midroader from
Georgia. Many populists hoped for a joint Bryan-Watson ticket, but
the Democrats refused any compromise. In the election that year the
"plutocrat" "goldbug" McKinley won; Watson recorded a dismal
vote. Although it survived as a remnant for a number of years, the
People's Party had torn itself asunder at St. Louis and ceased thereafter to pose a serious threat to the established political order.[12]

From the conflict between midroaders and fusionists to the more
prosaic Social Credit versus CCF struggles during the depression of
the 1930s, populist strategies polarized in three important domains:
the nature of the electoral alliance to be sought, the extent of the
critique of contemporary capitalist society, and the scope of reforms
advocated. Left populist strategy attempted to build a farm-labour
alliance; right populists minimized conflict among groups within the
prairies and attempted a regional alliance of all classes indigenous to
the plains against Eastern interests. Second, left populism erected a
relatively general critique of all sectors of corporate capitalism – the
railroads, mining companies, manufacturing trusts, as well as financial institutions; right populists concentrated their critique, to the
point of obsession, upon the power of banks to limit the money supply and control the cost of credit. Finally, all populists consistently
supported the institution of the individual family-owned farm, and to
that extent all were "capitalists" defending private property. However left populist organizations typically emerged from the extensive
rural co-operatives of the plains and tended to a chiliastic belief in
co-operatives as the morally just way to organize economic activity.
Beyond agriculture, left populists often spoke in terms of increased
competition (of "breaking up the trusts") as a solution to farmers'
problems, but here competition was a tactic to use against concentrated corporate power, not a goal in itself. Left populism demanded
of government not only a regulatory role to promote competition,

but also the generation of countervailing power on farmers' behalf by a variety of entrepreneurial means – public ownership of utilities and railroads, and government-run marketing agencies. Conversely right populism had few links to the co-operative movement and, beyond the use of the state to break the stranglehold of banks over the money supply, it viewed the achievement of well-functioning competitive markets as a sufficient goal.

No populist organization was consistently "left" or "right" in the above sense, but it is important to understand that this distinction defines functionally equivalent strategies, each with a degree of internal consistency and a set of arguments against the other, and therefore populist organizations, or factions within them, tended to one side or the other. One should not conclude that left populists were naive radical romantics, while their right-wing counterparts were pragmatic opportunists. Among the radical founders of large agricultural co-operatives were some shrewd entrepreneurs, and the quixotic 1937 revolt (discussed later in this chapter) of the insurgent backbench members of the Alberta Social Credit caucus demonstrated the seriousness of intent of right populists to realize their reforms despite overwhelming opposition.

Populism – The American Heritage

The populists' interest in economic issues invariably had its origins in some aspect bearing directly upon rural income. However, with the birth of the People's Party in 1892, populists generalized their complaints into a radical critique of the unbridled concentration of power and wealth in the "gilded age" of American capitalism. In the St. Louis and Omaha platforms, and resolutions adopted during the year of its birth, the People's Party covered a wide gamut of issues. On money: "We demand a national currency, safe, sound, and flexible, issued by the general government only," and predictably, "We demand free and unlimited coinage of silver." On the subject of transportation: "We believe that the time has come when the railroad corporations will either own the people or the people must own the railroads ... the government should own and operate the railroads in the interests of the people." On land: "The land, including all the natural sources of wealth, is the heritage of the people, and should not be monopolized for speculative purposes, and alien ownership of land should be prohibited." On government aid to industry: "That we oppose any subsidy or national aid to any private corporation for any purpose." The party also passed resolutions in support of female suffrage, the initiative and recall as legislative procedures, a graduated income tax, the eight-hour work day, and abolition of Pinkerton's "army of mercenaries ... hired assassins of plutocracy."[13] The most ambitious, the most debated, and the most controversial single demand was for the so-called "subtreasury plan" – a combination of central bank, publicly owned banking system, and marketing agency for the most important agricultural crops.[14]

The basic motivation behind the party's economic policy was clearly control over the power of industrial trusts. While the interests of the family farmer figured prominently, for example in the design of the subtreasury plan, the program did not romanticize the yeoman farmer or decentralized competitive markets. The suggested reforms implied an aggressive role for the federal government – monetary reform, marketing boards, nationalization – that contrasts sharply with the timidity of contemporary reform advocated within established parties. The chief product of the latter, the Sherman Antitrust Act of 1890, merely proposed a limited application of the classic liberal economic doctrine that trusts be broken into competitive units. Significantly, early applications of the Sherman Act were against labour, not capital. The government broke the 1894 Pullman strike, for example, by charging the union under the Act with a conspiracy in restraint of interstate commerce.[15]

The ambitions of the People's Party, relative to the conventional wisdom of the day, were obviously high. Why did it accomplish so little? One reason is that throughout the agrarian revolt of the 1890s it was never able to gain complete control – governorship plus majorities in both houses of the legislature – of a single state government. The implementation of a major reform program was in such circumstances obviously no easy task.[16]

The attempt in Texas to regulate railroad abuses and bar Standard Oil from conducting business in the state illustrates a second aspect of the populist legacy – many of its reforms were implemented by other parties anxious to garner farm support and deny success to the emerging farm party. In this case the reforms were implemented by the "reform Democrats" led by Jim Hogg, first as state attorney-general and from 1890-94 as governor. In response to pressure from the radical Texas Farmers' Alliance Hogg secured passage of a tough antitrust law that for some years barred Standard Oil from the state, and created the Texas Railroad Commission with such powers that it regulated not only railroads but the state's petroleum industry which boomed after the original discoveries at Spindletop (near Houston) in 1901. For better and for worse the Commission has been responsible for much of the law governing the exploitation of petroleum on this continent. It served as the basis for the regulatory structure adopted by both Alberta and Saskatchewan.[17]

The third example of the American populist legacy, the Nonpartisan League, we shall discuss in somewhat more detail. The League has considerable significance as the American populist party geographically and temporally closest to the populism of the Canadian prairies. In fact the impact was reciprocal – the struggles of Canadian prairie farmers prior to World War I to build co-operatively owned elevator systems influenced the policies of the League. The League spread into Canada beginning in 1916. It had little electoral success in Saskatchewan but it elected two of four candidates it ran in the Alberta provincial election of 1917, and this success forced the United Farmers of Alberta (UFA) into electoral politics despite the reluctance of the UFA leadership.[18] UFA locals endorsed the League and threatened the organizational integrity of the UFA unless the leadership acquiesced to the new strategy. More important than the organizational links is that the League in North Dakota provided, just across the border, the example of an aggressive state government pursuing regional economic development. The means – co-operatives and state-owned industries – were not unknown to western farmers, although no previous administration had as consistently advanced them. But the assertion of independence from, and willingness to pursue political conflicts with, metropolitan interests was indeed of a different order of magnitude than anything the Canadian farmer had undertaken to date.

The League provides a number of parallels to the early CCF and Social Credit. Like the first CCF leaders, the League founders, A.C. Townley[19] and his close associates, considered themselves socialists but found their base of support among rural farmers as opposed to urban workers. Like CCF and Social Credit, the League had ambitions of becoming a national party, but the only government over which it established effective control was that of a rural state with an economy similar to Saskatchewan's and Alberta's. Given its electoral fortunes it evolved a regional program concerned to maximize the industrial development that it could initiate from its state base. As did Social Credit's attempt to legislate monetary policy at a regional level, the League's attempts to assert a degree of financial autonomy by launching the state-owned Bank of North Dakota (intended to finance the industrial program) sparked animated opposition from local and out-of-state bankers, convoluted legal battles, and unprecedented partisan controversy. As with the CCF and Social Credit, its ambitions far exceeded its performance, but enough was achieved to inspire a generation of populist leaders north and south of the border, and to incur the antipathy of Eastern business interests – in Canada as well as the United States.[20]

From 1918 to 1920 the League enjoyed uncontested control of the state legislature and executive in North Dakota. Having successfully amended the state constitution by submitting proposals to the electorate as a referendum in the 1918 election, the League proceeded to establish an Industrial Commission "empowered and directed to manage, operate, control, and govern all utilities, industries, enterprises and business projects now or hereafter established, owned, undertaken, or operated by the State of North Dakota."[21] The Commission also supervised the Home Building Association which financed and built low-cost homes within the state. The state-owned Bank of North Dakota and a compulsory hail insurance scheme were launched.

Problems arose immediately. League opponents commenced numerous legal actions, including an injunction to prevent a major state bond issue, a challenge to the raising of the state borrowing limit, a challenge to the status of the Bank of North Dakota, and a suit alleging that the industrial program violated property rights ensconced in the fourteenth amendment of the federal constitution. The state supreme court generally ruled for the government in the cases it heard, but the right of the state to its bond issue was only established after a favourable decision by the Supreme Court in Washington. Meanwhile the post-war agricultural depression of 1920 had struck. Grain prices fell drastically and a number of the state-owned enterprises, including the bank, were financially embarrassed. Although none was bankrupted, some losses occurred; the bank was forced to extend loans due and restrict withdrawals. The opposition naturally charged administrative incompetence. By this time several senior state officers, elected as League supporters, had defected and joined the opposition. In the 1920 election the opposition gained control of the House and a number of state offices, although the incumbent League governor retained his office until the special recall election of 1921.

The activities of the League were a source of concern not only to the American but to the eastern Canadian elite. The prestigious Canadian Reconstruction Association was a Toronto-based organization comprising a number of prominent Canadians. Its honorary president was, until his death, Lord Shaughnessy, chairman and president of the Canadian Pacific Railway Company.[22] In 1921 the Association published a well researched but unremittingly hostile pamphlet[23] on the League, subtitled "A study of a class war and its disastrous consequences, together with a comparison of bank services in Canada and Western States." The pamphlet was intended as a warning against analogous Canadian movements: "It is difficult for a Canadian," confessed the pamphlet's author, "accustomed to the Canadian system of responsible party government, to understand a political situation such as has developed in North Dakota ... The fact is that political animosities have been so stirred that the State of North Dakota is today a veritable madhouse of intrigue and recrimination. ..."[24]

"If you put a lawyer, a banker, and an industrialist in a barrel and roll it down hill, there'll always be a son of a bitch on top,"[25] was one of Townley's more celebrated political quips. In somewhat more prosaic language the League had declared its object to be "the elimination of the profits of the middle-man through co-operation and public ownership of the means of production."[26] The League obviously embodied the populist concern to improve the terms at which the farmer bought and sold. However, it also developed an analysis of regional economic development, as reflected in its industrial program, that transcended the traditional argument over terms of trade. The industrial program was an attempt to exploit forward linkages (e.g. flour-milling) from the state's agricultural staples. Given the extent of political opposition, League leaders devoted more energy to preliminaries — amendment of the constitution, court battles, creation of the Industrial Commission and state bank — than to the substance of the program. The desire to foster forward-linked industries is certainly not itself a sign of radicalism. In order to force more transformation of staples within the province of Ontario, both Liberal and Conservative administrations imposed, after the 1890s, a "manufacturing condition" on leases for the production of crown-owned lumber and minerals.

A second aspect of League theory, an emphasis upon co-operative and public enterprise at the state level, flowed naturally enough from its left populist heritage, but it engendered a contradiction that neither it nor the later CCF was able adequately to resolve. As the Canadian Reconstruction Association argued, the League was primarily opposed to "big business" and had no intention of usurping the domain of the small commercial and financial interests within the state. However, given the small size of the state market, its policies could have little impact on "big business" and yet have serious repercussions on local businessmen. For example, the state mill and elevator system was intended to challenge large private grain handlers, but the most immediate consequence was the restriction on small local banks by the state-owned bank used to finance the venture. Local businesses were forced to contribute to a workers' compensation fund; local retailers were faced with direct competition from co-operatives, which furthermore enjoyed favourable government treatment. Many policies, to the extent they succeeded, effected an internal transfer of income within the state, from business to farm and labour. The logical consequence was an alliance of the local business community with metropolitan interests. At the end the League was struggling on two fronts – attempting unsuccessfully to market its long-delayed bond issue via unsympathetic major banks in Minneapolis and Chicago, amidst mounting local opposition from business and professional interests within and without the legislature.

The classic populist measures – organization of agricultural co-operatives, attempts to regulate banks, railroads, elevator companies, and commodity exchanges – were essentially concerned with the terms of trade between farmers and those from whom they bought and to whom they sold, within an economic environment created before the rise of populism. The issues raised by the control of new industries concerned not only income distribution, but the power to make entrepreneurial decisions with respect to the evolution of economic development. Both issues are intertwined in any society, and usually those with the power to make entrepreneurial decisions also benefit disproportionately in terms of income generated from their decisions. Nonetheless income distribution within a nation, region, or industry can change without any corresponding shift in the location of entrepreneurship, and a shift in entrepreneurial power need not, in the short run at least, be reflected in changed income distribution. To the extent political movements ever articulate theoretical issues, populists argued that both income distribution and control of entrepreneurship were important. However, there are reasons that militate strongly in favour of populists – or any other reform government – emphasizing the former over the latter. Any successes in the former are immediately apparent, whereas success in the latter entails measuring costs and benefits over a long-time horizon in a context of uncertainty and political conflict, and may well entail current sacrifices relative to a laissez-faire policy. Admittedly, in specifying goals for regional economic development, populists often ignored the most rudimentary constraints of comparative costs as a determinant of industry location. In other words, upon assuming office, populists found that they were limited by economic as well as political constraints.

The Beginnings of Canadian Populism
In Canada prairie populists' initial large-scale undertakings were of a commercial nature – in grain marketing. In 1906 the Grain Growers' Grain Company was organized as a farmer-owned co-operative to act as a dealer on the Winnipeg Grain Exchange. The major private companies on the market made their profits not by commissions on transactions undertaken for others but by trading on their own account, depending upon the spread between the prices at which they bought and sold. Theoretically competitive forces of supply and demand should have maintained the spread at a level permitting only a normal

profit to such dealers, but farmers were legitimately suspicious of the potential for major dealers to organize for their own profit speculative price movements unrelated to fundamental market conditions, and to destroy competitors by price manipulations in particular markets. The purpose of the new farmer-owned company was not to "play the market" but to maximize the prices farmers received, deducting only a commission to cover costs.

Shortly after it had purchased a seat on the Exchange and begun operations, the new company was expelled, ostensibly because patronage dividends[27] to its farmer members would constitute fee splitting and violate the Exchange rules. The ensuing controversy provided the new venture with precisely what it needed – wide publicity. The Grain Growers' Grain Company cast itself as David battling the Exchange, a pernicious closed club and collective Goliath. It sought the aid of the Manitoba government in securing reinstatement, threatening to oppose it in the forthcoming election were help not granted. The Premier requested the Exchange to reconsider. It baulked, but under threat of special legislation affecting its legislative charter, it finally relented.[28]

The Manitoba Grain Growers' Association convinced an unenthusiastic Conservative government under Premier Roblin to launch a government-owned country elevator system to be run as a regulated utility. From its beginning in 1910 until its transfer in 1912 to the Grain Growers' Grain Company it was, to quote Vernon Fowke, "an unqualified fiasco."[29] It provided a classic example of how not to run a crown corporation. The Minister of Public Works, responsible for elevator acquisition, relieved the line elevator companies of their least efficient elevators and compensated them at excessive prices. At some shipping points the government had three or four elevators; at others none. In Saskatchewan and Alberta the provincial governments resisted farmer demands for government-owned elevator systems, and given the Manitoba experience of a system operated by a disinterested government, farmers accepted the alternative of a co-operatively run system with government loans providing the bulk of the capital requirements.

In the 1920s a new generation of radical farm leaders further extended co-operative grain handling by importing the American idea of "pooling" crops and entrusting their sale to co-operatively owned marketing companies known, logically enough, as "Pools." The Wheat Pools of the prairie provinces absorbed much of the original co-operatively owned elevator system and sought, by selling directly to ultimate purchasers, to dispense with open marketing on the Grain Exchange. Under the slogan "orderly marketing," advocates of the Pools argued that pooling would permit farmers to exercise a degree of market power and realize higher average prices, and to minimize the price fluctuations on the Exchange. In all three provinces, including Manitoba after the farmers acquired the government elevator system (first by lease, later by purchase), the co-operatively owned systems thrived, marketing approximately half the prairie crop by the onset of the depression in 1930. The depression admittedly created severe losses for these systems and precipitated further government intervention, this time primarily at the federal level.

The co-operative grain handling ventures are significant early examples of regional entrepreneurship by farmers acting collectively and not as individual entrepreneurs. While the concerns of farmers who merely supported these ventures were relative prices – improved and more stable prices for grain sold, control over grading and dockage procedures, reduced handling charges, etc. – those farmers who also became managers and directors developed entrepreneurial skills that found outlet in populist politics.

At the provincial level the first successful populist parties in the Canadian prairies were the United Farmers of Alberta (UFA) and United Farmers of Manitoba (UFM), the Manitoba Grain Growers' Association renamed. The former governed Alberta from 1921 to 1935; the latter was elected to office in 1922, governed alone for ten years, and in 1932 returned to the ample bosom of political orthodoxy by forming an alliance with the provincial Liberals. At the level of federal politics the National Progressive Party was founded in 1920 – a left populist party with extensive support in the prairies and in rural Ontario (where, in 1919, the United Farmers of Ontario, supported by Labour members of the legislature, had formed a new provincial government). Although they elected the second largest caucus in the federal election of 1921, the Progressive leaders declined the position of official opposition to the smaller Conservative contingent. Instead they provided, in exchange for largely unfulfilled Liberal promises to lower tariffs, support for Prime Minister Mackenzie King's minority government. Mackenzie King, leading his first government, successfully wooed the Progressive leadership, many of whom were quite amenable to union with the Liberals and dubious of the prospects of establishing a successful left populist farm-labour political party. In the following election support for the Progressives collapsed, and the party's influence in federal politics promptly terminated.

In Saskatchewan, Liberal Premier Martin outmanoeuvred the populists. By taking prominent farm leaders into his cabinet and dissociating the provincial party at a critical moment from its federal counterpart, he partially satisfied the populist demand for political organization independent of the "old line" parties. In 1921, before farmers could decide to enter provincial politics, he called a snap election. He won, and by the time of the next election the immediate threat to the established party system had ebbed. In 1929 the Saskatchewan Liberals were defeated, and replaced by a coalition government headed by the Conservatives but also containing a minority of Progressives and independents.

Neither the UFA, nor the UFM, nor the Conservative/Progressive coalition government in Saskatchewan manifested any significant entrepreneurial thrust with respect to regional economic development. Admittedly there were flourishes, but they came to naught. For example the left wing of the UFA, following the precedent of the Nonpartisan League in North Dakota, succeeded in 1922 and 1923 in passing resolutions at the annual convention in support of a provincially owned bank. The government commissioned reports but refused to act, and in 1924 the left wing and cabinet collided as for two days the annual convention debated the issue. The left lost.

The UFA and UFM governments at the provincial level, and the Progressives at the national level, illustrate two social processes that in times of stable prosperity sap the drive of all reform movements — bureaucratic co-optation at the top and political apathy at the base. By the 1920s the UFA and UFM, and their Saskatchewan counterpart the Saskatchewan Grain Growers' Association, had established themselves as stable farm lobbies, elements in an emerging political equilibrium. Their leadership had penetrated into the regional political elite, occupying provincial and even federal cabinet positions. The post-war depression aroused their base and forced the leadership, in Alberta and Manitoba, to break formally with the traditional parties and lead electoral campaigns on the basis of the left populist demands, demands which had been ritually endorsed in convention year after year by these organizations, but on which the leadership was not expected to produce results because only a government could do so. The farm leadership thus were very reluctant radicals. Once elected they provided little innovation, although, in the words of one sympathetic historian, they gave "thoroughly competent administration."[30] Having fought earlier battles to establish their farm organizations and the closely aligned co-operative elevator companies, they had won a degree of market power and political respectability. This they did not intend to jeopardize by aggressively pursuing the remainder of the left populist agenda. It would be inaccurate to emphasize solely bureaucratic co-optation at the top. With the return of high prices in the middle of the 1920s farmers displayed increasing political apathy, in effect acquiescing to their leaders' arguments that it was more important to conserve and administer the achievements of the past than to endanger them by further radical ventures.

The depression and drought of the 1930s shattered the credibility of the moderates who presided over the previous decade. More militant populists – adhering to the left and right tradition – now dominated farmers' meetings. In Manitoba the UFM leaders saved themselves by seeking refuge in an alliance with the provincial Liberals. UFM Premier Bracken remained in office from 1922 until becoming federal Conservative leader in 1942. In Alberta there occurred a re-enactment of the 1917 scenario, with the CCF now in the role of the Nonpartisan League. Many in the UFA, including some of the UFA leadership outside the government, played a major role in the founding of the CCF. The founding took place at a conference held in Calgary in 1932 to which the UFA had invited kindred urban and rural groups across the country, with the intention of exploring united action. In 1933 the UFA convention voted to affiliate with the new party, but most of the UFA caucus and cabinet were dubious of, if not actually opposed to, the CCF, and had no intention of implementing its program. They resisted as impractical or beyond provincial authority all radical reforms proposed – debt adjustment and moratorium, public ownership of resources, and of course, the idea of social credit.

Social Credit
The association, in Alberta, of the left populist strategy with a tired co-opted government opened the field to a right populist alternative. Its champion was to be a Calgary high school principal and gifted lay preacher, William Aberhart. In 1932 "Bible Bill" Aberhart became a convert to Major Douglas' theories that financial interests, via their withdrawals of interest from the income stream, were the fundamental cause of economic depressions, and that additional purchasing power in the form of "social credit" was the requisite reform to restore full employment. Thereafter he devoted the considerable propaganda resources available to him as head of the Calgary Prophetic Bible Institute to the popularization of Douglas' ideas.[31]

The essence of Major Douglas' economic theory was contained in his so-called "A + B Theorem."[32] Income received by individuals (wages, salaries, and dividends) constituted the A items, and was available to purchase the goods and services produced by society. However the prices of goods and services, if they were to cover total costs of production, must reflect not only A items but payments to other organizations (interest on debt, cost of capital, and intermediate goods), constituting the B items. The market value of all goods and services produced in a period, if priced to cover costs, must equal A + B. Available to purchase the goods was income equal to A. Thus there was a deficiency of demand, equal to the sum of B items. Full employment of resources required an appropriate injection of social credit equal to B.

Douglas was correct to emphasize that withdrawals from the income flow could, in Keynesian terms, create a deficiency of aggregate demand. His identification of such withdrawals, in the so-called B items, was quite unsatisfactory. Payments for intermediate goods, for example, would appear as income to the factors of production in the intermediate goods industries. The withdrawal via interest paid to financial institutions was a more relevant item since there is no guarantee that the receipts of financial institutions will in any period be offset by equal injections of demand in the form of consumption or investment financed by new loans. The instability of investment demand, dependent as it is upon unstable expectations about the future on the part of borrowers and lenders, was a central component of Keynes' theory of aggregate demand.

It is important to realize that the call for government to stimulate aggregate demand – by means of public expenditures, fiscal policy, or even the issue of some form of social credit – was in the midst of the depression entirely apposite. The theory of social credit was in that sense an intellectual advance relative to contemporary economic orthodoxy of budgetary constraint and statements of faith in the temporary nature of the current depression. On this score it is worth quoting Keynes: "Since [World War I] there has been a spate of heretical theories of under-consumption, of which those of Major Douglas are the most famous. ... Major Douglas is entitled to claim, as against some of his orthodox adversaries, that he at least has not been wholly oblivious of the outstanding problem of our economic system." Douglas was, Keynes concluded in pun, "a private, perhaps, but not a major in the brave army of heretics – with Mandeville, Malthus, Gesell and Hobson, who, following their intuitions, have preferred to see the truth obscurely and imperfectly rather than to maintain error, reached indeed with clearness and consistency and by easy logic but on hypotheses inappropriate to the facts."[33]

Failing to persuade any party to include Douglas' scheme in its platform, Aberhart organized the Social Credit League only six months prior to its victory in the 1935 provincial election. Not surprisingly Alberta farmers preferred a right populist movement that "has not been wholly oblivious of the outstanding problem of our economic system," whatever the technical economic and constitutional problems of implementing social credit, to the ambiguous UFA-CCF alternative.

Once in office Aberhart and his cabinet were forced to confront the impediments to any program hoping to restore regional economic prosperity by setting, in effect, monetary policy at the provincial level. By early 1937 the government had already had legislation (dealing with debt adjustment) struck down as ultra vires by a hostile provincial supreme court, and incurred the opprobrium of Eastern financial interests. "Recent debt legislation," intoned the *Financial Post*, "is akin to confiscation of private property. It strikes at the very roots of commerce, business and finance in a way which characterized the early stages of the Russian Revolution."[34] The caucus became suspicious that the cabinet was faltering under the attack, and would not engage the central battle over implementation of social credit. In the spring of 1937 the caucus mutinied, and a group of "insurgent" members refused to pass the budget until the government introduced enabling legislation (Alberta Social Credit Act) for the long-promised addition to the money supply, to be known as "Alberta credit." This legislation created a Social Credit Board of five insurgent members, named in the bill, empowered to prepare a specific proposal and thereafter to appoint a commission to operate it. The first bills prepared by this Board were intended to regulate private banks operating in the province. They were disallowed within two weeks of their enactment. Through disallowance by the federal government, ultra vires court rulings, or reservation of royal assent by the lieutenant governor, all legislation emanating from the Board or government, affecting the chartered banks and debt management, was struck down. Social Credit thus failed to implement social credit.

By the end of 1937 the insurgency had been contained and cabinet authority re-established, but Social Credit had attempted enough to consolidate the opposition to its right into an electoral alliance for the 1940 election. The CCF and UFA had by this time dissociated themselves. The CCF campaigned heavily on resource nationalization, but figured no more prominently than in the previous election. The major confrontation pitted Social Credit against the united forces of political and financial orthodoxy within the province. Social Credit survived, although with a much reduced legislative majority.

In 1943 Aberhart died and was replaced as Premier by his close associate, Ernest Manning. Manning presided over a process of bureaucratic co-optation analogous to that undergone by the UFA and UFM governments two decades earlier. After 1937, Social Credit leaders de-emphasized the attack on financial power and presented themselves as able administrators. A new political reality permitted Manning to overcome the accumulated distrust of business and financial interests (local and national) resulting from the legislative struggles of the first term of office. That new reality was the rise of the CCF as a left populist party with a national base and, faced with the CCF threat, Prime Minister Mackenzie King's conversion to the Keynesian doctrines of government responsibility for full employment and welfare state reforms. For the 1944 provincial election Manning posed as a bulwark against socialism and federal encroachment upon provincial rights. As Manning's major target, the CCF finally became a serious contender in Alberta politics. With a quarter of the vote in 1944, its highest before or since, it ranked second in votes cast but won only two seats and failed to become the official opposition. Social Credit won re-election with an increased majority.

The remnants of the true believers loyal to Douglas' ideas continued to control the *Canadian Social Crediter*, official organ of the party, and the Social Credit Board, which had no administrative functions after abandonment of attempts to legislate social credit. As prospects for implementation of his scheme waned, Douglas' writings became increasingly cranky, anti-democratic, anti-socialist, and anti-semitic. He alleged that a Jewish conspiracy was in control of both high finance and the international communist movement. The symbolic end of Social Credit as a right populist movement came in the year oil was discovered at Leduc. That year Manning dissociated the government and party from the Board after its annual report to the legislature had discreetly supported Douglas' politically unacceptable ideas. Shortly thereafter the Board was dissolved and the "Douglasites" lost control of the *Social Crediter*. Although Social Credit remained in office until 1971, in Alberta the populist thrust was spent.

The Co-operative Commonwealth Federation
The CCF was undoubtedly the most ambitious of the populist parties to emerge from the great plains. It was, as its name implied, a federation – an amalgam both in its ideology and its organization. For many it was the culmination of attempts to create a national left populist party uniting farmer and labour; for others, the beginnings of a Canadian equivalent of the British Labour Party; and for a small minority, a potential vehicle for Marxism.[35]

In Chapters Five and Six we shall extensively discuss the ideological development of the CCF. However, to complete our general discussion of populism we here provide a sketch of the party's political history. Each of the provincial sections retained virtual independence throughout the party's lifetime. East of the Ottawa River the party remained marginal. The industrial workers of Sydney made Cape Breton an island of support in a region that remained largely indifferent to the party. The small Quebec section was dominated by anglophone academics close to McGill University. In Ontario the party most resembled the British Labour Party – its support concentrated in urban working-class ridings, its leaders primarily intellectuals imbued with the British Fabian socialist tradition and joined, after 1940, by a group of tough, pragmatic leaders from the non-communist industrial unions. Leadership of the national party came primarily from Ontario, and this despite the fact that an overwhelming majority of the elected members of parliament, including the party's three national leaders,[36] were Westerners. The principal reason for this anomaly lies in the centralist orientation of the Ontario leaders relative to those in the West who, being more concerned with regional issues, emphasized control of their respective provincial governments.

In Manitoba and Alberta the party remained small, due initially to the rural commitment to other populist parties. Despite large rural populations in both these provinces, support and leadership of the party came disproportionately from the cities – for example, Winnipeg's North End in the case of Manitoba. In British Columbia the working-class ridings of East Vancouver provided the core of CCF votes, although it also won support elsewhere in the province where the local economy was dominated by mining and forestry. Ideologically the distribution of the British Columbia leadership displayed a higher variance about its mean than elsewhere in the country – British Fabians, trade unionists, émigré prairie populists, and a sizeable minority of Marxists.

From its founding in Calgary in 1932 the party made little headway, outside Saskatchewan, until World War II. The decade of the 1940s encompassed both the rise and the fall of the CCF as a major party on the national stage. From 10 per cent in a Gallup poll in early 1942, support grew phenomenally until for one brief period in the fall of 1943, 29 per cent of Canadians backed the CCF; it was, according to Gallup, the most popular party in the country.[37] That year Premier Hepburn's Liberal administration in Ontario was defeated by the Conservatives; the CCF with no seats at dissolution came within four of forming the government – 38 Conservatives, 34 CCF, 15 Liberals. In 1944 the party formed what was to be its only government, in Saskatchewan.

In 1945 began the decline. In a new Ontario provincial election that year the party lost twenty-six seats, although its popular vote remained virtually unchanged. Mackenzie King forced the federal Liberal Party sufficiently left that it accepted responsibility for maintenance of full employment and a series of social security reforms, and the CCF did far less well than expected in the 1945 federal election. David Lewis, national secretary of the CCF from 1936 to 1950, has proffered three reasons to explain the inability of the CCF to secure its position as a major national party after World War II:

(1) massive contemporary business-financed publicity campaigns against the alleged evils of socialism, followed by Cold War hysteria; (2) post-war prosperity that discredited the CCF's prediction, based on the conclusions of orthodox Keynesian economists, that the decline of government expenditures for military purposes would engender a widespread post-war depression; and (3) an interpretation by many Canadians, tired of moral exhortations, that the CCF's demands for peacetime economic planning meant a continuation of wartime discipline.

Inexorably the party's popular vote in federal elections declined — from the peak of 15.6 per cent in 1945 to 9.5 per cent in 1958.[38] Frustration with the slowly eroding electoral support prompted the national leadership to explore new strategies. As indication of the new directions to be taken, the CCF in 1956 adopted the Winnipeg Declaration of Principles, a far less militant statement of party goals than the Regina Manifesto it replaced.[39] The electoral disaster of 1958, which reduced the CCF federal caucus from twenty-five to eight members, accelerated action by the national CCF and the newly formed Canadian Labour Congress (CLC) on behalf of "a broadly based people's political movement, which embraces the CCF, the Labour Movement, farm organizations, professional people and other liberally-minded persons."[40]

There was considerable resistance to reorganization of the CCF. The federal caucus and many long-time party members interpreted it to be a desiccated marriage of convenience arranged by the establishment of the respective organizations, and that CCFers would find themselves a minority within this amorphous new political party. A second source of resistance, overlapping the first, was based on ideology. The CCF left wing viewed substitution of the Winnipeg Declaration for the Regina Manifesto, the formal alliance with the CLC, and the appeal to the "liberally minded," as further adulteration of an already overly compromised party. Prairie populists saw that, relative to the CCF, the new party would be more urban, more interested in articulating the political demands of organized labour and less concerned with rural issues, attuned to the style of modern union politics and less interested in the political traditions of populism. The fatal weakness of the critics was that they implied a continuation of the status quo in a context where some form of revitalization was clearly necessary. The creative vitality of the constituent elements of the CCF had seriously waned and, faced with a choice between extrapolation of past trends or the "new party," the majority of CCF members opted for the latter. The New Democratic Party (NDP) was founded in 1961.

Although the CCF indirectly achieved many of its goals via the threat it posed in the mid-1940s to the survival of the federal Liberal government, the party ultimately failed to realize a left populist farm-labour alliance at a national level. The CCF's most dramatic impact was in Saskatchewan, the most rural of Canada's provinces and yet the only one, until the NDP victory in Manitoba in 1969, to elect a nom-inally socialist government. The CCF experience in Saskatchewan is important in its own right, but it should rightfully be read as the last and perhaps most significant chapter in the history of North American agrarian populism.

Populism, in both its left and right variants, involved strategies by those "at the bottom" to use the state to their advantage. After the 1930 transfer of resources from federal to provincial ownership, how-ever, relations "at the top" between provincial governments and resource corporations, of which those in oil and gas were the most important, underwent major changes in the areas of regulation over physical conservation and production, allocation of exploration and production rights for crown resources, and distribution of economic rent. Although populist pressures impinged on these changes, they essentially involved institutional bargaining between government and various corporate coalitions (the local independents often having divergent interests from those of the foreign-owned majors). In the prairies prior to 1950 virtually all oil and gas, and most other mineral resource discoveries, were in Alberta, and consequently it is to that province we shall now turn.

Notes

1. C. Martin, *"Dominion Lands" Policy*, edited by L.H. Thomas (Toronto: McClelland and Stewart, 1973), 9.
2. V.C. Fowke, *The National Policy and the Wheat Economy* (Toronto: University of Toronto Press, 1957), 58.
3. Manitoba Act, 1870, 33 Victoria, c. 3 (Canada), s.30.
4. L.G. Thomas, *The Liberal Party in Alberta: A History of Politics in the Province of Alberta, 1905-1921* (Toronto: University of Toronto Press, 1959), 4. The best study of the autonomy movements remains C.C. Lingard, *Territorial Government in Canada: The Autonomy Question in the Old North-West Territories* (Toronto: University of Toronto Press, 1946).
5. Lingard, *ibid.*, 242.
6. C.B. Macpherson, *Democracy in Alberta: Social Credit and the Party System*, 2nd edition (Toronto: University of Toronto Press, 1962), 21.
7. Stewart Bates, *Financial History of Canadian Governments: A Study Pre-pared for the Royal Commission on Dominion-Provincial Relations* (October 1938), 239-66.

8. On the utility and pitfalls of generalizing the concept to political movements beyond North America (such as the Russian narodniks) see P. Worsley, "The Concept of Populism," in G. Ionescu and E. Gellner (eds.), *Populism: Its Meanings and National Characteristics* (London: Weidenfeld and Nicolson, 1970), 212-50.

9. For an account of the complex radical-to-reactionary career of Tom Watson see C. Vann Woodward, *Tom Watson: Agrarian Rebel* (New York: Oxford University Press, 1963).

10. Two excellent comprehensive accounts of American populism in the nineteenth century are J.D. Hicks, *The Populist Revolt* (Lincoln: University of Nebraska Press, 1961) and L. Goodwyn, *Democratic Promise: The Populist Moment in America* (New York: Oxford University Press, 1976). For a discussion of the late nineteenth century agricultural economy see F.A. Shannon, *The Farmer's Last Frontier: Agriculture 1860-1897* (New York: Harper & Row, 1968), esp. chap. 13. Twentieth century American populist movements are treated by T. Saloutos and J.D. Hicks, *Twentieth Century Populism: Agricultural Discontent in the Middle West 1900-1939* (Lincoln: University of Nebraska Press, 1951). A useful collection of contemporary writings by populist leaders is G.B. Tindall (ed.), *A Populist Reader* (New York: Harper & Row, 1966).
Since World War II populism has been subject to widely divergent interpretations. On the right, it has been analysed as an example of irrational mass politics, as an early vehicle for many intolerant, anti-intellectual values in North American society. Among the best-argued indictments is R. Hofstadter, *The Age of Reform* (New York: Alfred A. Knopf and Random House, 1955). Irving treats Social Credit in Alberta as a case study in mass or collective behaviour (although he carefully avoids passing critical judgments): J.A. Irving, *The Social Credit Movement in Alberta* (Toronto: University of Toronto Press, 1959). A reasoned defence of American populism from its critics on the right is C. Vann Woodward, "The Populist Heritage and the Intellectual," reprinted in C. Vann Woodward, *The Burden of Southern History* (New York: New American Library, 1969), 104-20. On the left, populism has been treated both as a reactionary petit bourgeois movement of independent commodity producers and as the North American equivalent of contemporary European socialism. Two examples of the former treatment are William Appleman Williams, who attributes much of the responsibility for the growth of contemporary American imperialism to "farm businessmen" desirous of expanding international markets for American agricultural commodities, and C.B. Macpherson, whose critique of Social Credit in Alberta we discuss in Chapter Seven: W.A. Williams, *The Roots of the Modern American Empire* (New York: Random House, 1969), and C.B. Macpherson, *Democracy in Alberta: Social Credit and the Party System*, 2nd edition (Toronto: University of Toronto Press, 1962). Examples of the latter treatment are Seymour Martin Lipset, in his classic study of the Saskatchewan CCF, *Agrarian Socialism*, updated edition (New York: Doubleday and Company, 1968), and Norman Pol-

lack, *The Populist Response to Industrial America* (New York: W.W. Norton, 1966).

11. Lipset, *op. cit.*, 33-34.
12. *See* Goodwyn, *op. cit.*, chap. 15, and Hicks, *op. cit.*, chap. 13.
13. Quoted in Hicks, 438, 442-44.
14. Various versions of the subtreasury plan were advanced. In essence it envisaged the federal government establishing warehouses, to be known as "subtreasuries," throughout the country for the principal non-perishable crops, and loaning to farmers in paper money, and at a rate of one per cent per year, an amount up to 80 per cent of the value of crops delivered. Farmers were to sell their stored crops within twelve months (later versions allowed for the subtreasury itself to sell the crops direct to buyers) and out of the proceeds redeem the amount borrowed plus interest and storage charges. The subtreasury plan was thus a hybrid proposal—part central bank able to increase the money supply by the issue of paper money on the credit of stored agricultural produce, part commercial bank providing low interest credit to farmers, part marketing board permitting farmers to sell their crops direct to buyers at the most propitious moment eliminating the profits of speculators on commodity exchanges. The most valid criticism of the scheme was that the paper money issued by subtreasuries at any moment could be a vast and highly variable amount relative to the existing money supply, and could cause not only massive inflation but violent cycles in interest rates due to changes in the amount of paper money outstanding at different seasons of the year. Nonetheless the plan had considerable merit. Government-run marketing boards have proved essential to stabilize many agricultural markets, and undeniably monetary policy, then as now, was designed by bankers and conservative politicians primarily in the interests of creditor, not debtor, classes. An expansionary monetary policy, by lowering interest rates and increasing aggregate consumption by farmers, would have helped relieve the agricultural distress that prevailed from the end of the Civil War until the late 1890s. See W.P. Yohe, "An Economic Appraisal of the Subtreasury Plan," in Goodwyn, *op. cit.*, 571-81.
15. See H.U. Faulkner, *American Economic History*, 8th edition (New York: Harper & Row, 1963), 437-40.
16. See Hicks, *op. cit.*, chap. 10.
17. A concise discussion of the early years of the Standard Oil Trust and Texas oil politics is available in C. Solberg, *Oil Power* (New York: New American Library, 1976), chaps. 2 and 3.
18. See P.F. Sharp, *The Agrarian Revolt in Western Canada* (New York: Farrar, Strauss & Giroux, 1971), chaps. 5 and 6.
19. In 1914 Townley was a highly successful organizer in North Dakota for the Socialist Party, but the following year the party discontinued his work because he was attracting too many farmers and these new adher-

ents the party did not consider to have sufficient theoretical understanding of socialism. The rebuff from the Socialist Party was the immediate cause of Townley's turning his energies to the organization of a less explicitly ideological organization, the Nonpartisan League.

20. Details of the Nonpartisan League's industrial program are drawn primarily from Saloutos and Hicks, *op. cit.*, chaps. 6 and 7, and S.R. Weaver, "The Nonpartisan League in North Dakota" (Toronto: Canadian Reconstruction Association, 1921).

21. Quoted in Weavers, *op. cit.*, 19.

22. The Canadian Reconstruction Association conducted economic investigations and lobbied publicly on behalf of relatively sophisticated conservative issues of the day. It favoured the tariff and attempted to reconcile the West to the National Policy. It urged newly enfranchised women to participate in the labour force and to "apply themselves intelligently and with energy to the basic economic problems of national existence."

23. Weaver, "The Nonpartisan League in North Dakota," *op. cit.*

24. *Ibid.*, 71.

25. Quoted in R. Engler, *The Politics of Oil* (Chicago: University of Chicago Press, 1961), 16. Chapter 2 contains an interesting account of the impact on North Dakota politics of the discovery of commercial oil reserves in the state during the 1950s.

26. Quoted in Weaver, *op. cit.*, 15.

27. Patronage dividends are the traditional means whereby co-operatives distributed any surpluses at the end of the fiscal year to each member — in proportion to the extent of his patronage of its services, not in proportion to his investment.

28. Our brief discussion of co-operative grain marketing systems is drawn largely from Vernon Fowke's superb history of the Canadian prairie economy: V.C. Fowke, *The National Policy and the Wheat Economy* (Toronto: University of Toronto Press, 1957), chap. 8. For a lively contemporary journalistic account of the growth of prairie co-operatives and accompanying populist politics, see H. Moorhouse, *Deep Furrows* (Toronto: George J. McLeod, 1918). A sympathetic but uncritical account of populist politics in the Canadian prairies prior to 1935 is provided by Sharp, *The Agrarian Revolt in Western Canada, op. cit.* The standard work on the National Progressive Party, which also discusses the UFA and UFM, is W.L. Morton, *The Progressive Party in Canada* (Toronto: University of Toronto Press, 1950). Further information on the UFA is available in Macpherson, *Democracy in Alberta, op. cit.*; on the UFM in W.L. Morton, *Manitoba: A History* (Toronto: University of Toronto Press, 1957). William Irvine, one of the important leaders of this first wave of Canadian populism, provides, in a book first published in 1920, a lucid statement of the philosophy and goals, including group government, of contemporary populists: W. Irvine, *The Farmers in Politics*,

with introduction by Reginald Whitaker (Toronto: McClelland and Stewart, 1978).

29. Fowke, *op. cit.*, 141.
30. Sharp, *op. cit.*, 166.
31. For biographical material on Social Credit leaders, Aberhart in particular, see Irving, *The Social Credit Movement in Alberta, op. cit*, Macpherson (see Chapter Seven) provides a sophisticated Marxist critique of the UFA and Social Credit as petit bourgeois movements that failed to attack the fundamental issue of property ownership under capitalism: Macpherson, *Democracy in Alberta, op. cit.* Mallory analyses Social Credit's attempted monetary reforms from the perspective of conflicting interest groups and emphasizes the extent to which the constitutional division of powers between federal and provincial governments is the outcome not of abstract legal interpretations of the BNA Act, but of political bargaining and conflict: J.R. Mallory, *Social Credit and the Federal Power in Canada* (Toronto: University of Toronto Press, 1954). For an insightful analysis of the reasons for the failure of the CCF to establish itself in Alberta see M. Johnson, "The Failure of the CCF in Alberta: An Accident of History," unpublished paper presented at a conference sponsored by the Department of Sociology, University of Alberta, 1977.
32. See Macpherson, *op. cit.*, 107-12.
33. J.M. Keynes, *The General Theory of Employment, Interest and Money* (London, Macmillan & Co., 1936), 370-71.
34. *Financial Post*, September 19, 1936. Quoted in Mallory, *op. cit.*, 101.
35. A comprehensive history of the national CCF is available in W.D. Young, *The Anatomy of a Party: The National CCF 1932-61* (Toronto: University of Toronto Press, 1969). A highly favourable history of the CCF, at both the provincial and federal level, is D.E. McHenry, *The Third Force in Canada* (Berkeley: University of California Press, 1950). For the role of Canadian labour in the CCF and NDP, and the conflict between Communists and CCF for labour support, see G. Horowitz, *Canadian Labour in Politics* (Toronto: University of Toronto Press, 1968).
36. J.S. Woodsworth led the party from its founding until replaced by M.J. Coldwell in 1940. Hazen Argue was chosen house leader by the federal caucus upon Coldwell's defeat in the Diefenbaker sweep of 1958. From 1960 to 1961 Argue was national leader. In 1961 he ran for the leadership of the NDP, but lost to T.C. Douglas.
37. McHenry, *op. cit.*, 136.
38. Young, *op. cit.*, 319.
39. Both documents are reprinted in Young, *op. cit.*, Appendix A.
40. The quotation is from a resolution adopted by the 1958 CLC convention. Quoted in Horowitz, *op. cit.*, 192. The CLC had itself emerged only in 1956, upon the merger of separate congresses representing craft and industrial unions.

CHAPTER 3
Alienation and Resources: The Struggle for Conservation in Alberta

All over the North American continent a regrettable destruction of these resources was practised for many years. In many instances this destruction was selfish and unscrupulous. During the pioneer stage of development of all countries a certain and extravagant waste could not be avoided ... But, when such waste was continued, and no effort made to introduce efficient development, the continuance was criminal. ... In the oil and gas fields of the American continent strict Government control has never been possible, owing to the diverse ownership of the land and conflicting legal decisions, together with lack of unified legislation. This resulted in an orgy of waste which was introduced into these industries in the early years and has continued and been intensified with time. An ever-increasing greed was also noticeable, an adverse influence which the operation of a natural resource unfortunately appears to develop in the minds of operators and their employees. Owing to the lack of experienced labour, operators, developing oil and gas in Alberta, were forced to obtain the necessary personnel for their work from adjoining producing areas in the United States, and as the imported men had been trained under the above mentioned vicious methods of development, similar wasteful practices, when production was obtained in the Turner Valley, were introduced. These, unfortunately, at the time of introduction could not be controlled owing to the inadequacy of the regulations to cover work done on alienated lands.

Annual Report
Alberta Department of Lands and Mines
1932-1933

On November 20, 1946, an Imperial Oil Ltd. drilling crew headed by toolpush Vernon "Dry Hole" Hunter spudded in an exploratory well near the village of Leduc a few miles south of Edmonton, Alberta. Imperial's seismic crews had detected geological anomalies in the region, and Hunter's drilling crew had been instructed to drill to a deep level to test for formations discovered by another oil company elsewhere in the province. As Hunter's unflattering nickname suggested, Imperial's exploratory progress in western Canada since its arrival during World War I had been less than impressive. Imperial's first western Canadian wildcat had been drilled in Alberta in 1917. By the end of 1946 it had 133 dry holes and one discovery, Norman Wells, NWT, to its credit. Thanks to its control of the Turner Valley field, Imperial was the largest producer in the country, but production in Turner Valley had peaked at 28,000 barrels a day in 1942 and had declined to 20,000 barrels a day by 1946. Prairie refineries were becoming increasingly dependent on crude shipped by rail from as far as Texas and Oklahoma, at a cost laid down in Regina of $1.93 per barrel for transportation alone. Canada was importing 200,000 of its daily consumption of 221,000 barrels the year before Leduc.

Leduc #1 had been spudded in as a result of months of planning by a team of Imperial and Jersey Standard exploration and production executives. Imperial was considering the manufacture of synthetic oil from natural gas, but before committing itself to a high-cost synthetic fuel industry – the investment in which would be threatened by discovery of conventional oil fields – the company decided on another major exploratory campaign in the western Canadian sedimentary basin. In 1946 Imperial geologists explored along the eastern geosyncline for hundreds of miles in the vicinity of Edmonton before deciding on Leduc. Seismographs had detected a promising structure in a reef-type formation in deep Devonian limestone of the Paleozoic age.

By early February 1947, drilling at Leduc #1 had proceeded to a depth of 5000 feet when there were showings of high-gravity oil in the drilling mud. Imperial decided on a production test and, on February 13, with press, radio reporters, government officials and local farmers standing by, the well blew in. Vern Hunter later recalled the event: "By the morning of February 13 – the date set – we hadn't started to swab [a technique for sucking oil to the surface] and that operation sometimes takes days. However, we crossed our fingers and at daylight started in. Shortly before 4 p.m. the well started to show some signs of life. Then with a roar the well came in, flowing into the sump near the rig. We switched it to the flare line, lit the fire and the most beautiful smoke ring you ever saw went floating skywards."[1]

Leduc #1 triggered one of Canada's greatest resource booms, initiated a profound transformation in the Canadian energy economy, and ended nearly three decades of largely fruitless efforts by the international petroleum industry and many small independent explorers to prove the potential of the western Canadian sedimentary basin. The classic exploration and land play that followed in the wake of Imperial's first discovery well at Leduc lasted nearly a decade, and by the time the first oil rush tapered off several large and many small oil and natural gas fields had been discovered and tied into distant markets, in both Canada and the United States.

In part because of deliberate government policies, the pace of development was extraordinarily rapid. The first Leduc-Woodbend field was followed by Redwater (1948), Golden Spike (1949), Fenn-Big Valley (1950), Wizard Lake (1951), Bonnie Glen (1952) and Pembina (1953) – the latter a billion-barrel recoverable "elephant" pool located at Drayton Valley southwest of Edmonton. In these first expansionary years of the post-Leduc boom more than three billion barrels of crude oil and some eighteen trillion cubic feet of natural gas were proved up – just a fraction of the province's resource base, but more than enough to justify a continuing high level of capital investment by the major integrated companies, six of whom (Exxon-Imperial, Mobil, Shell Canada, Gulf Canada, Texaco, and Standard of Indiana) have dominated Alberta's oil industry since the 1950s. By the mid-1950s 70 per cent of the lands under reservation or lease and 80 per cent of proven oil reserves in the western producing provinces were under the control of American companies: the big six held about 40 per cent of acreage under reservation or lease and controlled three quarters of the proven reserves.[2] The same vertically integrated companies controlled the country's major oil pipelines and refineries; they also controlled Canadian oil policy until the early 1970s. The politics of natural gas were far more complex.

It is not our purpose to describe the post-Leduc boom in all its rich historical detail or to chronicle the tortuous paths of Canadian oil and gas policies in the 1950s and 1960s. The story of the oil boom has been told by other writers, albeit with a notable lack of critical perspective. In Chapter Seven we assess the impact of oil on Alberta's economy and society. In this and the following chapter our objective is twofold: to analyse the politics of development under Social Credit in the halcyon years of expansion and growth (1947 to 1955), but first to discuss the evolution of the provincial regulatory structure for oil and gas, and of the American structure on which it is based. Most administrative precedents were established in the late 1930s and in the years immediately following Leduc, and until the Lougheed Conservatives came to power in the 1970s these precedents remained essentially intact (indeed many of them still remain). We attempt to describe and to assess Social Credit's regulatory regime within a broad analytical framework for understanding bargaining relations between governments and large international firms over terms for resource development. Why did Social Credit choose certain policy instruments and reject others? Why did Alberta rely so heavily upon legislation and regulations borrowed from Texas and Oklahoma? Did the Manning government see realistic alternatives to an extreme dependence upon foreign capital? Why did most of the contentious political debate over the pattern of provincial development turn around the exports of natural gas? How efficient was Alberta's regulatory structure at capturing rents from oil and gas development?*

The Origins of Regulation

Following the transfer of prairie resources to the provinces in 1930, Alberta, Saskatchewan, and Manitoba set to the task of coping with the consequences of Dominion administration. In Alberta the agenda for resource management was largely defined, from 1930 to Leduc, by the struggles over waste and conservation, particularly in the Turner Valley south of Calgary – Canada's only major oil and gas field before Leduc. In this period rent maximization by the provincial government, as the new owner of crown oil and gas, was very much a secondary political issue for Alberta; not until the 1970s did bargaining over oil and gas rents displace the goal of increased markets or debates over physical conservation and prorationing as the central political concerns.

Although light conventional crude oil was not discovered in Turner Valley in commercial quantities until 1936, the field had been producing natural gas and naphtha since 1914 when a drilling company backed by a syndicate of Calgary businessmen, including Senator Lougheed, hit paydirt (the Dingman well) and triggered the province's first gaudy oil boom. Under Ottawa's indifferent jurisdiction Turner Valley was subjected to an irrationally fast pace of development – the result of fragmented ownership, unregulated drilling, and the complete absence of enforceable conservation laws. Concern was often expressed over the rapid depletion and loss of recoverable energy from the field but, until the 1930 transfer of public lands and resources, the province was helpless to prevent waste of its resources. Vast quantities of gas, for which there was little market, were flared at rates as high as 600 million cubic feet per day in Turner Valley, known locally as "Hell's Half Acre." Calgarians could sit on their front

* Unlike Saskatchewan's, Alberta's decision-making process must remain a subject for educated conjecture and speculation. We have used interviews and the public record wherever possible to answer certain questions, but until the files for the Social Credit years after Leduc are opened to the public the answers must be regarded as tentative.

porches on a summer's night and read their papers by the glow of the flares thirty miles away. From 1924 until 1938, when Alberta was finally able to establish a conservation authority with enough powers to force all operators to reduce the waste, the fearful flares burned night and day.

Alberta's dilemma in attempting to enforce a regime of conservation in the Turner Valley was a classic one: how to reconcile property rights with efficient resource management. In the early 1920s Standard Oil of New Jersey's Canadian affiliate, Imperial Oil, had moved into western Canada, partly as a consequence of Standard's postwar strategy of increasing its self-sufficiency in crude oil supply and partly in response to fears that Royal Dutch Shell (known among Standard personnel as "the yellow peril") was moving into the Canadian Northwest.[3] Imperial found no new oil in Alberta until 1947 but, following a pattern established by Standard in its early expansion in the United States, did very quickly succeed in establishing a position of dominance in the Turner Valley through its subsidiary, Royalite Oil Company. Royalite was created in 1921 to acquire the producing properties of the company which had opened up Turner Valley, following a disastrous fire in the latter's refinery in October 1920. Thereafter, Royalite and other Imperial-owned companies consolidated their control over Turner Valley, provoking much animosity among the many small independents in the field. Royalite had exclusive marketing arrangements with Calgary's gas utility and it also owned the only refineries purchasing naphtha and other oil products from the field. The independents had no markets for gas, so they simply flared it off; in the process they thereby reduced the energy drives in the field itself, and by the time the province received control of its resources in 1930 it was clear that, failing drastic political intervention, Turner Valley would quickly be depleted. The issue had been brought before the federal House of Commons by conservationists in the late 1920s, but Ottawa did little to slow the waste: indeed, its illogical allocation policies did a great deal to encourage it. Whether the field would have been developed much differently under provincial jurisdiction, given the very inexact contemporary knowledge of efficient reservoir development, is a legitimate conjecture; at the least it is reasonable to assume that the provincial government would have been forced into the learning by doing process somewhat earlier than 1930.

Oil and gas are resources whose peculiar physical properties virtually compel intervention by the state in order to prevent a chaotic pattern of destructive competition. Such intervention has occurred, largely at the behest of the oil industry itself, in areas such as Texas where individualism, property rights, and a distaste for government regulation have become almost a secular religion. To quote two leading authorities in petroleum law, the history of such intervention in North American oil jurisdictions has been "one of bitter conflicts on fundamental legal, scientific, economic and political issues. Belief in the right of an individual to do with his land as he wishes, so long as he does not commit nuisance, unwillingness to believe that engineering techniques could be applied to the production of substances from the bowels of the earth, only a gradually widening frontier of scientific knowledge upon which the validity of such techniques depended, and resistance to state regulation in any form were the motivations of legal and political attacks against all efforts to introduce conservation measures."[4] And yet, there were also powerful interests behind the movement toward regulation.

For both technical and economic reasons, competitive or common-property ownership of a "non-specific" resource such as petroleum leads to its waste and early depletion. The quantity of oil which can be produced from a reservoir depends on such factors as the loss of gas pressure caused by the drilling of wells, the placing of wells, and the rate of withdrawal of petroleum from the pool. Oil and gas are fugacious or migratory resources and will flow to the surface in whatever wells happen to be drilled in a field; where ownership and production rights are divided among many firms, producers of the common-property resource are of necessity placed in a furious competition with one another – each, in effect, attempting to rob his neighbour before his neighbour robs him. All operators favour the present over the future, and none has an interest in the maximization of aggregate recoverable reserves.

Such conditions invariably result in an excessive rate of depletion, whose costs must be borne by society. "Since each operator has a strong incentive to increase his share of production by developing his wells quickly, before the opportunity is lost to competitors on adjoining properties, all operators together create excessive productive capacity and produce at too fast a rate. Such competition for the common resource has an inevitable tendency towards development that is too early, wasteful of labour, capital and land, and hence depletive of the potential net value of the resource."[5] The obvious conclusion is that the reservoir itself is the natural unit for optimal resource management, and that the reservoir should therefore be developed under sole ownership. But the historical allocation of oil and gas rights in most North American jurisdictions, including Alberta, has not taken this into account. Fragmented ownership of mineral rights has been the norm; this has typically made it difficult to develop the reservoir as a unit and instead set in motion a cycle of rapid depletion and mineral waste. Indeed, it can be concluded on the basis of historical evidence that optimal development of the common reservoir under divided ownership is virtually impossible, save through legislative intervention or its threat.

To these inherent tendencies of the common-property resource towards waste, North American courts have added the so-called "rule of capture." A legal vestige of an earlier and more ruthless era of competitive capitalism, the rule of capture confers title to oil and gas on the person who can first reduce them to possession, i.e. bring them to the surface. Early legal decisions in U.S. oil-producing jurisdictions recognized an unrestrained right of capture which permitted the operator of an oil or gas well to produce it, regardless of the effects of such production on the rights of other producers or on the reservoir itself. The courts applied the common law principle that ownership is not confined to the surface but includes that which lies below as well. In coping with the problem that oil and gas are fugacious, the courts drew an analogy with migratory animals and birds, and established the rule that actual possession is required to obtain title.

This legal interpretation consequently stimulated free-booting resource exploitation that was both deeply anti-conservationist and the antithesis of Adam Smith's maxim about each man working for the common weal while pursuing his own greed and self-interest. The rule of capture, it has frequently been noted, encouraged the American oil industry to be conducted on principles of robbery. In Canada the rule of capture holds full sway apart from legislative intervention (discussed below), as the Privy Council confirmed in *Borys v. CPR and Imperial Oil Ltd.* (1953). "If any of the three substances [gas, oil and water]," Lord Porter observed, "is withdrawn from a portion of the property which does not belong to the appellant but lies within the same container and any oil or gas situated in his property thereby filters from it to the surrounding lands, admittedly he has no remedy. So, also, if any substance is withdrawn from his property, thereby causing any fugacious matter to enter his land, the surrounding owners have no remedy against him. The only safeguard is to be the first to get to work, in which case those who make the recovery become the owners of the material."[6]

North American Precedents
The rule of capture had encouraged the furious and destructive developments of the great "flush" oil fields of California, Texas, Oklahoma, and other areas of the United States in the early years of the petroleum industry. Conducted basically on the principles of a war of all against all, such development produced a catastrophic waste of energy re-

sources, but until the 1930s all segments of the U.S. oil industry fiercely resisted any movement towards state regulation. Then, in a brief and traumatic period between 1930 and 1935, relations between government and the petroleum industry were transformed by a series of far-reaching reforms at the state and federal levels. An industry that had uncompromisingly resisted government involvement "made a complete turn-about: in the early 1920s most important executives were repulsed by any governmental action at all; on the eve of World War II, few would have desired a return to the conditions that prevailed at the turn of the century."[7]

In essence, the American oil industry resolved its chronic dilemma of recurring crises of over-production, and unstable prices and markets, by working out a complex network of federal-state conservation policies, in reality "an intricate production-control mechanism"[8] at the domestic level designed to complement the international cartel arrangements of the major companies. While the details of this story are outside the scope of this book, some background on the origins of oil regulation in the United States is essential to an understanding of the conservation system as it has evolved since the 1930s in Alberta. Both Alberta's and Saskatchewan's institutional arrangements for planning the production of oil were consciously modelled on American precedents.

Early conservation statutes regulating the spacing of wells, the flaring of gas, and so forth, were enacted in some American oil-producing states between 1915 and 1919, but it was not until the early 1930s, following fierce political battles between the independent producers and the major companies, that the conservation authorities of Texas and Oklahoma were given enough legal powers to begin the controversial practice of prorationing the production of oil to market demand. Market demand prorationing is essentially an administrative mechanism for regulating the flow of crude oil into the market and preventing what the petroleum industry euphemistically calls "economic waste." This term has been applied to situations of unregulated supply in which producers sell at prices high enough to cover the costs of production but inadequate to yield a normal rate of return to the investor of capital or economic rent to the owner of the resource. However, what the oil industry considers a "normal" return on capital tends to be above the average rate of return on industrial capital, and to that extent market prorationing to prevent economic waste creates a situation of excessive profitability.

Prorationing is usually justified as a compromise between the need to prevent physical waste and the need to ensure that all operators in a given pool have the right to produce, but its fundamental underlying objective is supply management. Only coincidentally is it intended to prevent physical waste, i.e. waste of petroleum through evaporation, seepage, fire, or by the avoidable loss of the energy drives of the reservoir. While the production limitations entailed by market demand prorationing may prevent some physical waste, conservation agencies have a different and more efficient set of techniques for the latter task. Unitization of all pools and the abrogation of the rule of capture is the ideal. (To unitize a pool is to amalgamate the oil and gas rights of all those with claims upon it so that it can be developed as a coordinated unit, the costs and revenues thus generated being divided among those with claims upon the pool according to some pre-arranged formula.) Failing unitization, conservation agencies can and do regulate the spacing of wells, require enhanced recovery techniques, and impose on all wells a maximum rate of production (known as the maximum efficient rate, MER, or maximum permissible rate, MPR).

Although implementation has varied considerably in its complexity from one political jurisdiction to another, market-demand prorationing typically involves three distinct steps: (1) determination of market demand, (2) allocation of the market demand to pools, and (3) distribution of each pool allocation among individual wells. In oversimplified terms, under the U.S. prorationing system as it has evolved since the 1930s, state regulatory boards (such as the Texas Railroad Commission) are empowered to prohibit economic waste by setting monthly oil production quotas for the state based upon estimates of the reasonable market demand. Market demand is determined through monthly board hearings where refiners and other crude purchasers submit nominations (statements of their crude requirements) for the coming month. Once market demand has been established, the board then allocates to each producing pool in the state a production "allowable." Finally, each pool's allowable is distributed among its individual wells.

National coordination of state conservation activities has been achieved since the 1930s through the Interstate Oil Compact and through the monthly forecasts of national market demand issued by the Bureau of Mines in the Department of the Interior. The federal government also enforces oil conservation on its domain and prevents the interstate or foreign movement of any oil produced in excess of market demand through its administration of the Connally "Hot Oil" Act of 1935.

These interlocking pieces of federal-state machinery constitute an intricate system of public oil planning "that operates as smoothly and efficiently as the finest watch," to quote one U.S. Senate committee. The system was assembled between 1930 and 1935 as the U.S. petroleum industry's response to the combined crisis of world depression and domestic overproduction – a crisis that threatened the international production and market-sharing agreements worked out post-1928 by the world's three leading companies. In 1928 Sir Henri Deterding, head of Shell, invited his counterparts from Jersey Standard and Anglo-Iranian to shoot grouse at his castle at Achnacarry in Scotland. In between hunting and fishing, they arrived at the historic "as is" agreement. By it each agreed to adjust his respective production in order to maintain present market shares, and to apply a price system based on high-cost East Texas oil.

Although all segments of the industry were more or less united in their opposition to government intervention and regulation, a few of the large companies had begun in the 1920s to experiment with voluntary prorationing and unitization schemes. But in 1930 these schemes, and a 1929 American Petroleum Institute plan for "permanent" production sharing, collapsed under a flood of unregulated crude oil from two newly discovered fields: Oklahoma City in 1929 and the historic East Texas pool in 1930. The latter was a mammoth two-billion-barrel field, the largest strike to date in U.S. history, and it almost overwhelmed the industry. Neither the Oklahoma Corporation Commission nor the Texas Railroad Commission had enough power to enforce controls in the new fields, and by 1931 the industry's average wellhead price per barrel had been slashed in one year from $1.19 to $0.65: in East Texas oil dropped to ten cents a barrel, cheaper than water. Industry profits plunged. "From late 1929 to nearly the end of 1933 the pattern of crude oil production in these two fields threatened to disrupt all operations in the industry. In both areas, martial law was imposed for a brief period and a number of court cases, several finally reaching the U.S. Supreme Court, were instituted to test the legality of state statutes and the actions of regulatory commissions. It was a period marked by intra-industry conflict and direct threats of federal intervention."[9]

The conflict was especially sharp in Texas – the hub of the U.S. oil market – where the independent producers, who controlled the huge East Texas field, bitterly fought a campaign by the majors to introduce prorationing to the field. The independents were politically powerful, and Texas conservation statutes accordingly forbade the practice of regulating production to prevent economic waste. In 1931 the state legislature defiantly enacted an "Anti-Market Demand Act," annulling many of the orders of the Railroad Commission. At the behest of the major companies, martial law was finally declared and troops despatched to enforce order in the East Texas field. It was only when the integrated companies, who purchased the output of the field, used the club of ruinous prices (and, no doubt, a considerable amount of bribery) to enlist the backing of the legislature that the statute known as the "Market Demand Act" was passed in November 1932. This empowered the Railroad Commission to consider economic as well as physical waste: hearings were to be held monthly to determine the reasonable market demand, and waste was defined as any production in excess of this figure.

Its authority strengthened, the Texas Railroad Commission set to work to bring the East Texas field under control. But it soon found itself powerless to control the production of "hot" or contraband oil produced in excess of the Commission's allowables and marketed outside the state, and the politics of conservation and stabilization now moved to the federal level. President Franklin Roosevelt used the authority of the National Industrial Recovery Act of 1933 to ban the flow of "hot" oil across state borders, and meanwhile the American Petroleum Institute – galvanized by the threat of federal control over the entire industry – and the Governor of Oklahoma, Ernest Marland, initiated the formation of an Interstate Oil Compact among the leading oil-producing states. Texas, the leading producer, vigorously objected to the threat of federal intervention and protested that the compact was an attempt by a monopoly to impose a price-fixing scheme. The Texans were right. As one student of the period remarks: "Putting the issues bluntly, one might say that the Marland Group (Oklahoma) hoped to set up an organization closely resembling a cartel that would allocate the Bureau of Mines estimates of market demand to the oil producing states with the power to enforce production in accordance with this quota allocation. The Allred (Texas) Opposition was dead against this plan."[10] When it was made clear by Washington that the alternative could be as drastic as nationalization, however, these differences were resolved and the Interstate Compact to Conserve Oil and Gas was ratified by the leading oil states by 1935. In the same year Congress plugged the final loophole by enacting the Connally "Hot Oil" Act, thereby halting the interstate shipment of oil produced in excess of state allowables.

Thus did conservation and government regulation come to the American oil industry. The evidence is compelling that the system of output restrictions put together in the 1930s was designed rather more to conserve business profits than scarce resources. At the behest of its leading members, the oil industry was legally cartelized. The official biographers of the American petroleum business frankly note that the "main purposes of the conservation machinery as it had evolved by the end of 1935 were to restrict the flow of crude from new and old areas so as to keep current supply and demand more nearly balanced at profitable prices and at the same time to minimize the more flagrant 'wastes' and hopefully to increase the ultimate recovery of oil from a given pool." With the bogey of overproduction and distress oil eliminated, crude prices stabilized and the industry's average rate of return increased dramatically: from 4.3 per cent in 1933 to 13 per cent in 1936, 14.9 in 1937, 11.9 in 1938. Following the introduction of planned production, the average return on capital was nearly twice as high for firms with assets over $20 million as for those with assets between $10 and $20 million, and almost ten times higher than that of companies with assets below $2 million.[11] If the death of *laissez-faire* was painful, there were compensations for the survivors.

The Law of the Jungle: Conservation in Turner Valley

Against this dramatic backdrop of events in the oil fields of the United States, Alberta, first under the UFA government, then under Social Credit after 1935, struggled to devise its own conservation regime after the transfer of resources in 1930. Given the absence of alternatives and the province's proximity to the United States, Alberta's heavy reliance upon legislative precedents developed in Texas, California, Oklahoma, and other U.S. jurisdictions is hardly surprising. The situation in Turner Valley was acute, not unlike the typical early developments in the American oil fields. The combined impact of an illogical allocation system, the rule of capture, and Dominion indifference had created in Turner Valley what a provincial Royal Commission called "a law of the jungle." The waste of flared gas and potentially recoverable oil was scandalous: an estimated 1.8 trillion cubic feet of gas went up in flares between the wars, and the energy drives in the field were rapidly dissipated. A state of open warfare existed in the field between the dominant operator, Royalite, and the many small independent producers over the former's monopolistic marketing practices and the latters' refusal to enter into production sharing agreements.

After 1930 the newly formed provincial Department of Lands and Mines, empowered by sweeping legislation to control all aspects of the oil and gas industries in Alberta, attempted without success to devise enforceable conservation schemes in Turner Valley. The department commented in its annual reports on the "orgy of waste" that had attended oil development in the United States and blamed U.S. oilmen for introducing "vicious methods of development" into Turner Valley. The director of the department's Petroleum and Natural Gas Division proposed compulsory unitization for the province's oil fields, noting that "no matter how perfect any scheme may be it will only be possible by arbitrary action to enforce this form of development. Failing to

54

obtain the necessary co-operation from those now owning alienated mineral rights the latter should be nationalized on a purchase basis. ... Few if any industries have been developed with the same colossal waste and extravagance as that which has attended the development of oil and gas particularly in the United States where in the competitive race a vast amount of unnecessary capital has alone been squandered solely through a lack of confidence and co-operation between operators."[12] A Turner Valley Conservation Board was created in 1932 to restore order to the field, but resistance from the independents to production controls was so fierce that the board had to be disbanded.

In June of 1936, the year following the landslide election of William Aberhart's Social Credit movement, conditions in the Turner Valley deteriorated because of an important crude oil discovery – the Turner Valley Royalties well of Home Oil. Production boomed in spite of a lack of markets and pipeline capacity. "It became evident," the province noted, "that some wells were being produced at rates which would soon ruin them and which would result in terribly small ultimate recovery as compared with what might be expected if production was restricted and carried out on the basis of orderly development." Relations worsened between Imperial and the independent operators over the former's policies in Turner Valley. In the autumn of 1937 Imperial requested that the government establish potentials for individual wells so that the company could prorate its crude purchases; when the government complied, Imperial announced that it would not purchase more than 65 per cent of the production of any well; later this was cut by half. In the words of Imperial's own historian: "This raised a storm of criticism – reminiscent of early Standard Oil experience – by newspapers, politicians, and independent producers. The producers even considered building their own refinery."[13]

The decision of the Aberhart government to create the Oil and Gas Conservation Board in 1938 was partly a response to the campaign against Imperial, partly a reaction to pressures from Imperial for regulatory intervention in Turner Valley. Imperial was looking for an administrative buffer between it and the independents. Modelled on the Texas Railroad Commission, the Board was given a mandate to establish production quotas and to prevent physical waste, yet in another sense its true purpose was to stabilize the oil industry and to reconcile its warring factions. That same year, in a gesture to the independents and to Social Credit's populist constituency, the Alberta legislature passed a resolution calling upon the government "to give consideration to taking over the wholesale and retail distribution of petroleum products in the Province and/or to undertake a thorough inquiry into the spread between the field [i.e. wellhead] price of crude oil and the wholesale and retail prices of refined petroleum products with a view to bringing about a reduction in the consumer price of the said products."

The cabinet responded by setting up the McGillivray Commission to investigate the entire industry (we shall return to this commission in Chapter Four).[14] However, when the commissioners reported in April 1940, they attacked the concept of expropriation, defended the corporate behaviour of the integrated companies, and concluded "that the public in Alberta is adequately protected by the play of contending forces prompted by desire for gain." On the other hand, they urged the government to combat the "evils of over-production" through state-backed regulation, and taking their lead from the testimony of American oil conservation officials, the commissioners emphasized the need to mitigate the rule of capture either through compulsory unitization of pools (which they favoured) or prorationing. Regulation, not expropriation, was the watchword of the Commission. This was a prudent sentiment shared not only by the Aberhart administration but by every succeeding Alberta government. The rationale for positive government and the flight from competition lay in a convenient conjuncture of society's interest in the conservation of its resources and the oil industry's preference for stabilization at profitable price levels.

Greatly influenced by the practical experience of American conservation officials (the first chairman of the three-member Alberta Oil and Gas Conservation Board, W.F. Knode, was recruited from the Texas Railroad Commission), Alberta's Board began the difficult task of imposing order in the Turner Valley in 1938. Conservation raised daunting questions of equity. The Board's earliest efforts to prorate oil production and to prevent the wastage of gas provoked bitter protests from the independent operators, most of whom evidently viewed the new Board as an arm of the major companies. Lobbying the cabinet over the Board's head, the independents argued that the Board was not implementing conservation "but pro-ration, which will result in the major companies obtaining control of the production and development of the Turner Valley field." Given Imperial's exclusive marketing contracts with the Calgary gas company, it alone stood to benefit from the Board's restriction on gas waste. The prorating of oil was inequitable, the independents protested, since many small operators could not stay in business at the levels of production ordered by the Board: "the inevitable result of the policy of the Department of Lands and Mines and the Conservation Board will be that the independent companies operating in Turner Valley will gradually be hampered and restricted in the production which they can obtain, and the markets they can supply, to the effect that they will not be able to again carry on development and foster the oil industry in the Province."[15]

The coming of war and the extension of Alberta's markets eased the position of the independents: annual crude production in Alberta rose from 2.8 million barrels in 1937 to more than 10 million barrels in 1942, then dropped off steadily as Turner Valley went into decline. But the wastage of gas remained exorbitant, and American conservation engineers were retained by Alberta's Board during the war to work out a comprehensive scheme for conserving waste gases in the field. Imperial Oil decided, however, that "the economics of the situation were against it" and simply refused to comply with the Board's production quotas. Imperial informed the government that it would implement the Board's plan (which had been designed to be financially self-liquidating) only if Dominion assistance of $500,000 were forthcoming. Shortly before his death in 1943, Premier Aberhart advised the federal Minister of Munitions, C.D. Howe, that "there would appear to be no sound reason why any Crown assistance should be granted or why the companies who will be the chief beneficiaries of the plan should any longer be allowed to refuse to carry out this program of conservation so essential to the country as a whole." But neither level of government was prepared to force Imperial to comply. This placed the Conservation Board in a "completely impossible" position, its chairman complained, since the independents were also threatening non-compliance and accusing the board of "allowing Turner Valley to be stolen by the major companies."[16] The dispute was only resolved through a compromise proposed by Imperial: Royalite's exclusive marketing arrangements with Calgary's gas company would be terminated, in return for which the firm's pipelines would become a common carrier, operated on a utility rate of return, for all gas producers in the field.

Such episodes were highly revealing both of the limits of the Conservation Board's powers and of the broader pattern of Social Credit's relations with the integrated and independent fractions of the oil industry. The Board was not simply a tool of the major companies, but it did not believe that it could function without their compliance. And while Aberhart and his highly cautious successor, Ernest Manning, often professed an abhorrence of monopoly (private as well as state), through their policies and legislation governing the oil and gas industries they made it quite clear that their conception of the proper role of the state did not include intervention in the market to fight the battles of the independents or to roll back the power of corporations which were deemed indispensable to the economic future of the province.

Stabilization after Leduc

The great chain of crude oil discoveries which commenced at Leduc on February 13, 1947, quickly reproduced the familiar conditions of overproduction and surplus capacity that have always been so threatening to the stability of the petroleum industry. Production levels rapidly outgrew Alberta's limited markets, and in spite of the construction of the Inter-provincial Pipeline and the displacement of imported oil in Saskatchewan, Manitoba, and Ontario, excess capacity in the Redwater field (north-east of Edmonton) alone was estimated by 1950 to be 62,000 barrels per day, or 85 per cent of the province's average daily production. The overcapacity was largely caused by boom expectations and by the destructive competition that normally prevails under the rule of capture, but the situation was aggravated by government policies and the monopolistic structure of the industry. "Changes in the provincial land regulations in July, 1947, had introduced the requirement of surrender to the Crown of one half of the area under permit before conversion to a lease. This provision resulted in greater fragmentation of ownership of mineral rights in any producing field and, given the rule of capture, encouraged competitive development drilling. Imperial stated that it completed 286 producing wells in Redwater, where it owned 50% of the reservoir acreage, to meet the competition presented by twenty other companies that had acquired leases over the Crown acreage."[17]

In 1949 the integrated purchasers of crude – Imperial and British American – established a voluntary system of well acceptances under which the quotas purchased were substantially below the maximum permissible rates (MPRs), but intensive development of the Redwater and Leduc-Woodbend fields increased the problem of excess capacity. The independent producers found that their share of production was dependent upon the availability of a sales contract with one of the integrated majors, and a number of them complained of inequities within pools to the Oil and Gas Conservation Board. The Manning government introduced legislation in 1949 to permit prorationing to market demand, and the Conservation Board instituted the practice in December 1950 following public hearings. Planned oil had arrived in Alberta.

Did the Manning government consider alternatives to the creation of a producer's cartel? It seems unlikely. One critic has argued that if "the board was concerned by the market situation of many producers, few purchasers, and unpredictable additions to supplies ... it could have taken steps to break the power of the integrated companies by

requiring unitization of pools prior to production, by enforcing common purchaser requirements and, if necessary, by suggesting government entry into wellhead purchasing."[18] The reasoning is academic.
Later we shall argue that the last thing the Social Credit government
wished in the late 1940s was to "break the power" of the very companies it considered vital to the development of the province's oil industry. Under Ernest Manning's guidance, Aberhart's experiment in
radical right-wing populism had evolved by the early Cold War into a
"businesslike" conservative administration whose first priorities were
the preservation of political stability and the attraction of outside capital to Alberta. American conservation precedents loomed large, and
such a government would, in any event, naturally eschew concepts
such as compulsory unitization on the grounds that this method of
intervention would involve disturbance of property rights and might
even threaten its political entente with the American petroleum industry. The cabinet was also sensitive to pressures from the independents,
who now saw prorationing as a way of obtaining a larger share in
production, and it probably viewed cartelization as a compromise
necessary for the stabilization of the industry, as the only feasible way
of reconciling the interests of the independents and the integrated
major companies.

Alberta's procedure for prorationing the production of crude oil to
market demand is an adaptation of the American system discussed
earlier. The procedure has been revised substantially on a number of
occasions in response to changing conditions in the oil industry. Complex in its administrative detail, it follows the three-stage mechanism
outlined above: (1) determination of provincial market demand; (2)
allocation of market demand among pools; (3) distribution of each
pool's allowable among its wells. The initial step of receiving monthly
nominations from purchasers assumes a given price for crude and in
effect precludes price competition among producers.

Whether the price of oil ensuing from a typical prorationing system
dominated by the major producers is excessively high should be
judged in terms of the optimum price needed to ensure an inter-
temporally efficient allocation of the oil. Here we part company with
those economists who argue that a competitive free-for-all will better
perform that task. Usually the major oil companies have the technical
expertise and long-term planning horizon to make far better judgments on this score than the independents, and to that extent the
supply management restrictions of a prorationing system produce a
more efficient allocation of the oil over time than likely would ensue
from a competitive market with many producers. The real problem
raised by prorationing is the classic one of who gets the rent — the

owners of the oil via royalties, or the oil industry via excess profits; and within the industry, how are production and hence profits split among the majors and the independents? In general, one can conclude that, wittingly or otherwise, regulatory agencies charged with administration of market prorationing schemes have been successfully used by the major oil companies as instruments to realize their target rates of return and to perpetuate their dominant market shares. From the political point of view, such agencies also permit effective industrial cartelization without the dangers of anti-trust actions.

Prorationing is a decidedly inefficient mechanism for managing scarce resources. The allocation of market demand among pools and wells (steps 2 and 3) tends to substitute high-cost for low-cost production and therefore encourages inefficient operations. The original allocation formula adopted by the Oil and Gas Conservation Board in 1950, in response to conflicting pressure and advice from the majors and independents, guaranteed to each well owner an economic allowance sufficient to recover drilling, completion, and operating costs, provided the allowance did not exceed the well's maximum permissible rate (MPR). The sum total of such allowances was deducted from provincial market demand, and the residue was then allocated among pools and wells according to their MPRs. This procedure was used by the Board to guarantee the independents a share of production and was defended on grounds of equity, but it restricted the development of more prolific pools and wells and encouraged unnecessary drilling and investment in marginal reserves.

Faced with mounting criticism from the major companies, Alberta's Oil and Gas Conservation Board finally revised its allocation formula in 1964. The new plan, which became fully effective in 1969, phased out the economic allowable and replaced it with a minimum allowance for marginal wells which permits recovery of completion and production costs only. Other changes provide incentives for high-reserve pools and for reduction in the number of wells to be drilled, thereby lowering aggregate costs of producing oil. Yet the system still ensures production from high-cost reservoirs and marginal wells at the expense of low-cost pools. The new formula, while apparently weighted in favour of the larger, more efficient producers, can thus be seen as yet another compromise between the interests of the independents and the integrated majors.

Viewed from a broad political perspective, Alberta's Conservation Board performs several important functions. First, it stands as an administrative buffer between the oil and gas industries and the Alberta cabinet, thereby permitting potentially difficult political questions to be resolved in the sheltered environment of the regulatory tribunal.

Second, it performs the role of a cartel secretariat, supervising the output and allocation of production according to the industries' own rough definitions of equity. Third, it provides a forum (the National Energy Board is another) within which conflicts and grievances inside the oil and gas industries, notably those dividing independent and integrated producers, can be aired and legally resolved without concern for anti-trust actions. The latter role is particularly important. One of the central functions the state performs in capitalist society is to mediate and reconcile divisions within a capitalist class that is seldom, if ever, united as a class: in Marxist categories the state "organizes the unity of the bourgeoisie."

In the case of Alberta's Conservation Board, this mediating function has now been extended beyond the familiar confines of the petroleum industry. In the final months of Social Credit rule the agency was reconstituted as the Energy Resources Conservation Board and given broad authority across the province's entire energy industries, including coal, electrical generation and transmission, and non-conventional petroleum resources, such as the Athabasca tar sands and the Cold Lake and Peace River heavy oil deposits. Then, in 1974, the Lougheed administration empowered the ERCB to issue industrial permits for the local use of feedstocks, and thereby to regulate and promote the growth of the province's infant petrochemical industry – an industry, incidentally, in favour with the Board's leadership since the late 1940s. Traditionally tied to the interests and outlook of oil and gas producers, Alberta's Conservation Board is thus playing a more complex role in steering the development of the province.

The Politics of Natural Gas

To the limited extent that entrepreneurial initiatives, private as well as public, were taken by Albertans in the years after Leduc, they tended to occur in the development of the province's natural gas resources. There has historically been less integration and foreign ownership in the Canadian gas industry than in the oil industry, and since the 1950s the politics of gas have tended to revolve around regional rivalries pitting the consuming areas of the country against the western producing regions. Natural gas has been viewed as a crucial fuel for industrialization by "nation-builders" such as C.D. Howe as well as "province-builders" such as Peter Lougheed, and the reconciliation of national and provincial interests has tested the flexibility of Canada's federal political system on a number of occasions over the past three decades.

From Alberta's perspective, the most important economic and political influences on the growth of provincial powers over the gas industry were, first, pressures to prevent the wastage of gas through flaring or unsound methods of development; second, the threat of federal encroachments over provincial resource jurisdiction; and third, political pressures from Alberta consumers, industrial interests, opposition parties, and the media to give priority to provincial gas requirements. These combined to push Social Credit in the direction of provincial protectionism and encouraged some tentative experimentation with entrepreneurial policies.

Historically, Albertans have understood natural gas as a special birthright or natural endowment, and the resource has been closely linked to popular aspirations to industrialize and diversify the provincial economy. Accordingly, since 1949 the province has strictly controlled the production, sale and utilization of the resource through legislation such as the Gas Resources Preservation Act. The strong "Alberta first" opposition to the wastage or export of gas in the years after the Second World War was a logical precursor to the policies of the present-day Lougheed administration. Contemporary policies begin from the premise that Albertans have hitherto been denied a just return for the depletion of their gas reserves, including the opportunity to use the commodity as a catalyst for industrial development, and that outsiders have earned a disproportionate share of the benefits from the exploitation of the province's gas. It is because of the interventionist legacy of the Social Credit years that the Lougheed government is in a position today to use natural gas as the cornerstone of its development strategy.

No development issue was so contentious, so loaded with potential friction, in post-Leduc Alberta as the question of exporting gas from the province. On no other policy matter did Ernest Manning move with such extreme caution and trepidation. And with good reason: "... gas kept the street lights on and the barn warm and the house cheerful. The vast caverns of natural gas beneath the farm or the thousands of cubic feet running by in a pipe was part of the everyday life and folklore of Alberta. God had put it there for the enjoyment of His people. Woe betide the politician who sold such a birthright."[19] Natural gas was now widely understood to be both a cheap, clean fuel (a resident of Edmonton or Calgary could heat his or her home in the late 1940s for a few dollars a winter) and a valuable industrial feedstock, and there was virtually unanimous opposition within the province to any further wastage of the resource – the flares of Turner Valley were another part of the folklore of the province – and much popular resistance as well to the various pipeline promoters who planned to ship it out in large quantities to markets in eastern Canada and the United States. The *Calgary Herald* worried that "in five or ten years' time consumers in Calgary and elsewhere may find the price of their gas going up because it has to be drawn from more distant sources," while the *Edmonton Journal* fretted over the political implications of long-term exports to the United States:

> Once the export of gas ... is allowed to a foreign country, a "vested interest" is inevitably built up over the years. Ontario found this out long ago and again during recent years. That province consented, as a war measure, to the export of hydro power to the United States industries near the Niagara River. But when water levels fell and Ontario had to cut its industrial and domestic consumption of power, it discovered that it dare not reduce its exports to U.S. industrial plants. It had the legal right to do so, but had it done so retaliation was hinted, if not actually threatened, in the form of trade restrictions that would have been felt by Ontario producers and manufacturers. Alberta ... reserves the right to cut off gas exports in the event of any temporary emergency affecting this province's users of natural gas. But if it attempted to do so, it could find, as Ontario did, that the consequences would be unpleasant, to put it mildly.[20]

Both of Alberta's small but vocal opposition parties, the Liberals and CCF, opposed gas exports and the Alberta legislature saw several fierce shouting matches and donnybrooks over the issue between 1949 and 1954 (it was the central issue of the 1952 election). Liberal leader Harper Prowse vowed to be remembered by Albertans as "the man who delayed gas exports" and dared Manning to hold a plebiscite before approving removals from the province. Elmer Roper, leader of the CCF, linked the issue of gas exports to the takeover of the province's largest oil fields "by foreign imperialists," charging that Manning's choice of bidding system had permitted Redwater to pass into the hands of "rich and powerful foreign corporations who can put up the cash which Canadian co-operatives have not got."[21] But it cut more deeply than this. The president of the University of Alberta was speaking for an important segment of the community in 1949 when he privately told one pipeline promoter that "I may have a bit of prejudice against the proposal to export natural gas because I have always felt that this resource represented for Alberta what hydro-electric power represented to the St. Lawrence Valley. On this view it would seem unwise to sacrifice for immediate gain our long-range potentialities for industrial development."

This was a popular view. During province-wide hearings by the Dinning Natural Gas Commission, appointed by the province in November 1948 to investigate Alberta's gas reserves and requirements, the cities of Edmonton, Calgary, Medicine Hat, and Lethbridge, the Union of Alberta Municipalities, the provincial utilities, the chambers of commerce, the Coal Operators' Association of Western Canada, the Alberta Federation of Agriculture, the Alberta Research Council, and a variety of small manufacturers and businessmen all expressed varying degrees of opposition and outright hostility to the plans of the U.S. pipeline promoters, and many insisted that Alberta's own requirements be assured for up to fifty years before exports were approved (the province eventually settled for thirty years protection, a ruling still in effect). Business spokesmen wanted cheap gas protected as a catalyst for industrial growth; the Research Council anticipated major petrochemical developments; consumers in the cities and municipalities already dependent on gas wanted their supplies assured and worried that exports would force up local prices; more remote communities insisted that they be supplied before outside markets were served – in vain did Manning plead that this would be wildly uneconomic; while the declining coal industry was fearful of the effects that gas exports would have on its already dwindling markets. Much of the opposition was expressed in strong nationalist language, and the *Lethbridge Herald* was voicing popular sentiments when it editorialized in the summer of 1949: "Albertans want no wastage of this invaluable resource. There has been too much wastage already in the Turner Valley. The flares that lighted the skies for years over the Valley told their own story. More of our communities want natural gas for fuel. The demand for this clean fuel is growing and the *Herald* wants to see our needs guarded. If [export] is allowed it should be permitted only under strict control and not for the enrichment of absentee capitalists who have no real interest in the country."[22]

On the other hand, Manning's cabinet was clearly under very strong outside pressures to permit gas removals. No less than six consortia were actively lobbying the government in the late 1940s for permits – one of them, headed by Calgary promoter Frank McMahon, eventually became the Westcoast Transmission project, two others later merged into the Trans-Canada syndicate – and the major gas producers, such as Gulf, were equally keen to commence development. Unsure of its constitutional power to restrict the removal of gas but fearful that federally incorporated pipeline companies, most of them controlled by American interests, would try to make individual arrangements with the major producers, in July 1949 at a stormy special session of the legislature with most of the U.S. promoters sitting in the visitors' gallery, the Manning government pushed through several new pieces of legislation, including the Gas Resources Preservation Act, greatly strengthening its wellhead control over gas.

The new legislation provided for the protection of Alberta requirements, prohibited waste and – most important – empowered the Oil and Gas Conservation Board to control the removal of gas from the province by issuing export permits. This brought cries from the opposition parties that Manning was on the point of approving massive exports and that the bills were designed to place the power to do so in the hands of the Conservation Board and cabinet, and to emasculate the authority of the legislature. In fact, Manning appears to have been reacting defensively to a fear of outside encroachment, such encroachment being the classic motivation for provincial state intervention in Alberta. Social Credit had moved to protect its jurisdiction only after failing to convince the federal Liberal government to insert protective clauses in federal pipeline legislation requiring provincial permission before gas could be exported. Ottawa refused, Manning claimed, "90 per cent for political reasons," and left Alberta no option but to extend its wellhead control over provincial resources.[23]

As matters developed, it became clear that the Conservation Board was itself highly cautious and exports were not recommended until established gas reserves were substantially in excess of the province's own thirty-year needs. As discussed in Chapter Four, Ottawa had invoked the issue of continental military security to pressure Alberta to release gas to Anaconda Mining in Montana, and the same tactic was used by federal Trade and Commerce Minister C.D. Howe to push the province to approve exports to the Pacific Northwest. Howe, who was eager for gas exports for reasons of trade, informed the Alberta Minister of Mines in the early stages of the Korean War that, "I have recently been advised by the Chief of the International Program of the United States Munitions Board that the Board is seriously concerned about the lack of fuel in the Pacific northwest section of the United States, where the war-time industrial development, together with diversions of normal oil supplies to the Far East, has seriously accentuated the scarcity."[24] If Alberta supplies were not forthcoming, warned Howe, the market would be captured by a Texas franchise. Caught between external political and corporate pressure to export and local pressure to preserve the gas for ultimate use within the province, Manning insisted that gas reserves be proved up substantially beyond Alberta's needs before surplus gas was exported.

Ironically, such policies only worsened the government's dilemma since their effect was to encourage a rapid rate of accumulation of reserves and accentuate demands by producers that new markets be found for the capped gas. The opposition parties bitterly attacked the decision to approve gas exports to the Pacific Northwest via Westcoast Transmission in early 1952, and Manning evidently felt free to support the much larger Trans-Canada scheme only when he had fought and won the 1952 election on the issue of gas sales. Interestingly, whereas the Liberals and the CCF argued that gas exports would have a negative effect on Alberta's prospects for industrialization, Social Credit argued that such industrialization would not occur *without* exports: Alberta's best industrial opportunity lay in petrochemicals, an industry which would utilize the by-products extracted from gas before export. Failure to approve exports was restricting "an important phase of potential industrial growth," charged Manning. This seems to have been largely a political rationalization since he was privately skeptical and unenthusiastic about both petrochemicals and industrialization, given Alberta's distance from markets and the likelihood that secondary industries would require government subsidies.

Impending approval of the Trans-Canada project in early 1954 necessitated a further controversial intervention by Alberta into the natural gas industry. A precondition of new gas sales was the creation of a corporate instrument to defend the province from predatory encroachments into its resource base by outside monopolies backed by an acquisitive federal Liberal government. To appropriate a well-known idea of Professor Aitken, Social Credit required a new round of "defensive expansion."[25] On constitutional grounds the Manning government had long worried that federally incorporated pipelines could, by extending their gathering lines across Alberta's borders into its major gas fields, thereby also extend Ottawa's jurisdiction into the province and give the federal authorities wellhead control over Alberta's gas; this in turn could be used by the Dominion to undermine Alberta's emphasis on local priority in regard to supply and price, and to provide consumers in eastern Canada or the United States with cheap western Canadian gas.

In light of Howe's constant intercessions on behalf of American corporate and security interests and his single-minded pursuit of the Trans-Canada project, there was more than a little truth in this skeptical appraisal of federal policy. Fear of outside monopoly under federal jurisdiction was behind the enactment of the Gas Resources Preservation Act in 1949, and it was also the dominant consideration underlying the idea for a provincial monopoly over gas-gathering within the province. A single integrated gathering system would act as a common carrier inside Alberta, distributing pooled gas to export companies such as Trans-Canada at the provincial border. This would keep the export companies – and Ottawa – out, and prevent encroachments on the province's jurisdiction. If the ostensible threat was constitutional, it was Alberta's underlying fears of the empire-building instincts of Mr. Howe and his corporate allies that alerted Social Credit to the threat and provoked its defensive response. The parallels with the Lougheed administration's reaction in 1973 to the federal export tax on oil are striking.

The nature of the corporate vehicle created by Social Credit in 1954 was highly revealing of the ideological and political boundaries of its postwar policy. On the one hand, the government rejected an application by the two major provincial gas utilities and their parent, International Utilities of New York, to build such a grid, probably because of fear that it would be controlled from outside. On the other hand, Manning's cabinet rejected advice from its own lawyers that it create a crown corporation to shield Albertan interests and to put the province on its strongest constitutional ground. "Public ownership is bad in principle, worse in practice," Manning told the legislature. A crown corporation would impinge on industry rights and disturb the province's stable business climate – its most important asset in attracting new capital. Was Manning's aversion to public ownership based on specific representations from the oil and gas industries? There is no direct evidence of this, but it is worth noting that at least one major U.S.-controlled gas producer, Gulf, later threatened to cancel its marketing contracts with Trans-Canada if the federal government's crown equity in the pipeline was used to control it: Gulf had a long-standing international policy of refusing co-operation with any government which participated directly in oil and gas developments.[26]

As a half-way house, the Social Credit cabinet formulated the ingenious structure of the Alberta Gas Trunk Line Company. Incorporated under an act of the legislature passed in April 1954, Trunk Line was confined to the business of gathering and transmitting gas for export and was expressly forbidden to enter into any arrangements with gas export companies which could give the latter indirect control of the company. Two types of common stock, Classes A and B, were authorized: non-voting Class A shares numbering up to eight million; and voting Class B shares totalling 2002 and divided among four groups – the gas producers, gas exporters, Alberta's gas utilities, and the Alberta government (holding two shares and the right to nominate two of the company's board of directors). The voting shares were divided and appointments to the board so defined under the legislation that no single group would be able to gain hegemony; above all, it would be virtually impossible for the company to pass into the hands of external interests such as Trans-Canada. A large block of non-voting Class A shares were sold in 1957: initially restricted to bona fide Alberta residents, the issue was so heavily oversubscribed that sales had to be rationed. The ideological emphasis on people's capitalism – later invoked by the Lougheed government in launching the

Alberta Energy Company – was justified as the market value of the shares increased markedly. And, as Trans-Canada's own historian noted, "By forming this organization Premier Manning avoided the distasteful prospect of using a government department or crown corporation to control the direction or price of Alberta gas, while at the same time he effectively achieved the same thing by keeping jurisdiction over gas-gathering pipelines within Alberta."[27] Social Credit in effect had created a privately owned enterprise pursuing public, as well as business, aims.

Manning's refusal to make Trunk Line a crown corporation was, in retrospect, a crucial decision. He thereby made possible the eventual emergence of one of contemporary western Canada's largest and fastest-growing empires of indigenous private capital. Reflecting the new development priorities of Alberta under the Conservatives in the 1970s, Trunk Line has, under the management of Robert Blair and a board composed of representatives of oil, gas, agribusiness, and the oil-service industries, evolved well beyond its original purely defensive role and is engaged in a major programme of corporate expansion and diversification as well as an epic struggle with its ancient adversary, Trans-Canada, for control of Canada's natural gas industry. The victory of the Foothills group (Trunk Line and Westcoast Transmission) over the Arctic Gas consortium (dominated by Imperial Oil) for the right to transport Arctic gas south, the gas pricing disputes between Alberta and Trans-Canada at the opening of the 1970s, the rivalries within the gas industry over control of Alberta's growing gas surplus, and Trunk Line's participation in Alberta's first world-scale petrochemical complex are all aspects of the growth within Alberta of an arriviste bourgeoisie which has broken with the constrained role in life marked out for local capitalists by Ernest Manning. Trunk Line has been a leading force behind this movement, but it would not have been so as a crown company because the motivation – private accumulation – would have been missing. In creating Alberta Gas Trunk Line, Manning himself helped set the process of regional accumulation in motion – an interesting example of the unintended consequences of government intervention.[28]

Notes

1. E. Hanson, *Dynamic Decade* (Toronto: McClelland and Stewart, 1958), 68.
2. J. Davis, *Canadian Energy Prospects*, Royal Commission on Canadian Economic Prospects (1957), 143-8.

3. The best sources for Standard's policy are A.D. Chandler, Jr., *Strategy and Structure: Chapters in the History of the Industrial Enterprise* (New York: Doubleday, 1966), esp. chap. 4; and G.S. Gibb and E. Knowlton, *History of Standard Oil Company (New Jersey), The Resurgent Years, 1911-1927* (New York: Harper and Row, 1956) and in the same series, H. Larson, E. Knowlton and C. Popple, *New Horizons, 1927-1950* (New York: Harper and Row, 1971). Cf. also G. de Milne, *Oil in Canada West: The Early Years* (Calgary: Northwest Printing, 1969).

4. D.E. Lewis and A.R. Thompson, *Canadian Oil and Gas*, Vol. I (Toronto: Butterworths, 1971), Part X, at 166.

5. M. Crommelin, P. Pearse and A. Scott, *Management of Oil and Gas Resources in Alberta; An Economic Evaluation of Public Policy*, University of British Columbia, Department of Economics Discussion Paper, 76-19 (1976), 41.

6. *Borys v. Canadian Pacific Railway and Imperial Oil Ltd.* (1952-53), WWR (N.S.), 550.

7. H.F. Williamson et al., *The American Petroleum Industry: The Age of Energy 1899-1959* (Evanston: Northwestern University Press, 1963), 565.

8. J.M. Blair, *The Control of Oil* (New York: Pantheon, 1976), 153. On the history of conservation in the American oil industry see also E.W. Zimmerman, *Conservation in the Production of Petroleum* (New Haven: Yale University Press, 1957); Williamson et al., *op. cit.*, chap. 15; Larson et al., *New Horizons, op. cit.*; and R. Engler, *The Politics of Oil, op. cit.*, esp. chap. 6.

9. Williamson, et al., *The American Petroleum Industry, op. cit.*, 541.

10. Zimmerman, *op. cit.*, 207.

11. Williamson, et al., *op. cit.*, 554 and data at 563-64.

12. W. Calder, "Unitization Development Project," in Premier's Papers, 69.289/809 (Alberta Public Archives), December 1934.

13. Larson, et al., *New Horizons, op. cit.*, 112.

14. Hon. A.A. McGillivray (chairman), *Alberta's Oil Industry: The Report of a Royal Commission appointed by the Government of the Province of Alberta under the Public Inquiries Act to inquire into matters connected with Petroleum and Petroleum Products* (Imperial Oil Limited [publishers], 1940).

15. "Summary of representations made by the independent oil and gas producers in Turner Valley, re. Petroleum and Natural Gas Conservation Act 1938"; and also "Evidence Taken Before the Agriculture Committee in Connection with Bill No. 1, An Act for the Conservation of the Oil and Gas Resources of the Province of Alberta." Both are in Premiers' Papers, 69.289/812, Alberta Public Archives.

16. Correspondence is in Premiers' Papers, 69.289/811 and 812. The disputed gas conservation plans, the "Brown Plan" and the "Weymouth Plan," are also in these same files.

17. M. Crommelin, "Government Management of Oil and Gas in Alberta," *Alberta Law Review*, XIII, 2 (1975), 184.

18. *Ibid.* 185; cf. also G.C. Watkins, *Proration and the Economics of Oil Reser-*

voir Development, Province of Alberta, Canada, University of Leeds dissertation, 1971; and N.T. Khoury, "Prorationing and the Economic Efficiency of Crude Oil Production," *Canadian Journal of Economics,* II, 3 (1969), 443-48.

19. W. Kilbourn, *Pipeline* (Toronto: 1970), 18-19.
20. *Calgary Herald,* July 7, 1949; *Edmonton Journal,* July 7, 1949.
21. *Lethbridge Herald,* July 6, 1949.
22. R. Newton to J. Walker (Northwest Natural Gas Co.), January 31, 1949; *Report of the Province of Alberta Natural Gas Commission* (1949); and *Lethbridge Herald,* July 11, 1949. The *Medicine Hat News* worried (July 11, 1949) that "consent to export might well open industrial development elsewhere which could set back similar progress within the province for 50 to 100 years."
23. *Calgary Herald,* July 6, 1949.
24. Quoted in Gray, *The Great Canadian Oil Patch,* 166-67.
25. H.G.J. Aitken, "Defensive Expansion: The State and Economic Growth in Canada," in W. Easterbrook and M. Watkins (eds.), *Approaches to Canadian Economic History* (Toronto: McClelland and Stewart, 1967).
26. Kilbourn, *Pipeline, op. cit.*; *Edmonton Journal,* April 1 and 8, 1954.
27. The Alberta Gas Trunk Line Company Act (1954); Hanson, *Dynamic Decade, op. cit.,* 247; Kilbourn, *ibid.,* 56.
28. The best source of information on Alberta Gas Trunk Line is to be found in the company's *Annual Reports,* 1971-77.

CHAPTER 4
The Americanization of Oil: Social Credit and the Politics of Development

The oil rush has come
the broken bush and spruce country
have roads
one room schools have gone
the way of the out house
all the little Europes have disappeared
we have come from wood heated shacks
to pink gas palaces in ten years
the back ground is cutlined
marked square   blasted
drilled and pipelined
the torches burn forever at night
the plains are alive
with the campfires of millionaires

> Peter Christensen
> "Oil Rush," *NeWest Review*
> III 8 (April 1978), 8

The original concession agreements negotiated by the governments of Alberta and Saskatchewan with the international resource industries for the development of their oil, natural gas, and potash after the Second World War fall into a familiar pattern. Designed to induce foreign investors to commit risk capital to the rapid exploitation of non-agricultural staples, the concessions invariably provided favourable terms of access to resources, long-term leasing arrangements with royalty ceilings fixed at low levels, and assurances that crown-owned companies would not be placed in competition with private interests. Inevitably, the initial concessions were accompanied by solemn government undertakings to ensure political stability and a sound business climate, to respect the legal sanctity of contract, and to protect property rights. Renouncing any entrepreneurial role for the public sector, the provincial administrations of Social Credit and the post-1948 CCF in effect behaved like classic rentiers by encouraging large foreign companies to enclose their publicly-owned resources in return for minimal work commitments, some jobs, and a fraction of the proceeds from development.

Why did the provinces negotiate unequal concessions? In theory, any government assessing the prospects for the exploitation of a new resource has a broad range of alternative development strategies available to it. Assuming – as in the case of Alberta and Saskatchewan – that the state owns most of its mineral resources and has both proprietary rights and sovereign legislative powers, it can: (a) develop the resource itself through state-owned companies; (b) encourage domestic private investors to win the resource; (c) negotiate joint ventures between foreign companies and domestic concerns, private and/or public; (d) hire the skills and expertise of foreign corporations on a service contract basis; (e) rely exclusively on foreign investors and attempt to capture the economic rents through some mix of licensing and financial policies. Again in theory, the rational policy-maker optimizes his choice of development strategy after determining his goals and accounting for the availability and cost of risk capital, managerial skills, technology, access to markets, and so on.

But in the real world rational or strategic choice models of decision-making are unreliable guides to understanding why governments choose and act as they do. Bureaucratic inertia, incrementalism and the intrusion of domestic politics yield outcomes that could not be predicted with a model of rational optimizing behaviour. The full range of development options may not be considered. Ideological selection screens out certain alternatives, e.g. public ownership, and places government negotiators under a self-denying ordinance, thereby reducing their potential bargaining leverage. Moreover, given the oligopolistic nature of many resource industries, governments may find it impossible to organize a competitive market for the alienation of their resources. Rather than many firms bidding for development rights, governments may be faced with a few or often only one potential investor. In the extractive industries such as oil, copper, and potash, the terms of the original concession are struck "precisely at the points where the country [or province] is yielding of necessity to terms of an adversary at his strongest ... the formal contract with the ritual 20-40-99 year guarantee of 'inviolability' is a way of celebrating the foreign investors' moments of strength."[1] The large international firm begins from a position of monopoly control over information, expertise, and skills – a monopoly control that only a few alternative competitors can supply at a similar price. It has the experience, access to markets, and capital which the government needs to exploit its resource base, and it is initially in a powerful position to dictate terms for development. Government, on the other hand, typically starts with a very incomplete knowledge of its resource base or of the complex inner workings of the industry itself. It lacks bureaucratic expertise, often must rely on foreign consultants close to the industry to evaluate company feasibility studies and rates-of-return analyses, and is generally less qualified than the investor to assess and fairly discount the risk and uncertainty involved in new developments. Where a government is anxious for development to begin but has ruled out the economically and politically risky option of exploiting its resources itself, the international firm enjoys a monopoly veto power, and is literally in a position where its own lawyers and accountants can draft government contracts, legislation, and regulations.

Many students of resource development have emphasized the risks and costs of public investment, particularly at the stage of initial production. But the costs of being a rentier can be equally high. In assessing projected net revenues from any investment in an imperfectly understood political and geological environment where development has not previously occurred, a resource company will utilize a high discount rate (or, in what amounts to the same thing, will expect ex ante a high rate of return on invested capital). To an extent a realistic assessment of uncertainty may justify heavy discounting of expected revenues but, barring excessive cost overruns, the high discount rate will result in a capture of economic rent by the investing firm.

The distribution of economic rent (income in excess of a normal return to capital and labour employed) among the various claimants — owners of the resource, developing firms, consumers — depends crucially upon the degree of bargaining power each is able to deploy during the negotiation and renegotiation over the terms of development. Resource companies naturally exploit their "moments of strength" to maximize their share of the economic rent which arises due to a scarcity of the resource in question and/or barriers to entry characteristic of oligopoly in such industries. The power of resource companies to exact rent is greatest at the point before they have transformed their capital into fixed assets in place, and while they enjoy a temporary monopoly over skills and information; thereafter, this power tends to be whittled away until another round of major investments is pending. Companies exploit their initial bargaining advantage not only to exact high initial returns but to cement the initial asymmetries of power through long-term concessions. From the perspective of the corporation the concession — with its paraphernalia of

"sanctity of contract" and guarantees of stability and "inviolability" – is intended to postpone the erosion of its monopoly power,
and slow the cumulative shift in bargaining advantage towards the
government.

The price a government pays for risk-aversion and an unwillingness
to test its entrepreneurial skills can be very high indeed. The earliest
petroleum concessions obtained by the international oil companies in
countries such as Mexico, Venezuela, Persia (Iran), Iraq, Bahrain,
Saudi Arabia, and Kuwait were "negotiated" in a context of economic
imperialism and were so lucrative to the companies that they were
tantamount to outright plunder. Typically, one or several of the companies obtained exclusive rights to explore for oil over vast tracts of
land for up to ninety-nine years in return for a few thousand pounds
or dollars, a small annual payment or a very low per barrel royalty. In
many instances the codes setting out the rights and responsibilities of
the concessionaires were drafted by the companies themselves, after
only the most primitive exercises in bargaining. Lacking the most
rudimentary information about their oil reserves or the industry,
Third World countries had little choice but to accept the terms offered
by the companies. "It is inconceivable today," Edith Penrose has
noted, "that any government would accept the argument put forward
by the Anglo-Persian Oil Company in the negotiations over the revi-
sion of the D'Arcy Concession in 1933 that a 60-year concession was a
'necessary condition for the sinking of further large capital sums in the
installations in Persia'. At any reasonable rate of discount no business
firm would make a capital investment for a return on which it would
have to wait 60 years. Economists acting on behalf of the oil-
producing countries would today make hash of such an argument. ..."[2]

Because the original concessions tend to be so unequal, they are also
highly unstable. Once the foreign investor has sunk his capital into
fixed assets and as soon as the venture is financially successful, the
balance of power begins to shift away from the concessionaire towards
the landlord. Risk and uncertainty are reduced; the host government's entrepreneurial appetites are whetted as it "gazes out at a
profitable operation, carrying off resources the country was sure it had
all along, in which a large part of the revenue is flowing away to
foreigners."[3] Successful projects provide an incentive for government
to move gradually up a learning curve, and to develop the administrative expertise and negotiating skills which can decrease the asymmetries of bargaining power. Rapid development induced by the
favourable terms of the original concession brings urbanization and
social change in its wake. Fiscal pressures on the state increase until

the opportunity costs of inertia become intolerably high.[4]

The changing balance of internal classes, the growth of new ideological perspectives, and the impact of external events have all been crucial in the postwar development of oil, gas, and potash in western Canada, and it would be a mistake to ignore such variable factors. Within broad limits, however, and with the inevitable fluctuations that accompany the growth of resource industries, the above analysis of the bargaining cycle is a good approximation of the politics of development in Alberta and Saskatchewan over three decades. It is within this context that the early oil and gas policies of Social Credit must be reviewed.

The Populist Response to Oil

Farm mechanization after World War I contributed to a rapidly growing rural demand for petroleum, and as the co-operative movement diversified into wholesale and retail activities, it naturally developed co-operative bulk and retail gasoline outlets. These outlets bought much of their stock from small independent refiners who, by the 1930s, were being bought out by the majors as the latter concentrated refining into fewer and larger refineries. The emphasis of these initial ventures into oil distribution was merely to narrow the margin between the wholesale and retail price. With the disappearance of independent refiners it became obvious that the majors had considerable discretion over wholesale prices. Consequently the co-operatives considered the potential of backward integration. In 1934 ten co-operatives in the Regina area decided to build a co-operatively owned refinery. In the depth of the depression they raised as share capital from the farm community the meagre sum of $32,000. Nonetheless in 1935 they brought on stream Canada's only co-operatively owned refinery. With an original capacity of 500 barrels a day it was tiny, but it has proved itself in the intervening four decades to be a resounding financial success, and by the 1970s had expanded to a respectable capacity of 28,000 barrels per day.[5]

The farm co-operatives were unwilling to integrate further backwards into oil production. The capital requirements, the risks, the alien technology, the power of the major oil companies were forbidding obstacles. Instead they formulated demands for government intervention. Although the wasteful practices of overdrilling and gas flaring at Turner Valley offended the farmer's sense of wise husbanding of a resource, and the Alberta provincial government, under both the UFA and Social Credit, moved after the transfer of public lands in 1930 to establish conservation procedures, the perspective that farmers brought to the industry prior to World War II was essentially that of consumers. They did not perceive themselves as the ultimate owners, via the provincial government, of a resource whose economic rent they should seek to maximize. This limited consumer perception played its role in assuring that economic rents from early oil developments flowed to the producing companies.

This consumer orientation is amply illustrated by the McGillivray Commission (introduced in Chapter Three), established in response to a 1938 resolution of the provincial legislature.[6] The resolution – with its reference to spreads between wellhead, wholesale, and retail prices, and aim to reduce consumer prices – reflects precisely the contemporary conception of the problem by most populists. Aberhart's papers as Premier contain numerous pleas to tackle the oil industry from supporters who saw no contradiction in simultaneously backing Social Credit's attack upon finance and the more generalized anticorporate critique of the CCF. Aberhart's letters in reply (see below) are however quite explicit that, intent as he was upon monetary reform as the key to restored economic prosperity, there would be no major challenge to the oil industry from his government. In its choice as chairman of Alexander McGillivray – urban lawyer, Alberta Supreme Court judge, and former leader of the provincial Conservatives – the government could scarcely be accused of taking counsel from radical populists.

In addition to regulatory proposals for the prevention of waste discussed previously, the commissioners discussed in some detail the Texas Gulf pricing structure which had been formalized by the 1928 "as is" agreement among three of the largest oil companies.[7] The foundation of the structure was a "seaboard price" of East Texas oil delivered to a port on the Gulf of Mexico, this price to be high enough to guarantee a "reasonable" profit on the high-cost Texas fields. In principle the structure called for the delivered price, adjusted for grade and quality, in all markets throughout the world to equal this seaboard price plus the cost of transporting oil to the market in question from the Gulf of Mexico. In markets allocated by the "as is" or subsequent agreements to non-Texas oil the transport cost from Texas, being entirely hypothetical, became known as "phantom freight." Knowing the market for which it was intended, the appropriate wellhead price of oil from any field in the world equalled in principle the delivered price of Texas oil less the actual cost of transporting oil from the field in question to the designated market. The structure thus set prices for markets served by non-Texas oil on the basis of the price Texas producers would charge were they to supply them – a procedure that the oil company witnesses and commissioners rapturously described as "competitive forces bring[ing] the price of crude at each pool into dynamic equilibrium with the crudes from all other pools with which it is in competition, and so in dynamic equilibrium with all crudes throughout the world."[8] The commissioners freely admitted that under this system "it is to be recognized that there is no present close relationship between cost of production and [wellhead] price."[9] They even recognized the role of a price leader, Imperial Oil in the case of Turner Valley, in applying the formula to determine the appropriate wellhead price.

Having relied for its analysis of pricing primarily on American expert witnesses close to the oil industry, there were two basic questions the commissioners never asked. What justification was there for the foundation to the whole pricing edifice, the Texas Gulf seaboard price? Secondly, assuming the application of the Texas Gulf formula to Alberta oil, was the provincial government as owner of the oil in place, capturing the ensuing economic rent? The Texas Gulf pricing structure can only be fully understood in the context of the "as is" agreement that shut in much low-cost offshore oil in order to preserve the profitability of high-cost Texas fields. It assured large economic rents on the vast low-cost reserves of the Middle East (of which only a small fraction had at the time been discovered), on the recently discovered East Texas fields and, on a more humble scale, it created excess profits on Alberta oil. Prior to Leduc average production costs of Alberta oil were not low but, within the small prairie market supplied by Alberta crude, distances and hence transport costs were much lower than from Texas. Thus determination of the prairie crude oil price on the basis of a Texas seaboard price plus phantom freight provided a handsome wellhead price to Alberta producers – particularly to Imperial Oil which possessed the most productive least cost wells.

In assessing the populist allegation of an excessive spread between wellhead and retail price, the commissioners decided to examine the rate of profit of the Alberta refining and wholesale marketing operation of Imperial Oil, the largest integrated company in the province. If the spread was excessive, the commissioners argued, the rate of profit on these operations would be excessive. Using Imperial's accounting practices for capital valuation and determination of net income, the commissioners found for the year 1938 an after-tax rate of return on capital employed of 10.6 per cent[10] for the marketing operations and 12.7 per cent for refining.[11] Such returns, the commissioners concluded, were reasonable. In addressing the issue of the province nationalizing the petroleum distribution function or using legislative powers to set prices, they concluded "that there is no present need for government intervention."[12] We may object that for 1938, a depression year, the calculated rates of return are doubtless well above the year's average for industrial capital. The essential point however is not the rate of return on refining and distribution, but that the Texas Gulf pricing structure provided for the bulk of profits to be earned at the production level. Neither the commissioners, nor the more skeptical populists testifying, approached the problem of resource policy from the perspective of maximizing the returns to the province as owner of the oil in place. The perspective of both was that of consumers – the one attacking, the other justifying, retail price levels.

Social Credit's Entente with Oil

From the date of their landslide victory in 1935, Social Credit's leadership made it clear that the radical thrust of their right populist movement was not directed at the oil industry. In the desperate economic circumstances of the great depression, with Alberta deeply in debt, Social Credit was eager to entice outside capital into the search for oil. Premier Aberhart telegraphed assurances to the financial press and the oil trade bulletins that the province intended to give every incentive to risk capital.

In 1936 Aberhart appointed Nathan Eldon Tanner to be Minister of Lands and Mines (later Mines and Minerals). More than any other Alberta politician, including Ernest Manning, Tanner was the real author of the province's regulatory system for oil and gas. In his sixteen years in the portfolio (before leaving politics in 1952 to make his fortune in oil and gas, notably as the first president of Trans-Canada Pipelines; today he is a senior Elder in the Mormon Church hierarchy in Salt Lake City, Utah), Tanner put in place most of the complex administrative apparatus for allocating exploration and development rights to crown minerals, for regulating oil production, and for controlling the removal of gas from Alberta. It was Tanner who visited England in search of development capital and who toured the oil-producing states of the American Southwest in the late 1930s to study their methods for auctioning oil and gas rights and for preventing mineral waste. Tanner's department imported officials from the Texas Railroad Commission and other U.S. agencies to supervise the creation of Alberta's Oil and Gas Conservation Board and to devise schemes for reducing the wastage of oil and gas in the Turner Valley.

A conservative small businessman as well as former Mormon bishop and high school principal at Cardston, Alberta, "cast in the mold of those devout Mormons to whom hard work and self-reliance is both a way of life and a part of religion,"[13] Tanner launched a vigorous campaign to stimulate the search for Alberta's oil and gas. In 1936 revisions were made to Alberta's petroleum and natural gas regulations, permitting drilling companies to deduct their operating costs from their rentals of crown leases (companies drilling on freehold lands were allowed to write off half of their expenditures against rentals owing to the crown), and offering royalty rebates for wildcat discoveries of oil. At the same time the province's exploration permit and leasing regulations were amended in favour of private operators – all part of Social Credit's "endeavour to encourage introduction of new capital to the development of Alberta's great and widespread natural wealth."[14] The pattern of development established under Nathan Tanner in the first months of Social Credit rule laid the foundations for the growth of the province's oil industry after Leduc. While much of the legislation was incrementally amended and revised, and some new mechanisms were introduced after 1947 in response to the pressures of expansion, it was, as we have seen, in the late 1930s that the basis of the regulatory structure was conceived and passed into law. Profoundly conservative in its emphasis upon property rights and strongly influenced by the regulatory tradition of the southwest United States, much of this structure persists today and is now deeply imbedded in the statutes of Alberta and in the corpus of Canadian oil and gas law.

To some Social Credit supporters Nathan Tanner's campaign to attract development money to Alberta was nothing short of betrayal. Standard Oil was about as popular among prairie populists as the CPR or any other outside monopoly. Worse, Tanner had even enticed eastern Canadian capital into the hunt for oil! It was too much. One of Aberhart's admirers protested vigorously "that eastern interests have come in and have leased 40,000 acres to develop for oils":

> Here, Mr. Aberhart, is *just the thing we object to!* Prior to the election we were given assurance after assurance that such a despicable policy would end when Social Credit came into power. But what do we find? – the same old plundering of the west by the eastern capital as before. That is what the UFA government did and we put their selling out practices past the Social Credit government. I, for one, am definitely opposed to Russianism, Sovietism or anything of that nature, but I do believe that the province can develop its *own* natural resources with its *own* capital (using Social Credit if you please) without recourse to eastern capitalists ... what we want above all else is that our natural resources shall not be stolen from us and we in turn exploited to unmerciless [sic] degrees. If outside interests can come in and make big profits why can't we operate them ourselves and keep the money here? (emphasis in original)[15]

(This critic exceeded the usual populist demand. He hinted that the

79

economic rent arising from any crown development need not all be applied to oil price reduction; instead he implied that the alleged "big profits" of development be made available to the crown for general purposes.) Aberhart's reply was utterly conventional and can hardly have reassured his anxious supporter. The province's resources were of no value to anyone so long as they remained in an undeveloped state: "Our policy will be to encourage their development, thereby stimulating trade and industry within the Province, and giving employment to our own people. This does not mean that the Government itself will undertake the risks and actually conduct the enterprises required in development; but it does mean that the Government will exercise careful supervision and control through regulations and agreements which we have the power to make."[16]

Social Credit's attitude to the oil industry was not only limited by the consumer perception of most contemporary populists, but was also deformed by the ideological fixations of right populism. The true enemy was International Finance: "the core of the economic problem which confronts us," Aberhart insisted during a critique of CCF oil policies, "is to overthrow the domination of the money power and gain effective control of our credit resources."[17] By the late 1930s, as we noted in our earlier discussion of the origins of conservation in Alberta, the provincial oil industry was in a state of upheaval and there existed considerable public agitation for a government takeover of all or part of its phases. The discovery of crude oil in the Turner Valley in June, 1936, had set the independents at war with Imperial Oil; public outcry continued against the exorbitant wastage of resources in the field, and to this was added the populist sentiment that the major oil companies were exploiting the consumer through the spread between the wellhead crude oil price and the marketed price of gasoline and fuel oil. The CCF was leading the campaign for the takeover of the industry. Aberhart's cabinet had reacted by calling in Texan advisors who drafted legislation setting up an Oil and Gas Conservation Board closely patterned after the Texas Railroad Comgovernment takeover ("a government should not be in business in competition with its own citizens"), and Aberhart was in full agreement. Responding to CCF attacks on his oil policy, he argued that a takeover would only strengthen the hands of the great financial interests who were enslaving the common people. "Socialization" of the oil industry could only be accomplished through expropriation or with equitable compensation. "Expropriation can be ruled out. It is a vicious principle which strikes at the very roots of democratic institutions and ordered society. It would rapidly reduce the life of a country to chaos

80

and revolution." Compensation would involve taking over industries, and paying the owners with borrowed cash or bonds and debentures. Who would benefit? The financiers would be the sole beneficiaries of what the CCF proposed:

> On the other hand, given control of the financial system and their credit resources, a people's economy can be so ordered that socialization – or public ownership – is rendered unnecessary. So-called public ownership of Industry has been aptly described as a state of affairs under which everything belongs to everybody and nothing belongs to anybody. It involves centralization of control and large scale regimentation. Our objective is to confer the maximum Freedom and Security on the individual – in short, decentralization of control. National Socialism in Germany and Soviet Socialism in Russia are excellent examples of the out and out application of the social philosophy of so-called Socialism.[18]

Socialism, indeed, was fast supplanting international finance as the principal enemy of Aberhart and his followers (to some fundamentalist Social Crediters, the two were locked with international Jewry in a titanic plot against mankind). The CCF was on the rise in the early 1940s, and while it had fared poorly in Alberta, its successes in the rest of western Canada had thus far prevented Social Credit from becoming anything more than a single-province phenomenon. The war years saw Canada return to economic prosperity but they also called into being a strong central government armed with sweeping emergency powers: the provinces were little more than spectators in the movement toward a centrally planned war economy. Social Credit now perceived Alberta as a lonely ideological outpost threatened by the advancing forces of collectivism and centralization. Aberhart's young and shrewd successor, Ernest Manning, fought and handily won the provincial election of 1944 on the issues of provincial autonomy and the perils of socialism – a formula which, combined to the low taxation and growth accompanying oil, ensured Social Credit's political hegemony for another quarter of a century.

Social Credit now stood for free enterprise against the growing leftist trend in Canada: under Manning the movement left its agrarian heritage well behind, sought an accommodation with external capital and threw its propaganda resources into the Cold War struggle against communism. When Harper Prowse revived the provincial Liberal party of Alberta in 1947 he found businessmen reluctant to give him contributions. "We've got a business-oriented government now," they told him. "Why rock the boat and let in the CCF?"[19] By the 1948 election Manning was afraid of scaring off oil development capital, and he actively campaigned against a rural-backed plebiscite to bring the privately owned power companies, notably Calgary Power, under public ownership. Terming public ownership "risky" and predicting power shortages by 1951 if the plebiscite succeeded, Manning equated the "milk and water" socialism of the CCF with Naziism and communism: "You only need to look at a map to know why the Communists want socialist states in western Canada," he told one meeting. Alberta's public power plebiscite was defeated by a very slim margin (139,991 to 139,840 votes), with the conservative southern cities of Calgary, Lethbridge, and Medicine Hat tipping the balance by siding heavily with Manning and the private power companies, against the large majority of rural voters[20] who supported public power. Social Credit's metamorphosis into "businesslike" government was by now complete.

The conservative, almost xenophobic, ideological climate prevailing in Alberta in the early years of the Cold War smoothed the way for the Americanization of the province's oil and natural gas resources. The military security of the continent was invoked on numerous occasions to justify reliance upon U.S. capital or the approval of controversial exports of gas to Montana and the Pacific Northwest. Alberta's resources were to be committed to the free world's struggle with Godless communism. Following the outbreak of the Korean War in 1950, for example, the U.S. Department of Defense became concerned over the availability of natural gas supplies for the Anaconda Copper Mining Co., whose smelters at Butte, Montana, produced 23 per cent of America's zinc, 8 per cent of its copper and 85 per cent of its manganese. Alberta had not as yet approved any proposals to remove natural gas from the province, and so the Pentagon asked the Canadian Department of Defence to intercede with Alberta to ensure that the necessary supplementary supplies would be made available. A special law was duly enacted by the province in 1951 authorizing the removal of up to 10 billion cubic feet a year from Alberta's gas fields for the exclusive benefit of Anaconda, and a license to export was granted by Ottawa. Anaconda thereby obtained access, via the pricing arrangements worked out between it and Montana Power Co., to Canadian gas at a cost between one third and one half what it would otherwise have had to pay for energy in the form of coal or residual fuels (whether this was the real motive behind Washington's intervention is unclear).[21] The special arrangement was unpopular with the opposition CCF and Liberals in Alberta – they rightly saw it as the first in a series of export deals – and Social Credit's defence of the export was largely couched in terms of overriding strategic necessity. During the debate at the spring session of the 1951 legislature, one Social Credit cabinet minister brought forward the news that he had uncovered 500 to 600 spies and potential saboteurs working in Alberta's industries. "He based his calculations," the Calgary *Herald* reported, "on newspaper reports that there were 650,000 Communists or sympathizers in the United States, about 10 per cent of them potentially dangerous spies. The same sources estimated that there were 64,000 in Canada which meant 6,400 were potentially dangerous and 'he left it to the people to decide' whether the figure of 500 to 600 in Alberta was logical or not."[22] History, alas, does not record what the people thought of the minister's logic.

Alberta's regulatory structure was conditioned by rightist ideology – it was not an accident that much of Social Credit's legislation and regulations was based on Texas precedents – but more than the dread of collectivism lay behind Manning's entente with the American petroleum industry after Leduc. Social Credit, like the CCF in Saskatchewan, was eager to diversify Alberta's economic base out of its heavy dependence on agricultural commodities. Memories of the recent depression were still intense, and before Imperial's discovery of oil at Leduc in February 1947, the province's economic prospects were not particularly bright. Alberta's coal industry had been plagued for years with marketing problems; Turner Valley oil production was declining, and the outlook for agriculture was at best uncertain. Alberta's future, it seemed in 1946, would largely revolve around the wheat farm, the ranching and livestock industry and mixed farming: much would depend on the export demand for wheat and other farm products and on cost reductions in agricultural production. The mechanization of agriculture promised to reduce the number of farms: many anticipated a gradual long-run decline in both the rural and the total provincial population. Oil promised growth and the prospect of diversification; it also held out hope that Alberta's public debt burdens could be eliminated without increasing personal taxation.

Manning, however, perceived his government to be operating under several constraints which weakened Alberta's early bargaining position.[23] Capital was scarce. The province had gone to great lengths to entice eastern Canadian capital into the speculative search for Alberta's oil in the late 1930s and 1940s, with little or no response. Risk capital was not forthcoming from the large conservative financial institutions of Bay and St. James Streets (a fact still etched into Calgary's collective memory), and the small independents were far too weak to raise the large sums needed for exploration and development. The group of Calgary businessmen who eventually found oil in the

Turner Valley in 1936, and went on to create Home Oil, were able to do so only after turning to the major oil companies. A government delegation had visited Britain in 1939 in an attempt to interest the Admiralty in long-term access to Alberta's oil, but the war had intervened before anything came of this approach. The province was neither financially nor ideologically disposed to raising risk capital for highly speculative oil ventures – Imperial's long string of dry holes encouraged risk-aversion – through crown companies. Thus, as Manning saw it, there was no alternative to heavy reliance on American capital. One of his supporters later put it this way: "It was not, after all, that Alberta was being asked to leave a blissful state of nature in which she was economically free and independent, and exchange it for bondage; Alberta had spent her whole life as a province in the clutch of outside investors. The real question in 1947 and later was whether to exchange Bay Street and British investors for investors from New York and Houston. The answer seemed to be, why not? Next-door Saskatchewan had stuck up for her economic sovereignty, after all, and where had that gotten [sic] her? Her major export was people."[24]

In competing with other oil-producing regions of the world for development capital, Alberta, Manning recalled, suffered from other disadvantages. Relative to the vast deposits of cheap crude being opened up in the Middle East in the early 1950s, Alberta's oil was high-cost: for the most part the pools were not large by global standards, the transportation costs were high, and the province's markets were only penetrated and held with some difficulty. Throughout most of the 1950s and 1960s oil was in a glut and the provincial oil industry was producing at less than 50 per cent of its potential. Manning believed that in these circumstances the province was negotiating from a position of weakness and that it must offer the international companies something absent in most of the Third World: political stability. "We told them," he recalled, "that Alberta was a stable, sound place for long-range investment. The government would not get involved in the oil industry, but we would create a good business climate." Royalties would be fixed for ten-year periods, and private interests would have exclusive access through the allocative process (discussed below) to Alberta's resources. Implicit too in this strategy was a commitment not to hold back the pace of resource development unduly: this became an issue in the early 1950s when the companies successfully lobbied the province to permit removals of natural gas from Alberta, in spite of much public resistance to exports. These were the considerations which underlay the provincial regulatory regime. How successful was it?

Regulation and Private Rights: A Critique

The most striking feature of Alberta's oil regulatory process is its overwhelming emphasis upon private rights. This emphasis has been there from the beginning:

> The Crown in right of the province owns some 80 per cent of minerals in the ground, including oil and gas. Nevertheless, in many respects the Crown has been the passive partner of private enterprise in the development of these resources. The influence of private ownership has been disproportionately strong, perhaps because the earliest discoveries were made in areas where such ownership was significant, and certainly because experience in the development of these resources was gained from Texas, Louisiana, Oklahoma and California, where private ownership was the norm. Alberta has maintained an unbroken reliance upon private enterprise for the conduct of exploration and production operations for Crown minerals as well as for those subject to private ownership, and when problems have arisen requiring government intervention, the protection of private rights has been paramount in any solution adopted.[25]

We saw earlier how American precedents influenced Alberta's attempts to bring about physical conservation in the Turner Valley and how these were carried over into the post-Leduc era with the introduction of market-demand prorationing in 1950. U.S. legislation was no less important in shaping Alberta's allocative mechanisms for transferring exploration and production rights from the crown to private interests—a structure which, with minor variations, Saskatchewan adopted as well. "I must say that the cooperation we received from the governments in those states and from the industry for that matter was very good," Manning later remarked. "They gave us without reservation anything we asked for in the way of their legislation, their regulations, and we also had our people go down in some cases and talk to their government people and find out what the problems had been that they had encountered in the early period of development, and how their existing system had evolved. Now it was from that that we developed here a system of exploratory and development work." Texas had been selected as the model, according to Manning, because "they had moved further in the regulatory process" than states such as California where development had been "wide open."[26]

In its administrative detail Alberta's allocative structure is exceedingly complex, but its essential features—the exploration permit, the production lease, and crown reserves—can be readily grasped.[27] The structure distinguishes between two interrelated rights—first, the right to explore for oil and gas owned by the crown; second, the right to produce if commercial deposits are discovered – and provides the means whereby these rights can be transferred to private firms. The first stage in the process is represented by an exploration permit (or reservation) providing, for its duration, exclusive rights to the holder to explore for oil and gas on a designated block of land. In an unexplored area permits or reservations are granted, upon payment of a nominal fee, on a "first come first served" basis. In an area with known discoveries they are allocated by means of auction, known as "cash bonus bidding." To discourage speculation, the permit holder is required to undertake certain minimum exploratory work. If the permit holder makes a commercially exploitable discovery, he then has the exclusive right "to take to lease" up to 50 per cent of the land held under permit or reservation; the remainder is surrendered to the province as crown reserves. The long-term production lease is the instrument whereby the crown transfers to private interests the right to produce and sell oil and gas on a particular acreage, in exchange for payment of specified royalties and rentals, and subject to various regulations on well spacing, production limitations and other matters. Production rights are qualified by practices designed to prevent physical waste and by the Conservation Board's monthly allowables for individual pools and wells, as determined by prorationing to market demand. Government revenues are obtained from lease rentals, production royalties, and the sale of surrendered lands or crown reserves. In disposing of its crown reserves Alberta once again uses a competitive cash auction, although (as with Saskatchewan) there were early experiments with alternatives after Leduc.

Like most complex policies, Alberta's oil regulatory structure evolved incrementally as a compromise among conflicting goals and interests. How successful has it been? If one accepts the fundamental premise that all capital employed in the development of the provincial oil industry should be private, and that rapid development after Leduc was both appropriate and unavoidable, then relative to the experience in many jurisdictions, Alberta's regulatory system has probably been a good one. One authority in petroleum law has commented that: "The Alberta example shows a flexible system in which the public revenues increase both as a percentage of gross revenues from production and as a function of the market-place with respect to the present value of oil in place. It is a system particularly suited to the requirements of a government that does not possess a basic taxing power. It has resulted in a government that is the envy of others in Canada for its exceedingly large per capita public revenues derived otherwise than through taxation."[28] On the other hand, if one challenges the goal of accelerated development and the bias against public investment, the conclusion becomes more negative. Against the admittedly high revenues earned by the province must be balanced the costs of concentration and foreign ownership, an excessive pace of development, and lost economic rents.

Both Alberta and Saskatchewan encouraged a very rapid pace of development of their resources. One of the unavoidable prices paid for this policy was a high degree of concentration and foreign ownership in their natural resource industries. Had, for example, Canadian oil companies – all of which were small – been entrusted with the task of developing the western Canadian sedimentary basin after Leduc, they would have required massive infusions of external funds. But money markets would have considered such borrowing levels unreasonable given the restricted supply of equity capital and of managerial and technical expertise within the Canadian-owned industry. And since Canadian governments, both federal and provincial, were unwilling to invest in the industry, large-scale direct investment and ownership by foreign companies became inevitable.

With foreign capital came the high degree of corporate concentration characteristic of the international petroleum industry. This foreign takeover was facilitated by various federal and provincial policies, including the disposal of crown lands through a cash bonus bidding system. Under this system only the largest firms with substantial capital budgets could compete and offer cash in bidding for new or surrendered crown lands. Alternative methods of disposal, such as the auction of production rights on any acreage to the company prepared to pay the highest overriding royalty (in addition to payment of the standard gross production royalty), would have required the provincial government to share the risk of uncertain production from any acreage and to defer revenue collection. But because it entails no immediate cash payment at the time of auction, it would have encouraged smaller Canadian-owned companies to bid. Alberta considered (and briefly experimented with) an overriding royalty system but, according to Manning, rejected it for three reasons: cash bonus bidding would bring higher immediate revenues; under bonus bidding "the public treasury took no risk whatever"; based on U.S. experience, Alberta concluded that overriding royalties tended to encourage companies to shut down wells after production began to decline and thus provided an incentive to waste mineral resources (true if the overriding royalty is calculated on gross revenue, but not if calculated on net revenue).

Several features of Alberta's allocative process encouraged a rapid rate of development, creating an excessive accumulation of reserves.

The "first come first served" policy of allocating exploration permits, work requirements on permits, lease renewal provisions, fragmentation of ownership rights to pools, all encouraged the great land plays and too rapid a rate of development, leading in turn to shut-in production and marketing problems. Like the rule of capture, which impels each operator to produce at a maximum rate before the opportunity is lost to competitors on adjacent properties, provincial allocation policies had the effect of encouraging private exploration, development and the accumulation of reserves at faster-than-optimal rates, and thus dissipating economic rent. The application of a positive rate of time discount (a dollar spent today is worth more than one spent tomorrow), meant that discounted costs were higher than they would have been if the expenditures had been delayed, as would have occurred under more neutral policies. Put simply, accelerated development of oil reduced aggregate rent by increasing per barrel costs. The reduction was absorbed by governments who sacrificed some potential rents to induce private investors to advance the timing of investment.

The same pattern of excessive rate of development has been occurring in the late 1970s in Alberta, and once again provincial policies (e.g. drilling incentives and major new amendments to the allocation system) have helped to trigger a high level of investment. The new policies were designed to prevent the major oil companies from sitting on large tracts of land and to encourage explorers to develop deeper formations and to search for oil and gas in the costly, but relatively unexplored, regions of the province such as the foothills. Developed with the objective of sparking new exploration plays, the new policies have combined with higher producer returns (particularly in natural gas) to stimulate one of Alberta's greatest drilling booms. In turn, new gas reserves have accumulated at such a rate that the province has found itself under considerable pressure from producers to permit removals of gas to markets in eastern Canada or the United States. A less distorted pattern of timing presumably would have permitted the province to avert the marketing problems which have periodically plagued the oil and gas industry in Alberta since the early 1950s: to an extent that is not widely understood these problems are the consequence of Alberta's own policies.

How efficient is Alberta's regulatory structure at collecting resource rents? While revenue levels have been undeniably impressive, this is not in itself evidence of efficiency. Initially it is useful to consider the issue of rent as a zero-sum game involving bargaining among the various claimants over who gets what share of a pre-determined pie. But this is a static view of both resource development and bargaining. Associated with each of the feasible sequences of oil exploration and development is a unique level of rent. Power to determine the rate and sequencing of development (or whether it occurs at all) is divided among the various claimants to the rent. We have already argued that the excessive rate of development encouraged by Alberta's allocation system was costly in terms of lost economic rent.

The gross production royalty arrangements also led to lost rent. Royalty structures based on gross production raise marginal costs and lead to the premature abandonment of marginal wells which could still yield economic rent (i.e. revenue in excess of costs) if royalties were calculated on net rather than gross income. By graduating the royalty scale on a sliding basis up to a maximum 16⅔ per cent and basing the level of royalty on well productivity, Alberta attempted to compensate for the inverse relationship between per barrel production costs and well productivity. But a royalty structure so graduated encourages an inefficient overdrilling of wells in any pool in order to reduce aggregate royalty payments. Royalties based on net income rather than gross production could have resolved these inefficiencies, but the province felt, probably correctly, that such a system would be costly to administer and would only induce corporate cost padding.

Finally, the bonus bidding system used in the disposal of crown lands can be an efficient mechanism for collecting rents but only if a competitive market exists. In a competitive bidding market, the auction process should on average have generated a price sufficient to capture all the rent. But the law permits companies to keep confidential much of the geological information generated during exploration, and on many tracts only a few companies have sufficient information to make an intelligent bid. The fewer the firms bidding, the less keen the competition, the lower the bids. There is no evidence of bid rigging in Alberta (it has occurred in Texas), but even if we assume the bidding process to be competitive (i.e. bids equal the discounted present value to the bidder of the tract) it is reasonable to assume that the less information possessed by firms taking part in an auction, the higher would be the discount rate they apply to their estimates of the present value of crown reserves – and hence, the lower the bids.

Given the strong ideological bias against public investment and the overwhelming emphasis on the rights of private enterprise, many of these costs were probably inevitable. Had Alberta been prepared to assume a degree of the risk and to undertake government investment, it could arguably have increased its share of the rents generated by the development of its oil. One can, for instance, conceive a continuum of development policies ranked according to the degree of public investment and public assumption of risk. Consider the disposal of crown reserves – the lands surrendered to the crown at the time when exploration permit holders convert their acreage to production lease. For the most part Alberta and Saskatchewan have disposed of their crown reserves as would a rentier – avoiding the assumption of risk and uncertainty and exacting a fixed amount of rent per tract, an amount determined at the time of sale independent of the vagaries of actual future production. To a limited extent Saskatchewan and Alberta experimented with a second option, discussed above, in which the crown reserves were awarded to the firm offering the highest overriding royalty. This entailed no commitment of public capital, but under this option the crown did assume a portion of the risk inasmuch as the stream of future royalty receipts was dependent on the productivity of the reserve acreage. From the perspective of the firm, the amount of risk capital was reduced to that required to develop producing wells, and it can be assumed that in calculating present value the firm would employ a lower discount rate than it would under cash bonus bidding. This in turn suggests that firms place a higher value on crown reserves under an overriding royalty than under bonus bidding, and the ability of government to capture rent is consequently greater. A third option would have seen the province not only incur some uncertainty and risk but actually invest in the development of crown reserves through a crown corporation. Assuming a crown corporation could have achieved an efficiency comparable to its private competitors and that the government utilized a lower discount rate than the oil industry, then this option becomes the most attractive of all. In short, the presumption against both public investment and acceptance of entrepreneurial risk is a costly one for the owners of the resource. The costs of government entrepreneurship were always to the fore; the high costs entailed in the policies of a risk-averse rentier merit equal emphasis.

Conclusion

Summing up the politics of development under Social Credit is not easy. The arrival of oil and gas provoked some major public controversies within Alberta. To oversimplify issues and debates that seldom appeared anything but complex to the actual participants, the controversies frequently turned around the problem of conservation. But much more than the prevention of mineral waste is therein implied. The struggles over development in the Turner Valley in the 1930s, and the prolonged and often bitter disputes over natural gas exports between 1949 and 1954 were fundamentally about the conservation and utilization of publicly-owned resources, but these same conflicts also revolved around other far-reaching issues of development: foreign ownership versus local interests, the prospects for prairie economic diversification, the timing and pace of resource development, the distribution of rent, and, perhaps above all, the appropriate role of government in the process of economic growth and development. Oil and gas provoked a populist response in Alberta, part of the response in the great plains of North America to the westward advance of industrialism and corporate capitalism. Later we shall argue that for a variety of reasons the response was insufficiently strong by the late 1940s to change the rentier policies of the Manning government. Gradually the protests were overwhelmed in the harsh ideological climate of the early Cold War – a climate carefully nurtured by the pious heirs of Aberhart – by the sheer crushing advantages of foreign capital. Oil brought prosperity, urbanization, and the rise of a new middle class which lacked attachments or loyalties to populist concerns. Populism in Alberta was simply extinguished, swallowed up in the gaping maw of Americanization. Given this legacy, Social Credit's own fate was both inevitable and fitting.

Notes

1. Moran, *Multinational Corporations and the Politics of Dependence, op. cit.*, 168-69.
2. E. Penrose, *The Large International Firm in Developing Countries* (London: Allen and Unwin, 1968), 199.
3. Moran, *op. cit.*, 9.
4. See *ibid.*, 166.
5. J.F.C. Wright, *Saskatchewan: The History of a Province* (Toronto: McClelland and Stewart, 1955), 224-25.
6. Quoted in McGillivray, *Alberta's Oil Industry, op. cit.*, n. pag., and reproduced above in Chapter Three, pp. 55-56.
7. For a discussion of the Texas Gulf pricing system see J.M. Blair, *The Control of Oil* (New York: Pantheon, 1976), chaps. 3 and 5.
8. McGillivray, *op. cit.*, 60.
9. *Ibid.*, 45.
10. *Ibid.*, 124.
11. *Ibid.*, 98.
12. *Ibid.*, 265.
13. Earle Grey, *The Great Canadian Oil Patch* (Toronto: Maclean-Hunter Ltd., 1970), 183.
14. Alberta Department of Lands and Mines, *Annual Report*, 1936-37.
15. J. Anderson to W. Aberhart, Premiers' Papers, 0791, February 17, 1936.
16. Aberhart to Anderson, *ibid*, February 25, 1936.
17. Aberhart to Mrs. R. Syming, Premiers' Papers, 1241, March 8, 1940.

18. *Ibid.*
19. J. Barr, *The Dynasty* (Toronto: McClelland and Stewart Ltd., 1974), 124.
20. *Calgary Herald*, August 4, 10, 11, 13, and 14, 1948; and results of Province of Alberta Electrification Plebiscite, August 17, 1948.
21. Davis, *Canadian Energy Prospects, op. cit.*, 172 at note 13; and I. McDougall, "The Canadian National Energy Board: Economic 'Jurisprudence' in the National Interest or Symbolic Reassurance," *Alberta Law Review*, XI, 2 (1973), 354.
22. *Calgary Herald*, March 2, 1951.
23. Manning's views, including quotations, are taken from an on-the-record interview of July 28, 1976.
24. Barr, *The Dynasty, op. cit.*, 140.
25. Crommelin, "Government Management of Oil and Gas in Alberta," *op. cit.*, 146.
26. Manning Interview, *op. cit.*
27. Cf. Crommelin, *op. cit.*; and Crommelin, Pearse and Scott, *Management of Oil and Gas Resources in Alberta, op. cit.*, for critical overviews of Alberta's regulatory structure. Our own critique draws heavily on these studies.
28. A.R. Thompson, "Australian Petroleum Legislation and the Canadian Experience," *Melbourne University Law Review*, 6 (1968).

CHAPTER 5

The CCF in Saskatchewan:
The Years of Promise

... the only wealth there is comes from the labor of men and women applied to natural resources, that is, to land, water, forests, and mines. In Saskatchewan a tremendous amount of wealth has been produced in this way since the formation of the province in 1905. Thousands of men and women in the province have applied their labor to natural resources and have produced wealth. But what have they to show for their work? At the end of forty years they have [a] debt burden [on farm land] ... scanty social services ... deteriorating educational services ... In short, the lion's share of the wealth of the province has been stolen from the people who produced it. This must cease. No program of reform is worth the paper it is written on unless it provides for keeping this wealth within the province. The CCF maintains that our natural resources must henceforth be developed in the public interest and for the public benefit. They cannot continue to be exploited in a hit-and-miss manner for the benefit of promoters, investors, and absentee capitalists. The CCF stands for the planned development of the economic life of the province and the social ownership of natural resources.

"CCF Program for Saskatchewan"
(1944 election program)

The Regina Manifesto,[1] adopted by the CCF as its program at its first national convention held in Regina in 1933, is one of the classic documents of the Canadian left. Read in the context of four decades of populist demands dating back to the 1890s, it does not seem particularly radical. Only in its opening and closing paragraphs did it assume the prophetic exhortatory style. The Manifesto began with the statement: "We aim to replace the present capitalist system, with its inherent injustice and inhumanity, by a social order from which the domination and exploitation of one class by another will be eliminated, in which economic planning will supersede unregulated private enterprise and competition, and in which genuine democratic self-

93

government, based upon economic equality, will be possible." It concluded with the celebrated commitment: "No CCF government will rest content until it has eradicated capitalism and put into operation the full programme of socialized planning which will lead to the establishment in Canada of the Co-operative Commonwealth."

The economic policy of the Manifesto contained all the traditional left populist demands – security of tenure for family farmers against foreclosure by creditors; crop insurance; inflationary monetary policy to raise agricultural prices; opposition to contemporary policies of economic protection as a barrier to exports (although significantly no mention was made of the other half of the free trade argument – farmer opposition to tariffs on imported manufactured goods); "encouragement by the public authority of both producers' and consumers' co-operative institutions"; "socialization of all financial machinery – banking, currency, credit, and insurance"; and of course a section calling for "socialization (dominion, provincial, or municipal) of transportation, communications, electric power and all other industries and services essential to social planning ..." (Natural resource industries were explicitly included.)

All these demands, to varying degrees, had figured in earlier populist platforms. What distinguished the Manifesto was the emphasis placed upon the role of the state in economic planning. The first section, entitled simply "Planning," called for creation of a "National Planning Commission consisting of a small body of economists, engineers, and statisticians assisted by an appropriate technical staff. The task of the Commission will be to plan for the production, distribution and exchange of all goods and services necessary to the efficient functioning of the economy; to co-ordinate the activities of the socialized industries; to provide for a satisfactory balance between the producing and consuming power; and to carry on continuous research. ..." Although the section on socialization of industry envisioned a much enhanced economic role for all three levels of government, the constitutional orientation of the Manifesto was unambiguously centralist. "What is chiefly needed today," according to the section on the British North America Act, "is the placing in the hands of the national government of more power to control national economic development. ... The present division of powers between Dominion and Provinces reflects the conditions of a pioneer, mainly agricultural, community in 1867. Our constitution must be brought into line with the increasing industrialization of the country and the consequent centralization of economic and financial power. ..."

The emphasis upon planning was primarily due to the League for Social Reconstruction, an organization based at the universities of Toronto and McGill, and self-consciously modelled on the British Fabian Society. The League, although not formally linked to the CCF, served as a "brains trust" for the new party, and within the community of senior party leaders that developed across the country the League was particularly influential.

To give a fair assessment of the League is a difficult task. Are we to judge it by how well it articulated contemporary ideas on the left, or by the relevance of its ideas examined forty years later? It fares far better by the former criterion than the latter. It did provide a useful synthesis of many of the sources of CCF ideology. In describing the gist of the Manifesto, whose first draft was written by Frank Underhill (then a League member), one author has summarized it well as a "mixture of Christian, Fabian, and Marxian socialism, shot through with progressive reformism."[2] With the exception of the progressive (i.e. populist) component, the quotation serves also to describe the League itself. In 1935 the League published *Social Planning for Canada*,[3] a lengthy book which analyzed the social and economic problems of the day and the instability of an unplanned capitalist economy – particularly one such as Canada's where export staples figure so prominently – and which proposed the League's version of a socialist alternative. The book is important as the most comprehensive statement of the thinking of the League, and hence of the national CCF leadership.

The League was very much a creature of its time – an eclectic synthesis of contemporary thinking among cosmopolitan Canadian left-wing academics. It was, for example, uncritically admiring of the Soviet experience of forced industrialization under Stalin relative to the earlier policies of the New Economic Plan. "After various experiments with different methods of control," the League concluded, "Russia has led the way in economic planning; the development of a remarkable administrative machinery made possible the formulation and amazingly successful execution of the first Five Year Plan. ..."[4] It viewed provincial governments, with some justification given contemporary experience, as bastions of reaction, and looked to the conquest of power in a much enhanced federal government as the only sensible strategy. The consequence of such a singleminded attention on exercise of power at the centre, however, was that the League contributed little to an assessment of the potential for regional development strategies that various provincial sections of the party could pursue. There has arisen the glaring anomaly that within English-speaking Canada the bulk of what intellectual resources have been available to the left have been devoted to federal policy while the electoral successes of the CCF and NDP have all occurred at a provincial level west of the Lakehead. Its centralism has of course set the CCF and NDP leadership adamantly against most political traditions of Quebec and, in this decade, against the Parti Québécois which, apart from the crucial constitutional issue, is ideologically close to the NDP.

Two closely related characteristics of the League were communicated to the Saskatchewan CCF when it assumed office. The first was a tactical naiveté; the second an emphasis, to the point of disingenuousness, that the appropriate socialist goal was the elaboration and perfection of the British tradition of cabinet rule. The League envisioned neatly designated line and staff organizations, departments, commissions, and nationalized industries with their formal lines of authority explicitly rising to the cabinet, the cabinet itself perched at the pinnacle of this bureaucratic pyramid. "In the planned state," wrote the League, "the final authority of government is to rest, as it does theoretically today, in Parliament. More specifically, this means that the nation's primary executive is the Cabinet, subject only to the established democratic convention that it shall have the confidence of the House of Commons."[5] It viewed with equanimity "the growth in power of the executive at the expense of the power of the legislature, and the extension of the practice of government by independent experts."[6]

The League shared the Marxist critique of monopoly capital but rejected the Leninist conclusions drawn by contemporary communists that only a revolutionary "dictatorship of the proletariat" would suffice to conquer the power of private capital. Instead the League made "the prime assumption. ... that it is possible for a democracy to control economic policy intelligently."[7] Communist tactics of a vanguard party exercising dictatorial powers may have appeared to most Canadians as worse than the disease they were designed to cure, but communists at least had the virtue of stating how they proposed to deal with the awesome power – and here both the CCF and communists seemingly agreed – of the capitalist. By contrast what did the democratic road to socialism look like? What industries were to be nationalized? How did the CCF propose to handle the political and economic pressures brought against it? Were the cabinet and its panoply of professional experts really capable of the tasks they would face? What role would the party, or farmer and labour organizations, play? League members who presumably would be called upon to staff many of the senior positions in any CCF government had not even the limited experience in challenging private capital of the various co-operative ventures of the West. The League made some mention of industrial democracy in the running of nationalized industries, and the role of a disciplined party in organizing the electorate and presenting issues. But such ideas were vague and undeveloped. The essence of the theory of social change implicit within the League was the preordinate role of cabinet abetted by the ideologically compatible members of a centralized bureaucracy.

1934 to 1944

The ideology of the Saskatchewan CCF during the decade between its first provincial election in 1934 and ultimate victory ten years later veered from left to right and, to an extent, back to the left again. In 1934 the party campaigned on an uncompromising program of social ownership of all major industries, including agriculture. In the case of agricultural land the CCF proposed that farmers exchange, on a voluntary basis, their standard freehold titles, for "usehold titles."[8] In effect farmers would lease their land from the provincial government. They would have certain rights of transfer to sons or daughters, but usehold titles would, unlike freehold titles, not be marketable. The administrative details of such a plan were never elaborated, and the other political parties proceeded to equate it with contemporary Soviet land collectivization. Whatever the opposition allegations, the CCF had not of course deviated from the traditional populist adherence to the sanctity of the family farm. Far from proposing collectivized farming, the CCF argued that usehold titles were the most effective means to stop foreclosures and preserve security of tenure for the family farmer.[9]

The CCF was decisively beaten in the election, although with five seats it became the official opposition. The Liberals, who had ruled the province uninterrupted from 1905 to 1929, were re-elected to office. The incumbent Conservative/Progressive coalition government lost its entire representation in the legislature. The CCF performance keenly disappointed the party leadership and during the next four years they moderated the program, and attempted to co-operate with the other opposition parties – Conservatives, Social Credit, and to a degree even the Communists. In a number of individual constituencies deals were struck among the opposition parties at the local level to field a single "unity" candidate. But this period encompassed the initial years of national ambition of the Social Credit movement, and Aberhart was not about to enter into a formal alliance with the CCF when there was a distinct possibility of Social Credit's winning on its own. In 1938 while the Saskatchewan Liberals won re-election, the electorate showed a preference for a left over a right populist movement. Having run in fewer seats than Social Credit (the CCF ran in 30 out of 52; Social Credit in 41) the CCF ranked second to the Liberals in total votes cast and won ten seats to Social Credit's two. Two "unity" candidates also won election.

The CCF leadership was now convinced of ultimate victory, and began a process that culminated in undoubtedly the most ambitious program on which a Canadian provincial government has ever been elected. The 1944 election program, first published in late 1943 as a twenty-page pamphlet,[10] devoted its first section to security of land tenure for farmers and, emphasizing a farm-labour alliance, paralleled farm security to the rights of workers to organize trade unions and bargain collectively. The second section dealt with expansion of social services, including "a complete system of socialized health services with special emphasis on preventive medicine."[11] The third concerned educational reform. The fourth, "Planning, Public Ownership and Finance" contained the discussion of economic policy.

The context of rural populism in which the party program evolved was far removed from that of the League for Social Reconstruction. Political debates eclectically integrated a wide range of ideas, and were pursued with passion and gusto. A 1939 debate on resource policy in the legislature and an excerpt from a 1944 radio program can serve the dual function of communicating something of the flavour of contemporary political discussion, and of introducing two of the future leaders of the CCF government.

In 1939 George Williams,[12] then Saskatchewan CCF leader, moved an amendment to a government bill calling "for the said Bill to be so amended to include the principle of direct governmental development of Natural Resources."[13] Among the CCF members to speak in support of Williams' amendment was a successful farmer, defeated at the polls in 1934 but elected in the previous year's election. Joe Phelps was to play a central and controversial role in the unfolding of CCF economic policy during the decade to come, and already as a freshman member he introduced passion into a potentially arid subject. "Mr. Phelps," wrote the *Leader Post* legislative reporter, "condemned and condemned in the best Phelps style – indignant, hands waving, arms flying, at times so vehement that one expected him to take off like a whip-lashed aeroplane."[14] T.C. Davis, the attorney general, became sufficiently annoyed to propose that upon Phelps' death the latter's head be placed over the Speaker's chair, adding that it would be to the CCF's advantage if someone slit the honourable member's throat.[15] In the wake of the political controversy Phelps was to instigate as minister during the first term of office of the CCF, many party leaders may privately have wished they had followed Davis' advice.

In the following transcript of a 1944 radio broadcast Tommy Douglas, the Baptist preacher who succeeded Williams as provincial leader, combined ideas ranging from Marx to Keynes in a classic example of left populist oratory:

Last week we discussed the fact that the present economic system would lead inevitably to another world-wide depression after the war. Tonight I want to suggest an alternative economic system to the one we have at present. I have often likened our present capitalist economy to a cream separator. The farmer pours in the milk – he is the primary producer without whom society would collapse. Then there is the worker – he turns the handle of the cream separator – and it doesn't matter whether he is a coal miner, a railroader, or a storekeeper, it is his labor which makes our economy function. The farmer pours in the milk and the industrial worker turns the handle.

However, there is another person in the picture – he is the capitalist who owns the machine. And because he owns it the machine is run exclusively for his benefit – that is why it is called the 'capitalist' system. Now the capitalist doesn't put in any milk nor does he turn the handle. He merely sits on a little stool with the cream spout fixed firmly in his mouth while the farmer and the worker take turns on the skim milk spout. Of course you can stay alive on skim milk – you will not get very fat, but you will at least be able to live – providing the skim milk keeps on coming; but it doesn't. Periodically the capitalist gets so full of cream that he has indigestion, so he shuts off the machine, which means that the skim milk stops too. When he feels that he can use some more cream, the capitalist starts up the machine again and for a little while he gets the cream and you get skim milk. That has been the story of capitalism ever since we became a nation – we have a period of prosperity during which *he* gets cream and *you* get skim milk – followed by a depression during which you don't even get skim milk.[16]

The decade of the depression made blatantly obvious the extent to which the entire prairie economy was dependent upon income derived from agriculture, and the instability of that income due to variable export demand and climate – both variables over which prairie residents had virtually no control. Thus in the early 1940s there was universal agreement across all indigenous interest groups, that economic diversification was a major goal. Whatever else divided them they were all desirous to lessen the preponderance of agriculture in the prairie economy. The debate over appropriate government policy for diversification was most enthusiastically pursued in Saskatchewan. The reasons are fairly obvious. While the economies of all three prairie provinces depended disproportionately on agriculture, Saskatchewan's was the most dependent. Secondly, the emergence of the Saskatchewan CCF as a successful left populist movement in a cultural context that placed exceptional emphasis upon politics assured that debate would be vigorously joined. Conversely the entrepreneurial energy of the United Farmers of Manitoba had been long since exhausted, and that of Social Credit, which had been devoted almost exclusively to financial issues, was rapidly waning under Manning, Aberhart's successor.

"Diversification" became a political slogan. Everybody was for it, but what precisely it entailed was far from certain. At the risk of imposing more order on the contemporary debates than they in fact displayed, it is worth isolating two issues. The first was the role of public versus private enterprise; the second, the relative emphasis to place on the development of non-agricultural staples as opposed to import substitution secondary manufacturing. Within and without the CCF these issues were intensely debated during the decade of the 1940s. In 1942, for example, the Boards of Trade of the urban municipalities formed the Saskatchewan Industrial Board with, as first priority, the attraction of war industries to the province.[17] The main arena for the debate was, however, neither in the business community nor the universities, but in the CCF — in the party prior to 1944, in the senior ranks of government thereafter.

Advocacy of public ownership of the means of production has been such a prominent policy of the left that it has frequently been the basis, albeit a simplistic basis, for defining socialism. But how precisely did the CCF propose to go about the task? Which industries, what priorities? In a summary fashion the League for Social Reconstruction had proposed certain criteria: "the question as to which industries should be taken over first can be answered by reference to four tests. (1) Is it a key industry? (2) Is it operated under conditions of monopoly? (3) Is it seriously inefficient? (4) Does it control important natural resources?"[18] Whereas the League vaguely implied that socialization of industry would be a continuous process ultimately approaching complete public ownership, the party in Saskatchewan became quite specific that it perceived a limit to the process once "public property" had been socialized. Farm land was explicitly included in the category of "private property" which was to remain exempt, because "A man may own a farm, or a house, or a store without having the power to fleece the community. ..."[19]

Had the provincial party fully subscribed to the constitutional theses of the Regina Manifesto, it would have condemned itself to impotence. While recognizing that "it is not constitutionally possible to set up a complete co-operative commonwealth within the boundaries of a single province," the 1944 program stated the party's intention to carry the province as far as possible towards the goal by using the "very definite powers vested in a Provincial Government by the Constitution of Canada."[20] Gone were any references to amending the British North America Act to transfer provincial jurisdiction to Ottawa. In a preliminary fashion the party parcelled out, among the three levels of government, jurisdiction to tackle various industries:

[T]here are certain enterprises which can best be operated by the federal government such as the railroads, telegraph lines, our banking institutions, and shipping facilities. In the same way there are elements in our economy which could best be managed by provincial governments, as for instance, the development of hydro-electric power, mineral resources and the lumbering industry. There are projects which lend themselves naturally to operation by municipal bodies as, for example, milk boards for the distribution of milk and other important consumer commodities. But social ownership does not necessarily mean government ownership. There are other forms of social ownership – the most successful to date has been the co-operative movement. ...[21]

Its populist heritage prompted the CCF to view state ownership as only one category within the broader concept of "social ownership" defined to include co-operatives, "the most effective form of social ownership ... wherever that is feasible."[22]

In 1943 the CCF established a Planning Committee which in turn designated a number of subcommittees to prepare policy in specific areas. The Natural Resources and Industrial Development subcommittee was headed by Phelps, opposition resources critic in the legislature. It recommended in January 1944 that "the CCF provincial government plan for the eventual and complete socialization under provincial administration of all natural resources now controlled by the province."[23] The significance of Phelps' subcommittee was to confirm that the natural resource sector had by 1944 become the central candidate for social ownership.

With the advent of the CCF, populists advanced from perceiving resource issues essentially as consumers interested in low prices. Parallel to the oil and gas conservation debates in Alberta, discussion turned to government responsibility for conducting geological surveys and taking inventory of depleted forest reserves. Surpluses generated by public development of resources – coal and lumber were tentatively designated as the first priority – were perceived as a means of financing expanded government programs. The 1944 program drew the obvious parallel between land and other natural resources – all served as the foundation of staple-led economic development. It would hence-

101

forth be the government's responsibility to plan the development of such industries, and bargain for "the lion's share" of rents arising from them.

Prior to the CCF's assumption of office no commercial reserves of oil or potash had been discovered in Saskatchewan. Therefore public development of either did not figure in the policy debates leading up to the 1944 election. The populist concern over the spread between wholesale and retail oil prices was reflected in the program, but not from the consumer's perspective of reducing it. Instead the program incorporated a scheme put forward in the legislature by the CCF caucus. The program "proposed, for the purpose of financing education, the setting up of a Governmental Fuel and Petroleum Board to handle the wholesaling of gasoline and fuel oils. Why should the earnings from this source go to monopolistic oil companies rather than to the people of the province who use the products and make the earnings possible?"[24]

Let us summarize at this stage the party rationale for social ownership. Private development of natural resources, it was argued, had resulted in quick profits being taken without adequate concern for the long run (e.g. overcutting of forests) and had returned insufficient economic rent to the provincial government as owner of crown resources. Party leaders made a closely related argument that public ownership would reduce the outflow of interest and profits from the province to external corporations with capital invested in resource industries. The surpluses of crown corporations disbursed via improved social services or transfer payments would help equalize income distribution. In effect the party held to a countervailing power theory with respect to the distribution of economic rent from resources. Public ownership was to be a means of shifting power, and hence the share of rents, from the private to public sector. Public investment was also required to supplement private investment if full employment was to be assured. Private eastern Canadian investors, indifferent to the economic fate of the province or anxious to preserve prairie markets for eastern manufacturers, had allegedly ignored potentially profitable projects. Finally, economic arguments were frequently supplemented by an ethical argument that social ownership would advance popular participation in, and control of, economic institutions – by workers within public enterprises, by members within producer and consumer co-operatives.

The 1944 program, and Douglas' personal position at the time, reflected the left wing of the spectrum within the CCF on social ownership. It would be a mistake to imply that the program accurately reflected the thinking of all within the party. Although the program and attendant policy debates were far more specific than the League had been a decade earlier, a tactical naiveté persisted. Phelps' sub-committee, for example, at one meeting listed twenty-five industries as potential candidates for public investment, but the economic feasibility of a crown corporation in each was only superficially pursued. The tactical naiveté and inadequacies of party policy towards social ownership were, to an extent, visible to party leaders even before assuming office. How to resolve them was not. As often happens in contexts where uncertainty prevents the delineation of a transparently rational policy, arguments tended to polarize into ideological positions having a degree of internal consistency and generalized hostility to alternatives.

The moderate position emphasized the constraints – limited markets, lack of skilled management, limited access to capital, widespread political opposition – as sufficient reasons to place a low priority on social ownership. Extensive social ownership was purported by the radicals to be necessary to achieve the party's goals. But was it? Perhaps government regulation of private forestry operations and mines would suffice. Appropriate taxation could assure a fair return to the people of the province as owners of crown resources. When the postwar depression failed to materialize, moderates could, and did, argue there to be no need for public investment to maintain full employment. The radicals considered crown corporations a means of reducing income accruing to those outside the province but, cautioned the moderates, how was the takeover of existing assets or the building of new plant and equipment to be financed? Clearly borrowing in external money markets would be necessary for major crown ventures; they could not be financed from ordinary tax revenue all of which was required for current expenditures. What guarantee was there that the return on capital in any crown corporation would exceed its interest cost, inevitably high for such purposes, if the capital were available at all? If bond issues for crown ventures carried a government guarantee the interest rate on any particular project might be lower, but the saving would be offset by a rise in the overall cost of financing the government debt. The slogan "public ownership if necessary, but not necessarily public ownership" came to summarize the moderate position. Better to emphasize "bread and butter" social programs, they concluded.

If the radicals' lack of attention to the practical questions of business exasperated the moderates, conversely, the moderates' willingness to adapt to the current balance of political forces and the state of conventional wisdom exasperated the radicals. Only by explicitly stating the case for social ownership, giving it prominence within the program, could the party hope to persuade people to discard their accumulated pro-capitalist values, argued the latter. Did the moderates really think regulation and taxation were adequate to the task of directing economic policy and constraining corporate power? Surely not. Maybe a crown corporation in any sector would initially be less efficient than its private competitors, but only by actually engaging in the business and learning by doing would the government discover the potential in any sector.

The debate over social ownership was one dimension of the concern for economic diversification. A second was the relative emphasis to give to the development of new non-agricultural staples as opposed to import substitution manufacturing. Initially this dimension did not appear to entail any choice at all. Why not do both – for example manufacture shoes for the local market and simultaneously develop sodium sulphate reserves for export? Only after the CCF had been in office several years and had experienced serious difficulties with its crown ventures in secondary manufacturing did the distinction really manifest itself, and then only the Planning Board made any serious attempt to draw the appropriate conclusion – that the failures in manufacturing need not preclude further public investment, but that priority should shift to new staples.

The assumptions lying behind the arguments for import substitution manufacturing were rarely articulated. Again at the risk of imposing more order on the contemporary debates than they displayed, the following assumptions were implicit. First was a denial that the obvious comparative advantage of the provincial economy in agricultural staples should be permitted to dictate as great a specialization as in the past. A second related assumption was that institutional factors, such as federal political power and the biases of eastern Canadian banks against financing western Canadian industries, had significantly affected the location of industry independently of comparative advantage. Alternatively, this assumption was expressed as a belief that there existed considerable untapped potential for secondary manufacturing in the West that had been ignored. Third was the assumption that in interregional trade – whether in staple exports or manufactured imports – the terms of trade reflected unequal market power between East and West. The obvious conclusion was that Saskatchewan should not be content with a situation in which, by the 1941 census, its share of Canadian manufacturing employment was less than one sixth the province's share of the Canadian labour force (including agriculture).[25]

A priori, investment in manufacturing offered a number of attractions. Typically manufacturing technologies are more labour intensive per dollar of capital invested than those of staple industries, agriculture excepted. Contemporary politicians realized that sizeable new sources of employment would be necessary to avoid the painful economic alternative that has in fact been the lot of many in postwar Saskatchewan – either to incur the costs of migration out of the province or to endure underemployment, undercapitalization, and low incomes if choosing to remain on the farm. The trend towards substitution of capital for labour in agriculture became significant with the advent of the internal combustion engine after World War I. Extension of the agricultural frontier north into the parklands temporarily offset the labour-saving technological changes, but by the end of the 1930s the physical limits of the Canadian prairies had been reached, and it was obvious that agricultural employment would henceforth decline in the province. World War II resolved for its duration the unemployment problems of the depression, but politicians rightfully feared the postwar aftermath of returning demobilized soldiers. With a disastrous agricultural depression prominent in public consciousness, and given the populist mistrust of manipulation of terms of trade on imports and exports, the prospect of increasing regional economic self-sufficiency by import substitution had an obvious appeal.

The essence of the argument for development of new staples was that the comparative advantage of the province lay, initially at least, overwhelmingly in resource-based industries and that the export market would outweigh the domestic.[26] The development of secondary manufacturing, while desirable, should be allowed to develop via one of the linkage processes described in Chapter Twelve. The emphasis of the limited public entrepreneurial ability and capital should be devoted to the successful implantation of the new staples on a basis assuring maximum accrual of rents to the provincial treasury.

The serious disadvantages of secondary manufacturing in the province only became apparent after the CCF government found itself encumbered with a number of publicly owned manufacturing concerns, most of them registering embarrassing financial losses. Some of the reasons for failure were related to the fact of public ownership (e.g. refusal of some merchants to stock government products), but more fundamentally the failures turned on the recurrent problem that high transport costs restricted the available market to the province, and unit costs for the small Saskatchewan market could not be brought low enough to permit successful competition by the crown manufacturing concerns. In other words economies of scale in production are important. To anticipate the fundamental conclusion of this and the following chapter, the cabinet after 1946 made a basic error when, in

105

the wake of controversies over its crown manufacturing ventures, it abandoned all attempts at public investment beyond utilities, and in particular failed to secure effective public control, which inevitably would have required a degree of public ownership, of the emerging major staple industries of oil and potash. Private development of these industries occurred, but in a decidedly suboptimal manner from the perspective of the province.

The Initial Enthusiasm, 1944-45

In 1938 the Liberals had formed the government with thirty-eight seats to the CCF's eleven. By law the length of a legislature is not to exceed five years but, fearful of defeat, the Liberals in 1943 passed legislation extending the life of the sitting legislature for a year. Saskatchewan's contribution to the Allied war effort could not be endangered, they argued, by the partisan squabbling of an election. Liberal fortunes did not revive during the year of reprieve and, when they did finally call an election, for June 1944, the vituperation of their attacks had an air of desperation. They conjured up nightmares of rampant bureaucracy, authoritarianism, and expropriation of private property should the CCF win. They linked the CCF to communism and, for good measure, to fascism. Mussolini and Hitler, suggested the Liberal premier, were a variety of socialists. The results were decisive. The CCF won forty-seven seats to the Liberals' five; the other parties failed to elect any members at all.[27]

The first task of Tommy Douglas as Premier was choice of a cabinet. He kept for himself the Public Health portfolio, an indication of his personal priorities. In addition to the Planning Board (which was not created until 1946) the two agencies destined to bear most directly upon economic policy were the Department of Natural Resources and the Treasury. To the former Douglas appointed Joe Phelps, whom we have already had occasion to meet; to the latter Clarence Fines, a school teacher from Regina with a remarkable financial acumen.

Better than any other ministers, Fines and Phelps personally embodied the tensions within the government – between the moderate and the radical, between the urge for financial responsibility to prove the party's credibility and the need for agressive entrepreneurship to fulfil the party's program, between the relatively cosmopolitan urban Fabian socialist tradition and the rural populist tradition. While many external forces would bear upon the new government and constrain its options, it had also to effect a successful synthesis of the different strengths and limitations that Phelps and Fines represented. Knowing the history of failures of state enterprises launched by populist governments lacking financial and administrative acumen, and the intellectual weaknesses of the Fabian tradition in Canada as manifested by the League for Social Reconstruction, one could safely predict that were either Phelps or Fines to dominate to the exclusion of the other, the net result would be far from satisfactory.

Why, one might well ask, in a province whose economy depended so overwhelmingly upon agriculture, did that ministry not figure prominently in the determination of economic policy? The answer is to be found in the limits of populism. Populism, in both its left and right variants, made the farmer acutely conscious of external institutions – merchants, banks, railroads, commodity markets – whose depredations threatened his income and even his survival on the land. But by the mid-1940s there was in place a set of counter-institutions that, however imperfectly, protected him from his external enemies. A range of co-operative ventures provided grain storage and retail and wholesale distribution of most consumer goods and farm inputs. Farmers who patronized co-operatives benefited directly (although the intermittent disbursement of patronage dividends implied a measure of forced saving that some farmers could ill afford), but to the extent co-operatives served as price leaders constraining the prices of private competitors, all benefited. The Wheat Board, which after 1943 ceased to be merely a voluntary marketing agency, was marketing all wheat and thereby put an end to speculative manipulations on the Winnipeg Grain Exchange for the principal prairie crop. Via long-term contracts with major customers such as Great Britain, the Wheat Board guaranteed a degree of price stability.

Farmers continued to subscribe to a terms-of-trade exploitation theory – that the prices of agricultural exports reflected a low return on their capital and labour whereas the prices of manufactured goods imported into the prairies reflected higher returns on capital and labour characteristic of the manufacturing sector. But there was little to be done about the regional terms of trade at the level of the provincial government, and since net farm incomes had risen sufficiently to permit the average farmer a life style approaching that of an urban worker, political pressure on the federal government to change the terms of trade – by price supports, tariff reductions, etc. – abated.

While the accumulation of populist-inspired reforms had seemingly contained the external threats, populism had few answers to the more insidious internal threat posed by changing farm technology that remorselessly favoured increased capitalization and larger units. Farmers were doing to themselves what they had prevented external institutions from doing – forcing one another off the land as the big bought out the small, creating class divisions between large, well capitalized farmers often using hired labour and small, undercapitalized farmers increasingly reduced to tenant status. The very success of the earlier populist reforms accelerated capitalization of farming by increasing the certainty of a positive return on new investments entailing a lengthy payback period. Because it pitted farmer against farmer, this new dynamic posed a far more intractable political problem than the earlier populist crusades which had united farmers against external foes. Adjustments to changing farm technology and consolidation of the small original homesteads were obviously required but, if the social basis of populism was to survive, the provincial government had to control the process closely. If consolidation dramatically increased the degree of inequality of farm wealth and income distribution, if the entrepreneurial dynamic in the rural economy shifted predominantly to the larger farmers become private entrepreneurs and bypassed the co-operative movement, then the consequences would be fatal for the culture and politics of populism.

Farm leaders were cognizant of these dangers, but the contradictory pressures within the farm community paralyzed their organizations, and denied to the Department of Agriculture support for more than timid ventures into rural planning. Community pastures were developed, thereby enabling farmers to diversify into livestock without acquiring large private tracts of pasture land. The Department also encouraged creation of co-operative farms which would permit their members to realize economies of scale without necessarily reducing the number of families on the land, but few were launched and even fewer survived. The Farmers' Union and CCF debated the idea of legislating a maximum limit to farm size but widespread opposition, primarily from large farmers desirous of becoming larger, existed to such an idea and nothing came of it.

The CCF government remained in office from 1944 to 1964 but, with the important exception of a universal medical care insurance program introduced in 1962, virtually all of the major initiatives were launched in the first term – and most of them in the first two years. During the crucial first two years the more aggressive ministers devoted their energies to new programs within their respective departments, and thereby reduced cabinet to little more than the ratifier of departmental initiatives. Initially the central bureaucracy responsible to cabinet was minimal. A small Economic Advisory Committee composed of three ideologically sympathetic senior faculty members at the University of Saskatchewan was appointed by cabinet in the fall of 1944, only to be disbanded in the summer of 1945. During its brief lifetime it prepared a number of academic and relatively superficial reports on additional sources of government revenue, equity of the provincial tax structure, amending the distribution of federal and provincial jurisdictions under the British North America Act, and on industrial development. In July 1945 it cautiously advised that "the government should enter any particular industrial field only after searching investigation and on competent technical advice."[28] Since Phelps had by this time already committed the government to several crown corporations, such advice can be interpreted as an implicit critique of Phelps' impetuosity, or as a plea for the government to procure the requisite economic expertise, or both. In either case, at this stage neither the Committee nor cabinet was directing economic policy.

Douglas has described his early role as Premier as that of a circus ringmaster with many performers each wanting maximum time for his act. It was a brilliant circus for such a humble provincial circuit; the show changed at frequent intervals as different performers grabbed star billing, and no one, not even the ringmaster, was quite sure from month to month what acts would be playing and in what order.

Douglas in his capacity as Minister of Public Health was himself a major performer. The Health Services Planning Commission, created in 1944 as a research and planning agency within the Public Health Department, provided a detailed agenda for health policy that had not been completed by 1964. Among its recommendations was of course universal prepaid health insurance, but also centralized treatment for diseases (such as cancer) requiring specialized medical services, and a province-wide field service capable of providing preventive services. In retrospect health services are the domain in which the CCF made its most durable and extensive contributions as a government. Universal hospital and medical insurance in Saskatchewan served as a precedent for analogous programs throughout the country. The Public Health Department came closest to the Fabian model of social change discussed by the League a decade earlier. While any comprehensive account of the evolution of health policy would have to begin with the fact that socialized health services figured prominently in both the populist and Labour Party heritage of the CCF, here is a case where the initiative for particular programs came from the upper reaches of a highly professional civil service and, of course, from Douglas himself.[29]

Phelps' style of administration bore little resemblance to anything advocated by the League. It might better be compared to that of a new general manager in a corporation anxious to diversify its line of activities. While cabinet in principle favoured such a diversification, certain ministers were wary of their colleague's entrepreneurial ambitions. Phelps in turn chafed at the constraints upon his ability to act – whether it be the recalcitrance of cautious bureaucrats within his department (of the senior staff he inherited he dismissed the deputy minister plus four of six senior branch heads), budgetary controls exercised by the Treasury (he insisted on a single budget vote for the "conservation and development of resources" in order to minimize the details of accountability), or the necessity of procuring cabinet approval. One of the more celebrated incidents in Phelps' stormy relationship with cabinet concerns the purchase of a brick plant. Phelps proposed the purchase to cabinet and a lengthy discussion ensued during which Fines protested the lack of adequate economic research to justify such a government investment. The consensus of cabinet was against Phelps but he refused to let the matter drop, admitting finally cabinet had no choice – he had already bought the plant.[30]

Within the first twelve months of office Phelps had added an Industrial Development Branch to his department (appropriately renamed Natural Resources and Industrial Development), had launched several crown ventures, had raised metal mining royalty rates,[31] and had guided two important bills through the fall 1944 legislative session. The first gave the Minister of Natural Resources extensive powers to acquire any lands or works by purchase, lease or expropriation, and to "do all such things as he deems necessary to develop and utilize the resources of the province. ... which are the property of the crown."[32] The Liberals vigorously attacked the bill for the sweeping discretionary power it gave the minister.

Enactment of the second bill, the Mineral Taxation Act, 1944, was the first move in an eight-year legal and political battle containing many of the elements that have defined the resource conflicts of the 1970s. The purpose of this bill was twofold: to raise a modest tax revenue from freehold mineral rights (i.e. mineral rights owned privately and not by the crown) but more important, by levying a tax on undeveloped mineral rights (three cents per acre per year) as well as on producing properties, to encourage holders of the former to allow their mineral rights to revert to the crown. Early settlers who received title to their homesteads from the crown received both surface and mineral rights; later settlers got surface rights only. However several million acres of prairie land were retained by the Hudson's Bay Company at the time of transfer of Rupert's Land to the Dominion of Canada, and additional land grants were made by Ottawa to various railway companies as inducement to lay track. These companies, upon selling their lands to settlers, generally retained the mineral rights. "The policy of allowing mineral rights to become alienated from the Crown, as followed out by Dominion authority in the past was wrong in principle," the provincial government admonished, "was not in the best interests of the people and militated against the proper conservation of the country's natural resources."[33]

The companies principally affected by this early attempt to extend provincial resource ownership responded with a lengthy legal campaign that successfully thwarted the Act's intent. Initially the Hudson's Bay Company requested federal disallowance; Ottawa refrained. The CPR paid the mineral tax – under protest and on less than one fifth of its mineral acreage – and in January 1948 commenced a constitutional challenge to the Mineral Taxation Act, alleging it imposed an indirect and hence ultra vires tax.[34] (In connection with this case the Regina sheriff peremptorily interrupted a session of cabinet to serve Phelps and the provincial Attorney General with court summonses.) Later that year the CPR secured an injunction halting any further forfeiture of its freehold mineral rights for non-payment of the tax. The province decided to halt all forfeiture proceedings under the Act for the duration of the court challenge. Although the CPR appealed the case to the Supreme Court (which did not render a judgment until 1952), at all levels the Act was ruled intra vires. The province's formal legal victory meant little however, because it acceded to political pressure from the interested companies and from individual farmers to permit revesting of freehold rights upon payment of mineral tax owing. At the time of the 1948 injunction a large proportion of freehold owners were delinquent on the tax, but the province had conducted forfeiture proceedings on less than a million acres (four per cent of total freehold rights) and virtually all these rights later reverted to their former owners.[35]

"Going into Business"

"My colleagues and myself [sic] are working overtime in order to get the wheels of progress in motion," declared Phelps enthusiastically during a December 1944 radio broadcast. "An improved program of social services as well as education and health is being planned by the other departments. ... [T]o finance this new social program we have three choices: first, increased taxation; second, borrowing money and going into debt; or third, going into business. Following out the CCF program we have decided to undertake the third and, as a result, we have set up an industrial development branch of this department and numerous undertakings are now receiving very careful study." At this early optimistic stage Phelps justified crown investment not only in terms of economic diversification but as a source of revenue for new welfare state programs. "[M]oney did not grow on gooseberry bushes,"[36] he reminded his audience. The main feature of economic policy during the CCF's first two years would be the attempts at "going into business," and the minister most intimately associated

111

with these endeavours would be Phelps.

At this point it is useful to resort to a brief exercise in economic taxonomy. During its first term the CCF established ten corporations which can be classified as competitive. Phelps' role was central in the launching of all but two (the box factory and bus company). With the date of the order-in-council establishing each in parentheses, they comprised: a brick manufacturing plant (May 1945), a shoe factory (June 1945) to which was added a tannery (July 1946), a fish processing and marketing board (July 1945), a timber board (September 1945), a fur marketing service (October 1945), a box factory (November 1945), a provincial bus company[37] (January 1946), and a sodium sulphate mine (May 1946).[38] These corporations were competitive in the sense that private firms operated in the markets in which they sold their products or alternative private distribution agencies continued to operate. Government purchases, while significant in some cases, did not guarantee their financial solvency.

A second category were the utilities which, due to inherent economies of scale and the force of law, became monopolies in their respective markets. The publicly owned power and telephone systems inherited by the CCF obviously fall into this category as does the government insurance corporation (incorporated under its own statute in November 1944). While it competed with private firms in the field of general insurance, the majority of this company's revenue derived from the provision of no-fault vehicle insurance to which after 1946 all vehicle owners in the province were, and still are, required to subscribe as a condition for vehicle registration.

The third and least-significant category contained the corporations created as a means of performing certain traditional government functions of a commercial nature. The CCF established a printing company (June 1945) that fulfilled the majority of government printing requirements. It had only the government as customer. Two temporary corporations were created (in May and August 1945) that disposed of surplus war assets, basically at cost, primarily to public institutions. The government organized a northern airline (July 1947) for which government charter work was, initially at least, the mainstay of operations. The airline was sold by the Liberal government during the 1960s.

The competitive corporations obviously hold the most interest, for they were the experiments whose success or failure would determine whether the government undertook a major development strategy, or accepted welfare state reforms as the limits of its mandate. Nonetheless development of the utilities did entail considerable public entrepreneurship; it was not merely a case of passively exploiting monopoly markets created by the technology of the industries and the force of law.

Provincially and municipally owned telephone systems have long been the norm on the prairies. In Saskatchewan there has existed since 1908 a Department of Telephones with the primary function of aiding the latter systems. With the progressive consolidation of municipal companies by the provincial system, the CCF in 1947 created Saskatchewan Government Telephones, a formal crown corporation. After absorbing virtually all municipal systems, its monopoly on provincial telecommunications has been for the last two decades virtually complete.

The CCF's decision to treat automobile insurance as a utility has provided a subject for political controversy for three decades. The Saskatchewan Government Insurance Office (SGIO) has served as the precedent for analogous crown corporations launched by the Manitoba and British Columbia NDP, and by the Parti Québécois. The argument for economies of scale is not as clear as with power or telephones, but the low administrative costs and rates of litigation per claim experienced by SGIO are indicative that scale economies do exist for a universal no-fault insurance system relative to the private market alternative. Apart from an insignificant $12,000 government advance, SGIO generated its capital from premium income and had by the end of 1948 a capital reserve of $1.5 million, much of which was directed to investments within the province.

Publicly owned power first came to Saskatchewan in 1929 when the Liberal government of the day organized the Saskatchewan Power Commission. The following year the newly elected Conservative/ Progressive government bravely promised that "Saskatchewan is definitely committed to a scheme of public ownership of the power utility. ... The Saskatchewan Power Commission. ... is an expression of the popular will to ensure for all time an abundance of cheap power for industrial development and expansion and to make available to the agricultural community, at the earliest possible moment, a supply of electrical energy not only for agricultural operations but to remove the remnants of pioneer drudgery still clinging to the farm home in some areas."[39] The promise was made at the beginning of the depression that postponed, among many other projects, the commitment to public power and to rural electrification. After 1944, with Phelps the responsible minister until his defeat in 1948, the Commission completed the process of buying up the private systems, and undertook the extensive task of integrating them into an efficient province-wide grid. Conceived by the Liberals, blessed by the Conservatives, and delivered by the CCF, public power obviously did not pose ideological controversies in Saskatchewan. In fact the CCF rationale for public power was remarkably similar to that put forward by other Saskatchewan parties and by the Ontario Conservatives who, in the first decade of the century, established Ontario Hydro.[40] Ontario Hydro is the major precedent for publicly owned power in Canada, and one to which the CCF repeatedly referred. A public monopoly in power, claimed the CCF, would exploit all economies of scale, prevent private profiteering from such a basic commodity, and provide cheap power "at cost" in order to abet industrial growth and increase consumer demand.

Saskatchewan, a flat prairie province, lacks the massive hydroelectric potential of Niagara Falls that inspired Adam Beck and his Ontario colleagues to campaign for public power, but it does have bountiful coal and even a few hydroelectric sites, particularly in the North. Starting from an admittedly small base, the Saskatchewan Power Corporation (in 1949 it was formally organized as a crown corporation) experienced over the next two decades a rapid growth in its load, which it increasingly supplied from a few large thermal and hydroelectric plants. The economies of scale of centralized generation could have been achieved by integrating the relatively small Saskatchewan market into either a Manitoba or Alberta-based utility. Had such occurred, of course, the province would not have had available the sizeable pool of "human capital," of managerial and engineering expertise, that Saskatchewan Power (SPC) did in fact assemble.

If creation of a state monopoly in electrical power generation and distribution did not pose any substantial conflict with private interests, its extension to include natural gas distribution certainly did. Private companies developing newly discovered gas fields in the province were hostile to the government's intention of forcing them to sell all gas to SPC. For example, the president of one company, writing to the Minister of Natural Resources in 1951, claimed difficulty in raising capital in New York for drilling when the customer was to be a "corporation which has absolutely no experience in this field. ... we have the gas, Husky [and] Phillips have the gas; what does the Power Corporation intend to do, and when do they intend to do it?"[41] If the government insisted, despite all the disadvantages, on giving SPC a monopoly on distribution, industry wanted special incentives. The natural gas distribution decision was the only truly successful challenge by the CCF to the norm of Canadian government-corporate relations in the oil industry. As early as 1947 the Planning Board had concluded that gas distribution "would appear to be clearly a field for the Government," but immediately added "once the degree of risk is determined to be a minimum."[42] While the government in principle favoured public ownership of utilities, such caveats were always present. Without the pool of SPC managerial and engineering expertise, which provided competent in-house economic feasibility studies, it is doubtful the government would have resisted corporate pressure on the distribution issue.[43]

' The commitment to public gas distribution was tested in an interesting fashion when in 1952 Mannix, the large Calgary-based construction firm, proposed to launch a Saskatchewan subsidiary to undertake gas transmission within the province. Mannix made three basic arguments on behalf of its proposal: (1) the government could avoid the borrowing and public assumption of risk that the SPC proposal would entail, (2) a private utility would be better placed than a public utility to resist the pressure to extend service to unprofitable communities, and (3) Mannix had experience that SPC lacked.[44]

There is no evidence of any support within cabinet for the Mannix proposal, but it warranted a rebuttal from the government committee charged with preparing gas policy. The committee argued that SPC could buy whatever expertise it currently lacked and assumed that cabinet favoured extension of the distribution network to small high-cost communities (via a rate structure that permitted large cross-subsidization of rural by urban consumers) provided, overall, the system earned a reasonable return on capital. What, however, was a "reasonable" return on capital? For a capital intensive project with a high proportion of capital to operating costs (such as a pipeline network), a variation in the rate of return would have a substantial impact on the price of gas customers would be required to pay. The committee assumed Mannix would want a 6 per cent after-tax return, equivalent to 12 per cent before tax, compared to 4 per cent for SPC (which as a crown corporation could escape corporate income tax). The committee correctly insisted that, with competent management, there exists negligible uncertainty in the fundamental sense of the utility's ability in the long run to meet a pre-established target rate of return. Provided a government is prepared to resist political pressures for low rates, it can within limits achieve for a utility any target rate of return. Utility revenues are thus analogous to tax revenues. Within broad politically defined limits a government can realize whatever target it deems appropriate.

In his impatience to "get the wheels of progress in motion," Phelps despaired of the lack of entrepreneurial initiative among the career civil servants he had inherited in his department. Although he did create two royal commissions (on the forestry and fishing industries),[45] to rely on a powerful planning body of professionals did not appeal to Phelps' temperament. To do so would mean debate and delay. Had not these issues been endlessly debated by the party for the last decade? It was time to act, to experiment, to take risks. In addition to new senior bureaucrats he brought into the department, he entrusted the establishment and management of new crown ventures to a series of outside professionals and promoters. For many of the ambitious promoters who approached the new government, any ideological commitment to the CCF's development goals was secondary to their perception that here was a windfall opportunity to achieve the status and power of running a corporation. Whether the corporations over which they presided were public or private was of little concern. Unfortunately their ambitions often far exceeded their competence.

In the case of the shoe factory/tannery at Regina and the woollen mill at Moose Jaw, Phelps accepted completely inadequate feasibility studies on the capital and operating costs, and market potential. In both cases he appointed as general manager individuals who had themselves produced some of the more inflated assessments of feasibility. For example, the initial estimated capital cost of a woollen mill was $125,000; actual cost, $425,000. Daily output of the shoe factory was initially estimated at 800 pairs, but during the first seven months actual daily output averaged 130 pairs.[46] A 1949 Planning Board review was in passages as damning as the Liberal opposition. On the shoe factory/tannery: "the original investment was in second rate equipment and ... there is every evidence that those who laid out these two plants had little knowledge of modern techniques." On the woollen mill: "We now know that we made a very poor start. Our buildings and machinery were the best we could get but were inadequate, and there has had to be a great deal of costly replacement to bring the mill anywhere near to a reasonable cost basis."[47] If the problems had been solely the quality of initial planning and management they could presumably have been resolved. But there existed fundamental cost disadvantages to these secondary manufacturing ventures, disadvantages quite independent of the form of ownership or the competence of initial planning. The low quality of local wool and the breakage of threads aggravated by the dry prairie climate were, for example, continuing impediments to the competitive potential of the mill. The shoe factory, even with a much larger share of the Saskatchewan market, would still have suffered from too small a market to permit exploitation of scale economies. The shoe factory and tannery were shut down in 1949 with a cumulative combined deficit of $156,000. The woollen mill was maintained until 1954 by which time it had lost $830,000.[48]

The CCF entered two other manufacturing industries – purchasing a long-inactive brick plant at Estevan, a town in the southeast of the province, and expropriating a box factory at Prince Albert. The former incurred a series of deficits in all years but one prior to 1953. Extensive renovations in this period permitted the company thereafter to realize modest surpluses. During their term of office the Liberals argued that it was earning too low a return to justify retention; they sold it to a private firm. Acquisition of the box factory in November 1945 was the lone instance of use by the CCF of the wide expropriation powers contained in the Crown Corporation Act enacted earlier in the year. The provincial Labour Relations Board found the owners of the factory guilty of unfair labour practices against the local union, and issued an order to desist. In response the company transferred ownership to the general manager, thereby rendering technically inapplicable the order against the original owners, and simultaneously it dismissed all employees. The cabinet in turn decided to expropriate, with compensation. Incidentally Phelps did not participate in this particular decision. He was absent from cabinet at the time. The financial history of the box factory under public ownership was approximately the reverse of that of the brick plant. It initially lost money but by 1947 was generating modest surpluses. As paper products replaced wood as a packaging material, net income became negative in 1951, and the plant continued to lose money until closed in 1957, with a cumulative net deficit of $495,000.[49]

The CCF repeatedly charged that its public ventures were jeopardized by unfair market pressures from private competitors. Retail distribution of government boots and shoes was hindered because private shoe manufacturers threatened to embargo supplies to retailers who stocked them. Since the government shoe factory produced only a limited range (footwear for "people on the street, in the home, on the farm and at work. ... [no] style merchandise"[50] explained Phelps), such an embargo would leave retailers with half-empty shelves. On occasion the government found dealers in specialized machinery and patented items unwilling to sell to "socialist" crown corporations. Undoubtedly the opposition of external corporate interests and of the local business community did seriously hamper the government's freedom of initiative. But even without such opposition it is doubtful these manufacturing ventures could have overcome their basic cost disadvantages.

Whereas the strategy motivating the manufacturing ventures was primarily import substitution, that behind the remaining competitive ventures was the maximization of benefits from exploitation of primary staples – timber, fur, fish, sodium sulphate – whose primary markets were outside the province. This is most obvious in the case of the sodium sulphate mine, the last of the competitive crown corporations. It was established after the Planning Board came into existence, and the Board played a major role in recommending it to cabinet as a viable proposition. However Phelps had been instrumental in preventing the leasing to private interests of the province's largest sodium sulphate deposit, and in proposing crown development of the deposit, an alkaline lake located west of Moose Jaw. The mine was from its beginnings a financial success. During its first eleven fiscal years (1947-48 to 1958-59) its average annual net return on government equity, after payment of a modest royalty, was over 10 per cent.[51] The significance of this figure comes from the realization that, the basic market being the pulp and paper industry, all of the product had to be exported from the province. Clearly, in industries in which the province did have a comparative cost advantage, crown corporations could produce efficiently and negotiate sales successfully in external markets over which the CCF had no control.

Phelps' particular passion was development of the North. He was motivated in this by a complex of factors – a well-intentioned if somewhat paternal desire to relieve the abysmal poverty of the northern native population, a populist concern to conserve the poorly managed and overharvested provincial forests, and thirdly by the basic CCF goal of diversification of the provincial economy via public investment. The three northern corporations he established – in timber, fish, and fur – began as marketing agencies with the modest intention of applying "orderly marketing," as practised by analogous agencies in various agricultural markets, to raise the prices received by producers.

The most ambitious of the three was the Timber Board. Initially a voluntary marketing agency for the several hundred small sawmill operators, it rapidly evolved into the dominant corporation in the small provincial forestry industry. (In the winter of 1950-51 there were 511 sawmills in the province, of which 80 per cent produced annually under 100,000 board feet of timber.) By 1946 disposal to sawmill operators of crown timber stands "on the stump," in exchange for stipulated stumpage fees payable to the crown, had been terminated. Instead on crown forests, which comprised 80 per cent of the total, the government required operators to contract with the Timber Board for specified quantities of rough-sawn lumber and/or pulpwood. Until creation in the 1960s of a pulp mill, all pulpwood was exported; in most years a majority of lumber was marketed within the province.[52]

The Timber Board well illustrated the dilemmas of specifying goals for crown corporations. Initially conceived as a marketing agency for the benefit of small operators, it quickly became an instrument whereby the forestry branch of the Department of Natural Resources could regulate the annual harvest and restrict it to a level below the annual increment. A combination of uncontrolled cutting and disastrous fires during past years of drought had decimated the commercial forest. According to the 1947 *Report of the Royal Commission on Forestry*, continuation of prevailing harvesting rates would exhaust the commercial forest within a decade, and render extinct the most valuable species, white spruce. Calculation of the annual increment, the desired rate of growth of the forest stock, and hence the allowable annual harvest, involved a good deal of unsophisticated guestimating, but clearly here was a classic case of the social interest in a sustained yield, however defined, being at odds with the private interest of each individual operator in unregulated cutting rights for himself.

On occasion the Board attempted to protect domestic consumers against high lumber prices by selling in the provincial market at prices below levels prevailing elsewhere. The government also viewed the forest as a resource potentially capable of generating manufacturing jobs. It integrated its forest operations backwards by building a large centralized sawmill, and had ambitions to integrate forward, particularly into pulp and paper. But apart from the box factory and simple manufacturing operations that entailed only minor transformation (e.g. planned lumber, posts, poles, and ties) it did not realize any such goals prior to 1964. Finally, from its inception to the end of the 1950s, the government realized a 13 per cent[53] average annual net return on its equity in the Timber Board. The relative priority to attach to each of these goals – improving the net income of those currently engaged in forestry operations, conservation, lower lumber prices for provincial residents, linked industrial development, and extraction of economic rent for the treasury from a crown-owned resource – evolved in an entirely ad hoc fashion arousing considerable controversy.

It remained for the Liberals during their term of office in the 1960s to negotiate a pulp mill – a joint venture with Parsons and Whittemore, an American firm. The terms of the contract were extremely complicated. They gave majority equity to the private partner but, given a very high debt-equity ratio, little equity investment was entailed. The government assumed the bulk of the capital risk via a government guarantee of the loan to raise the debt capital. In addition the mill secured a large federal grant from the Department of Regional Economic Expansion, virtually exclusive access to nearly one third of the province's commercial forest, and establishment of a separate crown corporation to provide the necessary pulpwood at a subsidized price well below logging costs. The mill was built by a subsidiary to Parsons and Whittemore without recourse to tenders.[54]

There is a parallel between this mill and the CCF's manufacturing ventures. Both attempted to deny the comparative cost disadvantages of the province. Saskatchewan trees are, relative to those in British

Columbia, slow growing and stunted and, relative to Ontario and Quebec, distances to major markets are far longer. The Liberal opposition made much of the CCF's difficulties in launching manufacturing ventures. Analogously the NDP, during its stint in opposition, vehemently criticized the concessions extracted from the Liberal government by Parsons and Whittemore. The Liberals misjudged the extent of public opposition – on environmental as well as economic grounds – to projects providing such limited net benefits to the provinces. On the assumption that jobs at any price was the basic public concern, just prior to the 1971 election they entered into a similar deal with the same firm for a second pulp mill. The politics of pulp mills became a central issue in the campaign and, in general, one that redounded to the Liberals' electoral disadvantage. Rather than proceed with a marginal joint venture, the newly elected NDP government chose to pay a $6 million settlement to Parsons and Whittemore and cancel the contracts for the second mill. The obvious conclusion is that comparative costs cannot be ignored with impunity. Neither central Canadian financial and corporate power as argued by the CCF, nor the anti-business socialist attitudes of the CCF-NDP as claimed by the Liberals, suffices as an explanation for the small share of manufacturing in the province's industrial structure.

The modest yet unambiguously successful Fur Marketing Service established an alternative market for fur ranchers and trappers. The extensive use of this alternative to established buying agents, such as the Hudson's Bay Company, is evidence that it did improve net prices. Modelled on the Wheat Board, although without the latter's legal monopoly, it issued an initial payment and, after completing the auction of furs and deducting a fee to cover costs, any surplus was issued as a final payment.

The government attempted to perform a similar function for fishermen. Freshwater fishing on northern lakes has been a traditional but marginal economic activity, conducted primarily by natives. An internal government report described in unusually graphic terms the problems faced by the industry in the 1940s: "The fishing industry north of the prairies has always been a haphazard operation carried on by sharp traders whose policy is to operate only when the fish market is good, to pay the fishermen as little as necessary to get the fish produced, to charge the fishermen what the traffic will bear on supplies, and to make the highest possible profits. Since the fishermen are far from the markets and receive little information, they have been exploited unmercifully."[55]

The history of the Canadian freshwater fishing industry is a long and tortured one, characterized by many shifts in the policies of governments, both federal and provincial. In terms of establishing an industry in which native fishermen could earn reasonable net incomes, no policy has succeeded. Relative to this general pattern of failure, however, the provincial Fish Board, established in 1945, should be judged a success. The potential for the Board to have any impact on market prices of processed fish was negligible given Saskatchewan's small share of total production. It did, however, raise prices to fishermen at the loading dock by operating on low margins that resulted in intentional deficits. In an attempt to exercise better quality control the Board integrated forward, and established in the North its own packaging and filleting plants. Local employment was an obvious additional aim. The Board also integrated backward into the distribution, at lower prices than private traders, of fishing supplies and ultimately of general merchandise. With several reorganizations of corporate structure, the provincial government continued to market and process fish, to provide supplies and distribute retail goods until 1959, when these functions were transferred to co-operatives established for the purpose.[56]

All three northern corporations were attempts to export prairie populism to another cultural milieu. As part of a major program of northern development, which would have had to pay as much attention to the needs of natives for political as well as economic power, they would have been highly significant. But such a program was never forthcoming, and the benefits of the corporations remained fragmentary.

Conclusion

During the first two years of office the experiments in crown ventures were by far the most prominent of the government's economic initiatives but they were more the product of particular ministries, Natural Resources in particular, than of the government acting in concert. The role of cabinet was to veto or ratify ministerial initiatives, rarely to initiate itself. One reason for the extent of ministerial autonomy was that it provided at least a temporary solution to the disagreements among ministers on economic policy – an agreement to disagree. Recall the two central issues of economic policy to which we alluded in discussing the evolution of the 1944 CCF program: the role of public versus private enterprise and the relative emphasis to place on the development of non-agricultural staples as opposed to import substitution secondary manufacturing. The election of the CCF by no means resolved these issues; it merely transferred the forum from the inner councils of the party to the inner councils of the government.

Notes

1. Reprinted in Young, *op. cit.*, Appendix A.
2. *Ibid.*, 45.
3. *Social Planning for Canada*, the Research Committee of the League for Social Reconstruction, reprinted (Toronto: University of Toronto Press, 1975).
4. *Ibid.*, 217.
5. *Ibid.*, 229.
6. *Ibid.*, 494.
7. *Ibid.*, 229.
8. See T.C. Douglas, "Questions Invited," transcript of radio broadcast, *Saskatchewan Commonwealth*, January 1, 1943, and Lipset, *Agrarian Socialism, op. cit.*, chap. 6.
9. Although originally published in 1950, Lipset's remains the best single account of the history of the Saskatchewan CCF prior to 1948 and of its first term of office. Two doctoral theses written by senior Saskatchewan government officials during the later stages of the CCF administration provide a valuable internal perspective on the evolution of public policy: T.H. McLeod, "Public Enterprise in Saskatchewan: The Development of Public Policy and Administrative Controls," unpublished Ph.D. thesis, Harvard University, Cambridge, Massachusetts, 1959; A.W. Johnson, "Biography of a Government: Policy Formation in Saskatchewan 1944-1961," unpublished Ph.D. thesis, Harvard University, Cambridge, Massachusetts, 1963. McLeod occupied several senior positions, including Director of the Budget Bureau; Johnson became deputy provincial treasurer under Clarence Fines. Much useful information on the early CCF crown ventures is contained in B. Banks, "The Co-operative Commonwealth Federation Government and Economic Planning in Natural Resources and Industrial Development 1944-1946," unpublished honours essay, Department of History, University of Regina, 1977. A highly favourable biography of T.C. Douglas is available: D.F. Shackleton, *Tommy Douglas* (Toronto: McClelland and Stewart, 1975). For brief biographical information on other CCF leaders, including J.H. Brockelbank, Jack Corman, Clarence Fines, Tom Johnston, Woodrow Lloyd, I.C. Nollet and C.C. Williams, see C.H. Higginbotham, *Off the Record: The CCF in Saskatchewan* (Toronto: McClelland and Stewart, 1968), chap. 3.
10. "CCF Program for Saskatchewan" (Regina: CCF Saskatchewan Section, November 1943).
11. *Ibid.*, 7.
12. See F. Steininger, "George H. Williams: Agrarian Socialist," unpublished M.A. thesis, University of Regina, 1976. Williams was a maverick who fought with the CCF establishment, from Douglas to Woodsworth. Since most CCF history has been written from the perspective of that establishment, Williams has been virtually ignored. Stei-

ninger, impressed with Williams as a significant radical farm leader, here undertakes an exercise in rehabilitation.

13. Quoted in "CCF Program," *op. cit.*, 19.
14. *Regina Leader-Post*, March 3, 1939.
15. *Commonwealth*, March 8, 1939.
16. Douglas, "Cream Separator Economics," transcript of radio broadcast, *Commonwealth*, January 26, 1944.
17. McLeod, *op. cit.*, 105 ff.
18. *Social Planning for Canada, op. cit.*, 243.
19. Douglas, "Questions Invited," *op. cit.*
20. "CCF Program," *op. cit.*, 20.
21. Douglas, "The Two Main Classes: Exploiters and Exploited," transcript of radio broadcast, *Commonwealth*, February 24, 1943.
22. *Ibid.*
23. Quoted in Johnson, *op. cit.*, 134.
24. "CCF Program," *op. cit.*, 20.
25. Census data reproduced in J.C. Stabler, *Prairie Regional Development and Prospects* (Royal Commission on Consumer Problems and Inflation, 1968), 96.
26. In this discussion "domestic" refers to the Saskatchewan market. Analogously "export" and "import" refer to goods and services that cross the provincial border without reference to whether they also cross the national border.
27. For a description of the 1944 election campaign see D.E. Smith, *Prairie Liberalism: The Liberal Party in Saskatchewan 1905-71* (Toronto: University of Toronto Press, 1975), 244-53, and Shackleton, *op. cit.*, chap. 9.
28. "Report and Recommendations on Industry," Economic Advisory Committee, TCD Premier 136, July 1945.
29. See R.F. Badgley and S. Wolfe, *Doctors' Strike: Medical Care and Conflict in Saskatchewan* (Toronto: Macmillan, 1967), chap. 1. An important historical example of farmers co-operating to provide medical services is the municipal doctor scheme. The idea emerged during the decade of the 1910s, and was widely implemented in the two following decades. Many rural municipalities hired, on salary, a general practitioner who attended without direct charge to the medical needs of the residents of the municipality in question. The scheme constituted a limited form of medical insurance from the perspective of the patients, who paid a municipal tax to cover the costs of the physician's salary, and it assured stability of income to the physician who otherwise, under the normal system of fee-for-service, could expect payment of patients' bills to vary with the price of wheat.
30. Information in this paragraph is based on personal interviews with J.L. Phelps.
31. In 1945 quartz royalty rates (on metal mining) were raised to the lesser of 5 per cent of gross revenue or 10 per cent of net profits, and revenue under these regulations quadrupled – from $181,000 in 1944-45 to

$847,000 in 1945-46. The major company affected was Hudson's Bay Mining and Smelting with its copper-zinc mining complex at Flin Flon. Phelps reported that the company accepted the upward revision amicably, presumably having feared worse. "Amendment to the Quartz Mining Regulations," Order-in-Council [henceforth "o.c."] 837/45. *Commonwealth*, August 8, 1945. Data on royalty revenue for the 1940s is reproduced in *Annual Report 1949-50* (Department of Natural Resources [DNR]), 38.

32. An Act to Amend the Department of Natural Resources Act (Second Session 1944), "Development and Utilization of Natural Resources," s. 3.

33. *Annual Report 1947-48* (DNR), 36. Homesteads west of the third meridian (which approximately bisects Saskatchewan longitudinally) entered prior to October 31, 1887, and homesteads east of the third meridian entered prior to January 11, 1890, contained title to mineral and surface rights. Thereafter titles were granted for surface rights only. In Alberta, where less settlement had occurred prior to 1890, a smaller proportion of crown mineral rights was alienated than in either Saskatchewan or Manitoba. As of January 1953 nearly one third of the mineral rights acreage in the southern surveyed half of Saskatchewan was freehold. Of the freehold acreage in the province, nearly two fifths was owned by three companies – Hudson's Bay, Canadian Pacific Railway, Canadian National Railway. For a precise breakdown of ownership of mineral rights see *Interim Report of the Oil Policy Committee on Government Policy for the Development of Crown Reserves*, TCD Premier 168, June 1953, 2.

34. *Canadian Pacific Railway Co. v. A.G. for Saskatchewan et al.*, (1952) 4 DLR.

35. See *Commonwealth*, January 28, 1948. A chronology of administrative and legal actions is contained in *Annual Reports 1947-48 to 1952-53* (DNR).

36. J.L. Phelps, "Conserving Resources Developing Industries," transcript of radio broadcast, *Commonwealth*, December 12, 1944.

37. The existence of the private automobile as a close substitute to the bus as means of transport meant that the monopoly possessed by the company on many routes could not be exploited to guarantee a profit. Belonging neither to the primary nor manufacturing sector, it did not fit into any of the categories of the development debates. It has earned a modest surplus in most years and is still in existence.

38. The date of establishment and summary financial information for each crown corporation are available in "Summary of Results of Operations for Crown Corporations 1945 to 1959" (Regina: Government Finance Office, 1960). Besides the annual reports of the various corporations, much useful information on early operations is contained in "Crown Corporations Report," TCD Premier 152, October 19, 1949.

39. "The Province of Saskatchewan Canada: Its Development and Opportunities" (Regina: Bureau of Publications, Government of Saskatchewan, 1930), facing 38.

40. See H.V. Nelles, *The Politics of Development: Forests, Mines and Hydro-*

electric Power in Ontario 1849-1941 (Toronto: Macmillan, 1974), chaps. 6 and 7.

41. S.R. King (president, Albercan Oil Corporation) to J.H. Brockelbank, TCD Premier 166, September 8, 1951.

42. "Interim Report: Natural Gas in Saskatchewan," Economic Advisory and Planning Board [EAPB], TCD Premier 175, January 1947, 37.

43. In particular David Cass-Beggs, an engineer later to become SPC's general manager, played a leading role as ideological technocrat — committed in principle to maximum extension of public ownership in the resource sector, yet also capable of assuaging cabinet trepidations about technical complications.

44. See "A Proposal for the Co-ordinated Development of Natural Gas Utilities Throughout the Province of Saskatchewan," prepared for Government of Saskatchewan by Mannix Ltd. and Kramer Tractor Co., TCD Premier 166, July 23, 1952. Supporting arguments for the proposal are contained in Scott (assistant to Mannix) to Douglas, TCD Premier 166, September 8, 1952. Criticism by officials are contained in D.H. Black to Douglas, TCD Premier 166, September 2, 1952.

45. See *Report of the Royal Commission on Forestry* (1947), and *Report of the Royal Commission on the Fisheries of Saskatchewan* (1947).

46. Banks, *op. cit.*, 46.

47. "Notes on Crown Corporations," TCD Premier 152, February 11, 1949, 2 and 3.

48. "Summary Results of Operations for Crown Corporations 1945 to 1959," *op. cit.*, n. pag.

49. The expropriation decision is contained in o.c. 1612/45. See also *Commonwealth*, November 7, 1945, and "Summary Results of Operations," *op. cit.*

50. *Commonwealth*, December 5, 1945.

51. "Summary Results of Operations," *op. cit.*

52. Discussion of the Timber Board draws from McLeod, *op. cit.*, 86 ff.; Banks, *op. cit.*, 39-40; "The Forests of Saskatchewan," *Saskatchewan Economic Review*, I, 2 (1952); *Annual Reports* (Regina: Saskatchewan Forest Products).

53. "Summary of Operations," *op. cit.*

54. See P. Mathias, *Forced Growth* (Toronto: James Lewis & Samuel, 1971), chap. 4.

55. "Crown Corporations Report," TCD Premier 152, October 19, 1949, 2.

56. See J.N. Piper, "A Red Paper on the Commercial Fishing Industry in Saskatchewan" (1974), in papers of J. Richards, MLA, Saskatchewan Archives, University of Saskatchewan, Saskatoon.

CHAPTER 6

The CCF in Saskatchewan: Lowering Expectations

Whereas the existence of natural gas and oil in commercial quantities in the Province of Saskatchewan has been proven conclusively;
And whereas the CCF as a Socialist Party believes in and advocates the public ownership of the natural resources of this province for the benefit of the people of Saskatchewan;
And whereas a resolution was passed at the 1945 Provincial Convention urging the Government of Saskatchewan to undertake the development and distribution of natural gas and oil in this Province;
And whereas natural gas and oil in the Province of Saskatchewan continues to be extensively exploited by private persons and concerns;
Therefore be it resolved that the Government of Saskatchewan be called upon to show cause why the exploitation of these resources has been allowed to fall into private hands.
And be it further resolved that the Government of Saskatchewan be immediately called upon to place these resources under social ownership, control and operation for the immense benefit of the people of Saskatchewan.

> Resolution adopted by
> the 1946 Saskatchewan
> CCF convention

The prominence of Phelps' crown ventures suggests the cabinet had decided to adhere to the relatively radical stance ensconced in the 1944 program. "The Natural Resources of Saskatchewan," the first major policy document released by the Department of Natural Resources after the 1944 election, substantiates such a presumption. In a personal foreword Phelps reiterated the party program in an official context:

> It is the intention of the Government to effect an orderly change to social ownership in the industrial development of our Natural

Resources. The transition will be gradual and individual enterprise will no doubt continue to play a large part in the development of Saskatchewan's natural resources for some time to come. Eventually, it is hoped to establish complete social ownership and management of key industries in the development of our resources. The Natural Resources belong to society and their development should benefit all the people and, therefore, should not be exploited as a special privilege for the financial benefit of a small minority.[1]

The presumption however is wrong. The Natural Resources policy document contained Phelps' intent; cabinet as a whole was divided. As early as December 1944 a moderate current asserted itself in a cabinet study paper prepared for policy discussions within the party. In it the cabinet argued: "If Saskatchewan, or any other CCF provincial government in Canada is to ... share in new capital development in the mineral field ... then certain adjustments in policy must be made to make conditions favourable to investment of [private] capital comparable to capitalist governments. The province cannot afford to alienate all private interests who will be performing 70 to 80 per cent of the economic tasks."[2]

Within cabinet the most articulate exponent of moderation was Clarence Fines, Provincial Treasurer. His budget addresses during the CCF's first term constitute an invaluable record of the impact of office on a radical politician, the changing perceptions of the Regina school teacher once faced with the pressures of financing the budget of a "have not" province.

His first budget, in 1945, contained a lengthy discussion on the limitations of provincial power: "We have not the power over credit and monetary policy. ... We cannot create our own credit for capital development as can the Federal Government."[3] Nor could the province control the level of aggregate demand, regulate interprovincial trade, or halt the export of wealth "drained off to other parts of the country in interest and profits paid to the large, monopolistic, financial and industrial corporations."[4] At this stage Fines accepted the constitutional constraints as tolerable because, as with most of the CCF leadership across the country, he thought in terms of Ottawa playing the central role in implementing the welfare state and economic planning. Nonetheless constitutional limitations and external corporate/financial power were, in the immediate context, barriers to be overcome. "[W]e shall proceed with our program," concluded Fines, "taking full account of these limitations but not in the least daunted or deflected by them."[5]

By his second budget, in 1946, a fundamental shift had occurred.

The limitations upon the province, in particular financial limitations, had formerly been described as unpleasant realities, but cognizance of them would not deter him from proceeding as far as possible. In 1946 these constraints became an acceptable institutional framework in which he discovered he, as Provincial Treasurer, could operate successfully. Instead of a discussion of limitations on provincial power, this budget address contained a recounting of his travels, in conjunction with Douglas, to visit the financial houses of Toronto, Montreal, and New York that held large quantities of Saskatchewan bonds. They were apparently well received: "I cannot speak too highly of the courteous reception accorded us. ... We had to correct a great many false ideas that had been created in their minds, deliberately, by writers and speakers from this Province."[6] Fines was rewarded for his display of financial rectitude by a lowering of the interest rate on provincial treasury bills, and a dramatic rise in the market price of outstanding provincial bonds which had been selling at a heavy discount ever since the depression, but now were at a premium. In terms of interest rates, the rise meant the province could now borrow at a rate below 4.5 per cent, whereas it would formerly have paid 6 per cent.[7]

At times during the depression debt charges had absorbed over 40 per cent[8] of the provincial budget and, as Fines stated, the market for Saskatchewan bonds had been in a "chaotic state"[9] for fifteen years. Although the CCF had succeeded in raising over $5 million at a low interest cost in a special bond issue sold directly to Saskatchewan residents, it would continue to need recourse to money markets – to refund outstanding debt and to finance its proposed crown corporations. Obviously the CCF had to maintain some form of access to money markets, but there was a price to be paid for it, especially if access were to be at the new low interest rates of which Fines was so proud.

That price was the CCF's tacit agreement not seriously to exceed the contemporary norms for taxation of property income or conduct major transfers of entrepreneurial activity from the private to public sector. In other words, the experiments in social ownership must remain just that – small experiments, not wholesale takeovers as Phelps proposed. For Fines the price amounted to no more than common financial prudence. He believed in a mixed economy in which, apart from some increased investment in public utilities (broadly defined to include projects such as public automobile insurance), the current mix of public and private investment was quite tolerable. The failure of the post-war depression, oft predicted by the CCF, to materialize convinced him that private investment, particularly in the resource sector, would be forthcoming to ensure full employment. Thus he saw a double benefit to his liaison role between the hardheaded men of finance and the idealists within the party. In making the latter aware of financial realities he hoped to dissuade them from the quixotic and dogmatic pursuit of social ownership for its own sake and at great risk to the provincial treasury. In turn, once his colleagues had accepted his version of the mixed economy, he could persuade the former that the CCF were not latent revolutionaries.

In successive budget addresses he became more explicit about his economic policy. In 1947: "[S]o long as it is prepared to contribute to the economic advance and security of the people of Saskatchewan, private capital and enterprise need have no concern over the policies of this Government. We recognize fully that, under the existing framework of our national economy, there is wide scope for private capital. It may, with profit, engage in the utilization of our primary products, perform services and provide consumers' goods at lower cost, undertake speculative ventures, and provide training and employment for our people."[10] In 1948: "[S]ignificant and gratifying as [provincial crown corporations] may be, it is obvious that in relation to the overall productivity of the province, the great bulk of our economic life is dependent upon the enterprise of the thousands of private individuals, partnerships, co-operative organizations and private corporations. Nor has this Government any thought that this can or should be otherwise."[11] From 1945, when he warned "[i]f powerful forces from outside try to intimidate and embarrass us, they will find us unafraid and determined,"[12] Fines evolved to an acceptance of the present economic structure as a state of affairs that neither "can [n]or should be otherwise."

The Planning Board

The extent of ministerial autonomy we have witnessed was an unstable arrangement that could not persist. It clearly did violence to the priority within the CCF, especially among Fabian elements, of the idea of central planning. More specifically Fines had doubts about the economic viability of many of Phelps' proposals and was desirous of exercising a bureaucratic check. Douglas, as premier, wanted a more elaborate planning apparatus available to cabinet than that afforded by the small academic Economic Advisory Committee. The entire cabinet appreciated that economic development posed policy and administrative problems that surpassed the capacity of any one ministry.

The first organizational response was the decision to create a powerful planning board responsible to the cabinet. In June 1945 Douglas offered the chairmanship of such a board to George Cadbury, an English economist close to the Labour Party and a member of the family owning the celebrated chocolate firm. From the wide authority to be granted the chairman it is clear that Douglas, even at this early date before the economic difficulties of Phelps' manufacturing ventures had manifested themselves, intended the planning board to assume the central responsibility for future economic policy. "The duties involved," Douglas wrote Cadbury, "would be best described as those of planning the development of the economic resources of the province in the interests of the population with a view to development of new industries and relating them to the whole of the economic and social problems with which the government has to deal."[13] Cadbury accepted.

The Economic Advisory and Planning Board formally came into existence by order-in-council in January 1946. Apart from the chairman, secretary, and legal counsel, it was a committee of four (shortly expanded to six) cabinet ministers including Phelps and Fines but not Douglas, with a small professional staff of nine. The order-in-council confirmed the breadth of authority Douglas had proposed for it. It was "to advise the Executive Council [cabinet], through its President [Premier] upon all economic, industrial and commercial matters affecting the Province; to formulate a long term plan for the development of the economic life of the Province; ... to receive, for comment and appropriate action, ... all plans and proposals relating to the Government's existing or proposed participation in the economic, industrial and commercial fields in or without the Province."[14] In addition to chairmanship of the Planning Board, Cadbury assumed the impressive title of Chief Industrial Executive and Co-ordinating Officer, with wide powers over the management of all crown corporations.

Cadbury was the ideal Fabian – an administratively competent professional economist, ideologically committed to an active entrepreneurial state, imbued with a respect for British parliamentary practice and the rightful supremacy of cabinet within that system. He was also a shrewd bureaucrat who avoided sharp frontal conflicts with his nominal superiors in cabinet. In the written record at least, there are no explicit criticisms of ministers, although he was engaged in a process of challenging many of their presuppositions. Under his lead the Planning Board quickly assumed the full measure of the authority accorded it in principle. There were two basic tasks that lay before it. The first was to draw conclusions from the experiments in crown ventures and to resolve in some manner the divergences on economic policy within cabinet. The second was to impose administrative order upon the sundry crown undertakings. In general the Board succeeded to a far greater extent in the latter than in the former task.

The Planning Board's initial report on economic policy was conservative in its implications. It defined a much more restricted potential for government intervention than had been entertained to date by the left within the cabinet and party: "This government, despite its socialist aims and objectives, is still forced to function within the framework of a capitalist economy. Not only may it be forced to compete with capitalist institutions, and utilize their techniques, it may even be dependent upon these institutions ... to attain some of its immediate objectives."[15] The report emphasized the open nature of the provincial economy and the simple Keynesian argument that increased non-agricultural employment would depend on the aggregate level of investment by both the private and public sector. The report was pessimistic about the potential volume of public investment, from the federal or municipal levels of government or from the co-operative movement, and concluded: "private enterprise will (if not *must*) continue to operate in a wide field of investment, so long as the only government committed to extensive investment and social control on its own account is a provincial one."[16] Subject to government regulation that would provide for adequate royalties on exploitation of resources and preclude monopoly, and that would prevent excess profits, exploitation of labour, or undue competition with crown or co-operative ventures, the government should even encourage a wide range of private investment. It should provide loan capital, promotional facilities, and possibly wage subsidies. The list of caveats to increased private investment was long and the net policy direction implied would depend upon how seriously such caveats were taken.

To its authors this first report represented a needed lesson in common sense – the recognition that the government lived in a capitalist environment. To others the report went beyond a recognition of environmental constraints to an embrace of the present mixed economy as basically acceptable. The provincial party president, Carlyle King, after what he described as an "unsatisfactory discussion" with Cadbury about the report, wrote to Douglas in protest: "[Cadbury] was distinctly annoyed that I should have seen the [report] and I found him very vague as to what the sphere of government and co-operative enterprise was to be except that it was 'large'. He says that the sphere of private enterprise is 'residual', but I am not quite clear as to how you get at the 'residue' until you know what the main matter is."[17] King proposed that the whole subject be jointly discussed by representatives of the party and cabinet. There is no record of the outcome of this particular initiative, but it illustrates a general phenomenon. As the government proceeded to define an economic strategy independent of, and ultimately considerably to the right of, the program on which it was elected, conflict arose between government and party.

Each relied on an impeccable basis of legitimacy which, if pushed, implied a denial of the other's. Behind the cabinet and civil servants lay the venerable authority of a legislative majority in British parliamentary practice. Behind the leaders of the party outside government was the authority of election by party members, and the populist and socialist traditions whereby the parliamentary caucus is beholden to the party program. Tension between party and its elected legislators has been a recurrent theme in the annals of the left, a tension usually aggravated when the party forms a government. In the case of the CCF the key mechanisms of reconciliation were the private diplomacy and public oratory of a few leading MLAs, Douglas in particular, who usually succeeded in procuring party support for cabinet initiatives.

By the fall of 1946 Cadbury and the Planning Board did make considerable progress in removing the vagueness to which King had objected. "Planning Document No. 1,"[18] prepared by the Planning Board for cabinet in September 1946, represents the most ambitious attempt to define a general economic program for the government. The document remains disconcertingly ambiguous on many questions, but it does qualify as a program, however tentative, as opposed to an ad hoc response to immediate issues.

The document (p. 2) repeated the argument for diversification but insisted that new industries must be based on a better assessment, than in the past, of the comparative advantage afforded by the resource base of the province and of the available market: "there may be great but undiscovered mineral wealth in addition to the known lake and forest products. ... there is a small place for industrial development, especially in the processing of primary resources. ... However, such developments can never be large, and though a general diversification of the provincial economy is desirable, any attempted move towards a completely self-contained economy is foredoomed to failure in the face of the growing and inevitably cheaper output of industries in other parts of North America. Indeed, there is a legitimate question as to the efficacy of developing an area restricted by accidental political boundaries such as a province when necessity demands planning within a wider economic unit. ..." While the Board did not dismiss the possibility of import substitution manufacturing, it concluded that the "development of new industries within the province has been considerably overrated in the last two years."[19] The emphasis should be upon new non-agricultural staples: "It is quite clear that any substantial diversification of the provincial economy is most likely to arise from the development of our major natural resources. The provincial government should be directing much more time and money to the exploration of the mineral wealth of the province; to research and investigation into the uses to which our natural wealth can be put; and to assisting in the development and marketing of such products."[20]

The document did not preclude private investment from any field, and in that sense was a disappointment to the left. Conversely, it proposed considerable public investment in resource industries, and criticized excessive financial orthodoxy. Since the provincial credit had been restored, it was against "debt reduction for its own sake,"[21] and suggested annual capital spending for the government in the order of $25 million – in crown industries ($5 million), housing ($10 million), communications ($5 million), public works ($5 million). The amounts are small in absolute terms, but appear more significant relative to the size of the provincial budget, $39 million in ordinary non-capital expenditures for the 1945-46 fiscal year. Consideration was given to the idea of setting up a provincially owned savings bank as a relatively cheap source of capital. (Nothing came of the idea.) Further, in the domain of natural resources, the Board argued, albeit none too explicitly, that the provincial government should exert a dominant control: "there is the major battle to be fought with private interests over the control and exploitation of provincial natural resources."[22] In an appendix dealing with problems of northern development, the Board gave approval to the intent of Phelps' northern corporations in asserting public ownership and enforcing reasonable conservation policies: "It is time that the natural resources were conserved and perhaps redeveloped and their control brought back into state rather than private hands."[23]

The priorities at this stage were relatively clear. The major potential for economic diversification, argued the Board, lay in the rational expansion of non-agricultural staples. The inescapable conclusion reached by the Board, on the basis of the crown ventures launched, was that the potential for import substitution manufacturing had been greatly overestimated. As with any such distinction the affairs of man do not fit neatly. Thus investment in the brick plant was simultaneously motivated by the desire to substitute domestic for imported bricks and by the perception that the province had a comparative advantage in the industry in the form of local clays. Despite such obvious ambiguities the distinction is useful. Certain crown ventures (e.g. woollen mill, shoe factory/tannery) were launched in the hope of displacing imported manufactured goods; others (e.g. Timber Board, sodium sulphate mine) were based on the relatively simple transformation of particular primary resources, whose existence in the province assured a comparative advantage, into basic staples to be sold primarily in export markets. The first test of the Board's strategy was to be oil.

Oil and Potash

Shortly after the CCF assumed office, Imperial Oil proposed to the government a long-term agreement that would have given the company exclusive exploration rights, and leasing rights if it found commercial volumes of oil, over most of west central Saskatchewan.[24] The government rejected the proposal, but it is worth noting the advice proffered by Frank Scott, McGill law professor, prominent member of the League, and at the time chairman of the national CCF. In a memo addressed to Douglas and Phelps he first posed the question of using "an agency of Standard Oil." If the government relied on its own resources, lack of capital would delay exploration for many years. "In view of this fact, and in view of the highly speculative nature of oil exploration," Scott concluded, "I am inclined to think that the policy of using Imperial Oil is justified at this stage."[25] Scott objected to certain clauses of the proposed agreement, but he assumed without question that delay in development was intolerable, and that the risks inherent in the oil industry were inappropriate to a CCF provincial government. Such confidential advice was sharply at odds with the public stance of the national CCF. The lowest common denominator of all official CCF policy at the time was vehement opposition to cartelized industries in which producers exercised considerable monopoly power.

Commercial oil production began in Saskatchewan in 1945 – a mere 14,000 barrels of heavy oil from the Lloydminster area. After rejection by the government of its proposal, Imperial boycotted the province as a region for exploration, but certain independents, of which Husky Oil was the only one of size, invested in the Lloydminster area. In late 1946 Cadbury drafted a "Statement of Policy on Oil, Gas and Mineral Development" that in various guises received wide publicity as government policy: "The policy of this Government is to develop the resources of the Province on a planned basis. ... At the same time the Province is not equipped to enter all the possible fields of development immediately and when it therefore becomes obvious that new private capital can develop any particular project within the framework of the best plans for either the Province, the Prairies or the Nation as a whole, then such capital should be given an opportunity to operate in the Province."[26] Public investment was not excluded, but the evolution of government oil policy towards reliance on private capital excited ire within the party. In 1946 the annual convention adopted a resolution critical of the government for permitting private development of oil and gas. In 1947 the party again called for the government to "engage in the processing of oil on a public ownership basis as soon as such policy is economically sound and in the public interest." And again in 1948 a similar resolution was approved.[27]

By 1947 only a minority within cabinet, of which Phelps was the most vocal, placed a high priority on a crown oil development. Douglas apparently felt any crown venture to be unnecessary and undesirable.[28] On this issue he was presumably influenced strongly by the Planning Board, which concluded in 1947 that due to the heavy sour character of the only established fields and to the fact "[t]he petroleum industry is controlled by a highly integrated monopoly. ... [i]t is questionable whether or not the resources of the province should at this time be risked in this use at the expense of other more pressing (and more promising) alternatives."[29] Besides reversing the thrust of "Planning Document No. 1," this conclusion was obviously inconsistent with the Board's earlier stipulation that private capital should only by invited into industries where competition could be assured.

In early 1948 discussions took place among Husky, Saskatchewan Federated Co-operatives, and the provincial government with a view to expansion of provincial refinery capacity and joint exploration for petroleum. Cadbury was skeptical of the success of any joint venture and recommended against government participation in exploration or refining "even at the risk of letting the big oil companies get into the field."[30] The Planning Board did recommend shortly thereafter a joint petroleum exploration program with the co-operatives, but the latter decided ultimately to invest in Alberta.

In the light of the post-Leduc boom in Alberta the government became increasingly sensitive to opposition charges of stagnation in the provincial oil industry, and increasingly anxious to accelerate exploration. In February 1948 Douglas raised with the president of Imperial Oil the government's desire that Imperial return to the province and embark on an exploration program; the government would be happy to discuss any changes in provincial oil statutes and regulations Imperial thought desirable.[31]

The net result of a perceived political constraint on the minimum rate of exploration and development of provincial oil was effectively to preclude any public involvement and reduce the role of the co-operatives to that of a minor independent. In a lengthy memo to Douglas discussing policy to accelerate exploration, Cadbury did not rule out a "partial [public] participation if that is politically and economically feasible" but he was by now operating on the assumption that exploration must be more rapid than the capital budget of the government could possibly sustain. The first option Cadbury elaborated was to make the necessary concessions to bring the oil majors back into the province. In a revealing passage he examined the price that would have to be paid:

The main differentiation in the minds of the oil promoters and operators between Saskatchewan and other places is that the programme of this Government contains a policy of public ownership which in their minds could lead to expropriation of oil operations at some time in the future. The Government of Saskatchewan is, therefore, compelled to make concessions and firm commitments under this heading which would never be asked of their neighbours. If, however, the Government of Saskatchewan were prepared to make a definite statement and commitment to the effect that they would not expropriate oil operations, then it is possible that we could get a similar degree of interest in this Province to that in Alberta prior to the finding of the Leduc field. This has been confirmed in conversations with officials of the prominent companies.

The alternative, if the government was not prepared to make such a commitment, was "the possibility of making such other concessions as will attract the interest of smaller operators even if the major concerns are not interested."[32] Within this second option Cadbury considered the possibility of joint ventures. Joint ventures were possible, he stated, with certain private companies and with the co-ops which had a guaranteed market for crude oil in their Regina refinery and for refined products in their retail outlets. Cadbury did not recommend either option, but given his earlier stated hostility to any joint ventures, it seems fair to conclude he favoured the first. The party and Phelps, as the minister closest to the party's position, had clearly lost.

No decision was taken prior to the 1948 election, but shortly thereafter the CCF did indeed accept the first option. It reassured the oil industry via a series of individual letters, over the Premier's signature, to majors and independents:

It is the Government's policy in the next four years, to promote the maximum exploration and development of petroleum in Saskatchewan which natural circumstances will permit. This policy is based upon a recognition of two principles. First, it is necessary to secure to the people of the Province a fair return from the production of petroleum of which the people are the true owners, (a) by means of Crown reserves in all parts of the Province, and (b) in the form of royalties upon the petroleum that is produced. Secondly, the Province will stand by all agreements it enters into, and it has no intention of either expropriating or socializing the oil industry.[33]

The oil industry was delighted that the government had put an end to "the rash talk of 'confiscation' or 'nationalization' of oil and gas by certain of its members."[34]

What of potash? Blissfully ignorant of the consequences for resource politics half a century later, Sir Wilfrid Laurier's government,
when it created the new provinces of Alberta and Saskatchewan in
1905, drew the boundaries such that all the tar sands and most of the
conventional oil lay in Alberta, and all the commercially exploitable
potash in Saskatchewan. Except for a pittance of oil, Manitoba lost out
on both. The first evidence of potash deposits in the Canadian prairies
came in 1914. Reporting the results of their analysis of Manitoba
slough waters in the *Geological Survey of Canada* that year, two re-
searchers noted that "[t]he percentage of potash in the total solids
is ... unusually high – much higher than in most of the waters which
have been investigated for potash on this continent." They supplemented their geology with a few relevant political comments: "The
fact that a powerful monopoly has been established in the potash industry renders it difficult to forecast the success of a venture in this
field. ... "[35] The monopoly at the time was German, not American, but
their forebodings about the development of a Canadian industry
proved prophetic. Their findings were promptly forgotten until potash was accidentally discovered in 1942 in the core of a well being
drilled for oil in southeastern Saskatchewan. The discovery was at
7600 feet, too deep for conventional room and pillar mining techniques. In 1946 potash was again accidentally discovered while
drilling for oil, this time at Unity, a town approximately 100 miles
west of Saskatoon, at a commercially exploitable depth.

The first public statement of the existence of commercially exploitable reserves in Saskatchewan came in February 1947 from the
Honourable J.A. Glen, federal Minister of Mines and Resources, in
response to a question in Parliament from John Diefenbaker. The following day Phelps confirmed the discovery in the Saskatchewan legislature. Phelps was enthusiastic about the potential, adding that a
crown venture was the only rational means of proceeding.[36] However
Fines, while not explicitly contradicting Phelps, used the potash discovery in his 1947 budget address to "conjure up a scene of new enterprise and expansion. I see in it complete refutation of the prophecies
and the forebodings of those who. ... declared that advent of a CCF
government would drive private capital and private enterprise from
Saskatchewan." [37]

Initially the preponderant opinion within the provincial government was to preserve potash in the public domain. Douglas was
sufficiently interested in a crown development that he personally
approached Sir Stafford Cripps, Chancellor of the Exchequer in the
British Labour government, about British support. By agreeing to
long-term contracts to purchase Saskatchewan potash, the British

could overcome the major barrier to crown development perceived by the CCF—access to markets. They were agreeable, according to Douglas, and also willing to invest some equity capital, but as a precondition Cripps wanted Ottawa's assurance not to block the project.[38] In April 1947 Phelps' deputy minister reported to him on the current state of knowledge of reserves and recommended that potash be developed as a joint venture of the federal and provincial governments.[39] In May cabinet asked the Planning Board to prepare a proposal for a federal-provincial joint venture,[40] and Phelps wrote his federal counterpart proposing that Ottawa and Regina jointly undertake potash exploration to define the extent of reserves, sharing costs 75 per cent/25 per cent respectively. In the event that proved reserves justified development, the province would be prepared to invest the "major proportion" of the capital costs of a mine.[41]

Glen's reaction was decidedly negative: "In view of the difficulties in regard to the exploration, development, mining and treatment of the potash rock which are apparent from a study of the above reports, I do not feel justified in recommending to my colleagues financial participation by the Federal Government at the present time." He enumerated a series of problems: lower grade than at New Mexico (later exploration proved Saskatchewan to have the higher grade), high cost of exploratory drilling, high cost of shaft sinking due to depth and water-bearing formations, and high overland transport costs to markets in eastern Canada relative to cheaper ocean transport from offshore sources. Development would require the "highest specialized technical skill," available only to certain experienced private companies. Federal participation would be justified only if private enterprise were unwilling to invest and it became "a matter of national necessity" to develop the ore.[42] In the spring of 1948 Phelps made a second appeal to Glen for federal co-operation on the grounds the only private company having expressed interest was demanding excessive concessions. "Private interests," Phelps wrote, "[would] undertake development of the Potash deposits only under such terms and conditions which would not appear to be either in the interests of the people of Saskatchewan or of Canada."[43] The federal response was again negative.[44]

Meanwhile senior civil servants responsible for advising on potash policy lost their initial enthusiasm, and their counsel to cabinet diverged. A Planning Board subcommittee recommended in early 1948 against the province spending $2 million required for potash exploration.[45] Since the estimated costs of bringing a mine into production would be high ($15 million), the Planning Board urged modification of existing policy to permit private development,[46] albeit under the usual litany of safeguards to exclude promoters, to assure competitive negotiations by contacting as many companies as possible, and to "avoid entangling the government with the international potash cartel."[47] As with oil, the Planning Board feared the ability of a cartel of established producers to deny access to markets for the product of a crown mine. Cadbury demurred. Discussing both potash and potential uranium development, he argued that if public development was currently not feasible, the CCF had a responsibility to preserve these resources in the public domain until such time as it was, and not to allow their alienation from the crown. "I believe," he wrote to Douglas in March, "there is no need for such haste and that these minutes [Planning Board recommendations on potash and uranium] constitute an unnecessary retreat but I recognize the majority do not share my opinion."[48] Nor did cabinet share Cadbury's opinion, for shortly thereafter it decided to invite private capital into potash. Twenty-five years would elapse before public ownership of potash would again become a subject of cabinet deliberation.

"Socialist Planning"

One useful summary of the CCF's first term of office is to describe the first two years as a time of policy innovation, and the last two as a time of administrative innovation.[49] One obvious reason for the shift in emphasis was the inevitable accumulation of administrative problems posed by the rapid expansion of government activity. The most dramatic but by no means the only problems were those surrounding the new crown corporations. A second reason comes from a realization that the CCF government was a marriage between the leaders of a left populist movement and representatives of a generation of professional civil servants who, having been formed by depression and war, were radicals relative to their professional norms. After 1945 the tide of CCF support began nationally to ebb and the only dyke breached had been in Saskatchewan. Accordingly the CCF managed to attract to Regina a significant number of these professional civil servants who, in other circumstances, would never have congregated in such an isolated rural environment. They came from eastern Canada, the United States, Britain, and of course from Saskatchewan itself, attracted by the prospect of realizing, if only in one small province, their aspirations. Although they variously described themselves as "progressive," "socialist," and a few even as "Marxist," most were in effect Fabians. To the extent they shared a philosophy of social change it was the Fabian faith in the philosopher-bureaucrat who designs and implements change from the centre. They had a profound influence on the government, permitting the CCF to achieve a level of administrative competence far above that of previous populist administrations. Without them the CCF might have foundered in administrative difficulties analogous to those of the Nonpartisan League in North Dakota.

The impact of such Fabians was most evident in the Planning Board and its organizational offspring – the Budget Bureau and Government Finance Office.[50] The former, modelled on the U.S. Bureau of the Budget, was responsible for evaluation of all programs of line departments, and for budget preparation. The latter was intended by Cadbury to be the instrument whereby the cabinet, and the central bureaucrats of whom he was the most powerful, could control major policy and the capital budgets of all crown corporations. It was a holding company – the repository for government equity in, initially, all crown corporations. As with the Planning Board its members were senior cabinet ministers plus central bureaucrats; it had a small professional staff.

Much has been written, not least by the Fabian bureaucrats involved, about the rationale behind these administrative innovations.[51] Basically the arguments were the same as those put forward a decade earlier by the League for Social Reconstruction. Cadbury argued that policy and capital expenditure decisions for crown corporations were political in the sense that cabinet (and the central bureaucracy) should make them. To that end he insisted that each crown corporation have a cabinet minister as chairman of its board of directors. This policy was in marked contrast to the usual practice in Canada and Britain where ministers occupy no positions within the corporations, allegedly so that the corporations can operate on a "sound business basis" independent of "political considerations."

For Cadbury the administrative changes were themselves a valuable contribution to social change, combining a concern for efficiency with socialist goals. "We are in the middle of a process," he wrote Douglas in the summer of 1948, "by which we hope to establish a new pattern of operation for publicly owned enterprises which will not only measure up to the criteria of a capitalist balance sheet, but will also adopt patterns of human and financial relationships which are superior to those in private industry."[52] Such an assessment displays as much wishful thinking as Phelps' earlier pronouncements about ultimate social ownership for all resource industries. Administrative changes had effectively removed the ability of individual ministers, Phelps in particular, to initiate new crown ventures, and formally had given to cabinet as a whole the means, were it so inclined, to make more informed decisions concerning future public investments. In fact, however, this structure placed power with a few ministers, essentially Douglas, Fines, and Brockelbank (who replaced Phelps in the

Natural Resources portfolio after the latter's defeat in the 1948 election), and a few central bureaucrats. These men succeeded in preventing any further fiascos analogous to the shoe factory and woollen mill, but they proved unable or unwilling to launch any new crown ventures. They rationalized the crown ventures launched during the first two years, disbanding the blatantly unsuccessful and reorganizing the rest, but no new crown venture of a competitive nature was launched by the CCF after 1946. Significantly the only crown corporations that did undertake substantial expansion after 1946 all broke free from this structure and operated under special statutes that permitted them to bypass the Government Finance Office. Such was the case for government insurance and for the power and telephone utilities.

Upon his resignation from the government in 1951 Cadbury made his most explicit statement of the idea that cabinet government was the principal institution of a democratic society, and that the essence of socialism was to enable it to function well by providing it with "socialist planning." What Cadbury intended by the term "socialist planning" remained distressingly vague, although he more or less equated it with effective staff support to cabinet by ideologically progressive professionals. That government should become "the agent of the electorate for orderly planned progress rather than a necessary evil" he considered to be a "fundamental socialist concept." Within the Saskatchewan government he hoped that the Planning Board had become "the effective technical half of the planning process, with the Executive Council as the political and supreme portion of the partnership." Socialist planning and not public ownership, he concluded, was the essence of a socialist government: "To my mind Public Ownership is merely a tool to be used when applicable; but Socialist Planning is an essential process if a Government is to be able to claim any affinity to the world wide fraternity of those who believe in democratic socialism. ..."[53]

Given the emphasis upon effective exercise of cabinet authority, Cadbury and his associates did not, as we have seen in the case of oil policy, hold the authority of the party in high regard. Their primary commitment was to cabinet government, not to the culture of left populism. They were also hostile to what they identified as syndicalist currents within the crown corporations.[54] "Another problem with which we are faced," wrote Cadbury in 1947, "is the pressure for some measure of control by the workers over the management of our plants. This pressure does not originate so much with trade union representatives as with rank-and-file employees of CCF leanings who have been exposed in CCF circles to much loose thinking on this subject."[55] Labour relations in crown corporations were frequently tense. They were aggravated when financial losses prompted management to resist wage increases and when workers expected a socialist government to provide wages above the prevailing industry level which, for several industries in which crown corporations existed, was low.

Workers on occasion had wage demands which, if granted, would have entailed government subsidies to the crown corporation and, given the incidence of taxation and the low average contemporary provincial income, would have increased the inequality in overall provincial income distribution. The need to assert a managerial prerogative in such circumstances need not have precluded an interest in industrial democracy. The refusal even to experiment with it betrayed the unjustified faith of the Fabian tradition that the parliamentary system of cabinet government provides an adequate means for people to exercise control over their economic environment.

Conclusion

In assessing retrospectively policies formulated in a context of uncertainty, it is exceedingly difficult to be just. However, the first term of office betrayed a failure to grasp an essential aspect of private or public entrepreneurship, namely the willingness to risk. The only leaders who consistently displayed that willingness were Phelps and, to a lesser extent, Cadbury. The victors in the administrative reorganization of 1946-48 abandoned the relatively sophisticated analysis of the potential for public investment made by Cadbury and the Planning Board in late 1946. Instead of concentrating their limited capital and entrepreneurial resources in the new resource industries as then recommended, the government baulked at any further public ventures, or even joint ventures. To use a psychological analogy, after 1946 senior bureaucrats and ministers displaced their former ambitions to assert public control of economic development into an obsessive concern to perfect the machinery of government. After 1950 private development of these new resources did occur, but in a decidedly suboptimal fashion from the perspective of the province. In the interim considerable ambiguity reigned as to the government's intentions. In 1949 Walter Tucker, the Liberal leader, with some justification concluded with respect to oil and potash: "what has been done? Nothing! This government cannot make up its mind. ... whether it is socialist or free enterprise; and they are so hesitating between the two positions that nothing has been done."[56]

The failures among the initial crown ventures have assumed mythic proportions in Saskatchewan. The shoe factory, woollen mill, box factory and, to a degree, the brick plant remain political albatrosses for the NDP. So effectively has the opposition kept alive these case studies

142

in public misadministration that, in the heat of the controversy surrounding the NDP's 1975 enabling legislation for nationalization of the potash industry, a conservative national lobby chose as title for its large newspaper advertisements: "Can a government that failed at the shoe business learn the potash business?"[57] Clearly Phelps made some grievous errors in his choice of corporate managers and in his excessive faith in the potential for import substitution. He became the target for much internal criticism by the CCF, as well as external attacks from the opposition. The overall financial record of the competitive crown ventures was not however particularly grim. The total public investment in the competitive crown corporations by the end of the first term was $6.5 million. In the fiscal year 1947-48 the net return on this public investment was 3.1 per cent. This return was not high, but it included sizeable deficits in corporations shortly to be disbanded. Excluding the corporations registering losses, the net return for 1947-48 was 12.5 per cent.[58] As a final assessment, that by Al Johnson is worth noting. Johnson, who in 1952 became deputy provincial treasurer under Fines, found Phelps' impetuosity alien, but he allowed that Phelps' "unorthodox" approach produced the most substantial policy changes of any minister during the formative first two years of office.[59]

The year 1948 was in many ways the end of the beginning for the CCF, and the beginning of its end. The provincial election that year signalled the end (except for natural gas distribution) of any public investment in the resource sector. From 1948 until the post-1973 controversies, Saskatchewan resource policies paralleled very closely those of any other province.

Two political phenomena bear brief mention. First, the early optimism of the national CCF had given way by 1948 to a siege mentality in the face of highly successful business-financed publicity campaigns against socialism, and the rise of Cold War hysteria. No longer could the Saskatchewan leadership think of itself as a "beachhead of socialism" as Douglas was wont to say. Second, the actions of the government during its first term – from labour legislation to its crown corporations – were sufficiently beyond what the local business community would tolerate from a government that the CCF was unable, despite the desire of the more moderate leadership, to replicate the quasi-corporatist nature of Social Credit in Alberta. Class conflict and explicit ideological confrontation now became a feature of Saskatchewan politics to an extent unknown before. Having lost the support of most of the farm and labour leadership, the Liberals found their inner councils increasingly dominated by businessmen and professionals.[60] The Liberal party after 1944 defended free enterprise with a virulence it never displayed before when it had farm and labour support and could perform traditional brokerage politics. Although the Liberals did not win in 1948, their representation in the legislature rose from five to nineteen, the CCFs fell from forty-seven to thirty-one, and two other opposition MLAs were elected. In the 1949 federal election the Saskatchewan contingent of CCF MPs fell from eighteen to five. The CCF was clearly unable to rely on the united support, in times of conflict with Ottawa or external corporate pressures, of all local interests. Given the boom in Alberta after the discovery of oil at Leduc in 1947, the CCF became increasingly sensitive to opposition attacks of stagnation in Saskatchewan resource development, and to arguments that Saskatchewan could parallel Alberta were it not for the anti-business stance of the provincial government.

The net result was that after 1948 CCF leaders became anxious to adapt to new Cold War realities. The defeat of Phelps in the 1948 election and his replacement in the resources portfolio by J.H. Brockelbank, a far more cautious politician, hastened the demise of radical resource policies, but the trend was clearly independent of personalities. The cabinet assured private resource companies that there would be no nationalization, and more or less accepted the current conventional wisdom that the first priority of any resource policy was to encourage rapid private investment with collection of economic rent very much a secondary issue.

Notes

1. J.L. Phelps, foreword to W.H. Hastings, "The Natural Resources of Saskatchewan" (Regina: DNR, 1945) n. pag.
2. Quoted in Johnson, *op. cit.*, 188.
3. C.M. Fines, "Budget Speech," Legislative Assembly of Saskatchewan, March 15, 1945, 8.
4. *Ibid.*, 9.
5. *Ibid.*, 9.
6. Fines, "Budget Speech," March 14, 1946, 20.
7. A typical bond is a contract whereby the issuer agrees to pay to the lender the face value at some specified date in the future and, in the interim, to pay interest at a coupon rate. If the lender expects a higher rate of return than the coupon rate, he will only purchase it at a discount from the face value. Conversely, if he is content with less than the coupon rate, he will pay a premium above face value. Thus interest rate and market price of a given bond vary inversely.
8. See "Statements of Expenditure on Revenue Account" for fiscal years during the 1930s. Debt charges amounted, for example, to 42 per cent

of ordinary expenditures in the 1936-37 fiscal year. *Public Accounts of the Province of Saskatchewan 1937-38* (Regina: Government of Saskatchewan), xliv.

9. Fines, "Budget Speech," March 14, 1946, 20.
10. Fines, "Budget Speech," March 6, 1947, 9.
11. Fines, "Budget Speech," February 26, 1948, 12.
12. Fines, "Budget Speech," March 15, 1945, 9.
13. Douglas to Cadbury, TCD Premier 136, June 14, 1945.
14. o.c. 158/46.
15. "Report on Relationship Between Government and Private Enterprise," EAPB, TCD Premier 140, May 31, 1946, 1.
16. *Ibid.*, 2.
17. King to Douglas, TCD Premier 141, June 13, 1946.
18. "Program Planning: Planning Document No. 1," EAPB, TCD Premier 136, September 9, 1946.
19. *Ibid.*, 16.
20. *Ibid.*, 8.
21. *Ibid.*, 22.
22. *Ibid.*, 9.
23. *Ibid.*, 23-24.
24. "Memorandum of Agreement" (unsigned), between Minister of Natural Resources and Industrial Development and Imperial Oil Limited, TCD Ministerial files Natural Resources 45, 1945.
25. Scott to Douglas and Phelps, TCD Ministerial files Natural Resources 43, 1945.
26. "Statement of Policy on Oil, Gas and Mineral Development," TCD Premier 166, November 29, 1946.
27. Resolutions passed by Saskatchewan CCF Council (1947) and Saskatchewan CCF Convention (1948). Quoted in *Commonwealth*: August 13, 1947, July 28, 1948.
28. See Johnson, *op. cit.*, 186.
29. T.H. McLeod, "Oil Policy for the Provincial Government," TCD Premier 166, July 24, 1947.
30. Cadbury to Douglas, TCD Premier 166, January 9, 1948.
31. H.H. Hewetson (president, Imperial Oil) to Douglas, TCD Premier 166, June 14, 1948.
32. Cadbury to Douglas, TCD Premier 166, March 8, 1948.
33. The quotation is from one of many such letters. Douglas to B.F. Lundy (managing director, Inter-Provincial Petroleums), TCD Premier 166, March 21, 1949.
34. *Oil in Canada*, June 6, 1949.
35. A. MacLean and R.C. Wallace, "Gypsum and Salt in Manitoba," in *Summary Report of the Geological Survey 1913* (Ottawa: Department of Mines, 1914), 169.
36. *Regina Leader-Post*: February 18, 1947, February 20, 1947.
37. Fines, "Budget Speech," March 6, 1947, 8.

38. This information is based on a personal interview with T.C. Douglas in March 1976.
39. C.A.L. Hogg (deputy minister DNR) to Phelps, TCD Executive Assistant files 92, April 8, 1947.
40. "Report on Potash Development," EAPB, TCD Premier 140, May 9, 1947.
41. Phelps to J.A. Glen (Minister of Mines and Resources), TCD Executive Assistant files 92, May 22, 1947.
42. Glen to Phelps, TCD Executive Assistant files 92, November 28, 1947.
43. Phelps to Glen, TCD Executive Assistant files 92, March 16, 1948.
44. J.A. MacKinnon (Acting Minister of Mines) to Phelps, TCD Executive Assistant files 92, May 28, 1948.
45. Minutes of EAPB subcommittee on potash development, TCD EAPB files, May 3, 1947, May 10, 1947, January 16, 1948.
46. T.K. Shoyama (acting secretary, EAPB) to Douglas, TCD Premier 140, January 26, 1948.
47. Shoyama to Fines, TCD Premier 181, June 16, 1948.
48. Cadbury to Douglas, TCD Premier 140, March 9, 1948.
49. This distinction is made by Johnson, *op. cit.*, chap. 7.
50. The Budget Bureau came into existence in November 1946. The Government Finance Office, formed in 1947, had a statutory basis in the revised Crown Corporation Act of that year. The revised Act also created an Industrial Development Fund as a means for the government to provide debt capital to private companies and co-operatives. The Fund was a further symbol of the growing acceptance of private enterprise by the government, and it excited considerable opposition from the left within the caucus, and elsewhere in the party.
51. In addition to the theses of McLeod, *op. cit.*, and Johnson, *op. cit.*, a sample of the ideas of the central bureaucrats can be had from the following: A.E. Blakeney, "Saskatchewan's Crown Corporations: A Case Study," presented at Institute of Public Administration Conference in Saskatoon, Woodrow S. Lloyd Papers [henceforth "WSL"] Crown Corporation files I 10 d, 1953; G.W. Cadbury, "Public Enterprises in the Province of Saskatchewan," presented at International Institute of Administrative Sciences in Brussels, WSL Crown Corporation files 1 10 d, 1955; G.W. Cadbury, "Planning in Saskatchewan," in L. La Pierre et al. (eds.), *Essays on the Left* (Toronto: McClelland and Stewart, 1971), 51-64; M. Brownstone, "The Douglas-Lloyd Governments: Innovation and Bureaucratic Adaptation," in La Pierre, *ibid.*, 65-80.
52. Cadbury to Douglas, TCD Premier 152, August 9, 1948.
53. Cadbury, final comments upon resigning chairmanship of EAPB, TCD Premier 144, January 11, 1951.
54. See, for example, McLeod, *op. cit.*, chap. 7.
55. K. Bryden and Cadbury, "Relations Between Government Industries and Trade Unions," TCD Premier 172, August 12, 1947.
56. *Debates and Proceedings*, Legislative Assembly of Saskatchewan, 1st Ses-

sion of 11th Legislature (Regina: Legislative Assembly Office) February 15, 1949, 42-43.

57. *Saskatoon Star-Phoenix*, December 10, 1975.

58. Calculated from financial data in "Summary of Results of Operations for Crown Corporations 1945 to 1959," *op. cit.*

59. Johnson, *op. cit.*, 200.

60. See Smith, *Prairie Liberalism*, *op. cit.*, chap. 7.

CHAPTER 7

Oil and Social Class: The Making of the New West

The people filled with the spirit of capitalism to-day tend to be indifferent, if not hostile, to the Church. The thought of the pious boredom of paradise has little attraction for their active natures; religion appears to them as a means of drawing people away from labour in this world. If you ask them what is the meaning of their restless activity, why they are never satisfied with what they have, thus appearing so senseless to any purely worldly view of life, they would perhaps give the answer, if they know any at all: "to provide for my children and grandchildren". But more often and, since that motive is not peculiar to them, but was just as effective for the traditionalist, more correctly, simply: that business with its continuous work has become a necessary part of their lives. That is in fact the only possible motivation, but it at the same time expresses what is, seen from the view-point of personal happiness, so irrational about this sort of life, where a man exists for the sake of his business, instead of the reverse.

Max Weber
*The Protestant Ethic and
the Spirit of Capitalism*
(London: George Allen & Unwin, 1930), 70

Alberta's large and growing urban middle classes, nurtured by twenty-five years of oil and gas development, acceded to political power in the provincial election of August 30, 1971. That election, which saw Peter Lougheed's revived Progressive Conservatives win forty-nine seats to Social Credit's twenty-five and the NDP's one, was one of critical realignment – the political consolidation of major economic, demographic, and social changes which had occurred in Alberta in the generation of growth after Leduc. With the considerable advantage of hindsight, Lougheed's victory and the abrupt termination of the Social Credit dynasty represented an inevitable, albeit considerably delayed, response of the electoral system to rapid population growth, urbanization, and secularization – trends underway during and after World War II, but greatly accelerated by the oil boom. The meaning of Lougheed's victory was this: the political centre of gravity within Alberta had shifted in favour of metropolitan interests. The city, represented by an alliance of business and professional elites and led by a descendant of one of Alberta's ruling families, now dominated the towns and farms. Power had passed into the outstretched hands of Alberta's new bourgeoisie.

To understand the changes that helped bring Peter Lougheed to power, we require some historical perspective on the development of social class in Alberta and the other prairie provinces. Our primary concern is to sketch the rise to prominence of a new urban middle class in postwar Alberta, but the initial task must be to debunk the historical myth of prairie society as homogeneous and lacking most of the antagonistic relations that grow out of a modern capitalist economy.

Class in Alberta: Macpherson Revisited

Writing about Alberta's rural, small-town petite bourgeoisie and Social Credit, C.B. Macpherson, in his influential *Democracy in Alberta* (a book which has had a powerful impact on the left's understanding of the Canadian West), described "a society that is politically and economically a subordinate part of a mature capitalist economy, and whose people, at the same time, have preponderantly the outlook and assumptions of small-propertied independent commodity producers." The introduction of the party system to the prairies had been discouraged, Macpherson argued, by the West's "relatively homogeneous class composition" and its "quasi-colonial" relationship to the rest of Canada. The "absence of any serious opposition of class interests within the province meant that alternate parties were not needed to express or to moderate a perennial conflict of interests." For Macpherson, the outstanding features of the class composition of Alberta, as compared with the more industrialized provinces, were "(1) that independent commodity producers ... have been from 1921 until 1941 about 48 per cent of the whole gainfully occupied population while in Ontario they have been from 20 to 25 per cent, and in Canada about 30 per cent; (2) in Alberta the industrial wage and salary earners ... have been 41 per cent of the whole, in Ontario about 70 per cent, in Canada about 60 per cent."[1]

The preponderance of independent commodity producers ensured that class tensions within Alberta were muted: "the peculiarity of a society which is at once quasi-colonial and mainly petit-bourgeois is that the conflict of class interests is not so much within the society as between that society and the forces of outside capital." Alberta was not a classless society, but through Macpherson's eyes it approximated a one-class society. And the hegemony of commodity producers determined the limits of Social Credit's hinterland revolt. It was merely a regional revolt against eastern domination, not an attack on capital and the property system. Social Credit's petit bourgeois radicalism was inherently conservative. "Aberhart, from his first day in office, preferred to placate the established outside interests ... his economic radicalism was very limited .... nothing that he did was in conflict with a basic acceptance of the established order."[2]

Democracy in Alberta has been described as "the best political analysis in the Marxist tradition undertaken in Canada."[3] This is a rather uncritical endorsement. Macpherson is a political theorist and his discussions of the ideas and thought of Social Credit are undeniably brilliant. In other respects, notably its elucidation of the class structure of Alberta and prairie society generally, the work is flawed and seriously misleading.[4] Macpherson makes no attempt, for example, to analyse different variants of agrarian populism or to differentiate between what we have called left and right populism – the CCF in Saskatchewan, Social Credit in Alberta. He is unconvincing in his casual dismissal of Social Credit's controversial financial and debt adjustment legislation of the late 1930s. The assertion that such laws were not "in conflict with a basic acceptance of the established order" is clearly incorrect, unless we exclude Canada's banks, trust companies, insurance and financial houses, business press, and the Supreme Court and federal Liberal party from our conception of the established order. In 1938 the *Montreal Gazette* charged that Social Credit "has now run amok through a field of radical legislation that is without precedent in any country. It has legalized theft."[5] This implied at the very least that the bitter war between the province and its creditors was not merely rhetorical. That Aberhart did not intend to bring down the property system is true, but what is more interesting is that Social Credit's efforts to free the province's producers from the grip of external finance capital were close enough to the mark to provoke an unprecedented response by an overwhelming alliance of capital and federal political power.

The central flaw in Macpherson's study of Alberta society and politics – and it is an unusual failing in an avowedly Marxist work – is its consistent tendency toward single-class analysis. Alberta has never been as homogeneous or free of internal class conflict as is argued by Macpherson; nor has Manitoba or Saskatchewan. In Alberta tensions among rival metropolitan centres, between urban and agrarian interests, between ranchers and farmers, mine-owners and coalminers, between indigenous and external capital, and between capital and labour are recurring, not occasional, themes in the various stages of the province's development; and they can be ignored only at the risk of distortion. It is one thing to assert that Social Credit's base was mainly (though by no means exclusively) on the farms; that the independent commodity producer was numerically and politically dominant on the prairies between the wars; and that agriculture accounted for a majority of the West's income prior to Leduc, thus exposing the region to the vicissitudes and instabilities which overtook the wheat economy after 1928. It is quite another to argue that this society had been relatively homogeneous since its settlement, and that any serious opposition of class interests was absent in the prairie West between the wars. In the first place, by no means all of the farming population of Alberta or the other prairie provinces was engaged in the production of a single commodity, wheat; the farm economy also comprised ranching and mixed farming and was considerably less monolithic than Macpherson suggests. Second, the class structure of Alberta and the other prairie provinces also included urban labour, a professional middle class, small independent businessmen in the cities and towns, and the remnants of the bourgeoisies of Winnipeg and Calgary. Neither regional capital nor urbanized labour, each of which has played significant roles in the evolution of the Canadian West, feature at all in Macpherson's study. Thus he passes over in silence such developments as the radicalization of western labour during and after World War I, the considerable influence of the Communist party on the prairies, especially among East European and Ukrainian immigrants, the movement for a One Big Union, the Winnipeg General Strike, and the bitter and prolonged strikes in the coal mines of Drumheller, Estevan and the Crow's Nest Pass in the early 1930s – none of which is evidence of an insignificant working class or an absence of class divisions within prairie society.

Macpherson's emphasis on Alberta's dependence on metropolitan central Canadian capital is not misplaced for the early period of Social Credit. But his account ignores the presence of a significant Alberta-based bourgeoisie in an earlier stage (1885 to 1925) of the province's economic development, and he thus exaggerates the influence of metropolitan factors. Alberta's economic base, like Manitoba's, has always been a good deal more diversified than that of Saskatchewan. To wheatlands, Alberta added large-scale ranching, stock-raising and meat-packing, vast coal deposits, conventional oil and gas, tar sands, mixed farming, and a substantial business and financial community. Compared with Saskatchewan, Alberta has been considerably more urban since its settlement, and rivalries and conflicts among its urban business and political elites (notably the historic rivalry between Cal-

151

gary and Edmonton) have shaped its growth. Alberta has had "more business and industry and hence a larger and stronger business oriented bourgeoisie"[6] than its neighbour, and while this class was originally an offshoot of eastern and British capital, it developed strong roots, particularly in the prairie Southwest.

Sixty years before the oil boom of the 1950s, Calgary was an important regional centre of entrepreneurial and financial activity, thanks in large part to the establishment of the big ranching companies in southern Alberta following the critical decision of the Canadian Pacific in the early 1880s to take a southerly route across the prairies and through the Rockies. Induced by federal land grants and access to the railroad, and capitalized by British and central Canadian finance, the ranching interests of the South were the founding members of a vigorous Alberta business elite – complete with exclusive men's clubs, polo grounds, and private boys' schools. An alliance of ranchers and urban businessmen and professionals, notable among whom were Senator James A. Lougheed and his law partner, R.B. Bennett, owned and developed Calgary's waterworks, light, telephone and street-car utilities; raised the capital to develop the natural gas utilities of the cities of Medicine Hat, Calgary, and Edmonton; opened up the coal mines of Lethbridge and the foothills; and organized the syndicate which discovered oil in the Turner Valley in 1914, triggering Calgary's first bout of oil delirium. Nurtured in a context of metropolitanism by eastern and English capital and Tory patronage, by the turn of the century the ranching-landowning-urban business bourgeoisie of Alberta was a significant, albeit regional fraction of Canada's capitalist class.[7]

By contrast Saskatchewan, although it ranked as the third most populous province in Canada in the four censuses from 1911 to 1941, ahead of Alberta, offered fewer opportunities for regional capital accumulation. Lacking a diversified economic base, it actually corresponded better than did Alberta to the stereotype of a one-class society of independent commodity producers, although even in Saskatchewan there was sufficient diversity of interest between farmers and the local business community, composed largely of merchants, to create serious internal class tensions. (In Chapter Twelve we shall return to the subject of Saskatchewan's class structure, and in particular to the loss of homogeneity among farmers due to capitalization and technical change in agriculture since the depression.)

In his economic and class analysis Marx concentrated upon England, the society in which industrialization and capitalist class relations were the most fully developed by the mid-nineteenth century. But after the Chartist revolts of the 1840s English society failed to fulfil Marx's revolutionary political predictions, and he turned his political analysis increasingly to continental Europe where revolutions did occur. In an analogous fashion Macpherson's class analysis better fits Saskatchewan, but perhaps because that province has generated more internal class-based struggle than its neighbours, he uses Alberta to illustrate his thesis that a society of petit bourgeois farmers can produce only a critique of the terms of trade between themselves and the rest of society, not a full-blown critique of capitalist property relations. By ignoring the complexity of class relations within the prairie hinterland and assuming its social homogeneity, Macpherson overlooks substantial differences between Social Credit and the CCF – the same error committed by many contemporary Marxists eager to prove the CCF was merely a manifestation of petit bourgeois social democracy.

The Age of Prairie Elegance – Its Rise and Fall

Edgar Peter Lougheed was born in Calgary on July 26, 1928, the son of the late Edgar Donald and Edna Alexandria (Bauld) Lougheed, and the grandson of Senator Sir James A. Lougheed, one of Alberta's pioneering capitalists and among its most powerful political spokesmen in the formative years of the modern prairie West. The early successes, rapid decline, and subsequent rehabilitation of the Lougheed family across three generations and nearly a century of Alberta history cannot be chronicled here in any detail, but some background is essential to an understanding of the motivations and behaviour of the dominant political figure of the contemporary West.[8]

Like so many of the ruling members of his generation, James A. Lougheed was a lawyer by profession who shrewdly combined Conservative politics with railways and a sharp eye for real estate values. His life was devoted to the accumulation of property and capital and to the arts of political manipulation, and his place in the nation's history texts was therefore assured. He traded in land, patronage, and votes, and rose accordingly among the eminent to the highest reaches of Canadian politics and business. Born in Brampton, Ontario, the son of an Irish carpenter, he studied law in Toronto, then moved west, arriving in Fort Calgary on retainer to the CPR in 1883, shortly before the arrival of the railroad itself. ·

The Calgary townsite was then located on the east bank of the Elbow River near its confluence with the Bow, and most of its community of speculators, keenly anticipating the coming of the railroad, were trading in east bank properties. But Lougheed bought up large blocks of property on the west side of the Elbow, and when the CPR subsequently announced its decision to bypass the existing townsite and to build its station on the west bank, thereby outraging the businessmen and speculators of east Calgary, the young solicitor was in the enviable position of owning much of what is today downtown Calgary. He purchased more property, built a number of office blocks, and in one year reportedly paid half the city's tax bill. In 1884 he married Belle Hardisty, niece of Senator Richard Hardisty, whom he succeeded in the Senate in 1889 at the unlikely age of thirty-five. Later he built an imposing mansion on fashionable Mount Royal hill to entertain royalty, importing marble cutters from Italy to build the fireplaces to heat this ostentatious symbol of the new prairie wealth.

Lougheed also recruited from the Maritimes as a junior partner in his law firm the future prime minister, R.B. Bennett. Thus began a highly profitable alliance of political influence and property. The most prestigious law firm in Alberta, Lougheed and Bennett represented the CPR, the Bank of Montreal, the Hudson's Bay Company, and other leading corporate interests. They invested heavily in land and mineral developments, were part owners of both the *Calgary Herald* and *Albertan*, and founded companies such as Calgary Power, Canada Cement, and the drilling company which opened up the Turner Valley in 1914 (it was later acquired by Imperial Oil). Lougheed was also a director of the Canada Life Assurance Company, Canadian General Electric, and Canada Security Assurance, and reportedly left an estate worth some $12 million on his death in 1925. The Senator was also a powerful figure in the national Conservative party, although unlike his junior partner, Bennett, he died without attaining his life-long ambition, the Prime Minister's office. He was passed over for Arthur Meighen, it is said, because his wife's half-native ancestry was too exotic for the Tory hierarchy. He did however assume the Conservative leadership in the Senate, that august institution of the propertied which he once described as a necessary "bulwark against the clamour and caprice of the mob," and held ministerial posts in the Borden and Meighen governments. His Senatorial orations were notable for their passionate attacks on democracy and their equally fervent promotion of Alberta's mineral wealth.

The age of prairie elegance did not long outlive Sir James Lougheed. Like many other members of the old mansion set of Winnipeg, Edmonton, and Calgary, the Lougheed family did not fare well during the depression. Indeed, it very nearly wiped them out. The Lougheed estate, like the prairie economy itself, was overextended and exposed. The depression severely trimmed the values of the family properties, and the city of Calgary increased its levy on the Lougheed holdings. Following the death of the Senator's widow, the Royal Trust Company, which held the mortgages on the Lougheed properties, ordered the family mansion auctioned off (it is today the headquarters of the Red Cross in Calgary). The executor of the Senator's estate was Edgar Lougheed, one of four sons and the father of Peter. Edgar reportedly had many of the typical problems of the offspring of the privileged and powerful. An alcoholic who shared the Senator's taste for fine living but lacked his gifts of accumulation, he presided over the steady dissipation of the family fortune during the depression. "I wouldn't call him a weak man, but he sure as hell wasn't a strong one, and you soon learn that one of Peter's main drives is to restore the family name," a family friend says.[9] Peter's mother also suffered a nervous breakdown during the depression and spent some time in an asylum. These traumatic events all occurred before Peter Lougheed was a teenager, and their combined impact cannot have been a happy one. Without delving into the relationships between childhood experience and later political behaviour, we can speculate that at least some of Lougheed's better known traits – his driving ambition, his competitiveness, and his well known sensitivity to criticism – may be symptomatic of an insecurity and fear of failure and weakness which stem from his boyhood experience. Is it too fanciful to speculate that his family's sudden decline during the depression explains something of his near obsession with prairie economic diversification?

The decline of Alberta's original business class awaits its historian. The ranching-Conservative elite of southern Alberta was overwhelmed by the rapid influx of immigrants and settlement of the North by Clifford Sifton's "men in sheepskin coats." Edmonton was chosen over Calgary as the seat of political power, and after 1905 the Liberals dominated the provincial legislature. The Tories ceased to be a significant force in provincial Alberta politics until the 1960s. Alberta capitalists handed over the control of Turner Valley and the important gas utilities of Calgary and Edmonton to American interests during the 1920s, and the depression wiped out or severely trimmed many of the great prairie fortunes. Incomes declined less in Alberta than in Saskatchewan, thanks to the somewhat more diversified economy of the former, but the impact of the great collapse was traumatic across the West. The main lesson drawn from that experience, it cannot be too strongly emphasized, was the danger of economic specialization and the need to diversify away from an agriculture-dependent economy as swiftly as possible – even if such a transition implied a very great reliance on foreign capital. Indeed, given the indifference of eastern Canadian capital and the relatively undercapitalized state of Alberta business after World War Two, rapid development of new export staples would have been impossible without heavy foreign investment.

Instead of producing a resurgence of entrepreneurial activity (as it appears to have done in the 1970s) the push toward economic diversification in the late 1940s after Leduc encouraged the growth of a rentier mentality and an accommodation with American resource capital. The new export staple happened to be oil, and the fact that the oil industry was highly capital-intensive and traditionally dominated by a few integrated international firms further helped discourage domestic entrepreneurship in Alberta. We have seen how Imperial Oil early obtained a dominant foothold in the province's major producing field, Turner Valley, and how it consolidated its dominance over the province's oil industry in spite of an often bitter resistance from the independents. This set the pattern for the remarkable domination of the Alberta oil and gas economy by foreign capital after Leduc. "Development over the subsequent decades was dependent on a steady and plentiful supply of risk capital and while the persistent formation of Calgary-based exploration companies bears witness to the continued generation of capital in the Calgary area, it was never sufficient. This, with the general aloofness of eastern Canadian investors towards western Canadian oil ventures, accelerated the process of foreign acquisition of capital-starved enterprises."[10]

The striking failure of the post-Leduc resource boom to replicate the historical conditions of turn-of-the-century Texas and to nurture a powerful class of Alberta entrepreneurs united with populist farmers in hostility to a takeover by external corporate and political interests is one of the great puzzles of modern prairie development. It is easier to document the effects than to explain the failure itself. The absence of a vigorous entrepreneurial-populist reaction within the province permitted Social Credit to pursue its entente with American capital without fear of the political consequences – with economic effects which are discussed elsewhere in this book. No single factor adequately explains the phenomenon of the absent entrepreneur and the different responses of Texans and Albertans to the arrival of oil. Government policies certainly played their part, but this does not explain why the policies themselves met with such broad measure of popular support or acquiescence. The historian James H. Gray recalls in his autobiographical *Troublemaker!* how as the editor of the *Farm and Ranch Review* he had campaigned, indeed crusaded, on behalf of Alberta farmers in the late 1940s to have the province turn back its crown-owned mineral rights to the farmers. "The natural resources beneath the farmlands of Alberta had to be restored to the farmers on the land, to put them on a par with the farmers in Manitoba and in most of Saskatchewan who had received mineral rights with the title to their farms. Then it would be the farmers who got rich and, like the American farmers, they would plough their riches back into the development of the country." The central question facing Albertans, according to the Calgarians backing the *Farm and Ranch Review*, was whether they wanted a province of poor people with a rich government, or a province of rich people with a poor government. "A government that had to come to the people every year for every dollar it spent would be responsive to the wishes of the people. A government that, through oil income, could get along without taxing authority would be unresponsive to the people and might ultimately become completely dictatorial." But such noble populist sentiments notwithstanding, the *Farm and Ranch Review*'s crusade over mineral rights not only failed to change provincial policy, it met with little support from the farmers themselves. Whereas Texan farmers and ranchers had driven wildcatters from their land at the point of a gun, and then forced the state legislature to turn mineral rights over to the surface owners,

> Albertans, however, were more Caspar Milquetoast than Texan when it came to asserting their rights. Instead of fighting for the oil under their land, they were content to accept the law as it stood and haggle with the oil companies for an increase in the pittances they were offered for the use of ten-acre well sites, and later for the running of gathering lines and pipelines across their land. ... In some areas, the farmers barricaded access to their land until compensation claims were settled. The government then sided with the oil companies and passed the Right-of-Entry Act, which made it a criminal offence for farmers to bar their land to drilling rigs or seismic crews. The farmers accepted that order without even a whimper.[11]

Federal and provincial economic policies in the years immediately following the Leduc discovery tended to promote the external takeover of Alberta's oil and gas, and, with but a few exceptions, precluded the rapid expansion of the numerous Calgary-based independents formed in the 1940s and early 1950s. Under the guidance of C.D. Howe, successive postwar Liberal administrations in Ottawa pursued a strategy of rapid economic expansion and an open door to foreign investment. Resource industries such as oil and gas, developed for continental markets with large infusions of U.S. capital, would spearhead this expansion, while offsetting the balance-of-payments effects of Canada's manufacturing imports. In spite of his later support for an all-Canadian route for the Trans-Canada natural gas pipeline, Howe remained unsympathetic to, and unmoved by, the arguments of Canadian nationalists that his policies were fraught with dangerous long-term implications for Canada's political sovereignty and economic structure. Unapologetically centralist in design, his grand strategy for post-war development left little room for provincial economic autonomy, and, accordingly, he moved swiftly to pressure the Manning government to permit removals of natural gas on grounds of continental military strategy when protectionist sentiments began to build in Alberta in the early 1950s. Howe and his federal Liberal colleagues evidently viewed Alberta's new energy resources as potentially critical assets in, first, North America's international struggles with the Communist bloc, and, second, the industrial growth of the central Canadian heartland. Howe's impatience with Alberta protectionists and Canadian nationalists alike derived from his fear that parochialism would impede the country's rapid economic advance by discouraging the inward flow of foreign capital. When the owners of the small Alberta independents pleaded for changes in federal tax legislation to place them in a stronger position vis à vis the major American oil companies (after 1950 U.S. oil companies were permitted to write off substantial portions of their foreign exploration expenses against their American income tax), Ottawa's response was one of indifference. "I don't give a damn who owns this country, as you put it," James Gray recalls being told by the federal assistant deputy minister in the Department of Finance, "as long as we have the power to tax, because whoever has the power to tax calls the tune."[12]

Provincial development policies similarly had the effect, as we argued in Chapter Four, of strengthening the market power of the integrated firms and discouraging the entry into the industry of companies capitalized locally. The risk-averse allocation structure adopted by the Manning government on the basis of American experience guaranteed an immediate cash flow to the provincial treasury from the auction of crown lands, but it also favoured large companies with good financial reserves over small independents with limited access to capital. Alternative allocation structures would have required the provincial government to share, in varying degrees, in the uncertainty of development. Their rejection constituted implicitly a decision in favour of rentier development.

In such a political environment, with both the federal and provincial governments favouring foreign over local capital, yet another Texan precedent was precluded in Alberta. In Texas the economics and politics of oil have typically been dominated by the independents. At the end of the nineteenth century the populist movement in Texas successfully fought off domination of the state's infant oil industry by Rockefeller's Standard Oil trust, thereby creating the necessary conditions for expansion of the independents. By contrast, Alberta's independents were too small and lacking in capital to do much more than enter into unequal arrangements with the integrated companies and thereby ensure themselves a stable share of the province's crude oil markets. In conditions of surplus and soft markets, however, the independent producers typically do badly, and such were the conditions prevailing in Alberta's oil industry throughout much of the 1950s and the 1960s. At times the industry was operating at 30 per cent capacity. The province's system of prorationing oil to market demand attempted to strike a compromise between the interests of the integrated majors and the independents, sacrificing efficiency in order to guarantee the latter group a share of production, but the prolonged conditions of surplus capacity inevitably took their toll. The independents fought a lengthy political battle in the late 1950s to expand the domestic oil market by pushing the Interprovincial Pipeline into the Montreal area – supplied by the international companies from offshore sources – but they failed, and in the early 1960s a number of the larger independent producers passed into foreign ownership.

The presence or absence of entrepreneurship — the perception and rational pursuit of new market opportunities under conditions of uncertainty and risk — within a region can be an important factor in determining the degree of economic development and diversification obtained from any new export staple such as petroleum. Its absence may mean economic rents are foregone and investment is precluded in closely linked industries. This can lead to an over-concentration of resources in the export sector, thereby giving rise to a "staple trap."[13] An adequate supply of domestic entrepreneurship, whether private or governmental, is therefore crucial if the export staple is to be used to generate strong linkage effects and thus enable the economy to grow and diversify. Where the entrepreneurial function is left in the hands of foreigners and a passive rentier mentality exists among the dominant domestic groups, then the growth of a new staple is unlikely to generate a pattern of diversified development. In that event, the fate of the economy will depend in large part on the fortunes of its export markets, and any available domestic entrepreneurship is likely to be channeled into the conservative task of protecting these markets instead of creating new opportunities and "carrying out new combinations" – the true role of the entrepreneur in the classical literature on capitalist economic development.

The Impact of Oil
Enough has been said in this and previous chapters to demonstrate that local entrepreneurial decision-making, public as well as private, was largely absent during the development of Alberta's oil industry after 1947. But how much economic diversification actually did occur?

Did the rapid exploitation of the province's major oil and gas fields provide the stimulus for sustained economic development?

The answers to these questions are complex. At best we can arrive at a qualified negative. In the initial stages of petroleum development linkages were generated, but the pattern of diversification was not sufficient to enable the economy of Alberta to transcend its dependence on export staple industries – oil and gas essentially became a second export staple in addition to agriculture. Oil did not provide the spur to industrialization. (See Chapter Twelve for a discussion of staple-led economic development, and the concept of linkages.)

Under the heavy investment of the oil and gas industry in the years of rapid growth after Leduc, Alberta's economic base shifted dramatically from its prewar dependence on agriculture to a new reliance on the industrial staples of petroleum and natural gas. Between 1935 and 1971, agriculture's share of the total value added in goods-producing industries in the province declined from 54 to 14 per cent, while mining (essentially oil and gas extraction) increased its share from 11 to 39 per cent, manufacturing from 16 to 20 per cent, and construction from 14 to 23 per cent.[14] Professor Stabler has summarized the extent to which early oil and gas development did generate linkage effects:

> Once the importance of the oil fields had been ascertained, the building of storage facilities, pipelines, and refineries created a significant increase in demand for construction services and materials. A second round of induced investment came with the creation of petro-chemical and natural gas processing facilities. The increased activity directly stimulated the trade and transportation sectors as well as the construction industry. The local production of some manufactured inputs was begun or expanded, and legal, technical, managerial, maintenance, and other service activities directly serving the petroleum industry came into existence. The royalties collected by the province made it possible to expand government services and employment. The new jobs thus created further stimulated the population oriented trade and service activities as well as some manufacturing sectors. The end result of this expansion was the creation of jobs at a faster rate than they could be filled by the natural increase in the province's labour force even taking into account the release of surplus workers from agriculture. Labour, and population, was therefore attracted from outside the province.[15]

Shaffer, however, has argued persuasively that the early patterns of induced investment in backward- and forward-linked industries were insufficient to enable Alberta to make a transition from an oil-dependent economy.[16] (Backward linkages refer to additional income generated in industries that expand to provide inputs to the oil industry; forward linkages refer to additional income in industries that, using oil as an input, transform it further.) Backward-linked industries providing professional services slowly expanded, and the petroleum industry itself increased the number of its specialized employees trained within Alberta. But the backward linkages within Alberta for manufactured inputs (e.g. drilling equipment) were not substantial because the capital-intensive oil industry imported a very large percentage of its heavy equipment, engineering, and design technology. Nor, except for a brief spate of petrochemical development in the 1950s, the gradual transfer of prairie refining capacity to Alberta, and local pipeline construction, was there significant investment in forward-linked industries. Much of the early opposition to removals of gas from the province, we may recall, had its rationale in the fear that exports would have a negative impact on Alberta's chances for industrialization. But the real barriers to petroleum-linked industrial development appear to have been the traditional regional disadvantages of the prairies: the West's geographical isolation and distance from markets, high transportation costs, and the absence of developed infrastructure. The problem lay in "being small and isolated rather than with discriminatory treatment."[17]

Oil did not initiate the process of prairie industrialization many Albertans anticipated after Leduc, and in retrospect such anticipations were decidedly unrealistic. Consequently, as late as 1970, Alberta's manufacturing industries (by far the most important of which is the food and beverage group) employed merely 11 per cent of the province's non-agricultural labour force.[18] The political upshot was Social Credit's vulnerability to Conservative attacks that the province was too dependent on agriculture and oil and gas extraction, and that a "third phase" of development was necessary.

The greatest impact of oil occurred via final demand linkages. Oil called into being a large service economy, public as well as private, through the direct expenditures of income earned by those employed in the petroleum industry, and through the government's discretionary spending of resource rents – which have accounted for 40 to 50 per cent of Alberta government revenue since the late 1940s, a higher percentage than for any other province. Oil, according to Shaffer's estimates, accounted for over half of the new jobs created in Alberta during the 1960s. Of his estimated 87,000 oil-related new positions, more than half were in non-commercial services (e.g. teachers and hospital employees), commercial services (e.g. lawyers and hairdressers), wholesale and retail trade. Growth of a new urban and professional labour force, much of it in the public and para-public sectors, enlarged the ranks of a new middle class, but it also diminished the relative importance of Social Credit's rural base.

The demographic impact of the new mineral staples has been particularly striking. Rapid urbanization is not, of course, unique to Alberta, but in no other Canadian province has the domination of the city over the countryside been accomplished so abruptly. Dramatic population growth commenced in the late 1940s and continued through the 1950s, much of it caused by the in-migration of workers and their families from provinces such as Saskatchewan, Manitoba, and Ontario. Alberta's annual population growth rate exceeded the national average consistently until 1965, levelled off until the early 1970s, and then resurged under the impact of the energy crisis. Between 1946 and 1971 Alberta doubled its population, from roughly 800,000 to 1.6 million, and an overwhelming proportion of the growth was concentrated in the two major urban centres of Calgary and Edmonton, and to a lesser extent in Lethbridge, Medicine Hat, and Red Deer. The postwar growth rates of Alberta's two large cities have considerably outdistanced those of Canada's other principal metropolitan regions: between 1951 and 1971 Calgary and Edmonton increased their populations by 158 and 135 per cent respectively. Between 1911 and 1941 Alberta's rural-urban population distribution changed little (urban population grew from 29 to 32 per cent of the province's total) but in the next three decades, from 1941 to 1971, the demographic balance tilted decisively in favour of the cities (the urban percentage of the population escalated from 32 to 73 per cent). In 1941 approximately half of Alberta's population still lived on census farms and less than a quarter in Calgary and Edmonton; three decades later when Peter Lougheed's Conservatives swept to power, less than 20 per cent of the population was still on the farms while better than half of Alberta's citizens were concentrated in the big urban centres.[19]

The Rebirth of the Alberta Tories

The Lougheed family recovered some lost ground during the postwar oil boom – Edgar reportedly left some $3 million on his death in 1951. Peter, encouraged by his ambitious and highly competitive mother ("She was the one who gave me goals and objectives"), studied law at the University of Alberta, briefly ran back punts for the Edmonton Eskimos, and then went on to the Harvard Business School to study business administration. He spent a summer in the early 1950s working with the petroleum industry in Tulsa, Oklahoma, then in steep decline as an oil-producing state. Today he uses Tulsa as the model of what Alberta must avoid: "If you want to see what happens when the oil industry moves on, go to Tulsa. It's a dead city."[20] He returned to

Alberta and did a brief stint of legal practice; then in 1956 he joined the family-owned Mannix group, the large Calgary-based construction and engineering conglomerate that is today known as Loram (an acronym for "Long Range Mannix") Company Limited. Lougheed was a great success at Mannix, moving up the corporate escalator from Secretary to General Counsel, Vice-President and Director in five short years.

The Mannix connection is an intriguing one, and not merely because of Lougheed's close personal relationship with the family patriarch, Frederick C. Mannix, the second-generation head of the group.[21] The Mannixes, like the Lougheeds, are an Alberta dynasty — rich, politically influential, and dedicated to the concept of a strong conservative West. The group was founded by Frederick S. Mannix in the early years of this century. Mannix specialized in heavy earth moving and the construction of hydroelectric dams for Calgary Power, the province's big privately owned electrical utility. Recognizing that the utility would need to move into thermal power generation, Mannix bought up coal properties, then sold the strip mines to Calgary Power but retained the contracts to operate them. Mannix has since built most of Calgary Power's hydro dams and operates its strip mines. During the 1940s majority control of Mannix passed into the hands of Morrison-Knudsen Company of Boise, Idaho, one of the major U.S. construction groups, and it was through this connection that Mannix was able to break into the large postwar Canadian projects engineered and constructed by American companies: the St. Lawrence Seaway, Interprovincial Pipe Line, the Trans Mountain Pipe Line, and the Mid-Canada radar line.

In 1951, through a complicated financial arrangement, F.C. Mannix bought back control of the company and began to diversify. Mannix won Social Credit's approval to build and operate one of Alberta's largest oil-gathering systems, Pembina Pipe Lines, over the opposition of the major oil companies who controlled the big Pembina field. One of the few instances of entrepreneurial instincts displayed by the Manning administration, this proved to be of lasting benefit to the Mannixes. Today, in addition to its construction, engineering, and pipeline interests, the Loram-Mannix group of operating companies control a major coal producer, Manalta Coal, an oil and gas producer, Western Decalta, and land and ranching holdings. Loram is among the most important and influential Alberta-owned companies in western Canada.

Described as "rich, private, dynastic and inaccessible," the Mannix family is staunchly right-wing and fiercely dedicated to western regionalism. Fred C. Mannix, a close friend of both Ernest Manning and Peter Lougheed, has been called a "rabid Albertan" by the former, and the family foundation has been a major backer of the Canada West Foundation – an organization founded by a group of prominent Albertans and British Columbians dedicated to fostering the cultural and political identity of the West. Several former Mannix executives (including the present head of the Canadian Petroleum Association, Harold Millican) were recruited by Peter Lougheed to key positions in his first government, and there is little doubt that Lougheed's own managerial and quasi-corporatist style of government, as well as his penchant for strong executive government, were forged in the Mannix boardroom. More to the point, the Mannix group is among the handful of home-grown Alberta-based corporations which can successfully compete in national and world markets. It has been a model for the new capitalist West and an obvious training ground for Alberta's rising business class.

Peter Lougheed left Mannix in 1962 for law and politics. He considered running for the federal Tories, then opted to rebuild the nearly defunct provincial party. Why the Conservatives? In part because of family traditions and, according to one friend, "Once you accept that vaguely rightist position, it doesn't matter whether you're a Conservative or a Socred, but the Socreds were dominated by all those old guys ... by going Conservative, Peter was able to call his own shots."[22] He began by organizing a Lougheed Club (annual membership was $100) among his close friends, and planning strategy at weekly meetings in the Palliser Hotel in Calgary. In March 1965, he easily won the party's leadership.

When Peter Lougheed took over as leader, Alberta's provincial Conservatives were "a party only one step from outright decrepitude."[23] The Tories had been dormant in Alberta politics for decades and an attempt earlier in the 1960s to revitalize the party had collapsed. "The Conservatives have never been considered a threat to any government of Alberta," remarked the *Edmonton Journal* a year before Lougheed assumed the leadership. On the other hand, the NDP was relatively weak and the provincial Liberals, who had been a serious challenger in the late 1950s, had disintegrated because of internal leadership struggles. Lougheed and his small coterie of Calgary advisers sensed that Ernest Manning was close to retirement and that a more fluid political situation was opening up. The Tories were respectably conservative, but they differed from Social Credit in their emphasis upon political modernization and a more diversified economic base. The Conservatives, with their slogans "the future belongs to us" and "It's time for a change," "offered the electorate continued free-enterprise conservatism, but with the added bonuses of urban middle-class respectability, a comfortably vague social conscience and a little political excitement."[24]

The years 1965-67 were devoted to an intensive reorganization of the Conservatives at the grassroots level and to the mastery of television. Lougheed learned to use television as Aberhart had used radio in an earlier era – as a weapon of opposition politics. He attacked Social Credit as a "reactionary" government, but infuriated Manning by praising him personally. And he continued to hammer home his familiar critique of Alberta's economic policy. The province required a "third stage" of development, that of industrialization:

> We have been coasting on our petroleum revenues for the last decade – we have failed to use capital revenues from the petroleum industry – over one billion dollars – as an investment in the future by way of imaginative development, research and promotional programs ... we have utilized this one billion dollars from the petroleum industry to establish a built-in level of provincial government spending – far larger than any other province on a per capita basis ... we have been out-negotiated by the Federal Government and perhaps by other provinces. ...[25]

In the 1967 election Lougheed's revived Conservatives won 27 per cent of the popular vote and six seats – five from the upper-income suburbs of Calgary and Edmonton – to become the official opposition. The next year Manning retired, having failed to stimulate interest in his proposal for a "realignment" of Canadian politics on the right (it was rumoured at the time that Manning was, in effect, making a bid for the national Tory leadership, and that Lougheed was seen as his natural heir to the provincial leadership). The Tories managed to win Manning's seat, and they added several more through defections and by-elections. Without the pious Manning at the helm, Social Credit began the rapid slide toward political oblivion that has been the fate of most North American populist movements. Its new leader, Harry Strom, proved quite incapable of adapting the party to the province's changed economic and social environment. Would another leader have managed to stem the Tory tide? Probably not. Material circumstances were ultimately more significant than personalities in reshaping Alberta's political system. The economic and social base of Social Credit had been eroded by a generation of petroleum development and urbanization. Wheat had created Social Credit. Oil tamed it, then displaced it in favour of Lougheed's Conservatives.

On August 30, 1971, six years after Peter Lougheed entered politics, the Tories won a stunning upset victory, electing 49 MLAs to the 75-member Alberta legislature. The Conservatives swept both large cities (25 of the 29 seats), most of the smaller urban areas and the disaffected north of the province, increasing their share of the popular vote from 27 to 46.5 per cent. Much of this increased support came, interestingly, from Liberal and NDP supporters – the former party had captured 11 per cent of the popular vote in 1967, but in 1971 it was reduced to barely one per cent, while the NDP dropped from 16 to 11 per cent. Social Credit's popular support declined from 45 to 41 per cent, and the party managed to hold on to 25 seats – most of them from the traditional rural "heartland" of the south and south-central regions of the province. The Tories found their support among urbanites, new voters, and those of higher income, educational and occupational status – in brief, from the new middle class.

Some believed that the 1971 election had restored competitive party politics to Alberta, but this proved far from true. Demoralized and leaderless, Social Credit rapidly began to disintegrate as an effective political force. Internal leadership rivalries, between a fundamentalist "old guard" and reformers, spilled openly into public view, so that by 1975 the Social Credit corpse was in an advanced state of decomposition. In that year Alberta returned to its tradition of one-party rule, as Lougheed turned the election into a referendum on provincial rights and resources. Booming economic conditions and the Conservatives' mobilization of regional alienation decimated the ranks of the opposition parties. Lougheed's government won sixty-nine of seventy-five seats and fully 63 per cent of the popular vote; Social Credit returned four members; the NDP leader, Grant Notley, was narrowly re-elected; and a single independent was returned. This massive Tory consolidation of power was clearly assisted by Ottawa's heavy-handed interventions in 1973 and 1974, but even without the factor of regional protest it seems probable that the result would have been broadly similar. As of the late 1970s, no serious threat to the Conservative hegemony is yet posed by any of the three Alberta opposition parties and, barring completely gross mismanagement or serious scandal, none appears likely for at least a generation.

Alberta's Arriviste Bourgeoisie
By the opening of the 1970s, then, Alberta's population was substantially urbanized and its expanding labour force was oriented to the service sector and the managerial, professional, and white-collar occupations of the new middle class. Oil had induced little investment in manufacturing and Alberta's industrial working class remained relatively small, in spite of prolonged economic expansion. The new middle class was urban and secular in its outlook and impatient with Social Credit's blend of religious fundamentalism and the remnants of

its agrarian populist past. Social Credit, the Lougheed Conservatives were fond of saying, had grown isolationist and was outside the mainstream of North American culture, something which could never be said of Peter Lougheed. While the pious Manning was still delivering his weekly radio Back to the Bible Hour sermons ("in any unregenerate society, the will of the people is bound to come into conflict with the will of God" was the somewhat ominous theme of a typical 1966 broadcast), Lougheed was thumbing the pages of Theodore White's *The Making of the President 1960* and sharpening his television image in the Kennedy mould – the young, dynamic, and safely right-of-centre heir to a family dynasty.

A precondition for a movement away from the passive rentier behaviour which characterized provincial resource politics after the war was the development of domestic entrepreneurial ambitions and skills, private and governmental. In Saskatchewan a resurgence of Fabianism within the government bureaucracy and the leadership of the NDP in the 1970s has provided the requisite entrepreneurship, but it lacks a broad popular base and has antagonized local business elites. Its future is precarious. In Alberta, by contrast, local entrepreneurial energy is being generated by the province's upwardly mobile urban middle class – in effect, a rising urban bourgeoisie comprising leading indigenous entrepreneurs, managers and upper-income professionals – linking private and public sectors in a quasi-corporatist alliance of interests. This arriviste bourgeoisie is led by the owners and managers of the few Alberta-based corporations large enough to compete on a national and international scale – notably such firms as Alberta Gas Trunk Line, the Mannix-Loram group, ATCO Industries, the Alberta Energy Company – as well as some of the more dynamic oil-related businesses which have their head offices in Calgary. In addition, it includes a large body of well educated and upwardly mobile professionals, such as corporate lawyers, economic and financial consultants, engineers, geologists, and other scientists or technical experts providing services of a specialized nature to the petroleum industry and government. A third group, a state-administrative elite, occupies the top bureaucratic posts within the public sector, particularly, though not exclusively, in government departments and boards charged with the tasks of managing the province's resources, negotiating with other governments, investing the huge revenue surpluses of the 1970s and charting future economic directions. Confident of its own administrative competence and committed to a provincial strategy of development, this state-administrative elite sees Alberta as the logical arena for the advancement of its career opportunities and, like its private sector counterparts, is fiercely loyal to the province as a semi-sovereign political entity and deeply involved in the process of "province-building." As in Saskatchewan, bureaucracy in Alberta is an active and relatively autonomous participant in entrepreneurial debates and decisions concerning resource development. A good deal of the pressure to use Alberta's remaining energy supplies as bargaining leverage for economic diversification appears to originate, for example, within the provincial bureaucracy itself – which is hardly surprising, given its own heavy dependence on rents extracted from non-replenishable resources.

It is no exaggeration to suggest that Alberta's new bourgeoisie has begun to make arrangements for its own future in preparation for the inevitable day when the international oil industry leaves the province. What motivates this alliance of private and public interests is a fear of economic stagnation and secular decline. It is driven by an ambivalent sense of dependency and vulnerability and an acute awareness of the degree to which its own prospects rise and fall with the petroleum industry and the world oil market. The provincial Conservative party has been hammering at this theme since 1965, and not without success. "Since entering public life over nine years ago," Peter Lougheed told an audience of Calgary businessmen in 1974, "my theme has been that this province's economy is too *vulnerable*, it is too dependent upon the sale of depleting resources, particularly oil and gas for its continued prosperity. ... Frankly, I despair of the short-term thinking of a few Albertans who believe we can coast on the sale of our depleting resources for our continued prosperity."[26]

Throughout most of the 1950s and 1960s the central problem of Alberta's oil industry was that of markets. In the late 1950s a number of external factors (the resolution of the Suez crisis and the reopening of the Suez Canal to tankers, a recession in the United States, and a new U.S. oil import quota system) combined to depress demand for Alberta's crude. The decline in exports led to a demand by independent domestic producers to push the domestic market into Montreal, which was supplied exclusively by foreign oil. That proposal was strongly opposed by the international oil companies, who wanted to retain the Montreal market for their unprorated offshore oil, and by the U.S. State Department, which feared the political repercussions in Venezuela of a loss of one of the latter's key markets. The upshot was the compromise known as the National Oil Policy (NOP). The U.S. agreed to exempt Canada from its import restrictions, if Canada agreed to reserve the area east of the Ottawa Valley for imports. Under the NOP the increase in Alberta production was to be absorbed by the expansion of exports to the U.S. Midwest and West Coast and by the displacement of foreign oil in Ontario west of the Ottawa

Valley. While this compromise brought some measure of stability to the Alberta oil industry, it had the effect of tying the province into a continental oil policy. Alberta's economic prospects were intimately linked to U.S. quota politics.

The event which brought home to many Albertans the precariousness of their prosperity was the discovery of a major oil field at Prudhoe Bay on Alaska's North Slope in January 1968. Prudhoe Bay vividly emphasized the vulnerability of Alberta's oil-dependent economy to exogenous developments and, in particular, to the prospect that the Alaskan find might in the long run permit the United States to regain its self-sufficiency in oil and displace imports from western Canada. This fear caused Social Credit to delay approval of the Syncrude oil sands venture for another three years (because of marketing difficulties and pressure from conventional producers, Social Credit restricted oil sands development to one small-scale prototype plant, Sun Oil's Great Canadian Oil Sands). A more immediate concern was that Prudhoe Bay encouraged the major integrated companies to shift their exploratory activities out of Alberta to the northern Canadian frontier in search of new "elephant" pools. This movement out of the province, which had ominous implications for government revenues as well as for many small oil-service companies, was apparently based on a collective decision by the majors that the limits of Alberta's oil-producing potential had been reached and that new exploratory work would bring diminishing returns. While drilling activity in Alberta in the late 1960s was stable, the number of exploratory wells drilled by the majors fell off sharply between 1968 and 1970, while the smaller operators accounted for 75 to 80 per cent of new exploratory work in the province. New field wildcat wells drilled in Alberta fell from 421 in 1969 to 256 in 1971. Alberta's share of total Canadian net cash exploratory expenditures declined from a 1966 peak of 74 per cent to 54 per cent in 1970, and this had a predictable impact on provincial government revenues. Industry expenditures for crown reserves in Alberta dropped off abruptly. Revenues were becoming dependent to an ominous degree on royalties on production from declining reserves.[27]

The northward shift of the majors' exploration activities and the vulnerability of Alberta export markets in the U.S. after Prudhoe Bay were exploited by the Lougheed Conservative opposition in the late 1960s. Peter Lougheed attacked Social Credit for its "overdependence on the oil industry" and pressed for a "much higher priority to the field of industrial development. It's been kind of a lost cousin here in Alberta."[28] In his reply to the budget speech in 1969, Lougheed emphasized the weakness of the government's revenue position. "The dependence by Social Credit upon the continued prosperity of the oil industry has been evident for all to see for some time. In fact, they have established a framework of programmes and services as the largest spending province per capita in Canada – and it is dependent upon the ever-upward growth of petroleum revenue." With the oversupply then prevailing in North American oil markets, Lougheed, like Social Credit, at this point equated the maximization of production with optimal policy. But, unlike Social Credit, he intended the provincial government to "take the initiative":

> What role should the Alberta Government play in helping to develop new growth markets for Alberta oil? A fundamental question for the people and for this House. Social Credit policy seems to be ... to leave it to the Federal authority, be content to rely upon them to handle the negotiations and keep us informed. We disagree. We do not suggest at any time that any approach be taken directly by the Alberta Government with the United States Government ... without prior concurrence or co-operation and in joint conjunction with the Federal authorities. But we do suggest that the Alberta Government is definitely in the oil marketing business. That it must take the initiative.[29]

Lougheed was in effect giving notice that any Conservative government would consider itself an entrepreneurial actor in provincial economic development.

The Spirit of Capitalism
Change at the political level was a necessary but not sufficient prerequisite for the emergence in Alberta of provincial entrepreneurship. The development of bureaucratic competence and expertise and the growth of province-building elites in the public sector (e.g. at the Energy Resources Conservation Board) complemented the transition from Social Credit to the Conservatives, giving the latter an administrative advantage in bargaining over such issues as new royalty terms, the pricing of resources, the creation of an Alberta-based petrochemical industry, or development of the Athabasca tar sands. Of at least equal significance, however, was the growth among Alberta's business classes of what, borrowing from Max Weber, we might call "the spirit of capitalism."

So long as Social Credit's rentier approach to resource development governed relations between the province and the large international oil companies, Alberta businessmen had to be content with a highly limited and dependent, if relatively prosperous, role in life: either working for one of the branch plants of the foreign-controlled companies, or running one of the many small independent producers or ser-

vice companies which grew up in Calgary in the years after Leduc. As
we have seen, Social Credit's development philosophy grew out of
Manning's belief in the overriding necessity for an entente with
American capital. Without such an entente, accompanied by highly
favourable terms of development, Manning was convinced that
Alberta would lack the capital, expertise, technology, and markets to
exploit its energy resource potential: the province was bargaining
from a position of weakness, and its terms must therefore be attractive.
Recall that the accommodation negotiated between Social Credit and
the major oil companies after Leduc was designed to provide the latter
with a minimum of uncertainty over tenure, royalty charges, and property rights, and the assurance of long-term political stability. In return for their large capital investments in exploration and development after 1947, and sufficient royalties to enable the province to retire
its debt and to expand government services without increasing personal taxes, Manning's "businesslike" administration abjured intervention without consultation, and followed a policy based upon the
premise that the interests of the petroleum industry and the interests
of Alberta were roughly the same. By tacit, if not explicit, agreement
any entrepreneurial role by the province in the resource economy (e.g.
through the creation of crown exploration companies or a more innovative policy toward crown reserves) would have violated the spirit
of this broad entente.

In such a limited scheme of things, with both the province and an
indifferent federal government encouraging external capital to take
the leading role in development, Alberta business had to be satisfied to
eke out an existence on the fringes of the industry. Local capitalists
were far too small to compete with the integrated majors, and most
settled for a frustrated marginal role, often within the large oil-service
economy that developed in Calgary in the 1950s and 1960s. For the
most part they did not even play an important "comprador" function,
facilitating the takeover of Alberta's resources by foreign capital: that
function was largely performed by the traditional institutions of central Canadian finance capital and their branch plants in Calgary.
With a handful of notable exceptions, Alberta capitalists played a very
limited and subordinate role in the post-Leduc development of the
western Canadian sedimentary basin. In marked contrast to what had
occurred in Texas half a century earlier, the arrival of the majors did
not provoke a fierce defensive response by Alberta capital (although,
as we have seen, there was considerable friction in the Turner Valley
between Imperial Oil and the independents in the 1930s). Overwhelmed by the international petroleum industry and stifled by Social
Credit's preferential policies toward external capital, for twenty-five

171

years after Leduc indigenous Alberta capital settled for a marginal, dependent status in the shadows of Calgary's Americanized business environment. Calgary's gleaming new skyscrapers for the most part housed the branch offices of companies headquartered in New York, Houston, San Francisco, and Toronto. And since most of the economic surplus generated from the exploitation of Alberta's oil and gas was captured either by the provincial treasury or by multinational oil corporations, local capital had little prospect of growth. A less likely location for the emergence of a new regional bourgeoisie could scarcely be imagined.

A break with marginality and dependence has, however, occurred in the 1970s. While foreign capital continues to be preponderant within the provincial economy – indeed, measured on a percentage basis Alberta still leads the provinces in terms of foreign control of its industries – among Alberta's indigenous business elite there has been a definite awakening of expectations and ambitions in the past decade. A new consciousness, largely defined in regional imperatives, has emerged, a growing restlessness with the West's hinterland capitalist status and an awareness of the possibilities for accumulation. To an important extent, as we shall see in Chapter Nine, this is being deliberately nurtured by the development strategy of the Lougheed government, but the origins of the strategy lie in the aspirations and anxieties of an arriviste bourgeoisie. The break with dependence has occurred because of the fear of economic stagnation and secular decline and because of the threat of encroachments by eastern Canadian interests, but it has been reinforced by the sudden stimulus of the world oil crisis and by the relative "overdevelopment" of the Albertan economy since 1973 – an overdevelopment in sharp contrast to the conditions of recession and stagnation that have plagued the rest of Canada throughout the late 1970s. Once merely a hinterland service centre, Calgary is fast replacing Montreal as Canada's second largest financial centre (behind Toronto) and now ranks only behind Houston and London as a world capital for oil finance. It is the location of several hundred head offices, including those of postwar parvenus such as Alberta Gas Trunk Line, Ron Southern's ATCO Industries conglomerate, the Mannix-Loram group, Dome Petroleum (now under Canadian control) and many others. Much money is first or second generation wealth and the province still lacks large financial institutions which could compete with Bay or Wall Street, but it does have, as *Canadian Business* puts it, "the social energy and innovation that seem to have moved out of eastern Canada. Calgary's businessmen and their friends in the Alberta government are absolutely determined to make permanent capital out of the oil boom."[30]

172

The Shift of Power to Alberta

Powered by the shift in bargaining advantage from energy consumers to producers, Alberta's nascent bourgeoisie is in revolt against the uneven historical patterns of accumulation characteristic of Canadian capitalism. With interests in oil and gas, real estate, construction, petrochemicals, ranching and agribusiness, and the fast-growing sports and tourism industries, Calgary's business elite aims at nothing less than a transfer of wealth, industries, and decision-making from central Canada to the western periphery – "a fundamental change in the economy of Canada," as Premier Lougheed puts it. And to an important extent, this is already occurring. Measured by almost any standard of regional income distribution, the traditional hegemony of the central Canadian heartland has been slipping for well over a decade. Alberta's ability to exact a major regional transfer of income from the heavily populated oil-importing provinces can be seen in the huge surpluses accumulating in its Heritage Fund (discussed in Chapter Nine). Western business interests, headed by Calgary-based Alberta Gas Trunk Line, in 1977 defeated the powerful Arctic Gas consortium, composed of eastern-based firms, Canadian and foreign owned, for the right to transport Arctic gas south. It was an important step in the growth of western Canadian regional power in the natural gas industry. Allied with international chemical giants such as Dow, Trunk Line and Dome have played a major role in putting together Alberta's new petrochemical complex. Corporate empire-building is de rigueur among Alberta businessmen.

There are interesting parallels here with the politics of sectionalism in other advanced capitalist societies. Tom Nairn, for example, has written of a tendential relative "over-development" which lies behind the neo-nationalist movement in Scotland. "Obviously linked to the discovery and exploitation of North Sea oil, this new awareness has proved particularly effective in the face of English decline and political immiseration ... It has awakened the Scottish bourgeoisie to a new consciousness of its historic separateness, and fostered a frank, restless discontent with the expiring British world."[31] The inability of the Scots to capture the rents from North Sea oil in the highly centralized British unitary state provides fuel for secession, as will Westminster's spending of the rents to delay the process of English secular decline, but for the time being at least the Scottish middle class is severely disadvantaged by the absence of a federal political framework. One need only recall the role of the Alberta government in opposing new federal taxes on oil after 1973 to appreciate the advantages of constitutional decentralization to an ascendant regional bourgeoisie.

A closer parallel is to be found south of the 49th parallel. There the

American political agenda is increasingly defined by the sectional rivalries between "frostbelt" and "sunbelt" and the steady shift in power towards the latter – the so-called Southern Rim stretching from Virginia to California – since World War II. The traditional economic and political hegemony of the "Yankee" northeastern establishment has been undermined by the postwar military displacement of bases and defence industries to the sunbelt states, and by the rapid growth of the new technology, oil, agribusiness, real estate and leisure industries.[32]

The process of regional decline, symbolized by the threatened bankruptcy of New York City, has advanced to the stage where embattled northeastern politicians led by Massachusetts congressman Michael Harrington have launched a sixteen-state Northeastern-Midwest Economic Advancement Coalition to fight for "frostbelt" interests. Invoking memories of Franklin Roosevelt's attempts to assist the South in the 1930s, New York Senator Daniel P. Moynihan recently asked, "What happens to this tradition of national liberalism if it turns out, two generations later, that while the South was willing to accept the resources of the North to get it going, it has no intention to reciprocate now that the Northeast is in need?" Replying to his own question, he claimed there would be a "response in bitterness that would equal what the South expressed and endured after its defeat in the war between the states," adding that the bankruptcy of New York during a Carter Presidency "would be to the Northeast what Sherman's march was to the South."[33]

Conclusion
The rise of the Canadian West in the 1970s is a close parallel to the emergence of the American sunbelt, and the relative economic decline of the central Canadian heartland approximates the slipping hegemony of the American Northeast. The causes of regional decline are very similar: high energy costs, stagnating manufacturing industries, the outward flow of professionals and skilled labour to the periphery, a transfer of wealth and income via government policies (federal defence policies in the U.S., provincial resource policies in Canada). The shift in power is not as far advanced in Canada as it is below the 49th parallel – the periphery does not become the centre overnight – but it certainly has begun. That many observers in central Canada have not yet noticed it, let alone begun to mount a counter-assault on the West, does not make it any less real. It merely confirms the ancient psychological tendency of individuals to ignore that which they prefer not to happen – until it has already happened.

174

Notes

1. Macpherson, *Democracy in Alberta, op. cit.*, 21, 15-16.
2. *Ibid.*, 219-20.
3. L. Panitch, "The Role and Nature of the Canadian State," in Panitch (ed.), *The Canadian State: Political Economy and Political Power* (Toronto: University of Toronto Press, 1977), 10.
4. For an excellent critique, see A. Jackson, "Patterns of Hinterland Revolt: Alberta and Saskatchewan in the Inter-War Period," unpublished paper presented at the Canadian Political Science Association annual meetings, Fredericton, N.B., May 1977.
5. Quoted in J.R. Mallory, *Social Credit and the Federal Power* (Toronto: University of Toronto Press, 1954), 106.
6. Lorne Brown, as cited in Jackson, *op. cit.*, 14.
7. D.H. Breen, "Calgary: The City and the Petroleum Industry since World War Two," *Urban History Review* (1978); L.G. Thomas, "The Rancher and the City: Calgary and the Cattlemen, 1883-1914", *Transactions of the Royal Society of Canada*, VI (June 1968); A.R. McCormack and I. Macpherson (eds.), *Cities in the West* (Ottawa: National Museums of Canada, 1975).
8. The discussion of Lougheed's family and his career is substantially based on interviews; but see W. Stewart, "The Upwardly Mobile Mr. Lougheed," *Maclean's*, January 1972; *Edmonton Journal*, May 17, 1967; *Edmonton Journal*, March 22, 1965; R. Gwyn, "Impressions of Premier Lougheed," *Calgary Herald*, February 11, 1977; *Calgary Herald*, August 3, 1974.
9. Stewart, "The Upwardly Mobile Mr. Lougheed," *op. cit.*
10. Breen, *op. cit.*, 68.
11. James H. Gray, *Troublemaker! A Personal History* (Toronto: Macmillan of Canada, 1978), 201-2 and 211.
12. *Ibid.*, 232.
13. See M.H. Watkins, "A Staple Theory of Economic Growth," reprinted in W.T. Easterbrook and M.H. Watkins (eds.) *Approaches to Canadian Economic History* (Toronto: McClelland and Stewart, 1967), 49-73.
14. *Survey of Production, 1975*, 61-202 (Ottawa: Statistics Canada).
15. J.C. Stabler, *Prairie Regional Development and Prospects* (Royal Commission on Consumer Problems and Inflation, 1968), 53. See also Hanson, *Dynamic Decade, op. cit.*
16. E.H. Shaffer, "The Employment Impact of Oil and Natural Gas on Alberta 1961-70," University of Alberta, Faculty of Business Administration, mimeo, 1976.
17. K.H. Norrie, "Some Comments on Prairie Economic Alienation," *Canadian Public Policy*, II, 2 (1976), 223.
18. *Estimates of Employees by Province and Industry*, 72-008 (Ottawa: Statistics Canada), February 1971.
19. D.M. Ray, *et al.* (eds.), *Canadian Urban Trends* (Toronto: Copp Clark, and Ottawa: Ministry of State for Urban Affairs, 1976), I, 18-19.
20. Gwyn, "Impressions of Peter Lougheed," *op. cit.*

21. On the Mannix family and Lougheed's period with the firm, see the *Edmonton Journal*, December 7, 1977; and the *Financial Post*, November 26, 1977.

22. Stewart, *op. cit.*

23. J. Barr, *The Dynasty, op. cit.*, 216.

24. H. and T. Palmer, "The 1971 Election and the Fall of Social Credit," *Prairie Forum*, I, 2 (1976).

25. Cited in Barr, *op. cit.*, 218-19.

26. P. Lougheed, "Alberta's Industrial Strategy," speech to the Calgary Chamber of Commerce, September 6, 1974.

27. Data from *Tentative "Natural Resource Revenue Plan" for the Government of the Province of Alberta*, April 1972.

28. Lougheed speech in the Alberta legislature, March 12, 1971. Text in Provincial Legislative Library, Edmonton.

29. Lougheed speech in legislature, March 3, 1969; also his address to the Empire Club, May 7, 1973: "Essentials for a New Canadian Industrial Policy."

30. *Canadian Business*, March 1978, 54 ff.

31. T. Nairn, *The Break-up of Britain: Crisis and Neo-Nationalism* (London: New Left Books, 1977), 72.

32. K. Sale, *Power Shift: The Rise of the Southern Rim and Its Challenge to the Eastern Establishment* (New York: Random House, 1975), 6.

33. H. Sutton, "Sunbelt vs. Frostbelt: A Second Civil War," *Saturday Review*, April 15, 1978, 36. See also Kevin Phillips, "The Balkanization of America," *Harper's*, May 1978.

CHAPTER 8

Boom and Bust in the "New Saskatchewan"

Here is a broad outline of the CCF government's program for the next four years. ... (1) To consolidate the gains made in the last four years. ... (2) To expand as opportunity permits our Social, particularly our Health, services. ... (3) To press on with our program of industrial development. To this end, we propose to encourage private capital to come into Saskatchewan, and to co-operate with us in the development of industries based on our natural resources. All of these developments involve tremendous capital investments, far greater in amount than any provincial government dare venture from the limited sources of revenue they presently possess. So we propose to extend an earnest and sincere invitation to private capital to join us in this great task. We are prepared to participate with them in a joint program.

> Clarence Fines
> transcript of radio broadcast, 1948

Under the CCF until 1964, under the Liberals until 1971, and under the NDP until the resource controversies of 1973, the essence of Saskatchewan politics was a consolidation of the new programs initiated by the CCF during its first term, an expansion of social and health services (in particular the inauguration of medical care insurance in 1962), and encouragement of private capital to undertake the development of provincial resources. As Douglas stated in a contemporary series of letters to oil companies, the agenda for resources would henceforth be the "maximum exploration and development. ... which natural circumstances will permit."[1] It was not immediately apparent but this new agenda reduced the government's role to that of a largely passive rentier. It entailed an almost total abdication of any entrepreneurial role over the timing and level of resource investment, and a foresaking of considerable resource rent by the provincial treasury.

The new policies quickly vindicated themselves in the eyes of their authors. In 1949 both major and minor oil companies returned to the province, and by year end over 48 million acres of crown land (nearly 90 per cent of the total on which the crown held mineral rights) were under exploration permit or lease, or designated as crown reserves.[2] Oil companies also entered into contracts to explore a large proportion of the lands on which mineral rights were privately held. Debate over government oil policy again erupted at the 1949 provincial CCF convention as individual delegates denounced a policy that would "promiscuously give away rights the pioneers had fought for."[3] But the party was incapable of acting in concert to deflect government resource policy, and Brockelbank, Phelps' replacement in the resources portfolio, merely riposted that the choice was between private development and no development at all.

Most of the oil discovered in the province was a consequence of the initial exploration boom triggered in 1949. Three of four barrels discovered in Saskatchewan, from the beginning of exploration to the present, were added to reserves during the five-year period from 1952 to 1956. The high-grade potash discoveries occurred simultaneously. Nine of the ten mines currently in operation are mining one of two potash zones, both of which had been discovered, if not fully explored, by 1952. In the long run potash will prove far more valuable than oil to the province, but the relative ease of extracting oil induced a more rapid development of the latter. Already by 1947 Saskatchewan had become the country's second largest oil-producing province – albeit a very distant second – behind Alberta. At its peak in the mid-1960s, Saskatchewan oil production approached 50 per cent of Alberta's, although at the time prorationing shut in much of the latter's potential production. Cumulative discoveries in Saskatchewan to the end of 1976 amounted to 2.1 billion barrels of oil and 2.4 trillion cubic feet of natural gas, representing 19 per cent and 3 per cent respectively of oil and gas discoveries in Alberta.[4]

Oil – The Fabian's Last Stand
The years of the post-Leduc oil boom were simultaneously years of reaction against the political radicalism that had permeated much of North American society during the previous two decades. The desire of the CCF cabinet to adapt to the political realities of the Cold War, the inability of the party to levy any effective sanctions on the government for flouting party policy on crown oil and gas development, the CCF's electoral setbacks of 1948 and 1949, were local symptoms of the new political conservatism. It is ironic therefore that at precisely this juncture the Planning Board began a muffled bureaucratic resistance to the cabinet agenda for resources.

178

The Planning Board was fearful that inducements to rapid private development entailed too large a sacrifice of public economic rent, and argued the advantages of crown resource investment. Why did it articulate these concerns in the second and third terms of office whereas, during the first, it had come to view with equanimity the arrival of private capital into oil? The answer lies largely in the opportunity posed by the disposal of crown reserve acreage reverting to the crown when a company, having made a commercially exploitable discovery, went to lease. Whereas the government felt constrained to adopt Alberta precedent on royalties, the issues of crown reserves could not be handled so simply. They placed the government in the position of a competing oil company with a direct interest in the development of oil pools which, with a high probability, extended under the government's acreage. The risk associated with initial exploration was used by the Board as reason to recommend in 1947 against any public investment in oil, but the risks of public development of crown reserves were obviously much lower. Concerned to maximize economic rent accruing to the government from these reserves, the Planning Board became skeptical of the efficacy of the Alberta system of cash auctions as a means of disposal. Reduced risk and fear of lost rent prompted a return to the ideas of "Planning Document No. 1" and renewed advocacy within the board of a public entrepreneurial role.

In late 1948 the Planning Board proposed a ten-year program of public expenditure on exploration and development of crown reserves, with a capital budget of $500,000 annually, to be financed by a tax on the sale of petroleum products. Conscious of the political controversy such a scheme would engender, the Board was anxious that the government make a strong public case on the need for "positive action" – to counter the power of the major oil companies over retail prices and to assure the local availability of future supplies. Cabinet considered and rejected the idea.[5]

A year later the Planning Board returned to the frustrating task of convincing its political masters in cabinet of the need for a more aggressive oil policy. In November 1949 the Board prepared a lengthy and comprehensive study, the "Report on Fuel Policy." It included a history of the oil industry emphasizing the role of corporate power, and a discussion of issues ranging from policies for development of crown reserves, to physical conservation and the desirability of unitization, the extent of provincial jurisdiction to regulate retail petroleum prices, and the "socially desirable time pattern of production."[6] The thrust was evident. The Board was anxious that "[t]he intensive program of exploration for petroleum now under way in Saskatchewan has been purchased at the cost of important concessions to the private oil companies. ... The case for public ownership and development of the natural resources derives its greatest strength from the fact, amply demonstrated in the past, that their exploitation under a system of private ownership is often conducive to the extravagant depletion of irreplaceable sources of wealth." The Board argued in a familiar fashion that the government had a "threefold obligation to the public whose resources it administers": (1) full development to increase, stabilize, and diversify provincial income, (2) prevention of physical waste and "the weighing of present requirements against those of the future in order to achieve the long-run optimum use of resources" and (3) "that justice [be] done to the consumer by preventing the industry from exacting from him a greater tribute than is warranted by the service it provides or the risk it undertakes." The Board accepted that "[w]hatever policy is devised must be accommodated within the framework of the understanding which now exists between government and the private oil companies, an understanding which contemplates the continued operation of the latter in both the exploratory and subsequent production phases of petroleum development." But it was a reluctant acceptance: "when circumstances dictate a choice between development under private ownership and none at all, the adoption of the first alternative, in order to discharge one of the government's obligations, makes it doubly necessary, and in some ways more difficult, to avoid jeopardizing the fulfillment of the remaining ones."[7]

At the time of writing in 1949, before any major Saskatchewan discoveries, crown reserves had yet to become a significant asset. But given the evolution of resources policy the Board realized the disposal of crown reserves posed the most promising and perhaps only substantial area of potential innovation in oil policy. The Board presented, as it would repeatedly during the next five years, a continuum of options ranked according to degree of public investment and public assumption of risk; its own position consistently favoured the entrepreneurial options involving crown investment and risk-taking. The option entailing no public risk or capital was disposal by cash auction as in Alberta. A second option, a bidding system in which crown reserves would go to the firm offering the highest "overriding" (i.e. supplementary) royalty, entailed no public capital, but the crown assumed a portion of the uncertainty inasmuch as the stream of royalty receipts depended on productivity of the reserve acreage. A third option was "to make crown reserves available to selected organizations on the basis of private negotiations, in order to equalize the opportunities of entry regardless of bargaining power based on financial resources. This ... method would be open to attack on grounds of discrimination and favoritism, but could be used to particular advantage in rendering assistance to the co-ops without subjecting them to the disadvantages under which they labored in their Alberta venture." The final option was "to create a crown corporation for the purpose of drilling and operating on crown reserves over proven land. This ... method recommends itself most strongly when taken in conjunction with the policy of unitization. In other words, whether or not the necessity of drilling on a section reserved to the crown would be indicated by the geological characteristics of the structure, the government would participate in the prorated revenue in proportion to the volume of oil estimated to lie beneath the reserve." The Board wanted a combination of special arrangements with co-operatives and crown development; it opposed disposal by cash auction:

> This method ... has been the one adopted by the province of Alberta, ostensibly for the purpose of providing an opportunity for small operators to obtain a foothold on proven oil lands. In point of fact it has not been overly successful in accomplishing its objective, largely because of the overwhelmingly superior resources of the large American companies who have recently invaded the province. It has been questioned whether the advantage of certain and frequently substantial contributions to provincial revenue compensate for a greater revenue which would accrue over the life of the field in the form of an over-riding royalty or as the result of direct government operation.[8]

These arguments can be readily demonstrated by means of the algebra of discounted cash flows. Given the lower probability of suffering a loss, assume the discount rate used by firms to evaluate an overriding royalty system is less than that used in evaluating a cash auction bid and, as seems reasonable given the high expected rate of return in the oil industry, the government discount rate is less than either. Assume further that all firms, private or crown, could operate with equal efficiency, i.e. a crown corporation could reasonably estimate the same sequence of revenues and costs as a private firm. Under such assumptions it is a simple exercise to demonstrate that for any crown reserve (1) the present value to the government of expected overriding royalties exceeds that of a cash auction bid, and (2) a crown development offers the highest present value of expected rents of any of the three options.

The "Report on Fuel Policy" stated the case for vigorous conservation policy with an emphasis upon unitization to overcome the combination of rule of capture and divided ownership of oil pools. On price regulation, the third policy examined, the report arrived at the somewhat Machiavellian conclusion that "the essential precondition for regulation of crude prices is the discovery of an actual or potential volume of crude production capable of rendering Saskatchewan self-sufficient as to its petroleum requirements. In the interim nothing should be done to prejudice the program of discovery and development, and until that time, all attempts at regulation will be premature."[9]

The only recommendation of the Board to which cabinet responded promptly was to establish procedures for physical conservation. The government sought advice from the Interstate Oil Compact Commission in Oklahoma City, and the ensuing provincial conservation statute, The Oil and Gas Conservation Act, 1952, was based upon the Commission's model conservation statute.[10] Despite industry opposition, included in the statute was the power to impose unitization; the power has not been used extensively. The debate over crown reserves was to continue until 1955 but the Planning Board suffered its first setback when in 1951 the regulations governing the designation of reserves were relaxed, abandoning the checkerboard system.[11]

Sizeable oil discoveries persuaded cabinet by the end of 1951 to establish an interdepartmental Oil Policy Committee of senior bureaucrats, chaired by Tom Shoyama, who had replaced Cadbury as head of the Planning Board upon the latter's departure earlier in the year. (Shoyama joined the government during its first term and remained until Ross Thatcher's 1964 victory. He was one of the sizeable contingent of senior Saskatchewan civil servants who thereupon migrated from Regina to Ottawa. He has since become a senior mandarin occupying, at the time of writing, the position of deputy minister of finance.) This committee had a broad mandate to consider all options for disposal of crown reserves, the feasibility of government marketing crude oil, and the implications of retail price regulation within the province. The perspective was now that of a province about to become a net exporter of oil, and the earlier concern to control prices on behalf of provincial consumers was offset by concern that price controls would reduce revenue from oil exports, slow development of the industry, and hence delay royalty revenue.[12]

By the time Shoyama's committee reported in detail, in 1953, the policy debate had narrowed to the disposition of crown reserves. The committee had convinced cabinet to delay any disposal of reserves until a general policy had been determined. After 1953 production rapidly increased and began to drain oil from under reserve acreage; crown reserve policy could not be further delayed. The oil industry expected Saskatchewan to follow Alberta's precedent and to auction reserves on a cash basis, but the committee remained convinced such a policy would leave too much economic rent to the private sector.[13] Faced with the intrinsic uncertainties, Shoyama's committee recommended in a lengthy 1953 report that the government experiment with the entire gamut of options for disposition of crown reserves:

(1) direct development by the Crown, (2) unitization agreements, (3) development by a private operator for a management fee, (4) farmouts by competitive bid [a form of joint venture between government and the private firm offering the highest overriding royalty based on net income], (5) cash auction by competitive bid, (6) auction by competitive bid for overriding royalty [on gross revenue] and (7) specific pooling agreements for gas development. Consideration of the merits and feasibility of the above methods, and an evaluation of their respective value in terms of probable returns to the Government, indicates that the largest net return would be secured by adopting the first two methods where feasible. However, no rule capable of general application can be deduced, and the method to be employed will have to be determined by the circumstances particular to each reserve.[14]

In discussing the possible creation of a crown corporation to produce and market oil from crown reserves, Shoyama's committee envisioned an average annual capital budget of $6 to $10 million, sufficient to finance approximately 150 wells per year. The committee concluded "that from a financial point of view a careful and judicious program of government investment in its Crown Reserves should be both profitable and practicable."[15] It considered and dismissed a number of potential objections to a crown development: "Assuming the established methods of market proration which assure equitable access to the market on the part of all producers within the province, and which the Government has the statutory power to impose, no insoluble problems should be encountered in marketing crude oil."[16] "Some concern has ... been expressed that a government policy of investing in oil might prejudice the success of the anticipated bond flotations. ... A difficulty of this kind is impossible of precise measurement. If past experience is any guide, however, it is suggested that the problem is likely to be a short-run one. These short-run effects can be held to a minimum by choosing the best possible methods for financing and managing the oil investment program. They will be relieved as soon as the anticipated substantial earnings become available for the Treasury, and the net effect may in fact be a further strengthening of the Province's capacity to borrow externally."[17]

The intent of passages such as the above was to assuage cabinet trepidations. The obstacles to a crown venture lay both in the ideological opposition of the oil industry to public ownership and in the contemporary cabinet desire to accommodate the industry in the interest of rapid development. Brockelbank in particular was opposed to government development of crown reserves or any other policy that entailed conflict: "Our relations with the industry have been quite satisfactory and I consider it my responsibility to maintain that condition if at all possible."[18] Thus the committee considered it necessary to expend considerable energy to convince cabinet to adopt an entrepreneurial stance towards crown reserves, to study the problem from the perspective of maximizing provincial economic rents, to conceive the public interest as independent of and in opposition to that of the private oil companies:

> the Crown alienates from one-half to three-quarters of its acreage (less royalty) in return for the capital, organization and skill necessary to develop its potential petroleum resources. It follows from this that the Government, as owner of the Crown Reserves, has no further moral or legal obligation to the private operator in the development of a given field. Crown Reserves should have a "free ride" without being subjected to pressures other than those which are coincidental with [the] best economic interest of the Government. *The only obligation that the Government has with respect to Crown Reserves is to develop them by those methods that will maximize the total revenue to the public treasury from the Province's oil resources.*[19]

The first sale of crown reserves, in September 1953, was an orthodox cash auction,[20] but in December of that year the committee recommended a farm-out agreement for a proved low-risk crown reserve as "the first step toward a policy of retaining control over at least a part of the province's resources, without which government authority will never be effectively exercised."[21] It turned out to be an exceedingly modest first step – in March 1954 the government entered into a farm-out agreement for two sections with Co-operative Refineries Limited.[22]

Nonetheless the oil industry erupted in vehement rhetoric. The Saskatchewan division of the Canadian Petroleum Association concluded that the agreement "clearly puts the Saskatchewan government into the production and development phases of the oil business."[23] The agreement was allegedly unfair because it had been negotiated without competitive bidding, denying the possibility of access to those companies which had undertaken exploration in the field. The provincial media echoed the industry arguments, and in addition condemned any overriding royalty system as unjustified "gambling with the future well being of the people of Saskatchewan."[24] The repercussions were by no means restricted to the province. Carl Nickle, a Conservative Member of Parliament from Calgary closely linked to independent Alberta oil interests, ominously warned that, unless the government gave assurances that this was not to constitute a precedent, private oil capital could withdraw from the province.[25] In a "personal and confidential" letter from one of Toronto's most prominent investment firms Douglas received a more explicit warning: "I feel quite sure that a policy of this kind [i.e. farm-outs], if extended indiscriminately, would be sufficient to impair materially the Province's credit standing in the open market, which has been so carefully built up in recent years. In other words, there would be a number of corporations and institutions who would decline to buy Saskatchewan bonds as a protest to an apparently inequitable policy."[26]

The government attempted gamely to defend itself. "I think the oil companies need to be reminded," Douglas replied to the Toronto investment firm,

that when they take an exploratory permit the reward they get for their investment is 75% of the oil-bearing area while the Crown gets only 25% [under the checkerboard system]. It is therefore somewhat illogical to say that they are being cheated when they do not get as a reward for their investment the 25% which belongs to the Crown ... The only real complaint the oil companies have in the [farm-out] agreement is that they were not allowed to bid on the Crown Reserves and I agree that if the Government had made an agreement with any oil company other than a co-operative they would have a logical complaint. Many people will not agree with me but I maintain that the co-operatives are in a slightly different position to any other company for the reason that they represent many thousands of farmers and other consumers in the province and this agreement constitutes the one means by which the Government can enable the people of the province to participate in the utilization of their own resources.

But with only the CCF and the co-operatives behind it, the government retreated. "I am convinced that the agreement we have entered into with the co-ops will do two things," Douglas assured his Toronto interrogators,

(1) it will take the pressure off the Government to go into the oil business and develop the Crown Reserves and (2) it will make the farmers and other consumers of the province aware of some of the risks and heavy investments which oil companies have to make in

order to carry on their business. The main point we have tried to convey to those who were dismayed over this agreement is that the deal with the co-ops does not set a pattern for future disposition of Crown Reserves. The best proof of that is that we are this week putting up for auction many times the area that has been farmed out to the Co-op Refinery.[27]

In 1953 mining regulatory activities had been taken from the Department of Natural Resources and ensconced in a new Department of Mineral Resources headed by Brockelbank. Following the industry-backed barrage, the Planning Board's campaign to procure a degree of public investment in oil disintegrated; Brockelbank and his new department effectively wrested all authority over oil policy from the Planning Board. They transformed the farm-out option into a "net royalty lease" which, while preserving the overriding royalty, removed all joint venture features. Tom Shoyama impotently protested that certain companies had approached the government stating willingness to enter into farm-out agreements: "Formerly the Crown retained an effective share of ownership and a potential right to participate in important management decisions. This advantage (and accompanying risk) is now completely gone. ... under the new [net royalty] lease approach, the opportunity for Government personnel to observe, study and participate at first hand in the technical aspects of oil production will be sharply reduced from the scope possible under the true farm-out agreement."[28]

The significance of the Planning Board's six-year campaign over disposition of crown reserves lies not in the intricacies of the bureaucratic conflicts. It demonstrates the dilemmas facing a government in pursuing an entrepreneurial role on its own account in a hostile cultural milieu. How much more aggressive could the government have been? Public investment excited not only the predictable opposition of the oil industry, but in the cultural climate of the Cold War that opposition was echoed, if not amplified, by virtually all powerful institutions. Furthermore the CCF had collapsed as an effective left populist/social democratic movement at a national level. Thus to give a categorical answer to the question is impossible but, after making all due allowance for the environmental constraints, the cabinet could probably have been considerably more aggressive without endangering its electoral base. Apart from the timid experiments with farm-outs and the limited use of the net royalty lease, Saskatchewan accepted Alberta precedent. After 1948 most members of Douglas' cabinet shared a commitment to rapid development on terms acceptable to the oil industry – a commitment that precluded serious consideration of Planning Board arguments that such development entailed a high price in terms of rents lost and the abdication of a feasible public entrepreneurial role. Thus despite the past ideological differences between the CCF and Social Credit, their oil policies had by the mid-1950s converged and, in brief, in neither province did the government explore the limits of public policy during the first wave of post-Leduc resource development.

Potash – Establishing Precedents

The impact of oil on the politics and economy of Alberta has been overwhelming. In Saskatchewan no single resource has had as profound an impact but cumulatively oil and potash have wrought complex changes – as in the future will uranium. In the long run Saskatchewan's potash will prove far more valuable than its oil and gas. The undiscounted market value of potash accessible by conventional mining methods exceeds that of Alberta's remaining conventional oil and gas; the value of potash accessible by solution mining is approximately equal to the value of the Athabasca tar sands. These comparisons (based simply on a weighting of reserve estimates by market price and not on estimates of discounted present value) are of limited significance, except to suggest the magnitude of potash reserves. Saskatchewan reserves have been conservatively estimated at 5 billion tons attainable by conventional methods, an additional 69 billion tons by solution mining. (Throughout this book all quantities of potash are given in terms of K_2O equivalent.) These reserves, which will doubtless be revised upwards, allow the present annual rate of production, of approximately 5 million tons, to be maintained for 1000 years by the former method, and an additional 13,800 years by the latter.[29]

Saskatchewan potash provides an ideal case study to illustrate the central issues of postwar Canadian resource development – the effects of resource booms and ensuing contractions, political power and instability in international markets, foreign versus Canadian ownership, private versus public investment, distribution of economic rents, potential positive effects on industrial development via linkages versus the negative effects due to the crowding out of potential manufacturing investment by the demands of resource industries for available capital and labour. These issues are at the core of academic and political debates over economic policy since World War II. To summarize, our conclusion from the case of potash is that the comparative advantage afforded by vast provincial potash reserves clearly justified heavy capital investment in this as opposed to most alternative industries, but the provincial government's abnegation during the potash investment boom of any entrepreneurial responsibility to assess independently the market implications of large additions to world potash capacity, and to regulate the pace of investment accordingly, permitted a classic "staple trap" phenomenon to ensue. Any substantial rents that might have accrued to the provincial treasury from this resource were dissipated until the mid-1970s in low potash prices and the capital costs of excess capacity. (The only major benefit to the province until then was the several thousand jobs of potash miners at above-average wages.)

Before we tackle the politics of potash, it is necessary to introduce a minimum of geology and economics. In Saskatchewan the potash ore mined is a mixture of sylvite (potassium chloride) and common table salt (sodium chloride). Ninety-five per cent of potassium salts are used for agricultural fertilizers, potassium being the third element, after nitrogen and phosphorous, in which many soils are deficient.

The geology of the Elk Point Basin, in which the prairie potash deposits lie, became known as a side effect of oil exploration. Opening to the sea in what is now northwestern Alberta, the basin covered most of that province, the southern half of Saskatchewan, and extended into Montana, North Dakota, and Manitoba. Evaporation of this inland sea in the middle Devonian period, 300 million years ago, resulted in deposition of salt beds up to 1000 feet thick. Reefs limited the deposition of potash salts to the upper reaches of the basin east of Alberta. South of a line running west northwest through Prince Albert, potash deposits underlie most of Saskatchewan; they continue into Montana and North Dakota, and marginally into Manitoba. However the commercially recoverable reserves, all in Saskatchewan, are a small fraction of this vast volume. Much is too deep; some deposits are insufficiently separated from water-bearing formations to permit safe mining; elsewhere the concentration of sylvite is too low or the concentration of the undesirable potassium salt, carnallite, too high. Below 3500 feet the pressure of overlying strata is considered too great by most engineers to permit conventional room and pillar mining, although some have argued that conventional techniques can be safely extended to greater depths. Solution mining is not subject to such a constraint.

Nine of the ten mines constructed use conventional mining methods — one or more shafts permit men and machinery to reach the ore body and the ore to be raised. The tenth mine uses a solution method — the injection of hot water into the ore body via one set of pipes and extraction of a solution containing dissolved ore via another. Both methods display economies of scale dictating a large minimum size of mine. The capital costs of the solution method are lower because it avoids the expense of shaft sinking; conversely its operating costs are higher due primarily to the high energy input required to evaporate the ore solution. Post-1973 energy price increases have dramatically shifted relative costs against solution mining.

One geological problem deserves particular mention – shaft sinking through the many water-bearing formations lying above the potash. Of these the most daunting is the Blairmore. Ranging in thickness from 200 to 500 feet it consists of unconsolidated sand and gravel, and water under extremely high pressure. It has proved a formidable barrier. The Blairmore must be frozen in the region of the shaft; then the shaft is sunk through ice and lined. The first company to attempt shaft sinking did succeed in penetrating the Blairmore, but its shaft flooded even before the ore body was reached; the second company completed shaft sinking and began mining operations, but after a year water seepage forced a five-year closure for repairs. Only when the third company made use of tubbing, an expensive technique whereby the shaft is lined not with concrete but with cylindrical cast iron plates bolted together to form a watertight cylinder, was the Blairmore effectively conquered. Tubbing had been employed in deep potash mines in Germany, but this was its first application in North America. In a fourth mine an accident during shaft maintenance resulted in the entire mine being flooded; renovation required two years.

From 1948 to 1952 the CCF conducted protracted unsuccessful negotiations with several promoters and companies in an attempt to launch a potash industry. The government attempted to organize a competitive bidding process, but was repeatedly forced to amend the rules of the game to suit potential applicants. The process progressively assumed the character of very unequal bilateral negotiations. The balance of technical expertise, and of access to capital and to markets, lay overwhelmingly with the mining industry, which sought to translate its current advantages into long-term contracts for minimal royalties.

Initially in 1949 the government produced a "Tentative Terms of Agreement Between Private Industry and the Crown" embodying an exploration permit and production lease structure analogous to that for oil. The CCF at this stage still hoped for a joint venture; the agreement called for the government to have a one-third interest in any development. Altruistically and naively, a clause was inserted to the following effect – for the first five years the price of potash to be at the "discretion of [the] company," but thereafter price to be subject to negotiation between company and government "[t]o prevent monopoly practice insofar as Saskatchewan potash is concerned."[30] The two currently interested developers baulked, each wanting to enter into an exclusive agreement with the government that would preclude competitors. Thereupon the government dropped the crown participation and price control clauses and in May 1950 tendered for leases. None were received.[31]

The government next decided to draft potash regulations (gazetted in December 1950).[32] The royalty provisions called for payment of 5 per cent of the market value of potash produced, or 25 per cent of net profits (defined to permit a deduction for depreciation and interest costs at 8 per cent of book value of depreciable assets, but no allowance for depletion), whichever was less; a minimum of 80 per cent of ore was to be taken from crown, as opposed to freehold lands. Under these arrangements one inadequately financed company attempted unsuccessfully to develop a solution mining process. Thereafter, in 1952, it began shaft sinking which, after many delays caused by technical and financial problems, reached by 1960 a depth of 1800 feet before flooding from the Blairmore forced abandonment of the project.

In 1952 the Potash Company of America (PCA), an established producer in Carlsbad, New Mexico, discovered just east of Saskatoon a superior ore body to that at Unity. By the time royalty negotiations began in March 1953, six years had elapsed since the existence of commercially exploitable reserves had first been announced, and apart from the one ill-financed development mentioned above, the CCF had nothing to show for its effort. Its bargaining position was not strong. PCA categorically refused to operate on the basis of the royalty provisions of the 1950 regulations, and accordingly the latter became irrelevant. In a lengthy memorandum on royalties PCA's treasurer emphasized to the government just how dependent Saskatchewan was on his company's technical, financial, and marketing capacity:

> In summation, a Saskatchewan operation such as PCA is discussing. ... will be based on a venture where the risk factor is still of vital importance; financing will be undertaken from surplus and funds accumulated in the Carlsbad operation; technical skill and production knowledge will be supplied by the Carlsbad company; a ready-made market will be handed to the Canadian company by reason of the Carlsbad company foregoing that portion of the market. No company other than an existing potash producer could so smooth the road and thereby give reasonable assurance of an operation which will immediately be technically successful and operationally profitable. How, then can any argument be adduced in support of a royalty basis which is higher than that being paid by Carlsbad producers in an area where operating conditions are known and all other conditions are stable.

The initial PCA offer was to pay a gross royalty equal to 3.1 per cent of market value of potash mined from crown land. This, PCA noted, was somewhat above the equivalently calculated royalty rates paid in New Mexico – 2.5 per cent on federal leases, 2.7 per cent on state leases.[33]

On his own initiative Brockelbank undertook to amend the royalty clause by lowering the tax rate of the net profit option from 25 per cent to 12.5 per cent. Amended, the government regulations would have provided for a smaller royalty than the 3.1 per cent PCA proposal, provided, as was reasonable to predict, net profits as defined turned out to be less than 25 per cent of gross revenue. Furthermore the government's existing royalty structure forced the government to share in the risks. Should no profits be earned, no royalty would have to be paid. Nonetheless PCA rejected Brockelbank's proposal. Why? PCA may have been expecting an extremely high profit/sales ratio. It may also have rejected the net profit royalty because it entailed disclosure to the government of financial information it hoped to keep confidential.

PCA was concerned not only with the level of current royalties. It was intent upon using its bargaining power to fix a royalty structure over as long a period as possible. Originally PCA refused to negotiate except on the basis of a fixed royalty over the lifetime of the mine.

Brockelbank had no choice but to secure cabinet agreement to scrap the royalty structure laid out in the 1950 regulations. Cabinet agreed to negotiate down to a lower limit of 3.45 per cent of gross revenue. Final negotiations resulted in a complicated formula, graduated by quality of ore, which amounted to 3.5 per cent on the grade, 30 per cent K_2O, the government expected PCA to mine. (PCA refused, incidentally, to divulge to the government details of the grade of ore it would actually mine.) Finally, the minimum percentage PCA was required to take from crown land (the portion on which royalties could be levied) was reduced from 80 to 40 per cent.

As gazetted, the section of the 1953 regulations dealing with royalties began with a customary sentence: "The lessee shall pay to the Crown the following royalty, or such royalty as may from time to time be prescribed, by the Lieutenant Governor in Council. ..."[34] Seemingly PCA had dropped its demand for a fixed royalty structure over the lifetime of its mine. However on the adjacent page was an innocuous announcement that: "An Agreement, dated the 2nd day of November, 1953, has been entered into with the said Company [PCA], subject to the approval of the Lieutenant Governor in Council, which provides for the payment of substantial rentals for the lands therein described and for the construction and development of a potash mining industry. ..."[35] Nowhere was it publicly mentioned, but the above agreement committed the government not to change the royalty formula, as applied to PCA, before 1977, twenty-one years after the estimated start-up date in 1956. This agreement is still having repercussions. The 1953 royalty structure, combined with guarantees not to amend it for a fixed period, served as a precedent for both the CCF and Liberals in the development of all future mines. Alleged violation of the series of similar agreements covering PCA and other mines is one basis being used by the companies in their post-1975 challenges to government policy.

In 1954 PCA started preparations for shaft sinking. In 1958 it produced Saskatchewan's first potash. Within a year, however, water seepage from the Blairmore formation forced closure of the mine. Repairs and rehabilitation were not completed until 1965. The third company to attempt development, International Minerals and Chemical (IMC), also an established New Mexico producer, overcame the problem by use of tubbing, a technique described previously. The successful completion in 1962 of IMC's shaft dramatically lowered the uncertainty attached to development of the ore body and even without the additional factors that increased the value of Saskatchewan reserves, there would have been a significant influx of capital to the industry. Whether a crown corporation, had one been launched, would have suffered the fate of PCA, or conquered the Blairmore adequately as did IMC, is a hypothetical question. Clearly shaft sinking did pose serious technical problems that can be adduced to justify low initial royalties (although not for twenty-one years). With the Blairmore conquered, however, it was a logical moment to reassess potash policy, but 1962 was a year of crisis for the government, embroiled as it was with the implementation of medicare, and no one at a senior level in the cabinet or civil service was prepared to devote time and energy to the task.

More important than any particular crisis in preventing re-evaluation was the transformation since 1944 of the role played by the agencies responsible for resource policy—from Phelps' commitment to "an orderly change to social ownership"[36] as the basis of policy for the Department of Natural Resources, through a wary acceptance by the Planning Board of private resource development, to an attitude within the new Department of Mineral Resources that its role was to advocate within government the perspective of the mining industry. Resource policies after 1955 were in effect the result of a bargaining process *within* government among various departments representing different interests. A labour controversy during IMC's construction offers a convenient example.

192

In the spring of 1961 IMC changed construction contractors, and the new contractor laid off approximately 100 union members employed by the former contractor. The men protested vigorously to the government and after considering the case, the (acting) Minister of Labour concluded "that the parent company, in this case, is trying to do a little union busting. I believe we should do all possible to frustrate this."[37] IMC's operations manager protested to Brockelbank as Minister of Mineral Resources about the pro-labour interventions of the Labour Department. Brockelbank, albeit uncomfortable in the role, acted as the industry advocate within government against the Labour Department. He presented to Douglas the company's case that the union had irresponsibly extracted an unjustified wage settlement by striking in 1960 at a critical time during shaft sinking through the Blairmore: "I know I may be called a right wing reactionary, but I realize we do not live in a society where we can do without large corporations. As long as we need them and have to live with them I think we should ... be fair and consider a problem from both sides."[38] Ultimately negotiations involving Douglas and IMC head office produced a compromise solution.

The same obsession with rapid development that dominated cabinet response to oil policy was also present for potash. Predictably Brockelbank was the most adamant. In April 1961 he proposed to cabinet that the government accelerate investment in the industry by waiving all or a part of potash royalties until 1965. Cabinet rejected the idea, but did agree to a second proposal by Brockelbank that due to problems experienced by PCA, the fixed royalty agreement be extended from 1977 to 1981, and that the same terms be offered to IMC.[39] In late 1963 the government guaranteed the existing royalty structure, basically unchanged from that negotiated with PCA in 1953, for all new mines until 1974.[40] When the Liberals assumed office in 1964, they extended the guarantee of existing royalties to all producers until 1981.[41] The CCF, now in opposition, protested that this was an unjustified concession but given the evolution of royalty policy they had difficulty in convincing the public that the Liberals were doing other than extrapolating past policy trends. In fact the Liberals did marginally increase taxation on the industry by imposing a small production tax on potash produced from freehold potash lands.[42] Previously such production, nearly one half, was subject to no form of provincial taxation.

The Potash Boom
From 1962, the year of commencement of continuous production, until 1970, when the tenth and final mine came on stream, production

capacity grew at a phenomenal annual rate in excess of 25 per cent. By 1969 Canada had become, with a capital expenditure of $700 million, the world's largest potash producer. (After 1970 Canadian production was surpassed by the Soviet Union.) Six of the mines were within seventy miles of Saskatoon, and during the five-year period comprising the height of the construction boom, 1961-66, Saskatoon's growth rate was the fastest of the five major prairie cities; it exceeded that of both Calgary and Edmonton.[43] Saskatoon began calling itself the "potash capital of the world." Finally potash realized its potential as a regional staple, but what determined the timing and intensity of the boom?[44]

The first factor was simply the comparative advantage of the province's reserves, which constitute nearly half the world total. Given its uniform high grade over large areas and that it lies in horizontal beds uninterrupted by major faulting, the operating costs of extracting and refining Saskatchewan potash are among the lowest in the world. Given its depth (over 3000 feet) and the problems of the Blairmore, capital costs are obviously high but the successful application of tubbing dramatically lowered the uncertainty of capital costs and, provided mines are sufficiently large to exploit scale economies, total unit costs are decidedly lower than for potash from Carlsbad, New Mexico, the chief source of competition for Saskatchewan in the North American market.[45] To realize the cost advantages of the new large and expensive Saskatchewan mines, the capital costs had, of course, to be spread over full capacity production. Prairie soils are not deficient in potassium and the eastern Canadian market, even now in the 1970s, consumes approximately one third the capacity of one average Saskatchewan mine. Obviously growth of the Saskatchewan industry depended on exports, both offshore and to the United States. Since New Mexico deposits were of a lower grade and expected to reach the point of economic nonviability within one or two decades, producers invested in Saskatchewan with expectations of a proximate decline in New Mexico production.

The timing and extent of the potash boom depended on more than the technical breakthrough of tubbing and the comparative cost advantages. The United Nations "development decade" and the large fertilizer requirements of the new wheat and rice strains of the "green revolution" encouraged expectations of vast foreign-aid financed fertilizer demand in third world markets. In the five years prior to 1962 American potash demand grew at a modest average annual rate of 3 per cent; in the five years after 1962, the rate accelerated to 10 per cent. Potash producers profited from the shift in demand not only by selling more; from a trough in 1960 to a peak in 1965 they succeeded in raising average American prices by over 20 per cent.[46] A final factor influencing the boom was the provincial royalty and regulatory structure. The prospect of guaranteed low royalties for a specified period, with the obvious implication that thereafter they would be raised, encouraged firms to invest now. The government allocated permits and leases on an open "first come first served" basis, with work requirements to prevent acquisition for purely speculative motives, but with no intention of imposing any constraint on the rate of development.

The North American fertilizer industry had long been characterized by informal cartels among a few producers with close links to the large number of mainly small distributors. The initial Saskatchewan mines were built by established producers as extensions of their New Mexico operations or, in the case of the French-German mine, as an alternative source of supply for their traditional North American markets. These early companies invested in large new mines hoping to exploit the cost advantages of Saskatchewan reserves, and simultaneously to add sufficient new capacity to dissuade outsiders from risking the large sums required to build a mine. Under ordinary circumstances they probably would have succeeded.

But the 1960s were not ordinary. It was a decade of "bullish" corporate expectations of exponential growth, of corporate diversifications, of new conglomerates. To quote a sober economic study published by the federal government in Ottawa, the net result during the peak of the boom was after-tax profit margins for established North American potash producers that "ranged from significant to enormous."[47] The most successful financially was PCA, which for the years 1962-67 realized an average after-tax return on shareholder equity in excess of 19 per cent, and this despite its problems with its Saskatchewan mine. Oil companies, already engaged in the manufacture of nitrogenous fertilizer (ammonia from natural gas), diversified into the other two basic ingredients. Other established fertilizer firms producing one ingredient diversified into the others, and even companies with no previous experience in fertilizers invested heavily in the industry. Of particular significance for future political developments was the decision by Noranda, a Canadian mining company, to enter into partnership for construction of a potash mine, Central Canada Potash (CCP), with CF Industries, a company owned by regional farm co-operatives in the United States and Ontario. Together these co-operatives have a commanding one quarter of the North American fertilizer market. The partnership was a marriage of convenience guaranteeing the Canadian company access to the American market, and permitting the co-operatives to integrate backwards thereby weakening the power of traditional producers over potash prices. In this mine, plus one other, majority ownership was Canadian; for the remaining eight it was foreign. Majority ownership of six was American; one was owned by a French-German syndicate, and via a series of intermediate companies one was controlled by South African interests.[48]

"Big Business" – From Populist Ogre to Benign Benefactor

The large oil and potash deposits of Alberta and Saskatchewan were simultaneously a "gift of God" that offered the prospect of rapid relatively painless economic diversification, and opiates that for a quarter of a century sapped the entrepreneurial initiative of provincial governments both in Alberta and Saskatchewan. Although other phenomena – the uneven consolidation of farms creating internal divisions between rich and poor farmers, attendant rural depopulation, and the Cold War – diminished populism as a viable political culture, oil and potash developments contributed to the demise.

It comprised much more, but the core of populism was the organization of the small independent farmer against external corporate and financial power. It provided innumerable examples of attempts at economic entrepreneurship from the "bottom up" – the Nonpartisan League's industrial program, the Wheat Pools and other co-operatives, attempts to conduct an autonomous regional monetary policy by introducing "social credit," the CCF's crown ventures. As long as the prairie economy remained dependent upon the vagaries of agriculture, a majority of farmers and urban workers were prepared to support entrepreneurial farm leaders with ambitions to launch co-operatives, and populist politicians with analogous ambitions to use the provincial government for entrepreneurial ends. Individual populist organizations might undergo life cycles from youthful enthusiasm to mature conservatism, and the strength of popular agitation might vary inversely with the price of wheat, but populism remained an integral part of prairie culture.

For reasons discussed earlier, populist leaders failed, both in Saskatchewan and Alberta, to secure effective public control of the new non-agricultural staples, oil and potash. The failure of populist leaders to "diversify" their entrepreneurship from agriculture to new staples permitted the public perception of corporate/financial power to undergo a fundamental transformation. The populist image of Standard Oil monopolizing oil markets, of the CPR imposing exorbitant freight rates, of parasitic speculators on the Winnipeg Grain Exchange, yielded to the image of corporations, in particular those in the resource sector, as benign dynamic entrepreneurs capable of mobilizing the necessary capital and labour to diversify the regional economy. Both the renascent Fabianism of Allan Blakeney's government and the aggressive entrepreneurship of Alberta's new urban bourgeoisie are attempts to transcend this passive rentier ideology, but for a quarter of a century after Leduc a majority within all indigenous interest groups viewed resource corporations as benign benefactors. Why? The number employed directly at the exploration and production stages of the oil industry (excluding retail distribution) or in potash mining is small, and resource companies could afford to pay wages above the prevailing provincial average. This small well-paid work force has had few immediate reasons to protest, and the unions involved (in oil primarily Oil, Chemical and Atomic Workers, in potash primarily United Steelworkers) have generally practised a conservative "business unionism" that, despite official union support for the NDP and occasional union resolutions on behalf of public ownership in the resource sector, has restricted its demands to wage and work conditions. The thrust for change in resource politics, to the extent it has occurred, has come from elsewhere. For the remainder of the labour force natural resources offered the prospect of increased employment via the process of linkages. For the entire population resource royalties offered a pleasant combination of expanded government services and low taxation.

In Saskatchewan two men deserve particular mention as instruments of this transformation of the corporate image – Ross Thatcher, son of a Moose Jaw hardware merchant, and Thomas Ware, who succeeded his father as head of International Minerals and Chemical (IMC).[49]

The difference between the relatively modest heritage of Ross Thatcher and the imposing wealth and status of Peter Lougheed's forebears summarizes an essential difference between the indigenous business communities of the two provinces. With few exceptions there has been little substantial accumulation of capital by members of the indigenous Saskatchewan business community. It has comprised owners and managers of small wholesale, retail and service firms, of small market-oriented manufacturing establishments (e.g. brewers, bakers, printers) and self-employed professionals. Farm consolidation after World War II increased the inequality of rural income and wealth distribution. Small and average farmers continued to share work conditions and income levels comparable to those of an urban worker, but larger well-capitalized farmers, regularly employing farm labour, came increasingly to define themselves as part of this business community, and to dissociate themselves from left populist institutions such as the Farmers' Union and the CCF-NDP.

After receiving a Bachelor of Commerce degree from Queen's University, Ross Thatcher returned to Moose Jaw and expanded the family hardware business into a modest chain of four outlets. Despite his class background Thatcher in the 1940s supported the CCF, and in 1945 won election as a CCF Member of Parliament. In the decade that followed, however, he became dismayed at the anti-Americanism of "dogmatic" socialists, appalled by what he deemed the CCF's excessive enthusiasm for welfare state programs and big government, and disillusioned by Saskatchewan's experiments with public enterprise. In 1955 he left the CCF caucus, initially to sit as an independent. By the time he crossed the floor and joined the Liberals he had developed a fervent faith in the virtues of the private entrepreneur and the vices of the bungling socialist bureaucrat: "[the CCF] usually takes some teacher or preacher or someone who knows nothing about business and puts him in charge of an enterprise. ... the CCF can't sell nuts to chimps."[50] "There's nothing wrong with socialism," he was wont to say, "except it doesn't work."

The CCF was morally outraged; Douglas challenged the renegade to a public debate on the merits of public enterprise. The debate finally took place in the small town of Mossbank during Thatcher's attempt to secure re-election as a Liberal in the 1957 federal election. With contradictory biblical expectations over 900 people packed the town hall in this community of 700, and additional hundreds, unable to enter the overflowing hall, listened to the debate on their car radios. Some came expecting Douglas, one of the most skilled public orators of his generation, to humble this Judas from Moose Jaw; others hoped for David to smite the socialist Goliath. The entire province followed the battle as Douglas defended the CCF crown ventures and Thatcher attacked. "The crown corporation program," Thatcher concluded, "has bogged down in a morass of bungling, red tape and inefficiency and has demonstrated the futility of socialism."[51] Who won? Assessments were highly partisan, but even the CCF had to admit that Thatcher had proved the equal of Douglas in his command of political rhetoric. Thatcher lost his seat in Parliament to the CCF, but he won the respect of the provincial business community. It was delighted to discover a man who could articulate its political frustrations with such oratorical skill.

These frustrations were considerable. As with the Nonpartisan League in North Dakota, many CCF policies affected not "big business," the CCF's nominal target, but the local business community. The latter strongly resented the CCF's favourable treatment of co-operatives and provincial experiments in crown corporations that curtailed its freedom of action (e.g. constraints on private sawmill operators imposed by the Timber Board). The CCF's progressive labour legislation raised labour costs and abetted unionization, and its pioneering of welfare state reforms increased per capita taxes relative to other provinces and thus, it was argued, discouraged private investment in Saskatchewan.

After losing office in 1944 the Liberals went through three leaders – defeated Premier Patterson, Walter Tucker, and the gentlemanly but ineffectual Hammy McDonald – before choosing Ross Thatcher as leader in 1959. As we discussed in the conclusion to Chapter Six, the CCF had replaced the Liberals in the eyes of most farm and labour leaders as the legitimate brokerage party of the province, and the Liberals' inner councils after 1944 were more than ever dominated by businessmen and professionals. After four successive electoral defeats from 1944 to 1956 the party was desperate for revitalization, and quite willing to accept a conservative ideologue who distinguished himself as sharply from "left-wing" federal Liberals as he did from his former colleagues in the CCF. Thatcher brought to the Liberals the effective style of grass roots political organization he had learned within the CCF. In 1960 he overcame a concerted CCF attempt to deny him a seat in the legislature, and took his place as Leader of the Opposition. As the potash boom took off after 1962, many expected potash to do for Saskatchewan what oil had done for Alberta. In a political environment expecting bountiful prosperity from large corporate investments in potash, Thatcher's laissez-faire ideology flourished; it corresponded far better to contemporary expectations than the CCF's faded populism.

For the five years following 1962 a combination of strong export demand for wheat, oil production, and the potash boom brought per capita Saskatchewan income close to the national average. CCF leaders emphasized current prosperity relative to the depths of the depression, but Thatcher campaigned tirelessly that relative to the other prairie provinces Saskatchewan's rate of growth of manufacturing jobs and of total population was a "poor third." "Liberals refuse to accept the proposition," Thatcher told the legislature shortly before the 1964 election, "that our slow growth is caused by a lack of resources. We say it has been caused primarily by the theories, policies of this socialist government. ... Twenty years ago the CCF-NDP claimed that socially owned crown corporations were the answer to the industrial program. They tried to produce dozens of products in their own factories and mills. I wish I had time to go into the long and sad history of the crown corporation fiasco."[52] Thatcher concluded with a passionate statement of "a few personal views":

I am opposed to socialism and all that it stands for, because I think, given time, socialism erodes and destroys man's initiative and independence. I believe that a greater investment of capital in Saskatchewan is the one vital step towards the achievement of virtually every economic and social goal which we hold dear. I believe that you cannot make a nation or a province strong, united or productive, by fermenting [sic] class hatred. I believe in the dignity of labour and I support its reasonable and legitimate aspirations, but I do not believe that government is helping the wage earner, by trying to undermine the people who pay the wages.[53]

Paradoxically, despite its popular success, "medicare"[54] aided Thatcher in his crusade to defeat socialism. In 1962 the CCF introduced a universal medical care insurance program which covered all physician services and to which all provincial residents were required to subscribe. Independent of the government but inspired by the prevailing politics of health reform, there simultaneously blossomed a large number of co-operatively organized community clinics (most have since died but some, including the large Saskatoon clinic, have survived). From the business perspective medicare was an unwarranted infringement by the CCF and its allies in the co-operative movement upon the freedom of a sizeable segment of the provincial business community – namely the province's seven hundred doctors. When in July 1962 the doctors organized a withdrawal of services, in effect a strike, to oppose medicare, local businessmen gave them unqualified support. After three weeks the government and doctors negotiated a settlement in which the latter accepted the government's right to implement a universal insurance plan. The government made several administrative concessions and implicitly agreed that in no way would it abet community clinics, but seemingly it had won; the plan itself proved too popular for the Liberals to oppose in principle. But medicare galvanized the business community to unite behind the provincial Liberals. Although the Conservatives under Diefenbaker swept every federal seat in the province in 1963, they won only one in the provincial election of 1964; the Social Credit vote collapsed and it won no seats. The CCF vote remained unchanged from 1960, but consolidation behind the Liberals made Ross Thatcher premier, and ended twenty years of CCF rule.[55]

Thatcher was capable of brokerage politics. Ideologically he opposed the extent of the CCF's welfare state, but realizing its supporters far outnumbered its critics, he made few moves to curtail it. But his politics transcended political pragmatism. No orthodox Liberal would have enacted such tough back-to-work legislation as his Essential Services Act which effectively alienated all organized labour. He sold several crown corporations; dozens of senior civil servants suspected of

CCF sympathies he dismissed or forced to resign. His style of administration was autocratic, and he was personally responsible for virtually all substantial policy initiatives within his government. Most, but not all, of these initiatives concerned the furthering of private investment. (Among the exceptions was the creation of a ministry responsible for Indian and Métis affairs. Albeit his concern was paternalistic, under Thatcher native problems received more attention than they had since the CCF's first term.)

The Liberals' first term coincided with the height of the potash boom which in the short run justified Thatcher's faith that prosperity depended upon large dynamic corporate entrepreneurs. Representative of the class of entrepreneurs Thatcher cultivated was an American, Thomas Ware. His father, a self-made man, had risen to become president of International Minerals and Chemical, and built it into the world's largest supplier of agricultural fertilizers. Thomas Ware characterized the "bullish" corporate expectations of the decade. Upon succeeding his father, he launched new investments in all three basic fertilizer ingredients – a phosphate mine in Senegal, a fertilizer plant in India, a second potash mine in Saskatchewan, plus others. He envisioned the fertilizer industry, and par excellence his own company, fulfilling a mission to increase the world food supply. Speaking in Saskatoon at the 1965 Saskatchewan Potash Show, Ware compared potash to "a great new bridge over which we may reach out to the have-not areas, and help them across the ocean of human want which separates the world." Appealing to the less altruistic interests of his audience, he promised: "Nothing but growth lies ahead ... Saskatchewan can become the potash center of the world, producing as much as twelve million tons a year by 1975. ... It is not unreasonable to predict that investment by 1975 in new potash facilities can run to $750 million, employing 7,000 people. ... What an extraordinary opportunity exists for this Province!"[56] (His prediction of capital investment was remarkably accurate, but his production and employment estimates for 1975 were approximately double actual values.)

Speaking at the same conference Thatcher stressed the responsibility of private entrepreneurs to help him discredit socialism: "We are carrying out in Saskatchewan what I like to think is an 'Experiment in Private Enterprise'. It is our task to prove in the next few years that the private enterprise system can do more for our people than socialism." Thatcher had no qualms about the nationality of the entrepreneurs he was cultivating: "I believe, as I have said before, that the only thing wrong with American investment from Saskatchewan's viewpoint is that in the past we haven't been getting enough of it."[57]

Bust – Collapse of the "New Saskatchewan"

Ross Thatcher sought re-election in 1967. It was an opportune moment – just before the end of the potash investment boom, and at the peak of a cycle in farm income. In 1966 the volume of provincial oil production reached what was to be its global peak; thereafter it entered into an inexorable decline that, barring new discoveries or major investment in enhanced recovery, will continue. The election was esssential, Thatcher claimed, to assure potential investors of a favourable political climate that would continue to encourage private enterprise.[58]

From Joe Phelps to Ross Thatcher, Saskatchewan's political pendulum had completed as wide an arc as was feasible in the constricted Canadian institutional environment. Thatcher evoked the contemporary ethos with the slogan of the "New Saskatchewan" – the creation of an allegedly mutually advantageous accord among farm, labour, local business, and external corporate capital. Liberals emphasized the rapid growth of resource revenues, modest gains in manufacturing, and the fact that the value of non-agricultural production had finally surpassed that of agriculture. Besides potash investment Thatcher could point to the successful negotiation of a pulp mill for northern Saskatchewan. (See Chapter Five.) The CCF, Thatcher argued, was no longer a legitimate representative of farmers and workers but, since reorganizing as the NDP, had become the tool of "big labour." Sensitive to such attacks the Saskatchewan section of the NDP continued to campaign under the name "CCF". (From the NDP's formation in 1961 until November 1967, the Saskatchewan section had the cumbersome official title "Co-operative Commonwealth Federation, Saskatchewan Section of the New Democratic Party." After 1967 it finally accepted the name of the national party.) The CCF campaigned defensively, defending its record in office as if still the governing party, and far from launching a frontal attack on the "New Saskatchewan," it claimed credit for the central feature – potash. All but two of the companies active in 1967, claimed the CCF, had been in some stage of exploration or development before the Liberals took office.[59] The Liberals won as predicted, but the CCF reinforced its position as the major opposition party. The Liberals and CCF both increased their popular vote, attracting roughly equal shares of the disaffected Conservative voters who abandoned that party in the aftermath of Diefenbaker's defeat as national leader.[60]

After 1967 came the bust. Virtually all the assumptions upon which the potash boom and the "New Saskatchewan" had been based proved ephemeral. The effect of a new agricultural depression demonstrated the continued provincial dependence upon that sector. From a peak of $489 million in 1967, realized net farm income fell to a trough of $202 million by 1969. Average per capita income fell from 93 per cent of the national average in 1966 to 72 per cent four years later.[61] Potash was conceived as a means of economic diversification for the province, but the cycles of potash demand roughly overlap those in cereals. Thus development of potash served to amplify the intensity for the provincial economy of cycles in agricultural demand. It was not coincidental that the potash boom came to an abrupt halt in 1967 as the international market for wheat and other cereals collapsed; nor that the surge in international demand for cereals after 1972 led to a rapid recovery of potash markets.

The most illusory of the bases underlying the fertilizer boom in general, and potash in particular, was the projection of steady exponential growth in demand. The budgetary costs of the Vietnam War curtailed United States foreign aid expenditures on fertilizers. The average annual growth rate in North American potash consumption, 10 per cent for the five years prior to 1967, fell below 4 per cent for the next five years.[62] (What may appear as small changes in annual growth rates imply large changes in demand projections. For example, had North American potash demand continued to grow at 10 per cent annually during the decade after 1967, 1977 consumption would have been nearly twice its actual level – a difference equal to the full capacity of five average Saskatchewan mines.) With the decline in growth brought on by widespread agricultural depression those companies still at the exploration stage promptly abandoned their projects, but those with mines under construction had, quite literally, "sunk" so much capital that it was more profitable to complete than to halt construction. When all construction was complete in 1970, Saskatchewan's annual capacity, at 8.3 million tons, equalled *twice* the current level of North American consumption. The fertilizer boom had generated such optimistic expectations that additional potash investment in conventional mines, in a solution mine, and in brine recovery occurred during the decade in the United States. The operating costs of a typical American mine were higher than in Saskatchewan and the reserve base far inferior, but American capacity nonetheless grew, contradicting earlier expectations of its proximate decline. The combined Canadian and American capacity was nearly *three* times current North American consumption. Offshore sales (i.e. sales to countries beyond North America) could absorb some production, but when the Saskatchewan government belatedly in 1968 undertook its first serious independent study of supply and demand in potash markets, it came to the depressing conclusion that world capacity would exceed demand until 1976.[63] The most acute problem of overcapacity would be in North America, due to the massive investments in the province of Saskatchewan.

The essential economic argument, that both government and industry had ignored during the years of rapid demand growth, was the relationship between demand for potash and that for the crops to which fertilizers are applied. The stronger is the demand for fertilized crops, the more acres are seeded to them, the higher the fertilizer demand. Furthermore, increased applications of fertilizer induce progressively smaller increments in yield, until beyond some point the cost of additional fertilizer exceeds the value to the farmer of any additional yield. Once again the stronger is the demand for fertilized crops, the higher their market price, the higher is the optimum level of fertilizer application. Conversely the weaker the demand, the lower the level of crop production and prices, the lower the fertilizer demand. Admittedly many other variables also enter into potash demand – its price (although relatively insensitive to price, the decline in 1975 demand is in part due to previous exorbitant price increases), the price of other fertilizer ingredients, diffuse factors such as knowledge among farmers of the potential of fertilizers, and random events (e.g. a wet spring that can prevent farmers from realizing intended fertilizer applications).

Purely random events could obviously not be predicted, but after sixty years of experience with wheat as an export staple it is difficult to excuse the failure of all public authorities in Saskatchewan to take into account the significance of long and pronounced cycles in markets for agricultural commodities. For this failure the CCF was as responsible as the Liberals, for as late as the 1967 election its leaders made no criticism of the risks for Saskatchewan of yet another overextended staple industry; they merely attempted to claim credit for the boom. The only official voice of caution was in the federal Department of Mines which as early as 1965 warned that "[s]uch rapid development of a major industry cannot be justified on the basis of past potash consumption trends."[64] But who was to be believed – a dour Ottawa civil servant or an ebullient corporate head who promised "nothing but growth lies ahead"?

The economically efficient solution to the problem of excess capacity was to close the high-cost New Mexico mines and expand Saskatchewan production. After 1965 the large bi- or multinational producers with mines in both countries decided to do precisely that. From 1966 to 1968 American potash production declined by roughly 20 per cent.[65] The 1968 Saskatchewan government study, to which we referred above, accordingly recommended against prorationing on grounds it would delay the transfer of production from New Mexico. Its authors were also influenced by the opposition to prorationing of the major American fertilizer companies active in the province: "Most of the companies involved in Saskatchewan have long been established in the fertilizer business. Most of these producers are unyielding proponents of the private enterprise system and consider prorationing a negation of that system."[66] Such a conclusion was naive, but it did reflect contemporary thinking by established producers who rejected the idea when broached to them by Thatcher.

By 1969 the industry had further deteriorated. The combination of stagnant markets, new producers, and large debt burdens on new mines, sharply reduced profitability throughout the fertilizer industry. There occurred a series of mergers, sale of assets at prices below cost, withdrawal of companies from the industry, and firing of senior executives. As punishment for his optimism Thomas Ware suffered the ignominy of being deposed in an internal corporate coup. In an industry with heavy fixed costs there exist strong pressures on individual firms to attempt to maintain full capacity production by price cutting. During the stable years prior to 1962 the New Mexico producers had informally policed one another and maintained prices yielding handsome average returns on equity, but the presence of new entrants and the magnitude of overcapacity shattered the long-standing informal price control mechanism and, after 1965, prices fell precipitously as companies underbid one another. By 1969 potash was selling at only half its peak level in 1965, at prices scarcely sufficient – at least for New Mexico producers – to cover operating costs.

Elsewhere (in Chapter Seven) we have discussed the inadequacy of any theory that treats the prairies as a single-class, homogeneous hinterland. Analogously the political manoeuvres to determine who would bear the costs of the unwarranted excess investment in potash mines indicate the inadequacy of ascribing uniform interests to the various actors in the metropolitan country. The metropolis, like the hinterland, contains heterogeneous and sharply divergent interests. As early as 1967 an alliance of New Mexico interests – producers without Saskatchewan mines, the state governor and a congressional contingent representing sundry local interests, and the United Steelworkers representing the miners whose jobs were threatened – formed to oppose the transfer of production to Saskatchewan. In 1967 they initiated proceedings under the United States Antidumping Act alleging that Canadian and European potash was being dumped in the United States. (To dump is to practise price discrimination – to sell a product in an export market at a price below that charged in the domestic market. The Act provides for the imposition of dumping duties, a form of tariff, to protect a domestic industry in the event that (1) the Treasury Department determines dumping to have occurred, and (2) the Tariff Commission determines such dumping has materially injured a domestic industry.) In the following two years New Mexico congressmen, led by the state's senior senator, Joseph Montoya, introduced three separate bills designed to impose tariffs or quotas on foreign potash.[67] Political events reached a climax in the autumn of 1969, after the Treasury Department declared dumping had occurred and the Tariff Commission began hearings to determine the extent of damage to the American industry and whether dumping duties should be imposed.

The imposition of dumping duties or other forms of tariff was opposed by a counter-alliance – American farm organizations whose members had profited from low fertilizer prices, political representatives from large consuming states such as Illinois' Senator Percy, and producers with Saskatchewan mines. "The Antidumping Act should not be used," argued one representative leader of a farm co-operative, "as a substitute tariff wall to protect an uneconomic industry."[68] The margins of dumping by European producers on exports to North America were large and undeniable, but the Europeans accounted for only a small market share. On the large Canadian exports, argued the Saskatchewan producers, any dumping had been coincidental and the margin small – a symptom of rapidly falling prices in a chaotic market and not of intentional price discrimination. Injury to the American industry was due to North American overcapacity and its comparative disadvantage relative to Saskatchewan, not to dumping. Finally, the Saskatchewan producers argued that at the time of alleged dumping most Canadian production had been by American companies with American mines, and therefore any injury due to dumping was self-inflicted – by American companies upon themselves – and the industry should not qualify for protection under the Antidumping Act.

In November 1969 a majority of the Commission concluded that dumping from Canada and Europe had materially injured the domestic industry and recommended imposition of dumping duties. The majority dismissed the self-inflicted injury argument: "Such protected interests include not just the interests of the stockholders of the multinational corporations involved, but the interests of the workers in the U.S. plants as well."[69] So far so good, but the majority also dismissed with virtually no analysis the argument that injury to the domestic industry was due to North American overcapacity and its comparative disadvantage. The majority's position was sufficiently weak to prompt a dissenting minority statement: "dumping margins [on imports from Canada] in 1967 and 1968 were small ... and sporadic. In fact these years were marked by such instability of delivered purchase prices that dumping margins frequently had to be recomputed several times each day. Such unsettled market conditions make the concept of 'fair value' very difficult to apply – both on the part of producers seeking to avoid an equalizing dumping duty and on the part of enforcers seeking to determine whether a law has been violated."[70] It seems reasonable to conclude that the Tariff Commission was influenced as much by the New Mexico lobby as by economic argument.

The series of political measures initiated in Washington provided the New Mexico lobby with bargaining power to force the Saskatchewan producers to accommodate. The goal was protection; the means were secondary. If Saskatchewan producers had an alternative to tariffs, New Mexico interests were amenable to change tactics. The compromise that rapidly emerged was a prorationing system over Saskatchewan production to be administered by the provincial government. For Saskatchewan producers prorationing had distinct advantages over tariffs. It avoided the siphoning of revenue to the U.S. treasury, and would be administered by a compliant regional government, as opposed to the massive unpredictable Washington bureaucracy. The companies were fearful, with good reason given later events (see Chapter Ten), that any overt moves on their part to promote prorationing would be perceived by the Antitrust Division of the U.S. Justice Department as a conspiracy in restraint of trade, and accordingly virtually all public statements and deeds leading up to the imposition of prorationing were those of Saskatchewan and New Mexico politicians; the corporate role remains shrouded in secrecy. Nonetheless it is certain that Saskatchewan producers did privately approach the provincial government to suggest that the latter intervene to regulate production and prices, and two Saskatchewan producers (IMC and Duval) prepared draft plans.[71]

There was much coming and going in the fall of 1969 among politicians, senior bureaucrats, and corporate executives.[72] In September Ross Thatcher flew to Washington, to lobby against tariffs and also to meet privately with senior officials of IMC and Duval on the subject of prorationing. He returned to Regina convinced of the need for urgent action to avoid imposition of potash tariffs, but was unsure whether the province had the requisite jurisdiction. Shortly thereafter a delegation of Ottawa bureaucrats arrived in Regina to discuss the problems of the industry; they offered nothing tangible and warned that prorationing could well infringe federal jurisdiction over interprovincial trade and commerce. Early in October American potash executives flew to Regina to discuss options. Thatcher was worried that any program to restrict Saskatchewan production would encourage American and European producers to expand, and so he and several of his cabinet flew to Sante Fe, the capital of New Mexico – aboard a corporate jet owned by Pennzoil United, the parent company of Duval – to meet with Governor Cargo and representatives of New Mexico producers. Cargo was willing to abandon the strategy of protection via tariffs or dumping duties, and to support a prorationing system. The New Mexico government lacked jurisdiction to regulate production, but he could secure assurances not to expand from local producers and could monitor the companies to guarantee compliance. After the meeting Cargo urged that details be kept confidential and, to conceal the presence of the corporate representatives from the press, ushered them out a back door. The following week Cargo and his entourage flew up to Regina – on the Pennzoil plane – for a final meeting with Thatcher. Cargo provided Thatcher with the appropriate assurances from all New Mexico producers. In a joint press conference on October 18, 1969 the two politicians announced imposition of prorationing, and a minimum price of $33.75 (Canadian) per ton, 70 per cent above the current price. "Seldom in the economic annals of Canada," concluded Thatcher, "have we seen such responsible companies get in such an economic mess. Lack of co-operation and planning have brought major companies to the brink of disaster."[73] Cargo undertook to work against the imposition of tariffs or dumping duties. Despite the Tariff Commission's ruling a month later, duties were never imposed, and none of the tariff bills submitted to Congress were ever enacted.

Constitutionality of the system remained a potential problem, sufficiently worrisome to prompt Thatcher to fly to Ottawa to consult with Prime Minister Trudeau. "I am meeting with our Prime Minister ... ," Thatcher advised Cargo. "Unless he throws a monkey wrench into the situation I hope to announce our [potash prorationing] regulations on November 17 or 18."[74] The federal government was displeased but, it has been speculated, refrained from any intervention because it would be damaging to the electoral prospects of both the federal and provincial Liberals.[75]

Initially Saskatchewan mines were prorated on average to approximately one half of capacity; New Mexico production stabilized at roughly 80 per cent of capacity. The minimum regulated price, which promptly became the price at which all North American potash was sold, restored potash prices to the level prevailing ten years earlier. (According to a personal interview with ex-Governor Cargo in 1976, he and Thatcher determined the $33.75 minimum price on the basis of estimated average operating costs, royalties and depreciation, plus eighty cents per ton profit.) Very approximately the lower operating costs of Saskatchewan mines were offset by their higher per ton capital costs, inflated by prorationing which forced them to operate on average at only one half of capacity. As administered, quotas for individual

208

mines made some allowance for captive markets permitting therefore above-average quotas for the Noranda – CF Industries mine.

Conclusion

Who won in these complicated manoeuvres to prevent a competitive adjustment? (Had such an adjustment occurred, the largest low-cost mines would have run at full capacity, forcing the remainder to close down, either permanently or until market growth warranted reactivation. Bankruptcies, or sizeable capital losses in the case of divisions of larger corporations, could have been expected not only in New Mexico, but among certain Saskatchewan producers.) It would be a gross oversimplification to identify the winners as the American metropolis; the losers as the Saskatchewan hinterland. The unambiguous winner was the New Mexico lobby – an alliance of regional capital and labour – which succeeded in prolonging by probably two decades the life of its high-cost mines. The Saskatchewan producers lost inasmuch as they were forced to accommodate New Mexico production, but the minimum price permitted all new mines to earn at least a modest profit and forced farmers, via higher fertilizer prices, to bear the costs of irrational corporate decisions to overexpand. The new price prevented the latter from enjoying any benefits from the potentially lower-cost Saskatchewan reserves. Offshore consumers had more options, and one consequence of prorationing was a marked decline in offshore sales.

Relative to a competitive adjustment farmers lost – both those in the midwestern United States and Eastern Canada. So did Saskatchewan. A minor burden (except to those who bore it) was created in certain communities that experienced layoffs as the prorationing system reallocated production from established mines running at full capacity to the newest just commencing production. Ross Thatcher, and the CCF cabinet after 1948, had systematically denied the potential of conflict between the provincial interest and that of the resource companies invited to develop provincial oil and potash. Two decades later, the price of pursuing a passive rentier strategy, of abdicating any public entrepreneurial role over the rate of resource development, became evident. From a provincial perspective there were two rational strategies to have debated. Either the province collected limited rents, undercut New Mexico prices, and attempted to capture most of the latter's market; or, alternatively, it accepted a politically determined status as a large but residual supplier to the North American market and the prevailing price structure based on New Mexico costs and profit levels, and collected higher royalties per ton based on the difference in total unit costs between the two reserve basins. As we have seen, prorationing forced the province to accept the status of residual supplier, but without any of the advantages in terms of royalties. Given the inflated unit costs of large mines operating at half capacity, it could collect no more than nominal royalties.

Notes

1. See chap. 6, n. 33.
2. B. Sufrin, "Report on Fuel Policy," EAPB, WSL Minister of Education files G-19, November 1949, 5.
3. *Regina Leader-Post,* July 22, 1949.
4. The figures refer to proved ultimate recoverable reserves as defined by the Canadian Petroleum Association. The oil reserves quoted exclude the tar sands. *Statistical Handbook 1976* (Calgary: Canadian Petroleum Association).
5. "Ten Year Program of Petroleum Development," EAPB, WSL Minister of Education files G-19, December 1948; "Report on Fuel Policy," *op. cit.,* 5.
6. "Report on Fuel Policy," *op. cit.,* 25.
7. *Ibid.,* 1-2.
8. *Ibid.,* 27.
9. *Ibid.,* 33.
10. The Interstate Oil Compact Commission came into existence in 1935 as an instrument to realize market prorationing within the United States. Its major function has been to allocate quotas among oil producing states thereby controlling supply and maintaining a stable profitable price level. See Chapter Three, and B.V. Reed et al., "Preparing and Presenting a Conservation Board Hearing in Saskatchewan," *Alberta Law Review,* VII, 3 (1969), 417-28.
11. The original 1946 regulations had employed a checkerboard system which, in advance of any exploration permit being issued, designated random sections of the permit area as crown reserves. Crown reserves initially were set at 15 per cent of the total permit area, later raised to 25 per cent. This was a deviation from Alberta's practice by which the holder of an exploration permit could automatically take to lease any acreage under permit, subject to certain restrictions on the size of individual blocks, up to 50 per cent of the total permit area, the remainder becoming crown reserves. The oil industry objected to the checkerboard system and in 1951 Saskatchewan adopted Alberta's reserve allocation system. Given the small size of most Saskatchewan oil discoveries these new regulations usually permitted a company to lease out most of the area covering its discovery. See *Interim Report of the Oil Policy Committee on Government Policy for the Development of Crown Reserves,* TCD Premier 168, June 1953, 2-5.

12. "Memorandum on Study of Oil Development Policy," appendix to memo: Shoyama to chairman and members of EAPB, WSL Minister of Education files G-19, December 14, 1951.

13. When the committee, with access to the geological information generated by private exploration, attempted to estimate the discounted present value of particular crown reserves, uncertainty loomed so large that, for the example cited in its *Interim Report*, the upper limit of the estimate exceeded the lower limit by a ratio of six to one—and that after seven pages of calculations. With this range bids on a cash auction could be expected to exceed the lower limit, but on tracts demonstrating such uncertainty the discount rate applied by bidding firms would be high and bids correspondingly low. See *Interim Report of the Oil Policy Committee, op. cit.*, Part Two.

14. *Ibid.*, Summary, 3.

15. *Ibid.*, 22.

16. *Ibid.*, Summary, 3.

17. *Ibid.*, 23.

18. Quoted in Johnson, *op. cit.*, 505.

19. *Interim Report of the Oil Policy Committee, op. cit.*, 6.

20. *Saskatoon Star-Phoenix*, September 16, 1953.

21. Oil Policy Committee to Executive Council, Memo #1, WSL Minister of Education files G-19, December 21, 1953.

22. *Star-Phoenix*, March 6, 1954. By this farm-out agreement the co-operative paid all development costs plus standard royalties. Net income (gross income less operating costs and standard royalties) was divided between the government and co-operative as follows: the co-operative retained 85 per cent until it achieved payback of development costs; thereafter its share fell to 40 per cent. In total the government entered into four farm-out agreements, all with co-operatives, on a total of four and a half sections. See "Farm-Out Agreements," TCD Premier 383, June 12, 1961.

23. *Leader-Post*, March 8, 1954.

24. *Star-Phoenix*, editorial, March 9, 1954.

25. *Leader-Post*, March 9, 1954.

26. N.K. McKinnon (of Harris & Partners) to Douglas, TCD Premier 383, March 16, 1954.

27. Douglas to McKinnon, TCD Premier 383, March 19, 1954.

28. Shoyama to Hogg (deputy minister, Department of Mineral Resources [DMR]), WSL Minister of Education files G-19, February 8, 1955.

29. For geological and engineering information on the Saskatchewan potash industry see M.E. Holter, *The Middle Devonian Prairie Evaporite of Saskatchewan* (Regina: DMR, 1969), and "Potash in Saskatchewan" (Regina: DMR, 1973). The U.S. Bureau of Mines has estimated world potash reserves recoverable at 1974 prices to be 11 billion tons of which 45 per cent lies in Canada. Virtually all Canadian reserves are in Saskatchewan, but small reserves exist in New Brunswick. Other countries

possessing sizeable reserves (with percentage of total in parentheses) are: East Germany (25 per cent), West Germany (16 per cent), USSR (7 per cent), Israel and Jordan (2 per cent), USA (2 per cent), France (1 per cent), Spain (1 per cent). Small reserves exist in Britain, Congo (Brazzaville), Chile, Italy, Australia, and the People's Republic of China. Including reserves recoverable at higher prices (e.g. Saskatchewan potash recoverable by solution mining) world reserves are estimated to be 87 billion tons, of which 85 per cent lie in Canada. W.F. Keyes, "Potash," in *Mineral Facts and Problems*, 1975 edition (Washington: U.S. Bureau of Mines, 1976), 855-69.

30. "Tentative Terms of Agreement Between Private Industry and the Crown," attachment to minutes of potash committee, TCD Executive Assistant files 92, November 17, 1949.

31. On the details of proposals and counter-proposals by government and potential developers see numerous items in TCD Executive Assistant files 92, 1949-52.

32. "Potash Regulations," o.c. 2089/50.

33. Details of royalty negotiations are contained in documents attached to a memo: Hogg to T. Lee (executive assistant to Douglas), TCD Premier 181, July 6, 1953.

34. "Subsurface Mineral Regulations," o.c. 2276/53, s. 45 (1).

35. o.c. 2277/53. For details of the agreement and subsequent amendments see Brockelbank to Douglas, TCD Premier 181, October 27, 1961.

36. Phelps, foreword to "The Natural Resources of Saskatchewan," *op. cit.*

37. W. Davies (Acting Minister of Labour) to C.C. Williams (Minister of Labour), TCD Premier 181, April 18, 1961. This file contains extensive material on the conflict.

38. Brockelbank to Douglas, TCD Premier 181, April 28, 1961.

39. Brockelbank to Douglas, TCD Premier 181, October 27, 1961.

40. o.c. 2106/63.

41. The guarantee took the form of a series of bilateral agreements between the provincial government and the various producers. Details of most agreements are contained in the Statement of Claim filed by the potash companies, as plaintiffs, in *Duval et al. v. Government of Saskatchewan*, QB, No. 302, Regina, May 13, 1976.

42. W.E. Koepke, *Structure, Behaviour and Performance of the World Potash Industry*, MR 139 (Ottawa: Department of Energy, Mines and Resources, 1973), 31.

43. D.M. Ray, et al. (eds.), *Canadian Urban Trends*, I, *op. cit.*, 31-34.

44. The best source of historical and statistical information on the potash industry prior to 1971 is Koepke, *op. cit.* Good journalistic accounts of the potash boom and subsequent bust are to be had in R.J. Whalen, "IMC: The Miner Who Shook the Fertilizer Market," *Fortune*, March 1965, 108 ff., and T. O'Hanlon, "All that Fertilizer and No Place to Grow," *Fortune*, June 1, 1968, 92 ff.

45. For estimated unit production costs in New Mexico and Saskatchewan see Koepke, *op. cit.*, 14-22.

46. For American consumption and price data see respectively "Commercial Fertilizers: Consumption of Commercial Fertilizers, Primary Plant Nutrients, and Micronutrients," Statistical Bulletin 472 (Washington: U.S. Department of Agriculture, 1976), Table 1, 6, and Keyes, *op. cit.*, Table 10.

47. Koepke, *op. cit.*, 46. For time series of rate of return on equity for various potash companies, see Koepke, Tables A-10 to A-16.

48. "Potash: Challenge for Development" (Regina: DMR, 1976), 77-83.

49. For an account of Thomas Ware's career see the *Fortune* articles cited at n.44; for Ross Thatcher's the best source is Smith, *Prairie Liberalism, op. cit.*, chaps. 7 and 8.

50. Quoted in Smith, *op. cit.*, 275.

51. *Leader-Post*, May 19, 1957.

52. *Debates and Proceedings*, 6th Session of 14th Legislature, *op. cit.*, February 11, 1964, 41.

53. *Ibid.*, 51.

54. The best account of the "medicare" conflict in Saskatchewan is Badgley and Wolfe, *Doctors' Strike, op. cit.*

55. *Report of the Chief Electoral Officer: Eighteenth General Election 1975* (Regina: Chief Electoral Officer), Appendix VI, 113-15.

56. T.M. Ware, "Potash: Reward ... and Responsibility," in *Saskatchewan Potash Show Proceedings: Saskatoon 1965* (Regina: Department of Industry and Commerce), 15 and 17.

57. W.R. Thatcher, "Saskatchewan and World Hunger," in *ibid.*, 30 and 31.

58. *Leader-Post*, September 8, 1967.

59. Text of CCF television broadcast, WSL Leader of Opposition files 118 e, September 26, 1967.

60. *Report of the Chief Electoral Officer, op. cit.*, 113-15.

61. *Saskatchewan Economic Review 1977* (Regina: Saskatchewan Bureau of Statistics), Tables 21 and 39.

62. "Consumption of Commercial Fertilizers," *op. cit.*, Table 1, 6.

63. *World Supply and Demand for Potash and its Impact upon the Saskatchewan Economy* (Regina: DMR, 1968), chap. 5.

64. C.M. Bartley, "Potash," in *Canadian Minerals Yearbook 1964* (Ottawa: Department of Mines and Technical Surveys), 495.

65. E.A. Harre et al., *Fertilizer Trends 1976*, Bulletin Y-111 (Muscle Shoals, Alabama: National Fertilizer Development Center, Tennessee Valley Authority, 1977), 24.

66. *World Supply and Demand for Potash, op. cit.*, 68-69.

67. Koepke, *op. cit.*, 32.

68. *Star-Phoenix*, October 10, 1969.

69. "Potassium Chloride (Muriate of Potash) from Canada, France, and West Germany," TC Publication 303 (Washington: United States Tariff Commission, 1969), 23.

70. *Ibid.*, 30-31.

71. Considerable information became public in the course of the antitrust

case *U.S.A. v. Amax et al.* discussed in Chapter Ten. One piece of public evidence of the corporate initiative is an irate speech made by the Liberal Minister of Mineral Resources in early 1970 when potash companies blamed the government's new prorationing system for contemporary layoffs of miners in certain mines: "Our patience is wearing a bit thin with those who would weasel out of responsibility for unpopular decisions by attempting to make the government the scapegoat. ... I would remind the potash industry that the initial approaches for government measures were made by the producers themselves. It is evident to us that we have a sick potash industry in Saskatchewan and it is sick from self-inflicted wounds." *Globe and Mail* (Toronto), January 30, 1970.

72. For reports of these comings and goings see *Star-Phoenix*: September 17, 1969, October 10, 1969, October 18, 1969; *Leader-Post*: September 20, 1969, October 10, 1969; *Financial Post*, October 4, 1969; *Globe & Mail*, November 5, 1969.
73. *Globe and Mail*, October 18, 1969.
74. Quoted in Justice Disberry's decision in *Central Canada Potash Ltd. et al. v. Government of Saskatchewan et al.* (1975) 5 WWR, 260. Thatcher's reference is to "The Potash Conservation Regulations," o.c. 1733/69.
75. *Financial Post*, November 15, 1969.

CHAPTER 9
Empire Alberta:
The Province as Entrepreneur

But how long can it last? In my view, not very long; perhaps a decade at the most, unless we're able to put in place a more balanced economy for that inevitable day, Mr. Speaker, when oil and gas no longer provide such a large number of jobs, when production begins to decline, and resource revenue falls off. But it will not be easy to do so. There are going to be some failures and setbacks. It's not a place for timid people ... We can't rely on the federal bureaucrat or the establishment in Toronto to do it for us. For our objective means a fundamental change in the economy of Canada, a shift in the decision-making westward, and essentially to Alberta. Because of that, it will be vigorously opposed. ...

Peter Lougheed
speech in Alberta Legislature
October 13, 1976

The focus of this chapter is on the role of the provincial government as entrepreneur in regional capitalist development. Its themes are the role of the state in planning and promoting Alberta's economic growth since the advent of the Lougheed Conservatives to power in 1971 and the interplay between politics and business in the New West. Against the backdrop of the world energy crisis and the shift of power towards oil producers, the resources of an interventionist provincial government are being employed to nurture the development and defend the interests of an ascendant regional bourgeoisie. The purposes of this rising class are to strengthen its control over the Alberta economy, foster regional capital accumulation, reduce Alberta's dependence on external political and economic forces, and diversify the provincial economy out of its excessive reliance on oil and natural gas extraction.

The entrepreneurial role of the provincial government in creating and sustaining the conditions for successful regional accumulation has manifested itself in a variety of policy areas, and several of these are analysed later in the chapter. Here, in the interest of avoiding unnecessary misunderstanding about the general argument, we begin our discussion with four overriding generalizations concerning the methods and purposes of state intervention in Alberta in the 1970s. In the first place, except in circumstances of final resort, Alberta has eschewed public ownership and the creation of crown corporations as a mode of intervention, preferring to intervene through its unique quasi-state enterprises (such as the Alberta Energy Company) and through joint venture agreements with the private sector. With this has come an ideological emphasis on the nurturing of "people's capitalism" and more direct participation by Albertans and Alberta business in capital accumulation. In spite of this, the activism of the Lougheed government has occasionally given rise to conservative anxieties in a community where property rights and a hatred of socialism are virtually a secular religion.

Second, underlying the specific instances of state entrepreneurial activity in Alberta we can discern a relatively coherent development strategy which is best described as the provincial equivalent of economic nationalism – the ideological emblem of a rising middle class. Alberta's economic provincialism, with its emphasis on the use of the state to foster an indigenous industrial-technological core in the West, should be interpreted as the frustrated reaction of a hinterland elite to the unequal diffusions of industry, wealth, and power in the national political economy. The development strategy of the Lougheed government is to encourage local industrial processing of its energy and agricultural resources and, through its ownership of most of Canada's oil and natural gas, to negotiate a transfer of secondary industry, high-income jobs, and decision-making from central Canada to the West.

Third, it needs to be emphasized that the target against which this development strategy is primarily directed is central Canada. We are describing a classic struggle between a new rising capitalist class and an older entrenched bourgeoisie. The economic nationalists in power in Alberta have been in revolt since the early 1970s against what Peter Lougheed calls the "Toronto-Montreal establishment" and "its" federal government, and for the most part they see foreign capital and even foreign governments as potential allies. However, it is a serious error to conclude from this that the Lougheed government is merely an instrument of outside capital. The old alliance of interests and outlook between the major petroleum companies and the province has given way since 1973 to a much more fluid and ambivalent relationship. In part this has been a predictable consequence of Alberta's declining potential as an oil producing region; in part, the result of the province's aggressive pursuit of its own development plans.

Finally, it would be equally in error to suggest that the Lougheed government arrived in office with a fully articulated strategy of economic development and promptly set about implementing it. Some of Lougheed's ideas, as we have seen, can be traced back to his days in opposition in the 1960s. Others evolved as the Conservative government responded to the changing market conditions in world oil, and to policies of the federal government. Had the international energy crisis and the shift in oil markets from expectations of surplus to scarcity not occurred, Alberta's bargaining power and its ambitions would have been more limited than they have actually been. And had Ottawa not intervened in 1973-74 with its own heavy-handed resource policies, it seems improbable that any of the western producing provinces would have dared move as rapidly as they did, or that they would have risked a breach with the petroleum industry over the issue of rents. The western provinces naturally viewed the emerging seller's market in oil as an opportunity, but what above all else galvanized them into strong independent action was a political-constitutional threat to their jurisdiction. The provincial cabinets and bureaucracies of the West perceived Ottawa's resource policies as a fundamental attack on their own power, and they were forced to elaborate and implement defensive strategies in response.

World Crisis in Oil
When the Lougheed government took power in Alberta in the late summer of 1971, the international oil system was passing through a period of sudden transition from the conditions of surplus and low prices of the 1960s into a new era characterized by rapidly escalating prices and consumer concerns over the long term availability of petroleum supplies. The distribution of power in the world oil market was shifting from the multinational oil companies and the consuming countries toward the leading oil producers and exporters of the Third World, the Organization of Petroleum Exporting Countries (OPEC). This was to have a marked effect on the internal regional distribution of economic and political power in Canada as well. Although the full impact did not work its way into Canadian markets and federal-provincial relations until the traumatic autumn of 1973, oil was becoming a seller's market *extraordinaire.* Those who controlled the supply of this vital resource would henceforth be in a powerful bargaining position to dictate the terms of its future availability to energy consumers.[1]

The OPEC oil price revolution can conveniently be dated to the overthrow of King Idris of Libya in 1969 and the establishment of the militant regime of Colonel Khaddafi in that North African nation. During the 1960s Libya had become a significant oil exporter, and in 1970 Khaddafi's government successfully imposed new terms, involving higher posted prices and tax rates, on a group of independent and major American oil companies by threatening to curtail their production. It was immediately obvious that Libya's success would have to be generalized to the other members of OPEC. Meeting in Caracas in December 1970, the oil exporters agreed on a set of minimum terms and vowed concerted and simultaneous action by all member countries to force compliance.

In 1971, OPEC negotiated the so-called Teheran agreements with the international companies on higher prices and taxes, and new commitments were also made regarding government participation in the big concession-holding companies such as ARAMCO in Saudi Arabia. The new agreements were intended to provide at least five years of stability to the world oil market, but rising inflation in the West and successive devaluations of the American dollar wiped out much of OPEC's gain. Rapidly changing oil market conditions and the inflation in the prices of goods imported by the oil exporters created a situation between the companies and their host governments that became increasingly unfavourable to the latter. The *Middle East Economic Survey* calculated in September 1973, that the "notional profit split on realized prices between governments and companies may have changed from 80-20 in the governments' favor at the time of the Teheran agreement to around 64-36 in the governments' favor now."

Negotiations with the companies to revise the 1971 settlement opened in Vienna on October 8, 1973, two days after the outbreak of war in the Middle East. Later that month, OPEC unilaterally announced new posted prices, representing a 70 per cent increase in "reference" Arabian light crude (from $3.01 to $5.12 a barrel) and raising the government "take" from $1.77 to $3.05 a barrel. The output and destination restrictions imposed in late October by the Arab members of OPEC in support of their war against Israel further narrowed the market for oil, and in the chaotic weeks that followed some Iranian and Nigerian oil was auctioned at $17 and $20 a barrel! In December of 1973 some OPEC members, led by the Iranians, pushed for a new posted price of $16 or $17 a barrel, but Saudi Arabia, OPEC's leading producer, resisted, and a compromise was reached on a new posted price of $11.65 a barrel for Arabian light, yielding a government take of $7 a barrel. The Shah of Iran, announcing this bombshell to the world, noted that the price of oil would henceforth reflect the cost of the nearest competing substitutes – oil from tar sands, shale or coal liquefaction. "We have chosen the minimum necessary to establish equivalence with other comparable energy sources," the Shah explained.

OPEC's behaviour was in striking contrast to the historical performance of Third World petroleum exporters. Before Libya moved in 1970, unilateral action by individual oil producers had been constrained by fear that the international companies would cut back their investments and production in the offending nation, making it up in another part of the world. This fear was based on long experience in dealing with the "seven sisters," the handful of vertically integrated oil companies who dominated the international petroleum market for decades. At an early state in their corporate evolution the companies had learned that it could be fatal strategy to tie up all their overseas production in a single oil-exporting nation. This would leave them far too exposed to political pressure and the threat of nationalization. As insurance against expropriation and leverage in bargaining with oil producers, the companies learned that it was prudent to have a well-diversified supply of crude reserves. Surplus capacity based on diversified reserves permitted the companies, who typically bargained as a cartel, to play off individual producers one against the other and to bid down the terms for development – provided, of course, the producers themselves were not organized into a common bargaining front. This strategy paid off in the early 1950s when the cartel of international companies won a bitter struggle against the Mossadegh regime in Iran over the nationalization of British Petroleum. By increasing production in Kuwait and Venezuela, the companies were able to boycott Iran's nationalized oil and, with some friendly assistance from the American intelligence community, the offending Mossadegh was overthrown – and replaced by the re-instated Shah!

It was precisely in response to this weak and ineffective bargaining position that a few of the leading oil exporters, led by Venezuela, formed OPEC in 1960. But OPEC's initial tactics and its record of achievement in its first decade of existence were decidedly modest: real oil prices (adjusted for inflation) continued slowly to decline; the companies dominated negotiations with the producers, and OPEC's demands went largely unnoticed among industrialized consumers. Writing in the late 1960s about the place of the oil-exporting countries in international economic relations, Michael Tanzer remarked that "OPEC increasingly looks like an organization which is of more long-run value to the oil companies than to the oil-exporting countries." OPEC, Tanzer added, "has thus far utilized moderate methods and obtained only marginal gains. ... The danger for it, and for the international oil companies, is that OPEC will appear ultimately impotent and lose all influence."[2] In light of subsequent events, this was less than prophetic.

Why did Colonel Khaddafi and the Shah succeed in the Seventies where Mossadegh had failed in the Fifties? In part because international political circumstances had changed but, on a much more fundamental level, because the economics of world petroleum were ripe for political exploitation by 1970. Major changes in the international energy economy underlay OPEC's new bargaining power and ensured that this power would be enduring. On the demand side, these included the enormous postwar growth in aggregate energy consumption and the shift of the industrialized capitalist bloc from coal to oil-fired economies. On the supply side, additions of new oil reserves began to fall below demand levels in the late 1960s, while alternative energy resources have involved higher costs and longer development times than initially expected. OPEC's new power was a function of expectations of oil scarcity over the longer term, not merely the outcome of a temporary convergence of favourable economic and political circumstances.

The long economic boom of the capitalist West in the years following World War II was fired by cheap and apparently limitless supplies of hydrocarbons. The Cold War and the rapid recoveries of Western Europe and Japan encouraged the philosophy that resources existed to fuel industrial growth: the prevailing definition of progress as consumption discouraged the emergence of a conservationist ethic which might have triggered the alarm. Given the obsession with military security that dominated official thinking throughout the Cold War, surprisingly little attention appears to have been given to the wider political and strategic implications of the West's changing energy habit. By the 1960s the annual growth rate in world energy consumption was 6 per cent, and this rapidly escalating demand was essentially met by the accelerated depletion of the world's most accessible and least costly oil reserves. In the two decades before the energy crisis of the seventies, the world's consumption of oil grew at an annual rate of 7.6 per cent. Everywhere in the world, oil increased its share of the total energy market and displaced coal as the principal fuel. Oil and natural gas, combined, supplied 33 per cent of global energy in 1940, but by 1974 this figure had grown to 67 per cent. Over the same brief period the share of coal in the total energy market declined sharply from 75 to 31 per cent. Thanks in large part to the aggressive marketing strategies of the international oil companies (who enjoyed the official backing of successive American administrations), Japan and Western Europe made particularly rapid transitions from coal to oil. The political and strategic effects of this fundamental reshaping of the global energy economy were profound. The shift from coal to oil entailed a considerable erosion of the industrialized West's self-sufficiency in energy supply and a growing reliance on foreign oil – particularly oil from the giant fields of the Middle East and North Africa. Western Europe's dependence on North African oil following the 1967 Middle East war and the closure of the Suez Canal was Colonel Khaddafi's trump. Libya's threat to cut production of its highly desirable crudes was the first determined bid by the oil exporters to exploit this obvious source of bargaining leverage.

American energy supply and demand further opened the way to OPEC's successful exploitation of oil power in the 1970s. The crucial variable in the position of the United States was not so much a sharp movement to oil and gas – these had emerged as important energy sources in the U.S. earlier in the century – as it was the sudden acceleration in demand for oil in the late 1960s and the growth in the percentage of oil imported from Eastern Hemisphere sources. The essence of the problem was that the United States' demand for energy grew much faster than projected in the late 1960s (the growth rate in demand for gasoline was the prime culprit), while indigenous energy output fell increasingly behind. A bit earlier than Canada, the United States experienced a dramatic falling-off of annual gross-reserve additions of oil and thus of the country's share of world reserves, and a steady attrition of its share of world oil production. While the U.S. accounted for approximately one fifth of non-Communist oil reserves in the mid-1950s, its share of "free world" reserve additions during the next decade and a half was just 2.5 per cent. By the 1970s some 70 per cent of the world's known recoverable oil reserves was located in the Middle East, most of it in a handful of supergiant fields, each with more than five billion barrels recoverable.

The United States is still far more self-sufficient in energy than its major capitalist rivals. As of 1972, the percentage of total energy production provided by indigenous output was: United States, 85 per cent; Western Europe, 41 per cent; Japan, 13 per cent. Even so, after 1968 American oil imports began to rise steadily and were running at close to five million barrels a day (or 35 per cent of U.S. oil demand) on the outbreak of the 1973 Yom Kippur war. Of notable concern to American policy makers was the growing inability of Canada and Venezuela, America's traditional suppliers, to meet the rising demand. An increasing proportion of the new oil imports were coming from the Middle East. This implied, of course, a growing dependence on Arab oil, an unsettling prospect in light of existing U.S. political and strategic interests in the eastern Mediterranean, the Middle East and in the Gulf region. The American supply picture was further muddied by protracted delays in bringing Prudhoe Bay oil onstream, constraints on the use of coal, lags in the completion of nuclear power plants, and, in general, the long lead times and very high costs of bringing alternative energy sources into production. The growing reliance of the United States on imports from the oil fields of the Eastern Hemisphere coincided with, and clearly contributed to, the enhanced bargaining power of the oil exporters.

Expressed in overly simplified terms, the essence of the world energy crisis has been that reserve additions began to fall behind demand in 1967. In that year the demand curve for oil overtook the five-year moving average of discovery of large new fields. More than any other single factor, this event triggered the movement from a buyer's to a seller's market, and from expectations of unconstrained exponential growth of oil consumption to expectations of exhaustion of conventional oil reserves within one to two generations. The event also signalled a shift in geopolitical power towards the Middle East.

What gives OPEC its economic and political muscle is the spectre of long-term scarcity.[3] While the world is not facing imminent shortage of oil, there *is* compelling evidence that additions of new oil reserves have now fallen irretrievably behind the level of demand and that alternative energy resources – oil from nonconventional sources, coal, nuclear or renewable sources – may not come onstream rapidly enough to replace declining conventional production. Much, of course, depends upon the future growth rate in demand and whether or not higher prices and government policies will make a lasting impression on the energy consumption patterns of the industrialized countries. Failing a relatively drastic reduction in the rate of demand growth, it seems very probable that these countries will face adjustments even more painful than those of the 1970s. For the short- to mid-term, the world will remain largely a fossil-fuel economy, and crude oil could continue to be in a state of temporary surplus, particularly if recent recessionary conditions persist into the 1980s. For the longer run, however, a reasonable appreciation of the complex energy scarcity issue must be one of qualified pessimism. Minimally, this pessimistic perspective leads us to conclude that the high present world oil prices accurately reflect the cost and availability of alternative energy supplies, that real oil prices are unlikely to fall, and that OPEC's strong bargaining position is likely to be enduring. If this brave assessment, which is advanced subject to the usual ceteris paribus qualification, is correct, then it follows that the recent shift of economic and political power to the energy-producing provinces of western Canada is likewise unlikely to be a temporary phenomenon, and that Alberta in particular should be in a position of considerable strength to

222

negotiate a further transfer of wealth, decision-making, and power to the West in the 1980s.

Alberta: the Politics of Oil and Gas

After American oil production peaked in 1970, U.S. oil imports from Alberta began to rise dramatically. Between 1970 and 1973 Canadian oil exports to the United States increased from 659,000 to 1.1 million barrels a day before the Canadian government moved to control exports in March of 1973. Alberta's production of crude and petroleum products rose from 1967 levels of just 771,000 to 1.8 million barrels a day in 1973. Within the context of the abrupt changes in world prices discussed above, several upward adjustments were made to Alberta oil prices from 1970 to 1973 such that, by the spring of 1973, equality had been established between Canadian and United States delivered prices at Chicago. Canadian oil prices increased by a total of 95¢ a barrel in four successive escalations in 1972 and 1973 before the federal government moved, in September 1973, to freeze prices and to impose a tax on oil exported to the United States.

With the election of new provincial governments in British Columbia, Alberta, and Saskatchewan in 1971 and 1972, and the growing perception of a seller's market in energy, the producing provinces, led by Alberta, moved to increase their capture of oil and gas rents. Well before the tax fights with Ottawa of 1973-74, Alberta had taken several major initiatives on the energy front in order to improve its revenue position, to halt the decline in exploratory activity in the province and to beef up its falling reserves/annual production ratio. Annual crude oil production in Alberta had exceeded annual net additions to oil reserves in 1970 and 1971, and the ratio had dropped from 33.2 to 20.3 between 1966 and 1971. The shift of the major oil companies from Alberta to northern frontier exploration after discoveries at Prudhoe Bay seriously reduced revenues from land sales and, as Premier Lougheed informed the legislature in April 1972, Alberta's ability to maximize its capture of rents from its depleting oil reserves was constrained by past Social Credit policies:

> Regrettably, the former Social Credit government made – in our view – a very serious error in judgment many years ago in 1948 when it unnecessarily agreed to insert in petroleum and natural gas leases, a specific provision that the *maximum* royalty rate which would be payable by the producers under these leases would be limited on the petroleum to 16⅔% of gross production. The former government went even further. They enacted in 1949 sections in the Mines and Minerals Act which gave *statutory confirmation* to the maximum royalty provisions in the lease. ... The former govern-

ment clearly failed to give themselves any latitude on changing market conditions, which now exist in North America, and which have resulted in substantial increased levels of Alberta production and created a significant improvement in the profit margins of major Alberta producers. The current sellers' market conditions in all probability will continue during the next decade. ...[4]

The province's land tenure policies had allowed the major integrated companies to lease large tracts of potential oil-bearing land. Thirty companies accounted for 95 per cent of Alberta's production in 1970, and these same firms held 50 per cent of net acreage holdings in the province. Yet they had drilled just 28 per cent of Alberta's wells in the same year. In their perpetual search for large new fields to replace the reserves they deplete each year, the majors had evidently concluded that Alberta had reached the point of maturity where the return, in terms of barrels found per exploratory dollar expended, begins to decline. To the Lougheed government it was clear that the independents would have to take up an increasing share of new exploration work; the government's resource policies would have to reflect this if the province's prosperity was to be maintained.[5]

Alberta's response to this combination of constraints was its 1972 "Natural Resource Revenue Plan," which sought to boost royalties from their fixed maximum levels of $16\frac{2}{3}$ per cent without breaking contractual arrangements with the oil industry. After lengthy hearings the province superimposed on its royalty structure a mineral tax on remaining oil reserves (yielding the equivalent of about a 6 per cent gross royalty), and combined this with a new system of drilling incentives "designed to benefit those operators who actually undertake exploration for crude oil in Alberta." The incremental revenues would be used to

> stimulate substantial diversification of the Alberta economy over the next 10 to 15 years. The Government is aware that, as the conventional crude oil industry reaches maturity in Alberta, economic growth of the Province may tend to level off unless new and imaginative programs are initiated soon to diversify the Alberta economy along logical courses. ... Diversification of a significant nature will be difficult for a number of reasons, not the least of which are our relatively 'thin' consumer markets and transportation hurdles which affect the cost of inbound material and outbound products. It is the position of the Government that, in the Alberta public interest, significant expanded sources of Government revenues must begin to flow into the provincial treasury now in order to provide part of the funds for new programs specifically designed for such diversifica-

tion. ... Clearly, revenues from a depleting natural resource are an appropriate source of such funds.[6]

However, the prospect of increased federal taxation of Alberta's energy resources – first through the oil export tax of September 1973, later in the elimination by the May 1974 budget of provisions permitting resource companies to deduct provincial royalties when calculating federal taxable income[7] – jeopardized these early development plans. Federal intervention was a threat, but it was also a golden opportunity for the Conservatives: Ottawa's actions could be used as justification for abandoning Social Credit's dated inflexible royalty arrangements with the petroleum industry.

Predictably, federal encroachments resulted in a vigorous, albeit largely defensive, expansion of the province's own powers. In early October of 1973 – after Ottawa's imposition of an oil price freeze and the export tax, but before the major escalations in world oil prices – the Lougheed cabinet startled the oil industry by suddenly abandoning its new royalty plan, the subject of months of lengthy negotiations and public hearings, and announcing that royalties would henceforth rise with international oil prices. In a striking departure from the long-established practice of prior consultation, this decision was taken by cabinet with no advance discussion with representatives of the oil industry: in effect, the industry was handed a fait accompli. The province's primary objective was evidently to force Ottawa to withdraw its export levy by squeezing the industry; damage done to the oil industry could be repaired by Alberta later on. A secondary, but scarcely less important, aim was to free the government from the fixed royalty ceilings in existing contracts so that the province could take maximum advantage from rapidly changing market conditions.[8] Federal intervention had precipitated a fundamental break with the rentier policies of Social Credit. *Oilweek* magazine, speaking for the Calgary industry, rightly noted that "perhaps overriding everything is the tacit admission by Alberta, which has often publicly prided itself on being the last bastion of free enterprise in a socialist West, that the sanctity of contract is only valid so long as politics decree."[9]

As well as abandoning existing royalty arrangements, Alberta and Saskatchewan each announced new legislative packages at the end of 1973 designed to strengthen their constitutional control over the production, regulation, marketing, and pricing of their resources. Saskatchewan's sweeping oil royalty legislation, which was challenged in the courts and declared, in part, ultra vires by the Supreme Court in 1977, is discussed in detail in Chapter Eleven. Alberta's legislation was scarcely less comprehensive. A series of bills, introduced in the Alberta legislature in December 1973, had been drafted by a team of constitutional lawyers as a regulatory package aimed at consolidating provincial control of resources, resisting further federal incursions, and eliminating the federal oil export tax.[10] One bill, cancelling the maximum royalty rate of one sixth on oil and gas, provided for the government to set higher royalty rates as prices increased. Another bill, discussed below, provided for the incorporation of a provincial Petroleum Marketing Commission, a provincial crown corporation with broad responsibilities over the marketing and pricing of oil produced on crown leases. Broadly, the purpose of all the legislation was to strengthen the province's ownership and control of its resources, including the pricing of these resources in interprovincial and international commerce. We argue later that provincial jurisdiction over resources is subject to considerable constitutional ambiguity because of overlapping powers and changing court interpretations. Although Alberta's legislation, unlike Saskatchewan's, has not been challenged in the courts, there exists considerable uncertainty about its constitutional validity.

The general assertiveness of the producing provinces in turn provoked centralizing moves by Ottawa, including enactment of the sweeping Petroleum Administration Act of 1974, a bill granting federal officials broad powers over the pricing of oil in Canada. The federal budgets of May and November 1974 revised income tax regulations to disallow the deduction of provincial resource royalties in the calculation of federal taxable income — revisions designed to improve the federal treasury's position at the expense of the provinces. To the federal Department of Finance, Alberta and Saskatchewan's new higher royalties were "thinly disguised income taxes." Unquestionably, the simple facts of rising energy prices and the irresistible lure of new sources of revenue explain much of the aggressiveness and acquisitiveness of politicians and civil servants at both levels of government after 1973. And it should also be noted (although oil industry spokesmen took little comfort in the fact) that the interventionist behaviour of the producing provinces and Ottawa seems to have originated as much in a determination by governments to defend their constitutional prerogatives and powers as in any desire to undercut or to supplant the private sector.

Not surprisingly, Alberta's aggressive defence of its jurisdiction and its ambitious development plans put the province on a collision course with the international oil industry. Ottawa's tax policies drove a wedge between the Alberta government and the major companies, and the ensuing three-way feud over oil and gas rents lasted for the better part of two years. A major source of the industry's grievance with the Lougheed administration (and the Trudeau government) can be seen in the Table I, below, illustrating the changes in the distribution of revenue from 1973 to 1975 on a typical barrel of Alberta crown oil. In this two-year period the average wellhead price of Alberta crude oil increased from $3.80 to $8.00 per barrel. Alberta's percentage "take" on an average barrel (royalties plus provincial income tax) increased from 24 to 39 per cent, while the private producer's share of revenue declined from 51 to 34 per cent. That industry cash flow increased in absolute terms and that the major producers increased their net income in these two years do not alter the fact that the majority of the incremental rents from the rising oil prices went to Alberta – a fact emphasized by the oil-consuming provinces in opposing domestic oil price increases.

Following Ottawa's 1974 decision to disallow the deduction of provincial resource royalties in the calculation of federal taxable income, the major petroleum companies confronted all three western producing provinces with a well co-ordinated capital strike – withdrawing drilling rigs, cancelling new projects and investments, and laying off employees. This campaign was particularly effective in Alberta, as it threatened many of the province's oil-dependent businesses with sudden recession. The near-collapse of the giant Syncrude oil sands project (rescued in February 1975 through massive federal tax subsidies that will benefit the Alberta treasury as well as the private participants in the consortium) dealt a psychological blow to Alberta business, and the Lougheed government came under intensive pressure from local interest groups and the media. In December 1974 the province implemented a contingency plan, known as the Petroleum Exploration Plan, reducing royalties and introducing new drilling incentives for oil explorers.[11]

While this prolonged dispute over resource rents certainly confirmed the vulnerability of Alberta to pressure from international capital, perhaps the most revealing fact about the episode was that the major oil companies found it necessary to use such harsh methods in dealing with the Lougheed regime. Relations between the province and the majors have markedly improved in the late 1970s, thanks to somewhat reduced royalty rates and generous incentives which have sparked a classic drilling boom, but it would be absurd to conclude from this that the Lougheed government is merely an instrument of external capital or that Alberta's new bourgeoisie is "comprador" in nature – i.e. that its role is merely to facilitate the penetration of the local economy by foreign capital. The province's aggressive acquisition of rents, its stress on the local upgrading of hydrocarbons, its attempts to control the supply and pricing of feedstocks within Alberta have all created friction with the integrated major operators

227

who regard such practices as contrary to sound business logic. The traditional assumption – part of the mental apparatus of the rentier approach to development – that the interests of the major oil companies and of Alberta are identical, is now questioned on both sides, and this divergence of outlook could well increase in the future.

Table I
Distribution of Revenue per Barrel of Alberta Oil*

	September 1973		September 1975		Increase
Operating costs	$0.67	18%	$0.85	11%	$0.18
Taxes:					
Federal income tax	0.27	7	1.28	16	1.01
Alberta royalty and provincial income tax	0.92	24	3.12	39	2.20
Industry cash flow	1.94	51	2.75	34	$0.81
Average price	3.80	100	8.00	100	4.20

*"Old" Alberta Crown oil sold in Canada; ignores federal oil export tax revenue.

SOURCES: compiled from federal, Alberta, industry and *Financial Post* data. Reprinted from L. Pratt, "The State and Province – Building Alberta's Development Strategy," in L. Panitch (ed.), *The Canadian State: Political Economy and Political Power*, 155.

A second early initiative of the Lougheed government lay in the area of natural gas pricing. Here the province, closely allied to the producing companies, sought to challenge external economic and political forces which were keeping down gas prices and, according to the Lougheed cabinet, holding back expansion of the industry and exploration for new reserves. As we saw earlier, Alberta gas marketed outside the province, and all Canadian gas exported to the United States, were assigned under long-term export permits. Normally, for gas committed to permit, prices were constant, although provision was usually made for minor escalations and for periodic price redetermination. The Borden Royal Commission on Energy and the National Energy Board both found that Canadian gas exported to the United States in the 1950s and 1960s had tended to be underpriced, resulting in a loss of economic rent by the owners of the resource. The average Alberta field price for natural gas was stable and low in terms of BTU equivalence with crude oil throughout the Manning era, rising from 10.2 cents per thousand cubic feet (MCF) in 1957 to 15.7 cents in 1967.

By the late 1960s, however, looming shortages in the United States encouraged more American buyers to look to Alberta as a potential source of supply. Whether this would place upward pressure on gas prices depended in part on the willingness of the National Energy Board and the federal cabinet to approve additional exports. New exports were approved in 1970, but a year later the NEB, fearful that domestic users could face shortages if new permits to export were approved, rejected applications by two U.S. companies to sell more Alberta gas to American consumers. Canadian nationalists and consumers applauded the NEB's decision as long overdue, but Alberta and gas producers viewed it as a negative step. In effect, closure of the export market left gas purchasing in Alberta in a situation tantamount to monopsony (buyer's monopoly), given that TransCanada Pipelines was the sole buying agent for the big central Canadian distributors and utilities.

Following a comprehensive study of the field pricing of Alberta gas, the Energy Resources Conservation Board reported in 1972 that prevailing prices were substantially below commodity value (the BTU equivalent price per unit of energy in competing forms, such as oil) and argued that a lack of competition among buyers was the major cause of underpricing: "The current average field price for gas in Alberta ... is some 16 cents per MCF. The Board considers this to be less than the field value of the gas by at least 10 cents per MCF and thus finds that the current field price is not in the Alberta public interest."[12]

Acting on the Board's advice, the Lougheed cabinet intervened on the side of the producers to challenge TransCanada – a company historically understood by Albertans to be an instrument of and spokesman for eastern Canadian business interests. Approval was withheld from new applications to remove gas from the province until prices increased, and the province amended its arbitration legislation governing the redetermination of gas prices paid by pipelines to producers: such prices are now to be redetermined every two years on the basis of full commodity value. In the summer of 1972, the management of Alberta Gas Trunk Line, which, as we have seen, was created by the Manning cabinet in 1954 to keep Trans-Canada from extending its gathering lines past Alberta's border, created a new gas buyer, Pan Alberta Gas Limited, to gather gas not already committed to contract and to offer it for sale at prices substantially above Trans-Canada's best offers. Trunk Line's support for the cabinet's policy put competitive pressure on prices, as did the successive boosts in world oil prices. Alberta's policies, which were vigorously opposed and protested by Ontario manufacturers, utilities, and politicians, have had a major impact on gas pricing in Canada, although they did not come to fruition until

1975 when the impasse between TransCanada and the province was resolved.

"Sowing the Oil": Alberta's Strategy of Development

The phrase *sembrar el petroleo* ("to sow the oil") is a classic Venezuelan epigram. First coined during a 1936 debate over the uses of petroleum income, it has come to stand for the aspirations of successive Venezuelan governments to create an economic infrastructure independent of oil. Generally associated with the ideas of Venezuela's "petroleum philosopher," Juan Pablo Perez Alfonzo, formerly Minister of Mines and Hydrocarbons in the government of Romula Betancourt, the phrase captures the general development strategy not only of Venezuela, but also of other members of the Organization of Petroleum Exporting Countries and of non-OPEC oil producers such as Alberta.[13]

Perez Alfonzo's ideas concerning oil were fundamentally those of a strict conservationist. Obsessed with the prevention of waste and determined to impose efficient patterns of development on the foreign-controlled oil industry in Venezuela, he argued that oil has a high "intrinsic" value not always reflected in market prices because it is a depleting resource of critical importance to modern industrial societies. To prevent wasteful practices and to reduce Venezuela's dependence on volatile commodity markets, Perez Alfonzo argued that the private companies would have to come under government regulation and control. Further, he took the unpopular view that there are clear limits to the extent to which a country like Venezuela could absorb capital and use it efficiently to generate self-sustaining development. The problem of "economic indigestion" leads to the conclusion that the rate of production should be limited to a level such that government oil revenues are compatible with the country's capacity to absorb them. Oil revenue increases should come from price rises, taxed at the highest possible rate to capture the maximum rent for the owners of the resource, and not from boosts in production. The intrinsic value of oil ensures that it will grow in value lying in the ground; far from rushing to exploit it, the state should pursue a strategy designed to control production and to use petroleum income to fashion an infrastructure less dependent upon oil. "Sowing the oil" is thus a strategy of resource management based on long-term rent maximization, but at the same time it is a political doctrine aimed at the reduction of dependence on the multinational corporation and the industrialized consuming countries.

Such ideas took a long time to surface in Alberta. For decades Albertans defined the central problem of oil policy as the search for new markets and expansion of production in order to realize incremental royalty revenues. While conservation was, as we have seen, taken seriously in Alberta as early as the 1930s, many of the implications of conservation and long-term rent maximization did not work their way into the province's ideas on development until the 1970s. It was only after the Lougheed government had attempted the formidable task of "digesting" one Syncrude-scale oil sands project, for example, that it began deliberately to hold back the pace of oil sands development. It was only when it began to encounter the myriad headaches involved in managing multi-billion dollar surpluses that the province realized the necessity of timing large developments so as to slow the influx of new capital. Only with the arrival of a seller's market in world energy did Lougheed's cabinet grasp the potential of reserves appreciating in value in the ground.

On the other hand, the advantages of "sowing the oil" were well understood by Albertans who watched the major companies shift their new exploratory work into the Canadian North following the discovery of oil at Prudhoe Bay in 1968. Alberta resented its dependence on U.S. oil quota politics and feared economic stagnation as the province's oil industry approached maturity. We have seen that the provincial Conservatives, the party of Alberta's upper-income urban middle classes, began as early as 1965 to preach the need for a "third stage of development" – industrialization. Fiscal pressures promised to force up personal taxation unless petroleum royalties were increased and invested in diversification. These fears and anxieties underlay the new and relatively coherent economic development strategy of the Lougheed government, whose elements Professor Smiley has summarized as "the preservation of provincial autonomy in resource matters against federal influence; the creation of a strong petrochemical industry within the province; the establishment of arrangements by which Albertans are given preferential treatment in terms of employment and investment opportunities in the development of Alberta resources; the dispersal of economic development outside the Edmonton and Calgary metropolitan areas; adjustments in federal transportation and tariff policies to serve Alberta needs."[14]

The essentials of this strategy were evolved by Peter Lougheed and his closest political associates while in opposition in the 1960s, although much of the detail was not added until they took office. Perceiving that Alberta was overly dependent on depleting energy resources and that its position as a land-locked, thinly populated hinterland far from major markets was impeding industrial growth, the Conservatives accepted the need for an activist government to "sow the oil" and steer the province's future development. Government would play a central part in maximizing petroleum-linked industrialization. Lougheed argued the need to promote forward-linked industries such as petrochemicals and agricultural processing out of the province's strong resource base. An internal government memorandum, "The Management of Growth," dated May 1974, stated that the province was at the point of transition "from a primarily extractive economy, where our resources are exported for processing to other parts of Canada and the rest of the world, to an industrialized economy which will see further processing of our raw materials, increased manufacturing and ... satisfying employment opportunities for Albertans." But the same document noted that twenty-three of the twenty-eight largest development projects in Alberta in the mid-1970s were essentially extractive: unless the government managed growth and steered the economy in desired directions, the transition might not occur and "the economy could become even more dependent on the natural resource base of the Province."

Alberta's development strategy is rooted in the implicit assumption that regional economic growth typically occurs in a unilinear sequence of stages, the region evolving from an agricultural economy through the exploitation and export of its resources to the early and finally the advanced stages of industrialization.[15] A failure to make the difficult transition from an extractive to an industrial economy, according to this view of growth, dooms the region to stagnation and decay as emigration occurs and living standards fall behind the national average.

Where should we seek the determinants of Alberta's push for staple-linked diversification in the seventies and eighties? A major source of entrepreneurship lies in the accumulation, status, and occupational drives of a regional capitalist class or bourgeoisie that would transform the province from an extractive periphery into an industrial core where power, wealth, and attractive careers are located. This class, which has defined Alberta's recent agenda for economic development, views the West as an exploited dependency of central Canada: Confederation and its political and economic arrangements are perceived to be in the hands of Ontario and Quebec interests, the beneficiaries of Macdonald's National Policy. Discontent – with the lack of secondary industry on the prairies, the practices of Canada's financial institutions, freight rates, tariffs, and federal taxation of the resource industries – "can be seen as a mixture of dissatisfaction with the inevitable fate of a small region in a market economy, and unhappiness with distortions in such a system initiated or at least tolerated by the federal government."[16]

Prairie economic alienation is essentially a hinterland quarrel with the unequal distribution of growth that is characteristic of a capitalist economy, yet regional protest tends to focus on federal policies that are believed to buttress distortions and on demands for remedial state

232

intervention. A traditional western grievance, for example, is that federal policies have conspired to obstruct the normal evolution of economic development on the prairies, that institutional factors, such as national transportation policy and federal purchasing practice, have affected the regional distribution of secondary industry independently of comparative advantage. As with Saskatchewan's first experiments with economic diversification after the election of the CCF in 1944, underlying the development policies of the Lougheed Conservatives in Alberta is the assumption that there exists considerable untapped potential for manufacturing in the West. The validity of this assumption, and the rationality of the development policies that flow from it, are matters seldom debated in any of the prairie provinces. Those who suggest that the low percentage of manufacturing employment in the prairies is a logical consequence of the region's comparative advantages in other sectors, and rational cost-minimizing location decisions, are a distinct minority.

Underlying Alberta's recent development strategy is another assumption – verified by historical experience – that the West's narrow economic base, its great distance from the major population centres of North America, and its dependence on outside capital, communications, transportation, and volatile commodity markets have produced a society lacking in autonomy – whose well-being and security are precarious, always at the mercy of decisions taken by outsiders. This, of course, is compounded by awareness of Alberta's extreme reliance on the oil and gas industry. Speaking to Calgary's business community in the fall of 1974, Premier Lougheed warned his audience that the province had only a decade in which to diversify, adding that the government's development strategy was rooted in three fundamental objectives:

> The first one is to strengthen the control by Albertans over our future and to reduce the dependency for our continued quality of life on governments, institutions or corporations directed from outside the province. Secondly, to do this as much as possible through the private sector and only to move through the public sector if the private sector is not in a position to move in essential new directions and then only in exceptional and very specific circumstances. And thirdly, to strengthen competitive free enterprise by Albertans which to us means giving priority to our locally-owned businesses. Our basic guidepost [is] to maximize the number of our citizens controlling their own destiny.[17]

This "economic provincialism" has enormous political appeal among Alberta's urban middle classes. Thus *Edmonton Journal* columnist William Thorsell, in a gushing endorsement of Lougheed as "the right man in the right place at the right time," commented in mid-1977: "A more complex economy will create the choice in jobs that many of us desire and would go elsewhere to find if they were not here. We are Albertans too. If we want to manage complicated industries or financial affairs, if we want to pursue research in chemistry, make feature films or act on stage, we may want to do so without having to leave the province of our birth."

Taken to its extreme, Alberta's economic provincialism manifests itself on the right-wing fringe of the political spectrum, through the activities of organizations such as the neo-separatist Independent Association of Alberta, founded by an independent Calgary oilman devoted to the thought of Ayn Rand. But separatism is not a serious proposition in the West – nor is Ayn Rand – while the demand for regional political and economic autonomy is. Lougheed's avowed intention to shift decision-making and power to the West should be interpreted, in part, as an expression of the desire of Alberta's business class to be freed from its traditional dependence on eastern Canadian financial interests. "Half the businessmen you meet," one Ontario writer comments of Alberta, "from Carl Nickle, whose father was a Calgary shoe salesman who became enormously rich during the first oil strikes of the 1940s, to Don Getty [Minister of Energy and Natural Resources in Lougheed's second cabinet], who was born in the East but made his millions in oil in the 1960s before turning to politics – talk bitterly of how they were treated by officials in banks and investment houses on Bay or St. James Streets when they went there seeking development money."[18] This alienation of Alberta business was strongly reinforced in 1973 and 1974 by Ottawa's federal resource taxation policies. These were widely interpreted in Alberta as thinly disguised attempts by "the feds" to undermine the jurisdiction of the producing provinces and to gain indirect control of their energy resources. Business anxiety over further federal encroachments and interventions into the oil and gas industries provides the Alberta government and its regulatory arms with a powerful base of support for market interventions undertaken in defence of provincial rights. Western business supports constitutional decentralization and a strong, positive state at the provincial level as a buffer against a predatory national government.

Fear of economic stagnation and exhaustion of the province's oil and gas base provides a second crucial support for Alberta's interventionist policies. In spite of a recent spate of important discoveries of oil and natural gas in Alberta and British Columbia, the western Canadian sedimentary basin must be considered at the point of maturity. The greatest rate of hydrocarbon discovery in the basin occurred in the decade after the 1947 Leduc discovery, during the years of low wellhead prices and heavy prorationing of oil to market demand. During the 1960s the number of barrels of conventional crude discovered per exploratory footage drilled declined sharply, compared with the peak years of the late 1940s and early 1950s, and this decline has continued throughout the 1970s – that ratio has dropped from 1651 and 1141 barrels in 1947 and 1948 to 351 in 1960, 115 in 1965, and 27 in 1975.[19] This is the normal course of events in the development of a conventional oil basin approaching maturity. Since 1970 new reserve additions of conventional oil have been less than annual Canadian production for eight years in succession: the country has been living off its inventory and total proven and probable reserves stood at the end of 1977 at just over 7 billion barrels (6.3 billion located in Alberta). The producibility of most of Alberta's major oil fields (some fifteen fields account for better than 50 per cent of provincial production) has either levelled off or begun to decline, and it was the National Energy Board's belated recognition of this fact in late 1974 that prompted Ottawa to commence phasing out oil exports to the United States and to rescue the floundering Syncrude project. The discovery in 1977 of a new conventional oil field in deep geological structures at West Pembina – the first major discovery since 1966 in Alberta – has prompted a classic land and exploration play and some speculation that the province's declining capacity to produce conventional crude can be reversed. West Pembina's recoverable reserves have been variously estimated from 500 million to 1.5 billion barrels – the latter figure would rank it, along with the original (1953) Pembina field, as Alberta's largest – but at the time of writing the size of the field and its implications for Canadian oil supply in the 1980s remain uncertain. It is, of course, conceivable that additional new large fields will be discovered in the western sedimentary basin (natural gas reserves have increased for several years in succession), and higher prices will encourage producers to develop known reserves which would otherwise be beyond economic reach. This may well create temporary gluts and (as with gas) pressure for new oil exports, but the longer term oulook is that Canada's dependence on offshore imports will grow.[20]

In any event, Alberta's elites are well aware that the booming economic conditions of the 1970s have been largely a consequence of rising demand for non-renewable energy resources, and that little diversification of the province's economy has occurred as yet. How long can it last? Lougheed has suggested: "In my view, not very long; perhaps a decade at the most, unless we're able to put in place a more balanced economy for that inevitable day ... when oil and gas no longer provide such a large number of jobs, when production begins to decline, and resource revenue falls off."[21]

Uncertainty about the future gives Alberta professionals and businessmen an incentive to overcome their conservative dislike of bureaucracy and "big government" and to support a regime dedicated to the planning and promotion of an economy less dependent on staple extraction and less under outside control and ownership. But in a community whose political culture is overwhelmingly conservative and whose business community is often anti-leftist to the point of paranoia, it was inevitable that some of the province's interventions would create uneasy stirrings on the right. The creation of the Alberta Energy Company, the 1974 acquisition of Pacific Western Airlines, and some of the province's concessions to organized labour, have been unpopular with many Alberta businessmen. The labour issues have been particularly interesting, as it is clear that the agenda for provincial industrialization will require the support and co-operation of organized labour; and it is equally plain that local business fears the growth of powerful unions. The Lougheed government, for example, came under strong pressure over an incident involving the Alberta Energy Company (50 per cent owned by the province) and the awarding of the contract to build the Energy Company's pipeline from the Syncrude oil sands plant. In December 1975, on the urging of the Syncrude consortium, the Energy Company passed over the lowest tender, submitted by a non-union contractor, and gave the job to a unionized bidder. Syncrude had negotiated a deal with the unions on its site whereby the latter had agreed to no-strike, no-lockout agreements in return for assurances that the pipeline would be awarded to a union contractor. Feeling among the provincial Tories was so strongly anti-labour after this episode that the Lougheed cabinet was pressed to introduce "right to work" legislation, using some of the southern states as a model. Instead, the province outlawed the right to strike in the public sector. If there is a single political factor likely to restrain Alberta's push to industrialize, it is probably the small businessman's spectre of a growing and increasingly powerful provincial labour force.

Alberta First: The Role of the State

Closely resembling turn-of-the century Ontario's "manufacturing condition" (a set of policies with which that province sought to induce resource developers to process timber, nickel, and other natural resources in Ontario instead of exporting them in an unfinished state to the United States), Alberta's strategy of development puts great emphasis on the upgrading of energy resources at the source. By increasing its control over the pricing, supply, and local utilization of feedstocks—especially natural gas—the province can reduce the export of raw materials and industrial jobs to eastern Canada and the United States, and promote forward-linked secondary industries in the West. A viable manufacturing sector, based on the processing of energy and agricultural staples in western Canada, will, it is argued, attract new investment to the province, assist the development of a skilled labour force, and stimulate the growth of related industries. "Unless we seize the initiatives to diversify the economy of Alberta as they occur," Lougheed argued in May 1974, in the first flush of enthusiasm over petrochemicals, "we accept the risk that creation of new jobs will decline as the conventional petroleum industry headquartered in Alberta and its related service industries begin to level off. The most significant potential weakness in the Alberta economy is that well paid jobs in manufacturing are relatively limited due to the land-locked geography of Alberta and the cost—under existing freight rate structures—of shipping finished or semi-finished goods to market."[22]

Alberta's political and business elites believe that the world oil crisis, and the shift in bargaining power from consumers to producers, give the province the leverage to make the transition to a modern industrial economy. Using Alberta's remaining conventional oil and gas reserves and its immense untapped supplies of coal, tar sands, and heavy oils as bargaining tools, in a situation of energy scarcity and consumer concern about the long-term availability of fossil fuels, an aggressive provincial government may be able to negotiate a transfer of industry, high-income jobs, and political power from the central Canadian heartland to the West. This, of course, is what lay behind Alberta's lengthy struggles with Ontario in the mid-1970s over natural gas and domestic oil prices and the regional location of Canada's petrochemical industry.

Within the context of these development plans, the Lougheed government has exploited its constitutional powers to the fullest possible extent since the traumatic autumn of 1973 in an effort to extend its control over its resource base and to impede aggrandizement by Ottawa. Fear of new federal incursions and distrust of a market economy under outside control have manifested themselves in a series of related policy interventions, virtually all of which have been justified in the name of Alberta private enterprise. Through companies such as Alberta Gas Trunk Line and the Alberta Energy Company, Alberta capitalists and the provincial government have been involved in a close alliance for purposes of regional empire-building. The objectives of this business-state alliance are best grasped through a concluding discussion of specific policies.

237

First, Alberta has sought to extend its constitutional control over its oil and natural resources. Alberta takes the conventional view that the key to its constitutional position lies in its proprietary rights over crown oil – over 80 per cent of the recoverable oil and gas lying within its borders. A provincial government under the constitution "has vastly greater control over the natural resources it owns than it does over the natural resources it doesn't own," the former Attorney General of Alberta, Merv Leitch, remarked in Victoria in 1974. Basing his arguments on a decision of the Ontario Court of Appeal in 1900 (*Smylie v. the Queen*) upholding the proprietary right of the Ontario government to require firms cutting timber on crown lands to manufacture the sawn logs in Canada, Leitch asserted that "a province can with respect to natural resources it owns: (a) decide whether to develop them, (b) decide by whom, when and how they're going to be developed, (c) determine the degree of processing that's to take place within the province, (d) dispose of them upon conditions that they only be used in a certain way, or in a certain place, or by certain people, (e) determine the price at which they or the produce resulting from their processing will be sold."[23] Such assertions of faith in the extent of provincial constitutional jurisdiction over resources underlay the package of interventionist legislation passed through the special "energy session" of the Alberta legislature in December 1973.

How secure *is* Alberta's constitutional position? In light of Saskatchewan's difficulties and legal battles throughout most of the 1970s, can Alberta's constitutional position be held to be on safe foundations for the coming decades? This question can only be addressed through an assessment of specific legislation and regulations. Consider, by way of illustration, the Alberta Petroleum Marketing Act, passed as part of the province's campaign against the federal oil export tax. This legislation set up the Alberta Petroleum Marketing Commission, a provincial crown corporation with broad powers relating to the sale of oil produced from Alberta crown leases. Traditionally, Alberta's leases transferred ownership of oil at the wellhead from the province to the producing company. Once this occurred, the province lost its proprietary right over these resources, including its power to influence the pricing, processing, and marketing of crown-owned oil. One of the purposes of the legislation, and accompanying amendments of the Mines and Minerals Act, was to assert the province's control of oil after production at the wellhead by requiring all producers to sell their oil through the Marketing Commission and by providing that the royalty share of oil produced on crown leases (roughly a third of total production) remains the property of the province. The legislation is complex, and the powers granted to this new commission appear to be so broad that virtually any dealing with respect to petroleum produced from crown lands lies within its potential control. Thus far these powers have barely been exercised and the Marketing Commission has not substantially altered the operations of the oil industry in Alberta. Reportedly, however, it intends to take a much more activist role in marketing to ensure that new petrochemical industries locating in Alberta can be guaranteed supplies of feedstocks on a priority basis in furtherance of the province's diversification strategy. The oil industry opposes any movement by the Lougheed government to interfere with its traditional control over the marketing of oil and gas (Gulf Canada and other producers intervened during Energy Resources Conservation Board hearings on the petrochemical industry in 1976 on precisely this point), and any attempt to implement an "Alberta first" allocation policy that prejudiced customers in other provinces might well provoke a constitutional challenge. Such a challenge would almost certainly succeed on the grounds that the Marketing Commission legislation is an intrusion by Alberta upon the federal government's jurisdiction over interprovincial trade and commerce, and therefore ultra vires.

The pricing of oil, of course, determines the magnitude of economic rents arising from its production, and since the imposition of the federal oil export tax in September 1973 the producing provinces of Alberta, Saskatchewan, and British Columbia have all sought to enhance their regulation of oil and gas prices at the wellhead and to influence the terms on which their resources are sold into extraprovincial markets. It is in the latter case – attempts by provinces to use their legislative powers to regulate prices of commodities after they have entered the "interprovincial flow" – that there are grounds for questioning the constitutionality of certain provincial legislation. Since the Supreme Court of Canada's judgment on the CIGOL case (discussed in Chapter Eleven) there are also new ambiguities, concerning the legal definition of royalties as opposed to taxes, which seemingly apply to Alberta's post-1974 petroleum royalty structure as well as to Saskatchewan's. Earlier we argued that the practice of prorationing oil to market demand, implemented by the Oil and Gas Conservation Board and its successor, the Energy Resources Conservation Board, under conservation legislation since 1950, was more a complex procedure for balancing supply and demand and stabilizing oil prices than a method for preventing physical waste. Although there seems to be no consensus among constitutional authorities familiar with the legislation, there is at least a serious case to be made for the argument that oil prorationing is an encroachment by the province upon the federal trade and commerce power, given the broadened definition of the latter power in recent Supreme Court of Canada decisions. In October 1978 (as we shall see in Chapter Eleven) the Supreme Court held Saskatchewan's potash prorationing scheme to be invalid on grounds that the province had established a marketing scheme with price fixing as its central feature for a commodity exported into interprovincial and international trade. Failing a direct constitutional challenge, of course, that decision does not directly apply to Alberta's petroleum legislation. But it certainly does increase the uncertainty and ambiguity surrounding the limits of provincial jurisdiction over natural resources.

The constitutional debate is by no means academic, even if the arguments used by proponents of provincial and federal rights sometimes border on the metaphysical. Given the constitutional limitations on their legislative powers, the ability of the provinces to advance their separate paths of development is by no means open-ended, despite crown ownership of resources. And to the extent that Alberta's policies hinge – as do Saskatchewan's – on the province's ability to control its resource industries, the constitutional constraints become significant. The federal government and the consuming provinces have undoubtedly studied Alberta's energy legislation with an eye to potential challenges; and, even though none has yet occurred, Lougheed's administration has shared the fears of Saskatchewan that the Supreme Court is now pursuing, to use Premier Allan Blakeney's words, "a more activist, centralist role than its predecessors in creating policy through judicial decisions." Blakeney's charge that Ottawa has been engaged since the mid-1970s in an aggressive campaign through the courts "to limit and abridge the clear constitutional rights of the provinces in dealing with resources"[24] accurately reflects Alberta's position as well: Alberta's Attorney General has supported Saskatchewan in all of the latter's legal battles over resources (Alberta was also the only province to support the unions in their attempts to overturn the federal Anti-Inflation Act in the 1976 reference to the Supreme Court; this odd alliance originates in Alberta's fear that the same emergency powers which were invoked by Ottawa to justify wage and price controls might one day be turned toward the New West.) Saskatchewan's legal dilemmas have created anxiety and uncertainty in virtually every provincial capital, but above all in Edmonton, due to the significance of provincial resource revenues. We shall return to these issues in Chapter Eleven.

Secondly, in the interest of long-term diversification the Lougheed government has sought since 1972 to maximize its resource rents. Although the province was forced to retreat somewhat in the face of combined federal and oil industry pressure, the record is still undeniably impressive. Under the impact of rising prices and royalties and major new exploration plays, provincial resource revenues have swollen enormously since then. Aggregate oil revenues (comprising royalties, land sales, and rentals) increased from $516 million in 1973 to $2.7 billion in 1977, creating annual budget surpluses that have threatened to embarrass even the most acquisitive Alberta cabinet ministers.

In May 1976 Alberta established its Heritage Savings Trust Fund, with an initial allocation of $1.5 billion and a call on at least 30 per cent of the province's annual non-renewable resource revenues. The objective of the Heritage Fund is to mobilize capital to spur diversification. By March 1979 the assets in the Heritage Fund are expected to stand at $4.6 billion, and over and above the monies in the fund the province had, as of 1978, accumulated an additional $2.3 billion in successive budget surpluses. By the mid-1980s, assuming real oil prices do not fall, Alberta will have close to $15 billion in the Heritage Fund, earning as much in annual interest as some of the smaller provinces are able to earn in aggregate government revenues! How will this huge capital pool be invested? Under the bill authorizing the Heritage Fund,[25] at least 65 per cent of its assets must be invested in provincial projects which "will yield a reasonable return or profit to the Trust Fund and will tend to strengthen and diversify the economy of Alberta." Another 20 per cent is designated for Alberta investments that will provide long-term economic and social benefits for the province, and the remaining 15 per cent is reserved for investments in other parts of Canada (e.g. loans to the Maritime provinces). Most of the fund's assets are currently invested in short-term marketable securities, and no clear pattern of investment has yet developed. To date, its major investments have been in the Syncrude project, the province's shares in the Alberta Energy Company, debentures of the Alberta Housing Corporation, irrigation projects in southern Alberta, new medical research facilities in Edmonton, and the development of new processes for the economic recovery of oil from Alberta's immense deposits of tar sands and heavy oils. The Alaska Highway natural gas pipeline is a likely candidate for future investment.

Future political debates in Alberta will almost certainly centre on the management and discretionary spending of its huge revenue surpluses. The Heritage Fund is effectively controlled by cabinet, and the issue of executive accountability ensured that the bill authorizing the fund had a stormy passage through the Tory-dominated legislature (69 of 75 seats) in 1976. The Lougheed regime, run like a centralized business, with cabinet functioning as a board of directors, probably justifies its reputation among opposition party and media critics as one of the least accessible and most secretive executive branches of government in Canada. But the era of Tory hegemony in Alberta seems likely to persist for at least a generation, and the investments of the Heritage Fund in economic diversification will therefore bear the stamp of Conservative ideas about development. On that basis, we can anticipate that much of the surplus will be used to create the infrastructure for an industrial economy and to strengthen the position of Alberta corporations and entrepreneurs within the national capitalist system. Will the rest of Canada tolerate the large disparities and the investment of the surplus on an "Alberta first" basis?

Thirdly, the Lougheed government has consciously striven to nurture the development in Alberta of a strong indigenous class of entrepreneurs and managers capable of running a more complex and diversified economy. With this has come a pronounced ideological emphasis on people's capitalism, i.e. more participation by Albertans in local business developments. The Alberta Energy Company was created in 1973 as a joint public-private vehicle (50 per cent of its shares are held by the provincial government, 50 per cent by private investors) for the province's direct participation in the Syncrude oil sands venture and such developments as the Suffield natural gas field. AEC is expressly precluded from competing with the conventional oil and gas industry and is conceived by Premier Lougheed as "a unique partnership concept between public and private ownership." In a letter written to the company's first president and chief executive officer, David E. Mitchell, formerly the head of an independent oil company, Lougheed set out his philosophy of "participation": "Substantial direct citizen ownership will provide added stimulus and accountability for results that are inherent in the private enterprise system. ... Modern society is challenging the concept of private investment and sometimes with justification, the behaviour of corporations. It may well be that the Alberta Energy Company, by creating widespread ownership and corporate participation in the province, will foster better understanding between our citizens and our economic system."[26] To use a concept that has recently become debased currency, Lougheed's philosophy could be described as corporatism inspired by the purpose of winning business support for intervention and of giving the public a sense of participation in large-scale economic development. The philosophy manifested itself in a remarkable two weeks in November 1975 when Albertans were offered first crack at AEC shares. Brokers hustled pedestrians in shopping centres, shares were sold in banks and – where else? – at Grey Cup parties. Street hawking of shares in Calgary revived memories of the city's first wild oil boom in 1914. Within two weeks all of the 7.5 million shares, each worth $10, had been purchased by Albertans.

The Alberta Energy Company is engaged in several joint ventures with companies such as Alberta Gas Trunk Line and with multinational resource and petrochemical companies. Its function is to mobilize local capital, to increase regional participation in the growth sectors of Alberta's economy and to stimulate the "sowing of oil" — the transition to petroleum-linked industrialization. A further implicit function of companies such as AEC and Trunk Line is to train the managers and capitalists who can assume the direction of the Alberta economy after the major petroleum companies have left the province, as inevitably they must. In the long, gradual movement toward the full "provincialization" of the Alberta economy, a supply of domestic entrepreneurship is a critical prerequisite. Alberta enterprises are seen as the breeding-ground of a western Canadian bourgeoisie and as a logical area for the career advancement of hundreds of young professionals. There is much in common here with the role that provincial state enterprises such as Hydro-Quebec have played in advancing the interests of Quebec's francophone middle class since the early 1960s.

Finally, the cornerstone of Alberta's industrial diversification strategy and the area in which a great deal of its available entrepreneurship, public and private, is being committed is the petrochemical industry. The strategy is based on classic development economics. First, use the powers of the state to retard the export of valuable raw materials and their by-products (in this case, ethane — a natural gas liquid); then upgrade the feedstocks locally through an integrated complex of processing and derivative plants, thereby fostering a viable forward-linked manufacturing industry out of the province's resource base — attracting new technology, building an industrial labour force, and creating additional spinoff benefits through the growth of related "downstream" industrial activities. Like many other oil exporters, including Iran, Saudi Arabia, Norway, Britain, and Alaska, Alberta holds the now-conventional view of petrochemicals as a logical step forward from an export-dependent petroleum economy. And like other producers, the province believes that the emergence of scarcity conditions in world energy markets justifies the attempt to force a transfer of this industry from its traditional location in the industrialized core areas to the resource-exporting peripheries — in Canada, from the Sarnia region to Alberta. Lougheed has argued that in petrochemicals Alberta now enjoys "a natural economic advantage over other areas since the importance of assured feedstocks under current energy conditions is becoming as significant as proximity to markets".[27] Alberta's "natural" economic advantages depend more, however, on its political and constitutional power over resources than on regional differences in petrochemical production costs, which in all probability still continue to favour other regions.

Much of the entrepreneurial drive behind Alberta's venture into petrochemicals appears to originate in government. Lougheed personally has been interested in the industry since his days with Mannix in the late 1950s, and it fits naturally into the Tory strategy of diversification. Leading officials at the Energy Resources Conservation Board – some of whom come from backgrounds in chemical engineering – have also advocated petrochemical development since the late 1940s, but found Social Credit wary and unenthusiastic. Recalled one official, "The government of the day pretty well accepted that Alberta's huge distance from markets and the penalties involved with that were such that the time wasn't right for a petrochemical industry." But the Board found the Lougheed cabinet much more enthusiastic and knowledgeable – "There was an awakening to Alberta's resources," remarked the same official[28] – and the ERCB was encouraged to review the original proposal of Dow Chemical of Canada and Dome Petroleum (Dow-Dome proposed to manufacture ethylene in Alberta from ethane stripped from natural gas, then ship the ethylene to Dow's plants in Sarnia and Ohio). The Board was enthusiastic and the Dow-Dome project won the initial approval of the Lougheed cabinet. But in 1973-74 the situation changed radically. As part of its own strategy of corporate diversification, Robert Blair's empire-building Alberta Gas Trunk Line proposed an alternative petrochemical venture, involving far more upgrading of the ethylene "building-block" in Alberta. And the province became aware of the threat to its own plans for regional development posed by a third world-scale project, Petrosar – this one planned for Sarnia, the traditional centre of the Canadian petrochemical industry, and headed by a federal crown corporation. Petrosar would convert naphtha to ethylene and consume 170,000 barrels a day of Alberta crude oil – a classic example, from Alberta's perspective, of the West's resources being used to the detriment of western regional industrial prospects.

Confronted with the threat from Petrosar and aware that Alberta's own petrochemical industry might be closed out of the domestic market by Sarnia's expansion, the Lougheed government has pursued three separate strategies in support of provincial interests. First, Alberta attempted to block the Petrosar development, initially through arm-twisting and persuasion, then by threatening to deny the project feedstocks. This policy failed. Petrosar has been refused "approved" status as a purchaser of Alberta crude oil by Alberta's Petroleum Marketing Commission; but the province lacks the constitutional authority to deny oil to specific buyers once it enters interprovincial trade, and there is apparently nothing to prevent Petrosar from purchasing its 170,000 barrels per day from, say Imperial Oil, or another intermediary.

Second, the Alberta government took an active role in 1974 and 1975 as a mediator between the two other rival consortia proposing world-scale petrochemical complexes in the province. With the Lougheed cabinet acting as midwife, a forced merger of the competing projects was accomplished. The resulting hybrid was a compromise between the interests of the multinational corporation and those of local capitalists. The first phase of the project was announced in September 1975, and involves Dow Chemical and Dome in a complicated joint venture with the Alberta Gas Ethylene Company, a wholly-owned affiliate of Blair's Trunk Line. Ethane will be removed from Alberta's natural gas stream sufficient to manufacture 1.2 billion pounds of ethylene annually at Joffre, near Red Deer, by Alberta Gas Ethylene (using Dow technology); Dow and Trunk Line will then purchase a percentage of the ethylene for further upgrading (e.g. to vinyl chloride) in derivative plants near Edmonton, and Dow and Dome will remove the "surplus" ethane and ethylene via the Cochin pipeline to Dow's plants in central Canada and the United States. The complex ownership structure of the project is indicative of the web of state and corporate negotiations required to produce the deal. The province resisted company pressures for overt subsidies on feedstock prices, but it has left open the door for future subsidization should the project fail to be competitive with Sarnia and United States Gulf Coast plants.

The chances of Alberta's petrochemical ventures requiring subsidies, at least in the initial stages, appear rather high. Sarnia dominates the Canadian industry, with close to 50 per cent of total plant capacity, and Alberta has little competitive advantage, save that of access to plentiful and slightly cheaper feedstocks. Relative to the large Gulf Coast plants which dominate the North American market, the Canadian petrochemical industry was, as of 1976, estimated to be at a competitive disadvantage of at least 10 per cent. Measured against the capital costs of Gulf Coast plants, Canadian projects were higher by 20 per cent in Sarnia, 30 per cent in Montreal, and 35 per cent in Alberta, owing to factors such as higher labour costs, severe winters, and a lack of existing services and infrastructure.[29] Although the size of the cost disadvantage of the major petrochemical projects currently under construction cannot yet be known, Alberta's distance from markets, its lack of infrastructure and skilled labour, and its policy of pricing natural gas feedstocks close to full commodity value with oil, doubtless place the province at a cost disadvantage, and it is not clear that guaranteed access to feedstocks will be sufficient to ensure growth of an Alberta-based petrochemical industry. The incremental Canadian market is likely to be captured by Petrosar, while the United States market is protected by high tariffs. And because world-scale plants are being built to supply a demand that was forecast on higher past than present growth rates, the Canadian petrochemical industry faces the prospect of serious overcapacity in the 1980s.

This dismal prospect has led the Lougheed government into a third strategy – direct negotiations with the United States. Alberta has been sponsoring a new variant of an old idea: the continental energy pact. In return for reduced U.S. tariffs on petrochemical (and selected agricultural) products, Alberta would undertake, subject to federal approval, to increase sales of natural gas to the United States. As mentioned earlier, gas reserves have risen markedly in recent years (a leading factor in Ottawa's decision to refuse the application of Canadian Arctic Gas to build the controversial Mackenzie Valley gas pipeline) and western Canadian producers, not surprisingly, have been vocal in their demands for new markets. At the time of writing, several options are under more-or-less active consideration, including gas "swaps" with the U.S., penetration of eastern Canadian markets served by offshore oil imports, and new long-term export arrangements. The American Vice-President, Walter Mondale, visited Ottawa and Edmonton in January 1978 to discuss gas exports and the Alaska Highway gas pipeline, issues that will be inextricably linked in future Canadian-American negotiations. Mondale found federal officials eager to discuss new exports, but the Lougheed government took a tougher position: without concessions on trading issues, no new permits for the removal of gas would be approved. Whereas Ottawa views exports in classic rentier fashion as a way of improving its short-term balance of trade position with the U.S., Alberta, aware that its resources are likely to grow in value lying in the ground, sees exports from the perspective of its long-range strategy of creating a stronger regional capitalist base in western Canada.

Far more than Saskatchewan's brief experiments with crown ventures after 1944, Alberta's struggle to foster its world-scale petrochemical industry underlines the economic and institutional barriers to prairie diversification. Clearly, there are elements of irrationality in the province's development strategy. "Processing resources at the source" has unquestioned political appeal among businessmen and middle-class professionals eager for industrialization, but as a criterion for locating industries it may be less than sound economics. It is not at all apparent that Alberta – or any other oil exporter – does have the "natural" comparative advantage claimed by Peter Lougheed in petrochemicals; nor are security of supply considerations, which depend on Alberta's power to deny gas feedstocks to out-of-province plants, likely to be sufficient to induce the development of further derivative plants in the prairie West. However, a requirement for state subsidies would not, within the norms of capitalism, be atypical in a pattern of economic development. State-induced and subsidized industrialization has probably been the rule rather than the exception in the historical development of most of the advanced capitalist societies (certainly, as the National Policy attests, it has been the rule in Canadian history), and while comparative advantage will remain an important arbiter of the success of regional development strategies, too much emphasis can be given to orthodox location economics based on static cost estimates at any point in time. In the real, as opposed to the academic, world, power tends to be as important as the principles of textbook economics in determining the regional distribution of industry, jobs, and wealth in capitalist societies: a fact which can be confirmed through the most rudimentary survey of Ontario's historical hegemony within Confederation.

The rise of arriviste regional bourgeoisies and the decline of established capitalist core areas involve a complex struggle for ascendancy and power waged at the level of the state and politics, as much as in the realm of economics; and if the trends of the past decade are a reliable guide, power has shifted with the economic centre of gravity toward the West, particularly toward Alberta. Relative to the declining traditional power centres of central Canada, Alberta's bargaining position is steadily improving, and the future prospects for the province's strategy of economic development must remain an open question.

Notes

1. Our discussion of the world oil crisis is drawn from many sources, but see especially P. Odell, *Oil and World Power* (London: Penguin, 1974), 3rd ed.; J.M. Blair, *The Control of Oil* (New York: Pantheon, 1976); the special issue of *Daedalus* (Fall 1975) edited by R. Vernon, "The Oil Crisis: In Perspective"; G. Foley, *The Energy Question* (London: Penguin, 1976); C.T. Rand, *Making Democracy Safe for Oil* (Boston: Atlantic-Little, Brown, 1975); R. Engler, *The Brotherhood of Oil* (Chicago: University of Chicago Press, 1977).
2. M. Tanzer, *The Political Economy of International Oil and the Underdeveloped Countries* (Boston: Beacon Press, 1970), 72-73.
3. The debate over scarcity and the size of the world's recoverable oil reserves is a highly controversial one. The debate is conveniently summarized in Foley, *The Energy Question*, 132-46. See the classic exchange between a pessimist (Harry Warman) and an optimist (Peter Odell) in the *Geographical Journal*, September 1972 and June 1973. Our own

views have been considerably influenced by the studies of Ian McKay, whose assistance we gratefully acknowledge.

4. Statement by Lougheed re. maximum royalty limitation, Alberta legislature, April 17, 1972.
5. Cf. the province's *Tentative "Natural Resource Revenue Plan"* of April 1972 for relevant data.
6. *Ibid.*
7. See *Globe and Mail*, May 7, 1974.
8. Information derived from interviews with industry and government spokesmen, July-August 1976.
9. *Oilweek*, October 8, 1973.
10. The package of legislation included the Arbitration Amendment Act, 1973; the Freehold Mineral Taxation Act; the Mines and Minerals Amendment Act, 1973; the Alberta Petroleum Marketing Act; and the Gas Resources Preservation Amendment Act. See P. Tyerman, "The Pricing of Alberta's Oil," *Alberta Law Review*, XIV, 3 (1976), for a useful review of this legislation.
11. See the document, leaked to the press, entitled "Final Report of the Interdepartmental Working Group on the Oil and Gas Contingency Plan," dated October 22, 1974, for the rationale behind the Petroleum Exploration Plan. The document estimated the after-tax DCF rate of return on cumulative investment from 1947 to 1973 in Alberta's conventional oil industry would fall from a rate of 15-16 per cent prior to imposition of new federal tax and provincial royalty regulations to 9-10 per cent after their imposition. The latter range was considered too low and accordingly the document proposed provincial tax and royalty reductions. For a simulated assessment of the differential impact of the February 1975 agreements on the various participants in the Syncrude project, see J. Helliwell and G. May, "Taxes, Royalties, and Equity Participation as Alternative Methods of Dividing Resource Revenues: The Syncrude Example," in A. Scott (ed.), *Natural Resource Revenues: A Test of Federalism* (Vancouver: University of British Columbia Press, 1976), 153-80.
12. *Report on Field Pricing of Gas in Alberta* (ERCB), August 1972.
13. Cf. F. Tugwell, *The Politics of Oil in Venezuela* (Stanford: Stanford University Press, 1975), 32-37; and the essay on "The Oil Industry in Latin America" by Peter Odell in Penrose, *op. cit.* Odell correctly noted that implicit in Perez Alfonzo's view of the "intrinsic" value of oil was an optimistic assessment of future demand for oil, as well as an awareness that, to be effective, its policy of "no new concessions" and no increases in exports would require the support of other oil exporters. This was why Venezuela initiated the contacts which led to the formation of OPEC in 1960.
14. D.V. Smiley, "The Political Context of Resource Development in Canada," in A. Scott (ed.), *Natural Resource Revenues: A Test of Federalism, op. cit.*, 67.

15. Cf. D.C. North, "Location Theory and Regional Economic Growth," *Journal of Political Economy*, LXIII, 3 (1955), 243-58; and J.C. Stabler, "Exports and Evolution: The Process of Regional Change," *Land Economics*, XLIV, 1 (1968), 11-23.

16. K.H. Norrie, "Some Comments on Prairie Economic Alienation," *Canadian Public Policy*, XI, 2 (Spring 1976), 212.

17. P. Lougheed, "Alberta's Industrial Strategy," speech to the Calgary Chamber of Commerce, September 6, 1974.

18. C. Newman, "The New Power in the New West," *Saturday Night*, September 1976.

19. Communication received from Mr. Ian McKay, Department of Oil and Gas, The Bank of Montreal, Calgary.

20. The Canadian Petroleum Association and several of the major producers have begun to call for "short-term" oil exports as well as new gas exports to the U.S. Interestingly, Petro-Canada was one of the first oil companies to argue publicly that, given higher returns and freedom from prorationing, conventional oil producers might well discover another five billion barrels of commercially recoverable oil in western Canada. This is ten times higher than the most recent National Energy Board estimate. Petro-Canada's estimates appear to be predicated on the assumption of additional oil exports to the U.S.

21. P. Lougheed, speech in Alberta Legislature, October 13, 1976.

22. P. Lougheed, "Statement re. Petrochemicals," May 16, 1974.

23. M. Leitch, "The Constitutional Position of Natural Resources," November 21, 1974, reprinted in J.P. Meekison (ed.), *Canadian Federalism: Myth or Reality*, 3rd ed. (Toronto: Methuen, 1977), 170-8.

24. A. Blakeney, "Resources, the Constitution and Canadian Federalism," (delivered January 1977), reprinted in Meekison, *ibid.*, 179-88.

25. The Alberta Heritage Savings Trust Fund Act (1976).

26. P. Lougheed to D. Mitchell, October 9, 1974. As tabled in Alberta legislature.

27. Lougheed, Statement re. Petrochemicals, *op. cit.*

28. ERCB interviews, July and August, 1976. On the petrochemical industry, see also the *Annual Reports* of Alberta Gas Trunk Line, 1975-77; AGTL *Prospectus* of November 10, 1976; and the letters of intent exchanged between the participants in the project and Alberta's Minister of Business Development and Tourism in 1975.

29. Cost estimates of petrochemical plants are based on a federal sector profile on the industry, dated early 1978.

CHAPTER 10
Potash, Populists, and Fabians

I take great pride in moving second reading of The Potash
Development Act. ...

It is a step that was not taken lightly, a decision that was not made in
haste, and a course of action that was entered into only after other
alternatives had failed. It is the only measure by which we can ensure
that control of such a vital resource will remain in Regina and not
Houston, Chicago and Toronto. It is perhaps the single most important
step that this government has taken in its terms of office.

> Roy Romanow, Attorney General
> speech in the Saskatchewan Legislature
> upon introduction of enabling legislation
> to permit government acquisition of
> potash mines, 1975

During the 1970s there has occurred an unprecedented assertion of
entrepreneurship by provincial governments, most of it exercised in
the resource sector – from initiatives by the Parti Québécois government to nationalize part of the asbestos industry to the British Columbia NDP's sizable public investment in the forest industry. Closely
related to the increased public investment have been the experiments
by all provinces with new tax systems designed to collect a much
larger share of the economic rent generated from resources. In Alberta
the source of this enterpreneurship is a new urban bourgeoisie, a class
quite distinct from the dirt farmers who supported Social Credit's unsuccessful attempts to operate an independent provincial monetary
policy. Certain elements of this new Alberta elite, Peter Lougheed in
particular, are descendants of long-established and powerful Alberta
families whose prominence was eclipsed by the depression and the
preponderance of the oil majors in the years following Leduc. Thus to
a limited extent contemporary enterpreneurship in Alberta is a revival

of pre-depression phenomena, but essentially it is new – a break with the recent past. In Saskatchewan, by contrast, no substantial urban bourgeoisie has emerged, and support for the NDP's incursions into the resource sector has depended – to the extent support exists and it is much less unanimous than in Alberta – upon a partial revitalization of an essentially populist farm-labour alliance little changed from the 1940s. Further, the actual entrepreneurs within government can usefully be seen as a revival of the Fabian tradition of an earlier period. Without a brief discussion of the dynamic of revitalization that operated within the NDP during the years of the "New Saskatchewan," the events of the 1970s are incomprehensible.

Within a decade of their assuming office the governments of the United Farmers of Alberta and Social Credit had both been effectively co-opted by the business elites, local and national, they had originally set out to challenge. Although incomplete, an analogous process overtook the CCF, particularly within the ministries dealing with major corporate and financial interests. The Treasury, obsessed with maintaining a good credit rating for provincial securities on major money markets, came to reflect within government the hostility of such markets to projects entailing public risk capital. The Department of Mineral Resources became in effect an advocate of the perspective of the mining industry. Co-optation remained incomplete because the scope of the CCF's economic initiatives during its first term, and of its major welfare state initiatives – the most controversial of which, medical care insurance, did not occur until 1962 after eighteen years in office – nurtured a sustained mistrust by the local business community of the CCF.

But if the CCF escaped the Scylla of total co-optation, after 1964 it faced the Charybdis of an aging leadership and an eroding populist base. Douglas had departed for federal politics in 1961. Could his successor, Woodrow Lloyd, prevent the party's complete demise – the usual fate of North American populist parties after losing office – and equally important could he intellectually revitalize and rejuvenate its leadership?

Woodrow Lloyd grew up on a homestead in southwestern Saskatchewan. Lack of money during the depression forced him to abandon his university training after one year, but he later obtained teacher training and spent the depression as a rural teacher. By 1944, when he was first elected as a CCF MLA, he had become a prominent advocate of educational reform and was the obvious choice for the Education portfolio which he occupied until he replaced Fines as Provincial Treasurer in 1960. Upon his election to replace Douglas as provincial leader in 1961, he served as Premier until defeated in 1964.[1]

The collapse of the "New Saskatchewan" after 1967 was a necessary precondition to the NDP's re-election, but without the qualitative changes encouraged by Lloyd within the party the post-1971 NDP government might well have been a mere continuation of that of the CCF post-1948. He successfully made the transition after two decades of administrative politics and the powers of office to the radically different job of revitalizing a moribund political organization. Although education reform was to Lloyd what health reform was to Douglas, as early as 1965 he reintroduced discussion of public ownership of resources, joint ventures, increased royalties, foreign ownership, and a critique of the contemporary pro-development ethos. He began by acknowledging the obvious: "It cannot be claimed that CCF governments, in any substantial manner, altered the traditional pattern of ownership, or intervened extensively in the general procedures of resource exploitation." His language at this stage remained that of a long-experienced politician, chastened by the limitations of office, and he proffered more questions than answers:

> To what extent would, and could, the Saskatchewan people invest in. ... a publicly owned and operated oil or potash development? Could funds be borrowed from the usual commercial sources for this purpose? To what extent – having in mind elections at intervals of 4 or 5 years – would the voting public tolerate dry holes [in oil exploration] or the interest charges on investment of millions in a potash shaft which might require added millions of dollars and months (or years) of time to repair after technical difficulties? Would there be marketing obstacles ...? Would such a development (public ownership) interfere with access to needed capital for power, telephones, etc? How much can we rely on the strength of our near monopoly position in respect to known reserves of potash? In short are the potential returns such as to make the risk worthwhile?[2]

By the end of the decade a convergence of events revitalized traditional populist attitudes among much of the farm-labour constituency. The agricultural depression brought renewed support to the militant Farmers' Union; the crisis within the potash industry and Ross Thatcher's back-to-work legislation alienated labour from the Liberals' conservative economic ideology. Asserting that "[i]t is not the responsibility of the Saskatchewan government to make the world safe for U.S. potash,"[3] Lloyd dissociated the NDP from the potash prorationing system. Meanwhile, within the NDP, Lloyd's attempts at revitalization had succeeded sufficiently to produce animated policy debates analogous to those prior to 1944.

Many of the new policy initiatives originated with Saskatchewan supporters of the Waffle, and their success, in terms of policy debates, resulted in the 1971 program being the party's most radical since 1944. Albeit the proposal was couched in qualifiers, for the first time since the 1930s the party advocated a form of public ownership of farm land: "a Land Bank Commission which could purchase land offered voluntarily on the market at competitive prices and lease this land, guaranteeing tenure, on the basis of need, with option to buy, with the objective of promoting the maximum number of viable family farms in Saskatchewan."[4] The party evinced a strong bias against foreign capital and in favour of public investment. The debate over the final statement on resource policy was heated as moderate leaders, such as Allan Blakeney, sought to dilute proposals that would have barred all further foreign equity investment in provincial resource industries. The compromise adopted committed the NDP to "[o]ppose any further sellout of our resources. With respect to new development, the NDP will give first priority to public ownership through crown corporations. Co-operative ownership will be encouraged. Partnership arrangements between government and co-operatives or private developers will be undertaken when appropriate. Limits will be established with respect to foreign equity capital, and every effort will be made to limit foreign investment in resource development to non-equity capital."[5] On potash the NDP promised to "[e]nd the present government collaboration in a potash cartel that restricts Saskatchewan output and jobs. Because the present owners have generally shown unconcern about jobs for Saskatchewan miners, and because they have used their power to force farmers to pay exorbitant fertilizer prices, an NDP government will consider the feasibility of bringing the potash industry under public ownership."[6]

The Waffle originated in Ontario prior to the 1969 federal NDP convention, as an attempt at revitalization of the national party: "Our aim as democratic socialists is to build an independent socialist Canada. Our aim as supporters of the New Democratic Party is to make it a truly socialist party. ... [It] must be seen as the parliamentary wing of a movement dedicated to fundamental social change."[7] The 1969 Waffle Manifesto has been well described as having "the resonance of the Regina Manifesto ... in every line."[8] While it appealed to some as a return to the initial ideal of the CCF as a political movement for fundamental change as opposed to the moderate electoral party the NDP had become, it also attracted numerous Marxists, among them disillusioned ex-Communists, who hoped to render the NDP a more rigorously working class oriented and theoretically socialist organization. Finally, it introduced belatedly into the NDP many of the themes (if not the style) of the New Left – feminism, a critique of "business unionism" and advocacy of workers' control, opposition to American imperialism (in Vietnam in particular) and to the invidious influence of American-based multinational corporations and of American mass culture. The common denominator of the ultimately irreconcilable expectations of its supporters was an emphatically, at times stridently, anti-American version of Canadian nationalism. Given the Waffle's assumption that the "Canadian corporate elite has opted for a junior partnership with these American enterprises," the only means to assert Canadian economic independence was "extensive public control over investment and nationalization of the commanding heights of the economy, such as the key resource industries, finance and credit, and industries strategic to planning our economy."[9]

The Waffle achieved considerable influence on the policy of various provincial sections of the party – British Columbia, Saskatchewan, and Ontario – and considerable public attention during the 1971 federal leadership contest to choose a successor to Tommy Douglas. (The Waffle candidate for leader, James Laxer, succeeded in attracting 37 per cent of the delegate vote on the fourth and final ballot that pitted him against David Lewis, who won with 63 per cent of the vote.)

As a source of party revitalization, the Waffle attracted Lloyd and he gave it tacit support when, to the displeasure of most of the Saskatchewan NDP legislative caucus and the federal NDP leadership, he voted in support of the Waffle Manifesto. (The Manifesto, presented to the 1969 federal convention as a resolution, was defeated in favour of a substitute proposed by the federal party executive.) The few party leaders who lent any support to the Waffle were exceptions. For probably a majority of party members, and for an overwhelming majority of party leaders, the Waffle's claim to be a legitimate force for revitalization was bogus. They considered it a "party within a party," a radical sectarian group without public appeal, more committed to its own organizational advancement than to that of the NDP, and therefore a cancer to be eradicated. A dynamic of polarization ensued that confirmed the worst suspicions of all concerned. In particular in Saskatchewan (after Lloyd's ouster) and in Ontario, the party leadership lobbied systematically and in most cases successfully to deny any internal party offices or party nominations to Waffle sympathizers. The Waffle in turn lost much of its early creative diversity and after 1971 came increasingly to manifest a Marxist hostility to all aspects of the CCF-NDP heritage which it disparagingly dismissed as "social democracy." The climax of this polarization came with the expulsion of the Waffle by the Ontario NDP in 1972 and the voluntary withdrawal from the party of the Saskatchewan Waffle in 1973.

254

The history of the Waffle was, from the perspective of the Canadian left, a tragic fiasco. The NDP leadership, in its refusal to make any accommodations to a potentially significant force for revitalization, alienated many and retarded by at least a decade the intellectual renovation the party desperately needs. By its dogmatism the Waffle also alienated many and, outside the NDP, proved quite incapable of any impact upon Canadian politics, degenerating finally into a series of fractious and irrelevant Marxist sects.

The emergence of the Waffle – in 1969 its sympathizers controlled the Saskatchewan party executive including the party presidency – precipitated an internal coup against Lloyd's leadership. Many in the party, including a majority of the legislative caucus, feared that the new radical thrust endangered chances of electoral victory. In March 1970 a joint meeting of the party executive and caucus, called to discuss the participation in the Waffle by the party president, erupted into a general critique of Lloyd's leadership. Certain members of caucus had been meeting privately to discuss strategy in opposition to the Waffle, but the extent to which the caucus and the conservative minority of the executive plotted this coup in advance remains uncertain. Nonetheless the vehemence of the critique, and the number of individuals involved, forced Lloyd to choose between resignation for the sake of party unity or a bloody internal battle to re-establish his authority. He chose the former. The victor in the ensuing leadership contest was Allan Blakeney. Blakeney, while he had little empathy with the Waffle, was among the few MLAs who did not participate in any of the caucus cabals against Lloyd's leadership.

Blakeney and the Revival of the Fabian Tradition
In June 1971 the NDP received its highest popular vote since the CCF first entered Saskatchewan politics. The Liberals lost votes and, with two per cent of the vote and no elected members, the Conservatives seemingly faced electoral oblivion. Allan Blakeney led a government of forty-five MLAs, against an opposition of fifteen Liberals.[10] (Ross Thatcher's crusade against socialism ended not only in his government's defeat but in personal tragedy. Within a month of losing office he died of a heart attack.) The direction of the new government was problematic. In the wake of the caucus coup against Lloyd, conservative elements had defeated Waffle sympathizers on the executive and in most constituency nominations. Blakeney found himself between a program considerably to the left of his basic inclinations and a party leadership and caucus the majority of which was to his right. He opted for caution. Unlike the first CCF government when Douglas' cabinet contained members enthusiastic to implement the party's economic

program, Blakeney's initial choices for portfolios bearing on economic policy were – the Agriculture minister excepted – basically hostile or indifferent to the thrust of the party's economic policy.[11]

Allan Blakeney joined the Saskatchewan civil service in 1950, a lawyer and Rhodes scholar who had left his native province of Nova Scotia in search of a progressive political milieu. As a senior official within the Treasury Department he belonged to the small core of professional bureaucrats ideologically espousing Cadbury's ideal of "socialist planning." He left the civil service in 1958, but after two years of private law practice was elected to the legislature and returned to government as a senior minister in the last CCF cabinet, from 1960-64. If Woodrow Lloyd's goal as leader can be summarized as revival, within and without the party, of the diffuse culture of left populism, Allan Blakeney's goal has been revival of "socialist planning," revival of the professional competence of the CCF civil service which had withered under Thatcher's disdain for government bureaucracy.

Shortly after his election as Premier, Blakeney addressed the annual meeting of the Institute of Public Administration of Canada, the national association of professional civil servants. It was a significant address in its revelation of the priority he attached in the development of policy to the permanent senior bureaucracy relative to cabinet or, by implication, to any other body such as a political party. The source of policies rightly lay, he argued, with departmental officials: "the minister must hold himself aloof from the decision-making process until that process is in its final stages. ... The minister who permits himself to be enmeshed in that process finds that he has no time to perform his political function. Not only that, but by being implicated in the evolution of departmental polic[y] he finds he has lost his capacity to criticize it effectively in terms of its public acceptability." In addition to "his broader responsibility to his cabinet colleagues as a team," Blakeney claimed the appropriate functions of a minister are: "(1) [to] interpret and explain policies of the department to the public – and here I include both the particular publics which may be concerned and the general public, that is, the electorate as a whole. ... (2) to interpret to his departmental officials public reaction to the department's policies ..." The minister should in effect act as a sophisticated public opinion analyst who, given the policy options generated by his officials, determines which lie within the range of public acceptability: "For better or for worse, our system of government is a democracy, not a technocracy. Accordingly, an elected government is involved with providing leadership in developing policies which are in the range of public acceptability. In my view of democracy, we do not impose policies which fall outside this range. This is true, even though from a technical point of view, and in the eyes of the officials who designed them, the policies which the public reject happen to be superior."[12]

This vision of the political process (which quite accurately describes the operation of many departments dominated by their senior officials) contained the germ of the contradiction that, four years later, would explode in the controversies surrounding potash nationalization. Blakeney was determined to revive the progressive Fabian tradition of the professional CCF bureaucracy. Given their ideological proclivities, such bureaucrats would develop resource policy that bore an affinity to, if it did not converge upon, the party program, and one could predict an inevitable renewal of the long-dormant conflicts that during the early 1950s had divided the Planning Board under Shoyama from the Mineral Resources bureaucracy under Brockelbank. How then would Blakeney apply the criterion of pursuing policy within the "range of public acceptability"? To the extent the NDP's farm-labour constituency accepted the economic nationalist critique of foreign capital or the traditional left populist critique of concentrated corporate power, the "general public" would side with the new Fabians. But clearly the relevant "particular public," i.e. the mining industry, would not.

Another manner of expressing the contradiction with Blakeney's vision of the political process emerges from the observation that the Fabian tradition in the province, of which he was a product, placed an inordinate emphasis upon the role of ideologically progressive professionals in the formulation of policy but invested little in the diffuse process of cultivating an amenable political culture. To form a consistent whole the Fabian tradition required, as Lloyd came to realize as Leader of the Opposition, the existence of a political culture that encouraged people to think politically and to participate in the formulation of policy, and that was simultaneously capable of placing the Fabian reforms within the "range of public acceptability." Of what use was "superior" policy if no political movement existed to support it? Conversely why should people interest themselves in reforms designed by a small bureaucratic elite, nominally *for* the people but in no sense *with* the people? Admittedly it may be a difficult task to engage large numbers of people in technical economic and legal issues that bear only indirectly upon them, but the difficulty does not imply a dismissal of the need to do so.

Potash – The Dynamic of Polarization
After 1971 Blakeney slowly built up the central planning staff reporting directly to the Executive Council, and the regulatory capacity of the Finance Ministry (the Provincial Treasury renamed). Predictably

these bureaucrats rediscovered conflicts between the provincial interest and that of external corporations, and accentuated the need for public entrepreneurship in the diversification of the provincial economy. The following typical passage is from a 1972 planning paper on oil policy, written by Hubert Prefontaine, chief planning officer at the time, in the wake of decisions by the major oil companies to concentrate prairie petroleum refining in Alberta and to phase out their Saskatchewan and Manitoba refineries:

> It should be noted that Saskatchewan faces a major decision as to the degree of uniqueness and isolation of its economic development approach. If Saskatchewan follows the traditional path of being only marginally and superficially distinctive, a path into which provinces are pressed by the federal government, its future is predictable and bleak. If, on the other hand, Saskatchewan is to take its own development into its own hands, in its own interest, it will have to be distinctive. It will have to deal differently with economic issues and relationships, and with the dictates of power centres and of technology, than the North American norms. ... if we are to be other than a depopulated province, limited to the export of raw materials to more developed regions, we must strive to become a net exporter of various finished commodities. ... Clearly, if we wish to bring about these developments, we shouldn't be in the situation where large multi-national corporations can arbitrarily make decisions which make sense to them with respect to their own corporate interest, but which make little economic sense for Saskatchewan, and which, in fact, work harshly against the development of the Province.[13]

Prefontaine recommended the government enter the oil industry, first via a joint venture with the co-operatives to build a medium-sized refinery: "Beginning from the refinery, it is proposed that the government oil company should develop as an integrated company extending backward into exploration and crude production, and forward into the distribution and retail system."[14] True to form Mineral Resources officials opposed any major intervention in the industry, although in recognition of declining oil exploration in the province, they did propose some public investment in exploration on unalienated crown lands. When, in early 1973, the government created the Saskatchewan Oil and Gas Corporation (Sask Oil),[15] the Liberal opposition labelled it a sellout to the Waffle.[16] In fact it was nothing of the sort. With the Minister of Mineral Resources as chairman of the new corporation's board of directors, it remained closely affiliated to officials within his department. While its legislative authority was exceedingly broad, its actual mandate was to undertake a modest program of exploration. As a government priority it has ranked low, and as of March 1977 (the end of its third fiscal year) it had drilled a cumulative total of only 130 wells.[17] In addition Sask Oil has purchased some producing properties but, unlike the Alberta Energy Company, it has not become a vehicle for major public entrepreneurial initiatives.

Beyond the controversial increases in oil royalties following 1973 – and in this domain Saskatchewan continued to base the magnitude of its royalties largely on Alberta precedent – the central planners failed to prompt major government intervention in the oil industry. They secured creation of a crown corporation to undertake joint ventures in hardrock mining, uranium in particular, and undertook a major review of forest policy from which there arose several significant public forest investments.[18] However they, and Blakeney, rightly recognized the major potential for provincial intervention to be potash. In 1973 they finally began a thorough review of potash policy extending over taxation, constitutional jurisdiction, marketing, and alternative structural options for the industry. Among such options broached were: (1) abandonment of prorationing and return to a competitive market in the hope that Saskatchewan would emerge with a larger market share, (2) establishment of a government-run marketing board for the sale of all provincial potash, (3) investment in one or more new crown-owned mines, (4) purchase of a portion of the equity of one or more existing mines, (5) nationalization of the entire industry either by purchase or expropriation.

The Minister of Mineral Resources, Kim Thorson, and his departmental officials were wary of any structural changes in the resource sector, but the commodity price boom in oil and potash was of such magnitude and the opportunity cost of inertia so immense, in terms of foregone resource rents, that their resistance collapsed – particularly with respect to potash. As we argued in Chapter Eight, the demand for potash as a fertilizer depends critically on the demand for the crops to which it is applied. The resurgent international demand for cereals after 1972 created a demand for potash that by 1974 restored full capacity production and permitted companies to realize price increases of the same order of magnitude as for oil – a fourfold increase from the $20/ton trough of 1969 to the $80/ton peak in the spring of 1975. Blakeney became sufficiently enamoured of the potential for public entrepreneurial initiative in potash to back his central planners over Thorson and to risk alienating the "particular public" of the potash industry. (In January 1974 he finally replaced Thorson in the Mineral Resources portfolio with a minister, Elwood Cowley, who was ideologically closer to the central planners.)

The first fruit of this policy review was to redesign the potash tax system to restrict the return on capital to a normal level. Such an exercise is fraught with accounting conundrums in the choice of an appropriate rate of return and the definition of the capital base, but it marked an important advance to conduct rate of return analyses and to abandon ad hoc taxation formulas. Given the 1953 and subsequent agreements whereby the province had undertaken not to amend the royalty structure before 1981, the provincial tax reform consisted of a new "reserve tax" superimposed on already existing taxes. Due to this new tax, announced publicly in October 1974 and imposed retro-actively from July 1974, provincial government revenue from potash (excluding the provincial share of corporate income tax) increased by a factor of ten – from $9.9 million in the 1973-74 fiscal year to $105.8 million in 1975-76.[19]

Simultaneously the government invited the industry to expand its existing mines and stated its desire "to participate on an equity basis in such expansion plans." For all new mines the government intended to "participate. ... either as a majority partner in joint ventures, or as full owner."[20] A contemporary feasibility study commissioned by the government recommended construction of a massive crown mine that, with an annual capacity of 2.2 million tons and at a capital cost of $375 million (in 1975 dollars), would have increased current capacity by more than a quarter. Finally, in February 1975, the Potash Corporation of Saskatchewan was formed as a crown corporation empowered (to quote an official release) "to undertake mining developments, joint ventures with others, and to acquire interests in potash operations."[21]

A significant intellectual stimulus to the central planners was publication in 1973 of Eric Kierans' assessment on behalf of the Manitoba NDP government of that province's resource policy. Kierans wrote in the aftermath of the emasculation of the tax reforms proposed by the Royal Commission on Taxation (Carter Commission). He was convinced, as was the Carter Commission, that the combination of accelerated depreciation, expensing of exploration and development expenditures, and the depletion allowance had permitted resource companies to capture an excessive amount of the economic rent arising from growing natural resource scarcities.[22] If the federal government would not remove the special tax concessions enjoyed by the resource sector, perhaps he could persuade provincial governments to intervene. He articulated a strong provincial rights case, based on the fact that in Canada most resources belong to the crown and are thus being exploited under crown as opposed to freehold leases, and that, by Section 109 of the BNA Act, resources belong to the crown in the right of the provinces, and not that of the federal government.

Kierans urged upon the government of Manitoba a plethora of entrepreneurial initiatives to end the privileges of resource companies (Inco with its copper mine at Thompson being the most significant): "(1) Establishing crown corporations to explore and develop its resources through the mining and milling stages at least. ... (2) Investing in existing resource corporations. The continuation of existing leases could be made contingent upon the provincial government obtaining a substantial percentage of the equity. ... (3) Continuing the policy of granting licenses for exploration and development to all applicants but insisting on greater revenues by increasing royalties, taxing reserves, raising licensing fees and rentals and imposing heavier provincial income tax rates. ... (4) Closing the open access to the resources of the province. ... The adoption of such a policy requires that the province assume full and complete responsibility for [their] discovery and development. ..."[23]

Kierans wrote as a nationalist who had recently resigned from the federal cabinet in disappointment at its refusal to place a high priority on policy to counter foreign ownership of Canadian industry. His report was in effect a political manifesto. It eschewed radical rhetoric but it provided strong succour to the entrepreneurial ambitions of the Fabian bureaucrats within the central planning agencies of the three contemporary NDP governments across western Canada: "A new resource policy will undoubtedly bring the government of Manitoba into conflict with the federal government and the large multinational corporation, two formidable opponents. It will not, however, violate prevailing political or economic philosophies. A government is above all responsible to the people for using all their resources efficiently and wisely in accordance with the priorities that the people have set. If their credit and capital are squandered, if their labour is not employed and if their resources do not yield the highest possible returns, then the government must answer. It is not a question of capitalism or socialism. It is simply searching for the better way. In any event, one cannot nationalize what one already owns and it is clear that the province owns its own resources. What must be determined is the manner in which one can gain the highest returns from that wealth, both now and in the future. This is not a matter of questioning the rights or sanctity of private property. The issue of proprietorship has long been settled. It is public."[24]

Consistent with Kierans, the entrepreneurial initiatives to increase provincial potash rent collections and to expand the provincial share of world potash markets were conducted with scant reference to any rights of the federal government to a significant claim upon income derived from the resource. In Canada, however, the bargaining process over distribution of revenue between government treasury and corporate shareholders is rarely bilateral. It is a trilateral process involving the relevant provincial governments, the resource industry, and Ottawa. Given his intent of encouraging provincial entrepreneurship in the resource sector, Kierans diplomatically omitted any reference to occasions when the provinces had used their jurisdictional claims not on behalf of provincial rent maximization but in support of the resource industry lobby to maintain or expand special tax treatment. Ottawa's failure to implement most of the Carter Commission reforms on resource taxation was in no small way due to the support given by provincial governments to the resource industry lobby.[25] In 1974 all past alliances were severely strained and the struggle over rent shares, from oil and other resource industries, became acute as corporations and the two levels of government all insisted on their respective claims. The constitutional basis of the federal claim lies in its jurisdiction over "the raising of Money by any Mode or System of Taxation" (s. 91 (3)), a power it exercised by introduction in the May 1974 budget of a major amendment to the corporate income tax – elimination of provincial royalties and equivalent taxes (including the new potash reserve tax) as allowable tax deductions. (We earlier referred to this income tax amendment in Chapter Nine during discussion of rent distribution from Alberta oil.)

After twenty years during which successive provincial governments had been consistently solicitous of the industry's interests, potash executives were stunned and angry at the sudden changes in the rules of the game. They promptly announced cancellation of expansion plans that allegedly were to have been undertaken, and claimed the new tax rules could lose the province up to $600 million in foregone future potash investments. In a lengthy public brief they argued for the province to renounce its reserve tax in favour of an income tax set at a level such that joint federal and provincial taxation did not exceed one half of pre-tax profits. The effect of the provincial reserve tax plus federal tax amendments on nondeductibility of royalties had, they argued, reduced their after-tax return on capital to 3 per cent. For particular mines the government was willing to consider some relaxation of its taxation, but only on condition the companies disclose detailed company-by-company financial data. This they refused to do on grounds it would provide valuable information for the proposed crown mine, but their refusal lent credibility to Blakeney's counter claim that, properly calculated, the industry's 1975 after-tax rate of return on capital would be from 8 per cent to 12 per cent. It was at this juncture that the provincial election of 1975 interrupted the dynamic of increasing polarization.[26]

Potash Nationalization

Resource issues were present in the 1975 provincial election campaign but Blakeney was unsure to what extent the "general public" approved the entrepreneurial ambitions taking form among his central planners, and the NDP program was accordingly vague on the government's intentions for the provincial resource sector: "New Democrats will continue to act to see that Saskatchewan people get the greatest possible benefit from our resources. ... This may well involve new approaches to public ownership, to joint ventures between the government and private enterprises, and to resource royalties and taxation." There was a more specific promise to "[s]peed up direct government participation in exploration for and development of potash and hard rock minerals" – not a difficult promise to keep since there had been none at all to date. There was no hint of resource nationalization. The NDP sought of course to interpret the election as a mandate from the electorate for the provincial government's bargaining and constitutional stance over resource rents, and to that end the party program rhetorically asked: "who is to call the shots and reap the rewards from our rich store of resources: the multinational corporations, the federal government, or the owners of those resources – the people of Saskatchewan?"[27]

The provincial Liberals and Conservatives agreed upon the need to oppose Ottawa, but took strong exception to the rekindled anti-corporate Fabianism of the NDP. The Liberals posed in their program the choice between "more and more government control of our lives by a power-hungry NDP Socialist Government, or greater freedom of choice ... under a new Liberal government." "Mr. Blakeney," they accused, was "taking a dog-in-the-manger attitude saying, in effect, our resources should only be developed by the government through socialist enterprises. ... What the NDP fail to understand is that corporate income and activities can easily be controlled by taxation and government regulation."[28] Political licence for electoral effect granted, this was a truly remarkable conclusion to have drawn from the constitutional and political conflicts then raging over distribution of resource rents.

The election provided one clear example of how the Saskatchewan business community, unlike Alberta's, has opposed the provincial government in its attempts to intervene actively in the resource sector. In addition to the constitutional challenge to provincial oil royalty legislation (see Chapter Eleven), the oil industry responded by drastically reducing its already small exploration expenditures in the province. (From 1973 to 1974 the total footage of wells drilled in Saskatchewan fell by 60 per cent, and remained static at 1974 levels until a partial recovery in 1977.) A similar phenomenon initially occurred in Alberta, although in that province exploration quickly recovered. The small crown oil exploration company, Sask Oil, was completely unprepared to sustain the former exploration level, and considerable unemployment arose among employees of the small firms dependent upon drilling contracts from oil companies. Caught between the oil companies and the provincial government, these small firms in the oil service supply sector blamed the government for failure to offer exploration incentives as extensive as Alberta's. In January 1975 they organized a temporary withdrawal of field services in an attempt to curtail production from producing wells and hence force the rescinding of the royalty legislation. They failed to secure their stated goal, but did secure the election of Conservative candidates in two of the three principally affected provincial ridings – all of which the NDP had won in 1971. One of the NDP MLAs thus defeated was Kim Thorson, the ex-Minister of Mineral Resources.[29]

As expected given the current prosperity engendered by the boom in demand for the province's staple exports – wheat, oil, and potash – the NDP won re-election. But the results demonstrated the persistence of well-entrenched ideological and class antagonisms within Saskatchewan – in marked contrast to the quasi-corporatist unanimity of support among all indigenous classes within Alberta for the development policies pursued by Lougheed's government. The NDP popular vote fell substantially – to a level marginally below that garnered by the CCF in its 1964 election loss — and the party only retained office in 1975 due to the nearly even division of votes between the Liberals and a resurgent Conservative party. The latter, which in 1971 had appeared virtually extinct with 2 per cent of the popular vote and no elected members, in 1975, with 28 per cent of the vote, elected seven – its largest contingent since the Conservative/Progressive coalition government of 1929-34.[30] Although the Liberals retained the status of official opposition, the Conservatives emerged as the obvious party behind which conservative interests should rally to defeat the NDP.

Within four months of its 1975 re-election the NDP faced a third, fourth, and fifth constitutional challenge to its resource policy – in addition to the challenges to potash prorationing and its oil royalty structure (discussed in Chapter Eleven). The third was launched only nine days after the election. Presumably inspired by the challenge to the oil royalty legislation, all potash producers, except the two companies already engaged in the challenge to potash prorationing, filed a statement of claim contending that the reserve tax constituted an ultra vires indirect tax and infringed federal jurisdiction over interprovin-

264

cial trade and commerce. They demanded repayment plus interest. Simultaneously most producers refused any further payment of the reserve tax. The initial judgment, at the level of the Court of Queen's Bench, was not delivered until November 1978, long after the events leading to nationalization. It supported the government's claim that the reserve tax constituted a direct tax on property, a tax intended to be borne by the producers, and not an indirect tax to be passed on to customers. As we shall see in Chapter Eleven, the murky ambiguity surrounding the nineteenth century economic distinction between direct taxes, which both federal and provincial governments may levy, and indirect taxes, which are the prerogative of Ottawa alone, has become a major source of legal and political tension.[31]

When Noranda and CF Industries had launched their constitutional challenge to prorationing in 1972 (which we shall consider in detail in Chapter Eleven) most producers considered prorationing to be in their interest and had supported the province's constitutional position. But in the dynamic of accelerating polarization, the industry decided to exploit the initial court ruling against the scheme. Implemented in 1972, the "prorationing fee" was justified by the government as a levy for its services as administrator of prorationing. In a fourth constitutional challenge, launched in October 1975 by most of the producers, they alleged that the fee had been rendered unconstitutional by the court verdict on prorationing. For good measure they also alleged it to be an *ad valorem* commodity tax, hence indirect and ultra vires. To date this case remains untried.[32]

The fifth challenge was an extension of the reserve tax case. The province threatened legal action, including cancellation of leases, against companies refusing to pay the tax. Most producers refused to pay unless the government guaranteed to refund all payments plus interest should the tax be ruled ultra vires. This the government refused to do, citing a section of a long-standing provincial statute, The Proceedings Against the Crown Act, s. 5 (7), that explicitly prohibited any legal proceeding against the crown on the basis of a government action deriving from provincial legislation later ruled to be ultra vires. Producers thereupon asked the courts to permit them to pay under a court order that would facilitate their recuperation of the tax revenue should the reserve tax be struck down. At the level of Queen's Bench and Court of Appeal they received no satisfaction, but the Supreme Court agreed to hear the case, and to review the constitutionality of the statute. The federal government intervened against Saskatchewan; the province of Alberta intervened on the side of its provincial neighbour. Under British parliamentary practice a legislature is sovereign (within, if a federal state, its sphere of constitutional competence), and legal proceedings against the crown can only be undertaken to the extent a legislature permits. The province defended its statute as being within the province's jurisdiction to legislate the nature and extent of its immunity from court proceedings. In a decision delivered in October 1976 the Supreme Court refused the court order requested by the producers, but rendered it superfluous by ruling ultra vires the impugned section: "To allow moneys collected under compulsion, pursuant to an ultra vires statute, to be retained would be tantamount to allowing the provincial legislature to do indirectly what it could not do directly, and by covert means to impose illegal burdens."[33] Another provincial defeat.

To complete our discussion of the legal quagmire that has enveloped Saskatchewan resource policy we must make brief mention of the civil suit launched by most producers in May 1976, and the United States antitrust case against prorationing. In the former case producers sought repayment plus interest of revenues collected under the reserve tax and prorationing fee on the grounds these taxes were a breach of the series of agreements, dating back to the original agreement with Potash Company of America (discussed in Chapter Eight), not to amend the potash royalty structure before 1981.[34]

In June 1976 the U.S. Antitrust Division, on the basis of prorationing, filed an indictment in Chicago charging that from 1969 to 1974 five American fertilizer companies, plus over 150 unindicted co-conspirators, "engaged in a continuing combination and conspiracy in unreasonable restraint of ... interstate and foreign trade and commerce in violation of ... the Sherman Act." The intent of the alleged conspiracy was "to restrict the quantities of potash produced in the United States; to stabilize and raise the prices for potash produced and sold in the United States; and to restrict the export of potash from the United States and the import of potash from outside North America into the United States."[35] Among the alleged co-conspirators were ex-Governor Cargo of New Mexico, ex-Premier Thatcher, three Saskatchewan ex-Ministers of Mineral Resources (one Liberal, two NDP), three past or present Saskatchewan deputy ministers, and numerous corporate officers. In a rare display of bipartisan unanimity, the provincial Liberals and NDP both denounced the case as an intrusion upon Saskatchewan, and thus Canadian, sovereignty, and defended prorationing on grounds of the right of the province to regulate its natural resources. The irony was, of course, that the Saskatchewan government had exercised its sovereignty in this instance at the behest of, and on behalf of, the indicted American companies. And now the United States government, under pressure from midwestern farmers angered by fertilizer price increases, was prosecuting the industry leaders. The motivation of the contemporary Republican administration in pursuing this case, it has been speculated, was as much the winning of farm votes in the 1976 election as the attacking of corporate abuses. The case was not tried until early 1977, after the election. The judge acquitted one company and the jury a second. The jury failed to reach a decision on the remainder and in a retrial the judge acquitted all defendants concluding that, while some evidence was "damning," the prosecution had failed to prove criminal conspiracy. However, inspired by the antitrust case, over two dozen individual and class actions had also been launched by farmers claiming damages from the alleged conspiracy to raise potash prices. Most cases were dismissed but the companies indicted by the Antitrust Division ultimately paid a $3 million settlement in the remaining civil actions.[36]

The challenges to the reserve tax and prorationing fee, and the civil suit, remain outstanding at the time of writing. Since all were intended as bargaining tactics in the process of rent allocation, there may be out-of-court settlements. The only interest the producers have in constitutional distribution of power is to maximize the authority of whatever government is more amenable to the industry's interests and minimize the authority of the other. The nature of the bargaining process is, however, trilateral and, if Ottawa is intent on establishing legal judgments to limit provincial jurisdiction over resources, it may encourage producers to continue their constitutional challenges to the point of a Supreme Court judgment.

In the summer of 1975 the NDP cabinet faced in a dramatic manner the dilemmas inherent in Allan Blakeney's vision of politics. Would the cabinet support the aggressive entrepreneurial policies urged by its central planners? To do so would entail policies obviously beyond the "range of public acceptability" for the relevant "particular public" in the mining industry, but also beyond the range for a large segment of the "general public." The option was always open to do as in the past – to abandon the central planners' proposals as impractical and to seek an accommodation with the industry by lowering the level of taxation.

Why did the cabinet avoid compromise and resort to its ultimate weapon – nationalization? The first factor was simply that the uncertainty attached to the collection of resource rents via taxation or royalties had become as large as that inherent in the estimation of the potential profits of a crown corporation. The series of court challenges to the provincial authority to tax resource industries involved too many actors – potash producers, oil companies, provincial and federal governments – to be susceptible to an easy out-of-court compromise. Second, the province's jurisdiction over production, pricing, and allocation of economic rent in the industry would be enhanced were it operated directly as a crown corporation. If resources are not only owned but exploited by the crown, there is no question of potentially unconstitutional taxation – merely internal transfers among public bodies. Further, since the BNA Act states "No Lands or Property belonging to Canada or any Province shall be liable to Taxation" (s. 125) the federal government has to break long-standing precedent if it is to collect *any* income tax from a resource industry operated as a provincial crown corporation. Third, the four-year political time horizon of the next election militated in favour of investing public funds in the purchase of existing mines with established markets as opposed to a $375 million investment in a new crown mine that, requiring four years for construction, would come on stream in 1979.

Finally, the results of the 1975 election contributed to the decision. For some in the NDP leadership the obvious conclusion was that the majority of the electorate espoused the opposition critique of Fabianism within the NDP and, as in the post-1948 period, the NDP must adapt to retain office. For others the Conservative revival had exactly the opposite effect, convincing several cabinet ministers of the urgency to undertake a major reform, of the magnitude of medical care insurance, before losing office. Potash nationalization served that purpose. Allan Blakeney, for example, had long harboured the desire to leave a publicly owned potash industry as a heritage of his government, and this might be the only occasion to do so.

The decision to nationalize was taken by cabinet in August 1975. In the basement of the legislative building the potash task force seconded talent throughout the civil service and, in an atmosphere reminiscent of Phelps' early enthusiasm for social ownership, bureaucrats drafted legislation, studied the international law of expropriation, estimated costs and markets, searched for sympathetic engineers who knew how to run a mine, and finally wrote the Speech from the Throne to be read by the Lieutenant Governor.

In November 1975, upon the opening of the legislature, the decision became public. "You will therefore be asked at this Session," the Lieutenant Governor informed the assembled members, "to approve legislation which will enable my government to acquire the assets of some or all of the producing potash mines in the Province."[37] The government introduced two bills – one empowering the government to acquire by purchase or expropriation any relevant potash assets, the second providing a legislative status to the Potash Corporation of Saskatchewan.[38]

The most interesting issue posed was that of compensation to be paid. Bear in mind that within its sphere of constitutional competence a legislature is sovereign and is under no legal obligation to pay any compensation. In a famous 1908 Ontario case a mining company as plaintiff claimed compensation from the provincial government for an alleged expropriation of its mining rights. The government as defendant denied any compensation was due. In finding for the government the justice wrote what has become a celebrated statement of provincial rights and the legal omnipotence of parliament: "In short, the Legislature within its jurisdiction, can be anything which is not naturally impossible and is restrained by no rule, human or divine. If it be that the plaintiffs acquired any rights – which I am far from finding – the Legislature has the power to take them away. The prohibition 'Thou shalt not steal', has no legal force upon the sovereign body, and there would be no necessity for compensation to be given."[39] Legally there may have been no obligation to compensate; politically there obviously was. Compensation is a reef that has foundered many nationalization ventures. If the state pays compensation at a level satisfactory to the former private owner, it permits the latter to capitalize all expected future profits and vitiates much of the significance of the takeover. If the state pays too little, it runs the risk of serious legal and political retaliation. For example, Saskatchewan will inevitably remain dependent upon continued access to the United States fertilizer market, and it feared, on the basis of the Chilean experience with copper exports after nationalization under Allende, the possibility that expropriated producers, if dissatisfied with the level of compensation, might launch legal actions in the United States to block payment on imports of Saskatchewan potash.

Within the potash task force three principles of compensation were debated. The most generous was replacement value. Based on the unit capital cost of the feasibility study for the new crown mine ($170/ton of annual capacity), the compensation for all ten mines amounted to $1.4 billion (in 1975 dollars). This principle would require the government to pay for old partially depreciated mines the cost of ten new ones. A second principle, and the one embodied in the legislation, was "fair market value" defined as "the amount that would have been paid for such assets if, at the time of expropriation, such assets had been sold free and clear of all encumbrances, liens or charges in the open market by a willing seller to a willing buyer."[40] Essentially this meant that compensation be calculated on the basis of capitalized future net earnings. The conduct of such an exercise depends critically on assumptions about the life expectancy of the mines, operating costs, the rate of return used for discounting, future potash prices and sales volume, and tax policy. The legislation stipulated that fair market value be calculated as if the reserve tax and prorationing fee were constitutional, but compromised by assuming the deductibility of royalties from taxable income. On the basis of assumptions embodied in legislation and others used by the bureaucrats, the fair market value of all assets in the industry was in the order of $1.3 billion (in 1975 dollars), although under quite reasonable alternate assumptions the estimate could be raised or lowered by 50 per cent. Prompted by the uncertainty associated with a capitalization formula and the fear of the interpretation that a hostile court might place upon "fair market value" should, as the legislation allowed, a producer appeal his compensation award to the courts, some bureaucrats unsuccessfully advocated that compensation be based on the principle of depreciated book value of actual investment – a known figure of $565 million as of June 1975.[41] Compensation, so calculated, would permit producers to recoup only their initial investment plus whatever profits they had garnered to date. Producers would obviously object but, it was argued, the government should abandon the idea, implicit in prorationing, of any obligation to guarantee a particular rate of return to private risk capital in the industry.

Indirectly potash nationalization could be traced back to the revitalization of the NDP under Woodrow Lloyd's leadership, and to the nationalist critique of foreign ownership that had become a part of the province's left populist culture during the preceding decade. But unlike the political context surrounding the CCF crown ventures in the 1940s, the links between the central bureaucracy and any political movement, within or beyond the NDP, were in this case much more tenuous. A dynamic of polarization triggered by renascent Fabianism within the civil service had culminated in a significant new precedent for Canadian resource policy, but the cabinet and party leadership had only a limited desire to pursue its broader implications. Unsure of the extent of public support, cabinet avoided general ideological conclusions and presented nationalization as a good business deal bringing a corporate head office to the province, as the only rational response to the court challenges to the provincial claim on the resource rent, as an exception to the norm of amicable government-business relations.

The cabinet hoped that by minimizing the ideological content of nationalization, political controversy would be short-lived and insubstantial. It was not to be so. Within the legislature the Conservatives and Liberals, especially the latter, filibustered the legislation, while outside an impressive alliance of the potash producers, the Saskatchewan Mining Association, the Saskatoon Board of Trade, and the opposition parties mounted a massive media campaign in support of the status quo. An element of the federal cabinet also denounced the policy for discouraging foreign investment and as an attempt to evade federal taxation. Otto Lang, Saskatchewan's federal cabinet representative, threatened to tax a nationalized provincial potash industry, arguing the federal right to tax provincial crown corporations should that be required to protect the federal claim to a share of resource rents. For good measure the retiring United States ambassador to Ottawa cited potash nationalization as a barrier to cordial Canadian-American relations, and the United States Senate, in March 1976, passed a motion of concern, comparing Saskatchewan's potash policies to those of the Organization of Petroleum Exporting Countries.[42]

In January 1976 the potash producers released a public opinion poll purporting to show 52 per cent of those sampled opposed to nationalization, compared to only 22 per cent in favour, the rest undecided.[43] Given the source such results are suspect, but, after a highly effective two-month campaign by the industry and its allies, they deserve some credibility. By the summer of 1976, as the government and producers entered into tentative negotiations over compensation and rates of taxation, a de facto truce was called in the exchange of public attacks. The producers provided financial data to the government and recommenced paying the reserve tax. The potash producers had, however, contained the government's entrepreneurial thrust. Initially cabinet, and the senior bureaucrats involved, envisioned the progressive nationalization of the entire industry and the necessity of some forced expropriation. Faced with the extent of the opposition and the success of the producers in forging an alliance with the provincial business community, the government reduced its goal to ownership of one half the province's capacity and sought a modus vivendi with the largest producer, International Minerals and Chemical. Cabinet became increasingly anxious to avoid expropriation and offered attractive compensation to companies willing to break ranks and sell to the crown. The first to do so was Duval. By April 1978 the government had acquired 40 per cent of provincial capacity, purchasing all or majority equity in three additional mines plus the contract whereby International Minerals and Chemical mined potash ore belonging to a fifth fertilizer company.

In order to secure voluntary sales and avoid the political controversy of expropriation, the government offered extremely generous compensation levels. Duval, for example, received in 1976 (U.S.) $128.5 million for its mine, completed in 1968 at a cost of (Canadian) $80 million.[44] The two figures are not directly comparable due to inflation over the intervening eight years ($80 million 1968 dollars are approximately worth $140 million in 1976 dollars), but in terms of the cost per unit of annual capacity, Duval received a price nearly equal to the estimated unit cost of a new mine. Overall, the high level of compensation has resulted in a correspondingly low rate of return on the public investment in the crown potash company – under 4 per cent in fiscal 1977-78, a year of high fertilizer demand.[45] This rate of return is calculated, it must be remembered, after deduction of royalties and taxes imposed by the provincial government on all producers, public and private, and the magnitude of these latter revenues would in any case be far greater than that of the returns from the crown corporation. Thus inasmuch as potash nationalization constituted a necessary bargaining move in the government's campaign to tax away economic rent, the low rate of return is not particularly relevant. Nonetheless the private producers would protest vociferously were they constrained to a rate of return equal to that on public capital. The conclusion is inescapable: Lacking the political consensus to carry through a policy designed to capture all potash rents for the public sector, the government permitted those companies willing to sell to retain, via generous compensation, a portion of expected future rents.

The Saskatchewan government is now a member and major beneficiary of the North American potash cartel. It has a large financial interest in restricting aggregate supply sufficiently to sustain current potash price levels – levels which currently permit the province to garner in the order of one quarter of gross potash sales revenue as economic rent. However high prices combined with provincial insistence upon appropriating the ensuing rent have prompted producers to develop reserves elsewhere. In particular two Saskatchewan producers (Potash Company of America and International Minerals and Chemical) have explored the small but high grade New Brunswick reserves, which have a significant transportation cost advantage over Saskatchewan in the eastern seaboard market, and both intend to develop large mines in that province. By the mid-1980s Saskatchewan will have lost its monopoly on Canadian production and will face the threat of producers shifting production to New Brunswick whose provincial government, reenacting the Saskatchewan scenario of the 1950s, has already guaranteed low royalties over an extended period to these first two producers.[46]

Conclusion

Aggregate Saskatchewan government revenue from mineral and petroleum resources was $308 million in fiscal 1975-76, 28 per cent of locally generated revenue net of federal-provincial payments. The comparable figures in fiscal 1970-71 were $32 million and 8 per cent.[47] The ability to extract this additional resource revenue has provided the government with sufficient discretionary income to invest in the potash industry and other crown and joint ventures. But Saskatchewan is, as the Planning Board argued in 1946, an "area restricted by accidental political boundaries." The potential for secondary manufacturing employment has, due to the small dispersed market and high transportation costs, always been slight, and neither crown investments by the CCF nor concessions to private capital by the Liberals have achieved significant results. The benefits from non-agricultural staples, although very inadequately exploited until the 1970s, have been more substantial, but given the capital-intensive technologies of these new staples, they create little direct employment. Furthermore much of this resource revenue has been devoted not to capital investments but, given the NDP's ideological basis and electoral constituency, to new social services. To the extent Saskatchewan's resource rents are used to augment public consumption and not as a source of investment funds, the government may merely be retarding an inevitable process of contraction of the provincial population and infrastructure as agricultural employment continues to decline.

Such qualifications were predictably absent from the 1978 election campaign whose major theme was whether God's bounty, private enterprise, or the provincial government should be credited for the new wealth derived from oil, potash, and the rapidly expanding Saskatchewan uranium industry. The results suggest that the provincial government received most of the credit. The NDP won forty-four seats to the Conservatives' seventeen, and none for the Liberals. The NDP and Conservative popular vote rose, from 40 to 48 per cent and 28 to 38 per cent respectively; Liberal support declined from 32 to 14 per cent.[48] The rout of the Liberals completed a process that had earlier befallen provincial sections of the Liberal party in the three other western provinces. The popular vote statistics demonstrated nearly equal NDP and Conservative gains at the Liberals' expense, but the aggregate data probably disguised more complex shifts. In 1975 the Conservatives sprang forth as an ill-defined party. By 1978 it was apparent they were more intent upon laying claim to the anti-government, anti-"socialist" tradition of Saskatchewan politics than to the right populism of the Diefenbaker Conservatives. Given the tradition of ideological conservatism within the Liberal party, the Conservatives were probably the preferred alternative of most ex-Liberal voters, but simultaneously the NDP probably regained the support of a sizeable minority of 1975 Conservative supporters with populist inclinations. The NDP victory may have implied a partial rejection of the conservative trend, during the late 1970s, in Canadian politics but, as the evolution of potash policies since 1975 illustrates, the NDP itself has not been immune to the trend. The cabinet will conduct future provincial entrepreneurship in the resource sector subject to the self-imposed constraint that it be in co-operation with, not in opposition to, private capital.

In the longer run the Supreme Court decision in the Central Canada Potash case (see Chapter Eleven) may place a serious constitutional constraint on the provincial entrepreneurs of Saskatchewan and Alberta but, in the short run, delivery of the decision, during the election campaign, was a fortuitous random event from the NDP perspective. By resolving a constitutional ambiguity in favour of federal over provincial jurisdiction, the Supreme Court justices underlined the regional dimension of the resource debates and permitted the NDP to rally support on the basis of opposition to enhanced federal power. "The present Liberal government of Pierre Trudeau is making a determined effort to wrest control of our natural resources away from us through the Supreme Court," accused Allan Blakeney in a statement admittedly containing an element of electoral hyperbole.

> That court has consistently overturned the decisions of Saskatchewan courts. In the Central Canada case it upset the unanimous decision of the Saskatchewan Court of Appeal. And we are not alone. Alberta has now been told again what price it may have for its oil, and B.C. has been told what price it may have for its natural gas. But Ontario has not been told what price it may have for its nickel, nor has Quebec been told what price it can charge for its iron ore or its electricity. A clear double standard exists in this country. ... In the potash case, for example, the federal government intervened as a co-plaintiff – one of the very few times that has been done in the history of Canada. Standing at our side were the governments of Alberta, Manitoba, Quebec, New Brunswick and Newfoundland. Standing with the resource company was the federal government.[49]

After due allowance for all the ambiguities, the partial nationalization of potash marked a significant maturation of provincial politics from the years when the CCF feared to tackle the resource industry and the Liberals viewed external capital as totally benign. But the NDP in many respects resurrected ideas current within the CCF prior to 1948, ideas that for nearly three decades were absent from the cabinet agenda, that survived only as a minority political tradition, even within the NDP. The provincial Conservatives may yet return them to that status. The Conservative resurgence is proof that major social change effected by a bureaucratic and political elite with little attention to the cultivation of popular participation and support is fragile and tenuous – even *with* public participation the prospects are far from certain! To the extent reform politics have wrought important changes in western Canada, the formula for success has linked populists with Fabian social democrats. There are serious tensions between the vision of politics as seen from the platform of the populist politician and from the Fabian bureaucrat's desk. Both are partial visions. When policies reflect an excessive concern with one vision to the detriment of the other, there is one certain consequence. Whatever ensues is not socialism.

Notes

1. For brief biographical information on Lloyd see Higginbotham, *Off the Record, op. cit.*, chap. 3. On his relations with the Waffle and on the caucus coup against his leadership see the excerpt from his daughter's unpublished biography: D. Norton, "The Last Days of Woodrow Lloyd," *NeWest Review*, II, 3 (November 1976), 3-4.
2. Lloyd, "Ownership and Development of Resources," WSL Leader of Opposition files 106 n, May 26, 1965, 3 and 6-7.
3. *Globe and Mail*, December 1, 1969.
4. "New Deal for People: Program for Progress" (Regina: Saskatchewan NDP, February 1971), 1.
5. *Ibid.*, 8.
6. *Ibid.*, 6.
7. Waffle Manifesto, reprinted in M.S. Cross, *The Decline and Fall of a Good Idea* (Toronto: New Hogtown Press, 1974), 43.
8. Cross, *ibid.*, 16.
9. Waffle Manifesto, *ibid.*, 43 and 45.
10. Report of the Chief Electoral Officer, *op. cit.*, 113-15.
11. The first NDP Minister of Mineral Resources, Ted Bowerman, occupied the portfolio for only half a year before being replaced by Kim Thorson. The exception to this statement, the Minister of Agriculture, exercised considerable ministerial initiative in launching several major programs, including the land bank.
12. A.E. Blakeney, "The Relationship Between Provincial Ministers and their Deputy Ministers," reprinted in *Canadian Public Administration*, XV, 1 (Spring 1972), 42-45.
13. H. Prefontaine, "Public Policy Options for Saskatchewan Oil Industry Development," Planning and Research Executive Council, June 1972, 3-4.
14. *Ibid.*, 8-9.
15. Saskatchewan Oil and Gas Corporation Act, 1973.
16. *Star-Phoenix*, April 12, 1973.
17. *Annual Reports 1974-75 to 1976-77* (Regina: Saskatchewan Oil and Gas Corporation).
18. The political imbalance of the Fabian tradition was well illustrated by the emphasis upon rational forestry practices and increased public in-

vestment, at the expense of the potential role of native access to the provincial forest in the latter's economic development. The issue of native access to the forest finally emerged as a political issue when, in 1973, natives occupied for two days the legislative building. The immediate cause of the occupation was a demand for cutting rights for a series of small native cooperatives. The legacy of the years of neglect of native rights in the forest was that natives made few distinctions between private and public enterprise, it being largely indifferent to them whether profits accrued to corporate shareholders or the provincial treasury. Relations between natives and unions representing white workers in the forest industry were also tense. The former were suspicious of racism in union hiring practices, and the latter feared natives as a source of cheap labour and threat to white job security.

19. For comparative potash tax revenue see *Annual Report 1975-76* (DMR), 7. The reserve tax, a form of property taxation, was first announced privately to the potash industry in April 1974. It is based upon an assessed value times a mill rate. The assessed value in turn is an increasing function of the ore grade and the rate of capacity utilization, and a decreasing function of unit capital costs; the mill rate rises with the market price of potash. See "Saskatchewan Potash Policy," statement by E. Cowley, Minister of Mineral Resources, October 23, 1974, and "Potash Reserve Tax Regulations," o.c. 1756/74.

20. "Saskatchewan Potash Policy," *op. cit.*, 7.

21. SGIS, 75-081, February 5, 1975.

22. E. Kierans, "Report on Natural Resources Policy in Manitoba" (Winnipeg: Government of Manitoba, 1973). Accelerated depreciation permits a firm to deduct a larger sum than the actual depreciation charge entered in its financial accounts. By accelerating the rate of "writing off" a capital asset for tax purposes, a firm can delay the incidence of income tax. Expensing is an extreme form of accelerated depreciation whereby qualifying exploration and development expenditures can be treated for tax purposes as current (all of which can be deducted from current taxable income) as opposed to capital expenditures to be amortized over the productive lifetime of whatever reserves are discovered. The rationale behind all these concessions has been encouragement of exploration and rapid development. The result has been to accelerate unduly the rate of exploitation of domestic mineral reserves and bias the corporate income tax system. The least justifiable in principle is the depletion allowance which provides a deduction from taxable income for the "cost" incurred by depleting a nonrenewable resource – supposedly analogous to a depreciation allowance for the cost of using up a man-made asset. To the extent capital and labour must be invested to explore for mineral resources the market price of an undeveloped mineral property reflects actual costs incurred (defined to include the costs of unsuccessful as well as successful exploration) but in general the price also reflects a large component of capitalized economic rent, i.e. a capi-

tal gain to the seller. Although to a producing firm that buys a mineral property, the market price is a financial cost, only that portion reflecting discovery costs represents an expenditure of capital and labour analogous to that involved in producing a man-made asset, and only that portion – were it possible to determine it – should logically be deductible from taxable income. That portion is not readily calculable, and in fact the depletion allowance takes the form of a large deduction (in general one quarter, but one half in the case of qualifying nonconventional investments) from taxable income. Under the "reformed" Income Tax Act, containing the surviving remnants of the Carter Commission reforms, depletion must now be "earned" by undertaking sufficient exploration and development expenditures. Unlike depreciation allowances the total of depletion allowances from exploiting a particular mineral property can exceed the price paid.

23. Kierans, *op. cit.*, 9-10.
24. *Ibid.*, 2.
25. See M.W. Bucovetsky, "The Mining Industry and the Great Tax Reform Debate," in A.P. Pross (ed.), *Pressure Group Behaviour in Canadian Politics* (Toronto: McGraw-Hill Ryerson, 1975) 89-114.
26. See P.S. Jack (vice-president, Canadian operations, PCA), "Crisis in Potash," address to Saskatoon Board of Trade, February 6, 1975; *Potash ... Solution Imperative*, Canadian Potash Producers Association, February 10, 1975; *Star-Phoenix*: February 19, 1975, February 20, 1975. For an account of corporate-government relations in the potash industry, based on the theme of an escalating dynamic of confrontation, see R. Shaffner, "New Risks in Resource Development: The Potash Case" (Montreal: C.D. Howe Institute, 1976).
27. "New Deal '75" (Regina: Saskatchewan NDP, April 1975), 1 and 5.
28. "A New Direction: Saskatchewan Liberal Statement of Policy 75" (Regina: Saskatchewan Liberal Association, 1975), 1 and 4.
29. For data on oil exploration activity in Saskatchewan see *Annual Report 1976-77* (DMR), 8-9. On the withdrawal of services see numerous stories in *Star-Phoenix* and *Leader-Post*: January 16, 1975 to February 14, 1975. For the relevant constituency electoral results (Estevan, Swift Current, Weyburn) see *Report of the Chief Electoral Officer, op. cit.*
30. *Report of the Chief Electoral Officer, op. cit.*, 113-15.
31. *Leader-Post*, June 20, 1975; *Ideal Basic Industries et al. v. Government of Saskatchewan*, Judgment (unreported), QB, No. 331A, Regina, November 15, 1978.
32. *Financial Post*, October 11, 1975.
33. *Amax Potash Ltd. et al. v. Government of Saskatchewan*, (1976) 6 WWR, 73.
34. *Duval et al. v. Government of Saskatchewan*, Statement of Claim, QB, No. 302, Regina, May 13, 1976.
35. *U.S.A. v. Amax et al.*, Indictment, 76 CR 783.
36. For the political response to and the legal disposition of this and related cases see *Star-Phoenix*: August 28, 1976, August 31, 1976, May 8, 1977,

June 18, 1977; *Leader-Post*: February 19, 1977, October 5, 1977.

37. *Debates and Proceedings*, lst Session of 18th Legislature, *op. cit.*, Part 1, November 12, 1975, 8.

38. The Potash Development Act, 1976, and The Potash Corporation of Saskatchewan Act, 1976.

39. Mr. Justice Riddell, quoted in H.V. Nelles, *The Politics of Development* (Toronto: Macmillan, 1974), 173.

40. The Potash Development Act, 1976, s. 45 (2).

41. This figure is the value of property, plant, and equipment less accumulated depreciation as of June 30, 1975. See "Consolidated Financial Data of the Saskatchewan Potash Industry," Canadian Potash Producers Association, December 3, 1975.

42. *Leader-Post:* November 27, 1974, March 11, 1976; *Star-Phoenix*, December 17, 1975; *Saskatoon Commentator*, December 17, 1975. For a good account (with illustrations) of the media battle see D. Kerr, "Potash and Propaganda: A Managerial Melodrama," *NeWest Review*, III, 7 (March 1978), 5 ff.

43. *Star-Phoenix*, January 28, 1976.

44. *Star-Phoenix*: August 12, 1976, August 13, 1976.

45. The 4 per cent rate of return in 1977-78 is a weighted average of two items: the interest income received on a $75 million loan to the Potash Corporation at a rate of 8 3/8 per cent, plus the $11.3 million net earnings on the $418.6 million (as of June 1978) government equity in the crown corporation. See *Annual Report 1977-78* (Saskatoon: Potash Corporation of Saskatchewan).

46. *Globe and Mail*: October 28, 1977, January 19, 1978, March 30, 1978.

47. *Provincial Government Finance: Revenue and Expenditure*, 68-207 (Ottawa: Statistics Canada), 1970, 24-27; 1975, 20-23.

48. *Star-Phoenix*, October 19, 1978.

49. A.E. Blakeney, press statement, October 4, 1978.

CHAPTER 11
Regina v. Ottawa et al.

Federalism as we understand it in Canada ... means that in a case where provincial interest is paramount under our constitution it stands just as high and unassailable as does the federal power in a reverse circumstance. If it is to be overridden, it must be by an Act of Parliament which clearly establishes the emergent conditions which validate federal action. ...

I have become convinced that the present political leadership in Ottawa does not share this view. I have become convinced that their unrelenting attack on our resource policies is prompted – not by a belief that we are acting beyond our powers – as these have been understood for one hundred years – but rather by a desire to extend the central powers of the federal government at the expense of provincial powers.

They have a model to follow here. The required mix is an aggressive central government and an active, centralist Supreme Court. In the United States, over the decades, this mix has vastly diminished the powers of the states and firmly entrenched the federal government in a position of supremacy. So complete has been the transformation that one rarely hears these days about "states' rights." The result has been big federal government with a vengeance, with all the inflexibility and remoteness from the ordinary citizen which this involves.

> Allan Blakeney
> 1977 speech reprinted in J.P. Meekison (ed.)
> *Canadian Federalism: Myth or Reality*
> third edition (Toronto: Methuen, 1977)
> 179-88

What generalizations, if any, can be drawn from the historical record of prairie development politics? In this chapter we shall assess the role of natural resources in the conflict between regionalism, a persistent political force in the prairies as elsewhere, and the "national interest" as articulated by the central government. In the following chapter we shall address the debates over staple development and economic rent.

In a country of continental dimensions and ethnic diversity, significant regionalism must inevitably arise with or without legal sanction. But by providing it with a legal basis, the federal nature of the Canadian constitution has undoubtedly enhanced a regional identification by members of all social groups. Since the nature of the local endowment of land and other natural resources largely determines the distribution of industries within the economies of all regions except the heavily industrialized Quebec-Windsor corridor, it is not surprising that much regionalism has been directed towards provincial control of resources – the power to regulate production and, to the extent market structure permits, control price; to retain economic rent and secure the maximum linked industrial development. In a unitary state bargaining over these issues involves essentially two sets of actors – the state and the owners of capital invested in the resource industry. In Canada the claimants include not only capitalists and the federal government, but the provincial government in whose territory the resource industry resides and, on occasion, the governments of provinces importing the staple commodity produced.

The British North America Act was, to quote the prominent historian Donald Creighton, negotiated by "typical mid-Victorian colonial politicians who were intellectually as remote from the eighteenth-century preoccupation with first political principles as they were from the twentieth-century obsession with ethnic and cultural values. They thought of themselves as British subjects, and assumed that they were legitimate heirs of the British constitutional heritage and full participants in the British political experience."[1] Enacted by the Imperial Parliament in London, the BNA Act was certainly not a revolutionary declaration of independence. But nor was it the product of a subjugate people. It was a thoroughly pragmatic compromise negotiated by the political elites of disparate colonies – differing in economic interests, language, religion and race. Tentatively and with much mutual suspicion, the colonists of Canada, New Brunswick and Nova Scotia decided that federation into a "dominion," an ambiguous entity with internal but initially only limited external sovereignty, was preferable to the alternatives of continued colonial status or absorption by the aggressively expansionist United States.

Confederation was a marriage of convenience, not of passion. Unlike nation states born, amidst fervent affirmations of national identity, from an act of collective will that overthrew the old order – which may have derived from an imperial external source as in the case of British rule over the United States or from an internal source as with the

French ancien régime – the modern Canadian state emerged with no direct participation by the people from whom it claimed allegiance. The decision to federate was precise only in its rejection of continental integration — the extent of power and authority to be vested in Ottawa relative to London, or relative to the provinces, was far from settled by the BNA Act. Some contemporary politicians, Macdonald in particular, had ambitions of transforming British North America into a major industrial economy and would much have preferred a unitary state to realize their purpose. "The primary error at the formation of their [American] constitution," concluded Macdonald, "was that each state reserved to itself all sovereign rights, save the small portion delegated. We must reverse this process by strengthening the general government and conferring on the provincial bodies only such powers as may be required for local purposes."[2] Read from a perspective sympathetic to Macdonald's National Policy of an all-Canadian railroad, western settlement directed from and by Ottawa, and industrialization behind protective tariffs, the BNA Act can be seen as a charter for nation-building under the aegis of a strong central government. But to do so would be to ignore the regional aspirations that imposed a federal structure on the dominion – in particular the utilitarian Quebec sense of Confederation as an instrument for "la survivance." From this second perspective Confederation created a central government for the realization of certain goals (e.g. defence, a larger domestic market and tax base than that afforded by any individual colony), and provinces for the realization of others (e.g. control of education, social welfare programs, administration of crown-owned lands and resources). Provincial elites were prepared to accord absolute sovereignty to Ottawa within specific jurisdictional bounds but they intended that, within their sphere of constitutional competence, provincial legislatures should also be sovereign. Specific sections of the BNA Act, and specific statements of the Fathers of Confederation, can be adduced to support either interpretation. Consequently an assessment of the success and failure of the Canadian federation must be sought in an analysis of the political life that ensued, not in an appeal to any allegedly correct interpretation of the BNA Act.

Since 1867 Canadian politics have fluctuated in the importance attached to regional as opposed to national authority. Despite the successful utilization of federal power to implement the National Policy and extend the dominion "a mari usque ad mare," the trend during the first half century of Confederation was to enhance provincial power. Sir Oliver Mowat, Ontario Premier from 1872-96, was an early embodiment of the trend. In personal appearances before the Judicial Committee of the Privy Council in London (prior to 1949 the final court of appeal for interpretation of the BNA Act) Mowat won several key constitutional cases that buttressed the perspective that Ottawa and the provinces were both sovereign within their respective spheres of constitutional competence.

The Judicial Committee has been severely criticized by some for the decisions whereby it enhanced provincial jurisdiction. Such decisions, it has been alleged, distorted the "true intent" of the BNA Act and its authors. But the Judicial Committee was only guilty of distortion if one denies the underlying divergence of interests at Confederation. More importantly, it is usually a mistake to portray legal institutions as autonomous agents capable of bringing about major social change independently of more fundamental political and economic forces. As A.C. Cairns succinctly concluded, "It is impossible to believe that a few elderly men in London deciding two or three constitutional cases a year precipitated, sustained, and caused the development of Canada in a federalist direction the country would otherwise not have taken."[3] Such legal decisions did not prevent the expansion of political and fiscal power in Ottawa at a time, after the 1930s depression and World War II, when majority opinion considered the provinces to be inadequate political vehicles for the tasks at hand.

Turning from the Judicial Committee to the contemporary Supreme Court, we shall assess in this chapter the degree to which the latter is attempting to play an autonomous role in enhancing federal jurisdiction in the resource domain – at a time when Canadian regionalism, among all social groups and in all provinces, is at a peak. Given the economic magnitude of the resource rents at stake, in oil in particular, the delimiting of federal and provincial jurisdictions becomes a massively complex and controversial issue – one that can only be resolved, if at all, by resort to political compromise. It is not at all clear at this time to what extent Canadians, acting as individuals and as organized class and regional interests, wish to assert provincial control over resources or to see the central government exercise jurisdiction in order to realize national goals (such as, in the case of oil, maintenance throughout Canada of a price below world levels). The Supreme Court, however, appears to be pursuing a path of legal thought that will significantly enhance federal at the expense of provincial jurisdiction in this domain. For the Supreme Court to have adopted such a strategy, independently of a clear political will among Canadians to proceed in that direction, has exacerbated constitutional tensions.

The Constitutional Ambiguity
For "the purposes of the Dominion"[4] Ottawa initially retained title to all public lands and resources within the three prairie provinces and a

portion of British Columbia. As discussed in Chapter Two, these provinces finally achieved equal status with the others by the British North America Act, 1930,[5] which confirmed the transfer of title to public lands in the four western provinces from Ottawa to the province within whose borders they lay. The Canadian province with the highest percentage of its land and resources under crown ownership is Alberta where, for example, over 80 per cent of all oil is produced from crown as opposed to freehold leases.

The economic significance of federal retention of public lands and resources in the prairies can be exaggerated. Prairie politicians in general approved Ottawa's policies of granting homesteads to settlers and providing land grants to accelerate railroad construction. Had the lands been provincially owned, provincial legislatures would doubtless have undertaken similar programs to encourage rapid development at the expense of long-run rent maximization from the public domain. Federal retention of ownership constituted political "colonialism" and doubtless, in matters such as oil and gas conservation, it retarded the process of learning by doing on the part of provincial governments. But prior to 1930 the overly optimistic expectations, engendered by the wheat boom and other western resources, induced both federal and provincial governments, national and local business elites, to overinvest – particularly in railroads. Even without ownership of its public domain the Alberta government indulged its reckless enthusiasm for railroad construction and incurred an excessive burden of provincial debt. To the extent it constrained public investment in railroads, delayed provincial acquisition of the public domain may even have been to the prairie provinces' long-run economic advantage.[6]

A detailed examination of the respective federal and provincial powers granted by the BNA Act and of the tradition of their judicial interpretation is a daunting task well beyond our scope. Both levels of government have substantial bases of authority that frequently overlap – nowhere more so than in the management of natural resources, the area of most interest to us.[7] The motivation of the authors of the BNA Act is unclear, but by section 109 they retained for the founding provinces important proprietary rights – as the owners of all crown lands and resources lying within their boundaries, and as the recipients of royalties therefrom: "All Lands, Mines, Minerals and Royalties belonging to the several Provinces of Canada, Nova Scotia, and New Brunswick at the Union, and all Sums then due or payable for such Lands, Mines, Minerals or Royalties, shall belong to the several Provinces of Ontario, Quebec, Nova Scotia, and New Brunswick in which the same are situate or arise, subject to any Trusts existing in respect thereof, and to any Interest other than that of the Province in the same." (The BNA Act, 1930, amended section 109 to extend provincial ownership of crown lands and resources within its respective borders to each of the four western provinces.)

It has been argued that section 109 should be narrowly interpreted. By this token the major benefits of resource industries should flow to the nation as a whole via the federal government, and retention of federal title to western lands can be viewed as having been necessary to realize the goals of the National Policy. Conversely it has been argued that without autonomous revenue sources any provincial constitutional authority is ultimately meaningless. Under this latter interpretation the majority of the Fathers of Confederation – putting aside Macdonald and other ambitious centralists – intended "to make of the natural resources the cornerstone of provincial finance. The Provinces transferred to the Federal Government most of their other sources of revenue, including notably the collection of custom duties, but they retained for themselves the use and control of the Crown lands, mines, minerals and royalties as a source of income."[8]

Throughout the historical discussion we have referred to particular cases whose resolution has had important impact on the scope of potential provincial entrepreneurship over resources. An early example is *Spooner Oils v. Attorney General of Alberta*[9] which indirectly established the province's right to regulate over physical conservation of resources. In this case Spooner Oils sought to escape the provisions of Alberta legislation (The Turner Valley Gas Conservation Act, 1932) designed to prevent the waste of natural gas. Spooner Oils extracted naphtha from "wet gas" in Turner Valley and flared the natural gas for which it had no market. The Alberta statute, Spooner contended, constituted an infringement upon its contractual rights under a lease granted by Ottawa prior to the 1930 resource transfer. Furthermore since most of the naphtha entered into interprovincial trade, and since compliance with the Alberta conservation statute would increase the company's costs, it allegedly infringed upon the exclusive federal power to regulate interprovincial trade and commerce (BNA Act, s. 91 [2]). The Supreme Court accepted the first but not the second argument. It ruled that the Alberta legislature had exceeded its jurisdiction, that, in altering the rights of Spooner Oils under its federal lease, the province sought in effect to nullify partially the federal statute under which the lease had been granted. Thus Spooner could continue to flare waste gas, if it so desired. While Alberta lost out to Spooner, in rejecting the second argument the Court indirectly handed the province a far more significant victory. The Court ruled that in substance the impugned statute did not deal with trade and commerce but "provides for the regulation of the wells in that area from a point of view which is provincial and for a purpose which is provincial – the prevention of what the Legislature conceives to be a waste of natural gas in the working of them."[10] This case effectively determined that regulation for physical conservation of resources would be a provincial and not a federal matter.

Regulation by a provincial legislature of trade in a commodity is ordinarily constitutional if it is produced and primarily sold within the province in question. By long standing legal precedent such regulation is deemed to fall under provincial jurisdiction over "Property and Civil Rights in the Province" (BNA Act, s. 92 [13]) or "Matters of a merely local or private Nature in the Province" (s. 92 [16]). Furthermore a province has jurisdiction over the "Management and Sale of the Public Lands belonging to the Province and of the Timber and Wood thereon" (s. 92(5)). Provincial regulation of resource industries has, however, extended to matters not easily encompassed by the above sections – for instance, into market demand prorationing. Is the essence of prorationing the conservation and management of provincial property and hence intra vires the province, or is it in essence a means for supply management and price-fixing that eliminates free competition in the sale of particular commodities and hence constitutes an ultra vires intrusion into regulation of interprovincial trade and commerce? The Supreme Court decision in the Central Canada Potash case (see below) concluded the latter. Since Saskatchewan closely modelled its potash prorationing regulations on the Alberta analogues for oil, this decision increases the ambiguity concerning constitutionality of prorationing oil production to market demand by the government of Alberta.

The case challenging the Saskatchewan Mineral Taxation Act, *CPR v. Attorney General for Saskatchewan* (see Chapter Five), raised the crucial but confused issue of direct versus indirect taxation. The distinction nominally refers to the incidence of a tax. It was a prominent nineteenth-century doctrine succinctly expressed in the following oft-quoted passage from John Stuart Mill's *Principles of Political Economy*: "Taxes are either direct or indirect. A direct tax is one which is demanded from the very persons who, it is intended or desired, should pay it. Indirect taxes are those which are demanded from one person in the expectation and intention that he shall indemnify himself at the expense of another; such are the excise or customs."[11] The distinction was embodied in the BNA Act, which permitted the federal government to engage in "the raising of Money by any Mode or System of Taxation" (s. 91 [3]) whereas the provinces were restricted to "Direct Taxation within the Province in order to the raising of a Revenue for

Provincial Purposes" (s. 92 [2]). Courts, in interpreting this distinction, have been loath to examine the actual incidence of any particular tax and instead have usually relied on a basically ad hoc classification of certain taxes as being inherently direct or indirect.

In the nineteenth century revenue from the latter greatly exceeded that from the former, but the emergence of new taxes defined to be direct – in particular the income and sales tax – has strengthened the taxing power of the provinces relative to Ottawa. Income taxes have been classified by the courts as direct even though the nature of the market demand for a corporation's product may permit it to pass on via price increases any increase in corporate income tax. By contrast import and excise duties are deemed indirect even if the nature of the market demand prevents any price increase and forces the importer or exporter to bear the burden of such taxes. If provincial royalties are not "royalties" in the sense of section 109 of the BNA Act, they become ad valorem commodity taxes, and these in general have been considered indirect taxes – but not always. Sales taxes on commodities in retail trade have been classified as direct taxes borne by the consumer. Whatever virtue the legal meaning of direct versus indirect taxation may have, intellectual consistency is obviously not one of them.

In addition to specific legislative and proprietary rights already discussed, the BNA Act contains more general clauses that may be invoked. A province has jurisdiction over "all Matters of a merely local or private Nature in the Province" (s. 92 [16]), a clause however of limited generality. Far more important is the federal authority to declare certain "works" (i.e. capital investments such as railroads) "to be for the general Advantage of Canada or for the Advantage of Two or more of the Provinces" (s. 92 [10] [c]). Even when such "works" are entirely within one province, their regulation thereafter falls under federal jurisdiction. Finally there is the extremely general federal power "to make Laws for the Peace, Order and good Government of Canada in relation to all Matters not coming within the Classes of Subjects by this Act assigned exclusively to the Legislatures of the Provinces" (s. 91). The courts have limited the application of these sweeping powers, although they were successfully invoked, for example, to procure federal jurisdiction over uranium.

The only sure conclusion with respect to the constitutional division of authority is that both levels of government have a basis for bargaining and that conclusions drawn from a literal reading of the BNA Act, or of past legal interpretation of it, cannot be relied upon as guidelines for the future outcome of federal-provincial constitutional conflict. If the constitution provides the provinces with a basis for bargaining, the magnitude of economic rents created by the international commodity price boom in petroleum and other minerals during the 1970s provided Alberta and Saskatchewan, the two leading provinces in per capita resource revenues, with a strong incentive to "try harder." The opportunity costs of inertia became so large that broad alliances across indigenous classes have supported the provincial governments, more unanimously in Alberta than in Saskatchewan, in bargaining with Ottawa, foreign resource companies, and resource importing provinces.

Most jurisdictional conflicts have not been bilateral cases pitting one level of government directly against the other, but have involved trilateral conflicts in which typically a private corporation, adversely affected by some government levy or regulation, emanating from one or other level of government, mounts a constitutional challenge. The level of government whose jurisdiction stands to be enhanced by the success of the challenge has a coincidence of interest with the corporate plaintiff and, either independently or in alliance with the plaintiff, may intervene in the case. Two significant contemporary examples of this process are *CIGOL v. Government of Saskatchewan*[12] and *Central Canada Potash v. Government of Saskatchewan.*[13]

CIGOL v. Government of Saskatchewan

The central planners in Regina failed to persuade their political masters to intervene in the oil industry beyond the limited exploration and production activities undertaken by Sask Oil, and the increases in Saskatchewan oil royalties were closely related, in magnitude per barrel, to Alberta precedent. However, for several reasons the oil industry chose to mount a constitutional attack on provincial royalty claims in Saskatchewan and not Alberta. Why? A superficial answer lies in the fact that the average per barrel Saskatchewan royalty after 1973 exceeded somewhat that in Alberta, but both provinces simultaneously undertook drastic revisions in their royalty structures as the basis of their claim to the majority of the incremental rents created by oil price increases. A more plausible hypothesis is that the oil industry, which fundamentally objected to the royalty revisions in *both* provinces, chose to attack Saskatchewan because the NDP, despite the record of passive regulation by the Department of Mineral Resources, remained to the industry an alien unpredictable institution whose leadership had few links to the business community. The oil industry feared that, if unambiguously successful at rent collection, the NDP might proceed to more ambitious stages of entrepreneurship including nationalization of the industry. In the course of the constitutional challenge counsel for the oil company challenging Saskatchewan's oil royalties did resort to precisely such a political argument – claiming the Saskatchewan oil and gas legislation to be part of a "grand scheme" to take control of the provincial oil industry.[14] By contrast most oil executives retained confidence that the Alberta government, despite the unprecedented autonomy manifested in its royalty increases, would never seek to use its new power and wealth to revoke private property rights. Finally, it is worth stating the obvious: any court decision restricting the constitutional rights to impose royalties of one province created a precedent applicable to all others.

In December 1973 Saskatchewan enacted Bill 42, a complex piece of legislation whose central functions were to nationalize (with compensation) virtually all freehold oil and gas rights, and to impose a "royalty surcharge" on all crown oil production.[15] The royalty surcharge per barrel was defined to be the difference between the market price for oil and a lower price approximately equal to prices prevailing prior to the OPEC price increases in the fall of 1973. To prevent evasion of the surcharge by transfer pricing among divisions of an integrated oil company, Bill 42 empowered the Minister of Mineral Resources to specify, for purposes of calculating the surcharge due, the market price whenever he deemed oil was being sold at a price below it. The lower price could be adjusted by the Minister to allow for grade of oil, rising production costs, and drilling incentives, but in principle the royalty surcharge was to be a 100 per cent tax on all incremental rents arising from future price increases.

The Calgary-based oil industry decided that one of its members should challenge the constitutionality of Bill 42, and in February 1974 Canadian Industrial Gas and Oil Limited (CIGOL), an independent company producing oil in Saskatchewan, initiated such an action. It contended that the new royalty surcharge constituted an indirect and hence unconstitutional provincial tax, and that the bill's price-setting provisions infringed federal jurisdiction over trade and commerce. In response government counsel argued that the royalty surcharge was a legitimate royalty generated by a natural resource owned in the right of the province. As in the potash prorationing case, the federal government here intervened to argue against provincial rights. In appreciation of the significance of the case, the provincial governments of Quebec, Manitoba, and Alberta intervened on the side of Saskatchewan.[16]

It is always necessary to bear in mind the trilateral, if not quadrilateral, nature of bargaining over resource rents. Besides the oil industry and the provincial governments as claimants, there was the federal government and, fourthly, the oil-importing provinces which hoped to capture the rents via preservation of oil prices below world levels. In September 1973 the federal government had imposed a "voluntary freeze" on domestic crude oil prices and a tax on exported oil equal to the difference between the landed price of imported oil and the frozen price. At the time the volume of oil exports from western Canada to the United States exceeded the volume of offshore imports east of the Ottawa Valley, and therefore the export tax earnings sufficed to cover a federal subsidy on imported oil designed to maintain a uniform "frozen" oil price across the country. The oil-producing provinces protested vigorously that the sale of Canadian oil at prices below the international level constituted an unwarranted federal limitation of provincial rights to *all* economic rent created by natural resources. Saskatchewan and Alberta grudgingly accepted the price freeze as a temporary measure, but they insisted prices rise progressively towards the world level. As Canadian oil producibility peaked and Canada became a net oil importer (the transition occurred in 1975), the federal government could no longer cover the subsidy on imported oil from export tax earnings and it too supported a policy of raising domestic oil prices. Since 1974 the price of crude oil has become an administered price negotiated in federal-provincial conferences of the eleven Canadian governments.

The producing provinces intended, by taxing all incremental revenue accruing to the oil industry at a high enough level, to preclude any increase in federal corporate income tax collections from the industry. We have previously referred to the federal government's elimination in May 1974 of provincial royalties as an allowable income tax deduction for resource companies. This federal claim to a substantial share of resource rents exacerbated an already complex and acrimonious bargaining process. After May 1974 the constitutional challenge to Bill 42 assumed an enhanced significance. Whereas it began as a manifestation of the oil industry's traditional mistrust of the NDP, it became the arena for a major constitutional battle between the federal and provincial governments over resource jurisdiction.

At the level of the Court of Queen's Bench and the Saskatchewan Court of Appeal the constitutionality of Bill 42 was upheld, but in a significant decision delivered in November 1977, the Supreme Court ruled ultra vires those sections of the Act establishing the royalty surcharge; it upheld the nationalization by the province of freehold oil and gas rights. The court ordered repayment, with accumulated interest, of all tax revenue emanating from the royalty surcharge – an amount in the order of $500 million. The government has responded by introduction of a new retroactive income tax on oil revenue whereby it hopes to collect an equivalent sum, but the constitutionality of the enabling legislation for this new income tax may also be challenged.[17]

To appreciate the constitutional ambiguity surrounding resource taxation we must examine two legal distinctions – that between a tax and a royalty, and between direct and indirect taxation – both of which, as used by the courts, constitute dubious economic theory. Recall that economic rent is an excess income above that necessary to generate a normal return to the capital and labour employed and, by generalization, a normal return to all taxing authorities. Analytically a royalty is economic rent accruing to the government in its capacity as owner of the resource in question. Provided it does not reduce the return on capital and labour in the industry below normal, or squeeze out normal tax revenues, any government levy on a resource industry, whatever form it takes (a portion of the mineral produced or cash, a percentage of gross or net income, a lump sum or a stream of payments over time), constitutes economic rent and can analytically be defined as a royalty. By contrast, a tax is any other levy on private income deriving from the power of a sovereign state to collect revenues from its subjects.

Now, the Saskatchewan government calculated the royalty surcharge as the difference between the politically administered domestic Canadian oil price and the "frozen" 1973 price level. The surcharge varied as new oil price increases were negotiated, and as adjustments were made for rising production costs and incentives to producers. If we accept that, prior to its imposition, capital, labour and governments (considered as tax collectors) were receiving normal returns, then the royalty surcharge was analytically a levy on economic rent and hence a royalty, not a tax. One could argue that the surcharge could have been set equal to the world price less the "frozen" 1973 price level and still have constituted merely a capture of economic rent, but let us accept that economic rent and hence royalties should be defined with respect to the politically administered domestic oil price level. To the extent Alberta royalties and unit operating costs were somewhat lower, the rate of return on capital employed in the Alberta industry was higher than in Saskatchewan, but imposition of the royalty surcharge, in the context of pre-1974 income tax rules, still permitted Saskatchewan oil producers an average return on capital above the average for all Canadian industries. But after the OPEC oil price increases the federal government no longer considered its tax returns "normal" and in May 1974 proceeded to amend the corporate income tax. The combination of the royalty surcharge plus income tax calculated with nondeductible royalties certainly reduced profits, on Saskatchewan oil, below a normal level.[18]

What portion of the royalty surcharge ceased to be a levy on economic rent, and became a tax, turns on what portion of the increased federal income tax should be deemed normal taxation. Relative to the past tradition of tax concessions to the resource sector, virtually all the post-1974 increase can be considered "excessive," as charged by the oil-producing provinces and the industry. But if we take as a working definition of a normal income tax rate the average ratio for all industries of income tax to book value of capital (were the rate of profit on capital equal in all industries, the average ratio of tax to profits would yield the same definition of normal taxation) then the rate of income tax on resource industries had hitherto been below normal, and Ottawa did not act unreasonably by raising it. To the extent nondeductibility of royalties took federal income tax above the normal rate, so defined, the provinces were justified in claiming that Ottawa was using its taxing authority to erode provincial rights to collect resource rents via royalties. While the producing provinces complained bitterly about nondeductibility provisions, they implicitly granted Ottawa's right to some increase in the corporate income tax by reducing their royalty levies. The reductions were of course also a recognition of the bargaining power of the oil industry to preserve its traditional return on capital.

In assessing the royalty versus tax distinction, the Supreme Court paid absolutely no attention to the economic argument that royalties should vary as a function of economic rent. The justices made the appropriate distinction between a royalty as income derived from ownership of an asset and a tax as income derived from the authority of the state to impose levies on its subjects. They proceeded, however, to emasculate the proprietary right of the province to collect royalties, by concluding that any use of the province's legislative authority to enforce its royalty claims transformed the levy from royalty to tax. A royalty, they argued, is a payment to the crown arising from a *voluntary* contract between the producing company as lessee and the crown as lessor; a tax is an *involuntary* payment made under obligation of law. By historical precedent, the Court further implied, a royalty has been in the order of one eighth of gross revenue, and any levy significantly exceeding that norm becomes a tax. Arising from an imposed statute and not from voluntary negotiation between lessor and lessee, and being a 100 per cent levy on all income above the specified lower price, the royalty surcharge was, all justices concurred, a tax and not a royalty.

The Court's argument ignored the nature of bargaining inherent in the determination of royalty levels. If, in other jurisdictions, much of the economic rent is left with private producers, they will not voluntarily agree to contracts permitting any particular province to capture most or all of the economic rent. In such cases the province can capture rent only by use of legislative powers to determine the level of royalty payments. Analytically the revenues thus collected do not cease to constitute economic rent – unless they prevent normal returns to capital, labour and tax authorities. Legally, however, the Supreme Court has ruled that the use of legislative power, in and of itself, transforms the revenues collected from royalty to tax.

The Court's reasoning appears as ominous for Alberta's royalty structure as for Saskatchewan's. Alberta has divided the total price of oil into ranges, and within each range has levied different gross royalty rates. The mechanism differs from that of the royalty surcharge, but Alberta's new royalty rates were unilaterally imposed by the government and far exceed the historical one eighth formula. The Supreme Court might well, if called to rule, deem them to be a tax. The clear implication of the Court's reasoning is to limit the scope of provincial power, under section 109 of the BNA Act, to impose royalties on resources. There remains the second question of whether the provinces can defend their resource levies as direct taxation.

The distinction between a direct and indirect tax refers, nominally at least, to its incidence. In contemporary economics the assessment of incidence is an exercise in comparative statics – in which the tax in question is one of several variables in a system of equations describing the relevant functional relationships within the economy. Variation of the tax may generate potentially complex changes in prices, wages, and profits in several industries, although in this case the answer is relatively straightforward. Since the price of crude oil has become a politically administered price, oil companies could not pass on the surcharge and therefore it has in effect been a direct tax upon their income. The dissenting minority judgment agreed with this reasoning and concluded that the royalty surcharge, while not a royalty, was a direct tax and hence intra vires. The majority judgment placed great stress on the powers granted to the Minister by Bill 42 to specify, for purposes of calculating the surcharge, the market price of oil. The ministerial power to deem the price at which the producer bought and sold oil meant, the majority argued, that the producing company became a "conduit"[19] passing on the surcharge to the purchaser of crude oil. Thus the royalty surcharge has been ruled to be neither a royalty nor a direct tax. It was instead an indirect tax – and ultra vires.

As a secondary argument the majority judgment concluded that the price-setting powers of Bill 42 constituted an infringement of federal jurisdiction over trade and commerce: "the legislation [Bill 42] gave power to the minister to fix the price receivable by Saskatchewan oil producers on their export sales of a commodity that has almost no local market in Saskatchewan. Provincial legislative authority does not extend to fixing the price to be charged or received in respect of the sale of goods in the export market."[20] Such an unqualified conclusion buttressed the constitutionality of the 1974 federal Petroleum Administration Act which authorizes Ottawa to negotiate agreements with producing provinces for oil prices and, in the event of a failure to agree, to establish unilaterally the maximum price for oil entering into interprovincial trade.

In discussing the division between a federal power and a potentially conflicting provincial power (in this case the federal power over interprovincial trade and commerce versus the provincial power to collect royalties), the courts have frequently made use of the image of a "flow of commerce." Provincial jurisdiction obtains up to but not beyond the point a commodity enters the flow. The ambiguity of the image has always lain in the definition of the point at which a commodity enters the flow. "Implicit in the argument of the appellant [CIGOL]," observed the author of the dissenting judgment, "is the assumption that federal regulatory power pursuant to [trade and commerce] follows the flow of oil backward across provincial boundaries, back through provincial gathering systems and finally to the well-head. A secondary assumption is that sale at the well-head marks the start of the process of exportation. In the view I take of the case it is unnecessary to reach any conclusion as to the validity of either of these assumptions. It is, however, worth noting that neither American nor Canadian jurisprudence has ever gone that far."[21]

Obviously the general thrust of constitutional interpretation does not repose upon this one decision. However, from a provincial perspective, the intention of the Supreme Court does appear to go "that far" – to entrust to the federal government all power to regulate the price of a commodity destined for interprovincial trade. If the federal trade and commerce authority empowers Ottawa unilaterally to set oil prices, what remains of the province's constitutional claim to royalties? The answer appears to be, not much – even if prevailing practice continues for the interim to permit the provinces to gather large royalty revenues.

The uncertainty surrounding the current constitutional division of powers over resources has increasingly prompted Saskatchewan and Alberta (plus certain other provinces) to exercise their proprietary rights. Provincial jurisdiction over crown-owned resources (exploited by firms under crown leases) is stronger than that over privately owned resources (exploited under freehold leases). In the case of crown resources ownership of the commodity produced traditionally passes to the producing firm in exchange for payment of a royalty, but if a province retains ownership to the point of sale to a final consumer – by use of a crown corporation for example – it may be able to garner economic rent via the crown corporation's profits, potentially obviating the constitutional proscription on indirect taxation by a province. Potash nationalization in Saskatchewan is the most dramatic example of such an extension of provincial resources ownership in order to capture economic rent, but in December 1973 the province of Alberta enacted the Petroleum Marketing Act, thereby establishing a Petroleum Marketing Commission (see Chapter Nine), a crown corporation with broad powers extending over the production and pricing of all crown oil. Since the Commission retains ownership of all crown oil until the sale to a final consumer, and is empowered to determine the price paid to producers for their services in producing crown oil and the price at which it sells, the difference between these two prices could be used as an alternative to royalties as a mechanism for collecting economic rent. To date the mechanism remains a potential but unused tactic, and untested in the courts. Since one level of government does not traditionally tax another (BNA Act, s. 125), the federal government would have to break long-standing precedent to collect *any* income tax from a resource industry operated as a provincial crown corporation.

The advantage to a province of extending its resource ownership will always be limited by the courts. A province can do with provincial crown property whatever a private owner could do, but no more. It cannot, by extending its ownership, indirectly encroach upon what the courts rule to be legitimate federal areas of jurisdiction. Thus if the federal government has the constitutional authority unilaterally to set resource prices, it can presumably set them sufficiently low to eliminate any economic rent. There would then be no residual for the provinces to extract, whether via royalties or profits of provincial crown corporations.

Central Canada Potash v. Government of Saskatchewan

Although Blakeney slowly re-established the Fabian tradition within the central bureaucracy, it required the post-1973 commodity price boom in oil and potash to shatter the accumulated inertia of resource policy. The interlude from 1971 to 1973 constituted the final years of the accommodation to external resource capital that had been initiated by Clarence Fines and J.H. Brockelbank after 1948.

In a classic example of a regulatory agency co-opted by the industry it is intended to regulate, the bureaucrats within the Department of Mineral Resources sought to justify potash prorationing as the only feasible policy to pursue. Admittedly it was fulfilling its raison d'être admirably – permitting American producers to operate at nearly full capacity, transferring the costs of irrational investment decisions from corporate shareholders to fertilizer buying farmers, and thereby avoiding financial losses among either Saskatchewan or New Mexico producers.[22] With restriction of Saskatchewan supply to approximately half capacity, North American producers had even succeeded in raising prices somewhat above the $33.75/ton minimum regulated price. Thus between 1969 and 1971 the value of Saskatchewan production doubled while the volume rose only marginally; American production stabilized. Saskatchewan tax and royalty revenue from the industry remained static at nominal levels.[23]

A necessary (but not sufficient) condition to realize the NDP's commitment to increase provincial production significantly would have been for the government to ally itself with consuming interests – offshore and among American farmers – and sever its role as administrator of a cartel designed to protect profit rates among North American producers. The bureaucracy correctly argued that aggregate North American potash demand was relatively insensitive to price, and therefore it would not be significantly affected by price reductions. Thus market sharing in the continental market became essentially a zero-sum game with New Mexico, and officials had concluded that political power dictated Saskatchewan remain a large but residual supplier. Was this conclusion valid? It is impossible to offer a definite answer because, as with all such questions involving the limits of public policy, the constraints had not been tested since the time of Phelps' early ventures. However, the success of the New Mexico lobby in halting the transfer, by multinational producers, of production from New Mexico to Saskatchewan in the late 1960s, suggests that it probably was. The offshore demand for North American potash producers, however, has been sensitive to price changes.

In the negotiation of offshore sales and in allocation of quotas among individual mines, Thatcher had recognized the conflicts between Saskatchewan's interest in a larger market share and the producers' interest in Saskatchewan's acting as administrator of a producer cartel. While transportation costs barred offshore producers from the North American market, except the Eastern seaboard, offshore producers could, and did after imposition of regulated prices, undersell North American producers in the latter's offshore markets. In an attempt to preserve such markets Thatcher entered into a technically illegal agreement with Japanese importers to sell a large volume of Saskatchewan potash at an average price below the $33.75 minimum, thus violating his own government's regulations.[24] In the allocation of mine quotas Thatcher recognized the value to the province of organized American farm interests by awarding larger quotas to the producers having captive markets than to those without. A major beneficiary of such a quota formula was Central Canada Potash (CCP), the mine jointly owned by Noranda and the large farm co-operative, CF Industries. By 1971 it enjoyed the highest quota and its farmer owners indirectly benefitted via the profits of the mine, if not via low potash prices.

The bureaucracy was reluctant to admit any conflicts of interest. It considered the present situation basically satisfactory, and after June 1971 undertook to re-educate the new NDP minister: "Saskatchewan has been acknowledged," he was informed, "as the world leader in formulating a sound policy for conserving, developing and marketing potash."[25] Within six months it had succeeded sufficiently that in meeting representatives of the producers he (to quote a contemporary departmental press release) "dispelled any possibility that the plan would be abandoned ... [and] emphasized that the Saskatchewan government believes in the spirit, intent and purpose of the potash conservation regulations."[26] ("Potash conservation" was the euphemistic title given to the regulations covering prorationing.) Despite a few gestures to further offshore sales by forcing all producers to join Canpotex, a marketing agency for offshore sales of Canadian potash, and the imposition of a modest new tax, a "prorationing fee,"[27] officials were not interested in the income distribution consequences – upon farmers or the Saskatchewan treasury – of current arrangements. They were interested, however, in the constitutional question posed: does the province have the jurisdiction to regulate the production and hence price (since supply and market price are functionally related, jurisdiction over the former extends de facto to the latter) of a resource entering into interprovincial trade, or is such regulation an intrusion on federal jurisdiction over interprovincial trade and commerce? Seeking to establish an analogy to the conservation argument on behalf of oil prorationing, officials claimed that, prior to prorationing, potash was "being wasted by high grading and other wasteful mining tactics."[28] But potash is not a fugacious substance like oil. Dubious as the physical conservation argument is for oil prorationing (as with potash prorationing, the primary intent of oil prorationing is regulation of the supply and market price of oil in interprovincial trade, not physical conservation, which is controlled by other regulations), it is even more dubious for potash. Prorationing of potash had no impact upon mining practices.

The strongest argument developed by officials was to redefine the concept of conservation. The Mineral Resources Act empowers the Minister of Mineral Resources "to discover, develop, manage, utilize, and conserve the mineral resources of Saskatchewan."[29] Perhaps they could expand power over conservation to include the prevention of "economic waste" – a euphemism by which officials meant the sale of a commodity at a price below cost. Provincial jurisdiction over conservation, so defined, rationalized the Department taking whatever action was required to guarantee producers a profit. Inclusion of "economic waste" obviously strained the usual sense of conservation, but until the central constitutional question – jurisdiction over regulation of resource production – was posed by a constitutional challenge, it would stand.

Far from appreciating the contradictions of their role, officials sought to strengthen the cartel and unwittingly thereby precipitated the constitutional challenge they feared. The majority of producers, lacking captive markets and hence receiving below-average quotas, advocated a formula that allocated to each mine a percentage of the aggregate quota equal to its percentage of aggregate capacity. Departmental officials had their own reasons for supporting such a simplified formula. The possibility of a company increasing its quota by claiming to have captive markets resulted inevitably, given excess capacity and price far above operating costs, in hidden price discounts to allegedly captive customers. The need to police producers to enforce the regulated price exasperated officials. In 1972 they persuaded cabinet to adopt a formula based on capacity alone, thereby sharply reducing the Noranda-CF Industries quota, and forcing the latter to purchase a portion of its market requirements from competing producers.[30] (In the 1971-72 fertilizer year Central Canada Potash, the Noranda-CF Industries mine, enjoyed the highest quota, 71 per cent of capacity. The new formula reduced its 1972-73 quota to 49 per cent of capacity.)[31]

Infuriated at this turn of events, Noranda and CF Industries decided to defy the cartel. In July 1972 they sought a court order forcing the government to issue their mine a quota sufficiently large to produce the volume specified in contracts with the American co-operative. After defeat at the initial hearing they appealed twice, the final appeal being to the Supreme Court. At all three hearings they lost. Simultaneously they ignored their quota and operated their mine at full capacity until the government, threatening to cancel the mine's production lease, forced them to cut back. Thereupon, vociferously blaming the government, they laid off 120 miners. Finally in December 1972 they launched a second court action – suing the government for damages caused by the lowered quota, and challenging the constitutionality of the prorationing system. They were later joined in this second action by the federal government as co-plaintiff. Ottawa, as we have mentioned previously, considered potash prorationing an incursion upon federal jurisdiction but had refrained from launching its own challenge.[32]

This second case was not heard until late 1974,[33] and the initial decision, at the level of the Court of Queen's Bench, was only delivered in May 1975. The principal argument of government counsel was to defend prorationing as a measure intended primarily to conserve a crown-owned resource, not to regulate interprovincial trade. Conservation, it was predictably argued, must be broadly defined to include prevention of "economic waste." The argument of the plaintiffs was that prorationing "responded to market conditions, which existed outside the province, and was concerned with the regulating and the market for potash and was not in any way related to wasteful refining or mining practices. ... The regulations taken by themselves are ultra vires because they were passed under the guise of conservation regulations while in reality they are a powerful attempt to establish a scheme to regulate and fix the price of potash in the interprovincial and international market place."[34] The initial court decision explicitly rejected the government definition of conservation, ruled the entire prorationing system an unconstitutional invasion of the federal trade and commerce power, and awarded $1.5 million damages to the corporate plaintiffs.

The government promptly appealed to the provincial Court of Appeal, and to strengthen its argument amended the Mineral Resources Act to reinstate the prorationing system and to include a definition of conservation: "'conservation' includes the prevention of waste or improvident or uneconomic production or disposition of minerals. ... in excess of. ... reasonable market demand for any mineral produced, and includes the control in Saskatchewan of the production, transportation, distribution, sale, disposal and consumption of all minerals produced in Saskatchewan."[35] A great deal now turned on this definition of conservation. It embodied one of the strongest assertions ever legislated of provincial rights over natural resources.

What would the courts decide? In January 1977 the Saskatchewan Court of Appeal, in reversing the lower court decision, reasoned that, although it had some effect on interprovincial trade and commerce, the primary intent and purpose of potash prorationing was to overcome immediate problems in order to conserve the economic viability of the potash industry. It was a judgment redolent with the provincial rights philosophy of its author: "the potash industry had a right to seek assistance from whatever government had the power to grant that assistance. Natural resources being exclusively within the provincial jurisdiction, the industry turned to the province."[36]

In a unanimous judgment, written by Chief Justice Bora Laskin, the Supreme Court in October 1978 restored the initial decision. The judgment borrowed heavily upon the secondary argument in the Supreme Court's CIGOL decision, namely that provincial legislatures have *no* jurisdiction over the price of commodities entering into interprovincial trade. "It is, of course, true," concluded Laskin, that production controls and conservation measures with respect to natural resources in a Province are, ordinarily, matters within provincial legislative authority. ... The situation may be different, however, where a Province establishes a marketing scheme with price fixing as its central feature. Indeed, it has been held that provincial legislative authority does not extend to the control or regulation of the marketing of provincial products, whether minerals or natural resources, in interprovincial or export trade. ... The present case reduces itself therefore to a consideration of "the true nature and character" of the prorationing and price stabilization schemes which are before us. This Court cannot ignore the circumstances under which the Potash Conservation Regulations came into being, nor the market to which they were applied and in which they had their substantial operation. In [*CIGOL v. Government of Saskatchewan*] this Court. ... said that "provincial legislative authority does not extend to fixing the price to be charged or received in respect of the sale of goods in the export market". It may properly be said here of potash as it was said there of oil that "the legislation is directly aimed at the production of [potash] destined for export, and it has the effect of regulating the export price since the producer is effectively compelled to obtain that price on the sale of his product."[37]

"There is no accretion at all to federal power in this case," Laskin insisted, "which does not involve federal legislation, but simply a determination by this Court, in obedience to its duty, of a limitation on provincial legislative power."[38] This is a debatable conclusion. Since quantity supplied and market price of any commodity are functionally related, the constitutional authority to regulate the former implies de facto authority to affect, if not determine, the latter. Under most market conditions imposition of any tax or supply management scheme raises the market price of the affected commodity. Firms using the commodity as an input for further transformation will experience higher costs of production, and may raise the price of their output. The original commodity may or may not enter into interprovincial trade but, even if it does not, it is feasible that its higher price will affect the price of commodities that do. Interpreting the federal trade and commerce power broadly to imply that provincial legislatures have no jurisdiction over the price of commodities entering into interprovincial trade, it could be argued that much provincial regulatory and tax legislation is ultra vires. Since it has, in other cases, ruled intra vires provincial legislation that "incidentally" has an impact on the price of commodities entering into interprovincial trade, the Supreme

Court is obviously prepared to place some limit on the federal trade and commerce power. It matters a great deal where that limit is set. At stake are vast resource rents, and potentially the Supreme Court is determining the distribution of benefits, from oil as well as potash, among producing firms interested in higher profits, customers intent upon lower prices, and the federal and provincial governments. These conflicting claims are at the heart of current debates over Canadian economic policy, and while the present distribution of benefits may or may not be appropriate, it is an issue that transcends any reasonable scope for judicial review of statute law. The CIGOL and Central Canada Potash cases significantly enhance the federal trade and commerce power, restrict the constitutional interpretation of royalties, and curtail provincial powers to regulate resource production. Issues of this magnitude cannot be adequately resolved by the courts; they bear too fundamentally upon the nature of the Canadian federation. The solutions, if any, will be political, not legal.

Conclusion

While the CIGOL and Central Canada Potash cases directly concern Saskatchewan alone, they have created apprehension in other provinces, notably in Alberta.[39] There is a close relationship between Alberta's rising economic power and its defensive stance on political and constitutional decentralization. Alberta's political elites favour strong provincial governments as a buffer against a federal authority perceived as the predatory instrument of central Canadian interests. They do not favour the reform of federal institutions, such as the Senate, as a strategy of increasing regional representation in Ottawa: this, they fear, would weaken the position of the provincial governments. Ultimately, the Lougheed regime anticipates a major devolution of power in favour of the provinces as Canada is forced by the threat of Quebec secession to evolve a new set of constitutional arrangements. While the outcome is at this writing uncertain, Alberta will use all its bargaining power and its alliances with other provincial governments in the attempt to protect itself from fresh federal encroachments. Such encroachments, Alberta evidently believes, are virtually inevitable given the trend of Supreme Court interpretation – notwithstanding Chief Justice Laskin's protestation to the contrary in the Central Canada Potash case.

To entrench provincial powers in the area of resources Alberta is demanding, first, that sections of the BNA Act ensuring provincial ownership and control of natural resources be strengthened; second, that the constitution be clarified "in order to reaffirm the provinces' authority to tax and to collect royalties from the sale and management of their natural resources"; third, that provincial jurisdiction be established over offshore minerals; fourth, that the provinces be given access to both direct and indirect taxes; and, finally, that the constitution "include provisions that confirm the established legitimate role of the provinces in certain areas of international relations" – such "certain areas" remain unspecified. Beyond this, Alberta proposes the termination of the powers of disallowance and reservation and severe limitations on the federal declaratory and emergency power, advocates the creation of "a representative constitutional court" to resolve constitutional issues, and wants the provinces to have the right to appoint 40 per cent of the members of federal regulatory agencies such as the National Energy Board.[40]

Rejecting special status for Quebec, Lougheed's vision of a reformed Canadian federation can probably best be described as "voluntary special status" or "special status for all," wherein, as part of a constitutional package, each province would assume the substance of certain federal powers. Neither Lougheed nor his constitutional advisors have, to our knowledge, attempted to elaborate their conception of an appropriate set of functions for the federal government, and it is hard to avoid the conclusion that they would be happy to see federal power virtually emasculated. Lougheed's extreme provincial rights stance, which is not so far removed from the doctrine of nullification upheld by anti-federalists and the proponents of states' rights in the United States during the nineteenth century, has evolved as a largely defensive response to what Alberta and Saskatchewan believe is a federal campaign to reduce and abridge the powers of the provinces over natural resources.

Notes

1. D. Creighton, *Canada's First Century* (Toronto: Macmillan, 1971), 8.
2. Quoted in *ibid.*, 10-11.
3. A.C. Cairns, "The Judicial Committee and its Critics," *Canadian Journal of Political Science*, IV, 3 (September 1971), 319.
4. Manitoba Act, 33 Victoria, c. 3 (Canada), s. 30.
5. BNA Act 1930, 21 George V, c. 26 (Imperial).
6. See K.H. Norrie, "The National Policy and Prairie Economic Discrimination, 1870-1930," unpublished paper presented at a conference sponsored by the Departments of Economics and History, University of Manitoba, 1977.
7. For a comprehensive treatment of the subject see G.V. La Forest, *Natural Resources and Public Property under the Canadian Constitution* (Toronto:

University of Toronto Press, 1969). Useful summaries of the division of constitutional powers over management of natural resources are available in R.M. Burns, "Conflict and its Resolution in the Administration of Mineral Resources in Canada," Centre for Resource Studies (Kingston: Queen's University, 1976), chap. 3; M. Crommelin, "Jurisdiction Over Onshore Oil and Gas in Canada," *University of British Columbia Law Review*, X, 1 (1975), 86-144; W.R. Lederman, "The Constitution: A Basis for Bargaining," in A. Scott (ed.), *Natural Resource Revenues: A Test of Federalism* (Vancouver: University of British Columbia Press, 1976), 52-60; A.E. Safarian, *Canadian Federalism and Economic Integration* (Ottawa: Privy Council Office, Government of Canada, 1974), Part II.

8. *Report of the Royal Commission on the Transfer of the Natural Resources of Manitoba* (1929), quoted in E. Kierans, "Report on Natural Resources Policy in Manitoba" (Winnipeg: Government of Manitoba, 1973), 1.

9. *Spooner Oils Ltd. et al. v. Turner Valley Gas Conservation Board*, (1933) 4 DLR.

10. *Ibid.*, 563.

11. J.S. Mill, *Principles of Political Economy*, edited by J.M. Robson (Toronto: University of Toronto Press, 1965), Book V, chap. 3, 825.

12. *Canadian Industrial Gas & Oil Ltd. v. Government of Saskatchewan et al.*, QB, (1975) 2 WWR; SCA, (1976) 2 WWR; SCC, (1977) 6 WWR.

13. *Central Canada Potash Ltd. et al. v. Government of Saskatchewan et al.*, QB, (1975) 5 WWR; SCA, (1977) 1 WWR; SCC, (1978) 6 WWR.

14. *Star-Phoenix*, August 8, 1974.

15. The Oil and Gas Conservation, Stabilization and Development Act, 1973. On most of the small remaining freehold production Bill 42 imposed an identical tax but under a different name – the "mineral income tax." Like the royalty surcharge it has been declared ultra vires the province, and all tax revenue emanating from it the Supreme Court has ordered to be reimbursed.

16. *Star-Phoenix*, 12 February 1974. In December 1976 Imperial Oil initiated a second and similar legal action challenging the constitutionality of Bill 42. *Star-Phoenix*, December 24, 1976.

17. The Oil Well Income Tax Act, 1977 (Bill 47).

18. Although many of its calculations are subject to challenge, readers desirous of per barrel comparisons of revenue, costs and tax levies between Saskatchewan and Alberta may refer to "The Petroleum Industry and Canada" (Calgary: Canadian Petroleum Association and Independent Petroleum Association of Canada, 1974).

19. *CIGOL v. Government of Saskatchewan* (1977) 6 WWR, 624.

20. *Ibid.*, 626.

21. *Ibid.*, 652.

22. From information filed under the Canada Corporations Act, financial data for the period are available for only one mine. In 1972 and 1973 International Minerals and Chemical earned on its Canadian operations an after-tax return on net capital employed equal to 11.8 per cent

and 9.2 per cent respectively. Given its size and above-average quota, its rate of return was above average.

23. *Miscellaneous Non-Metal Mines*, 26-220 until 1974, thereafter *Potash Mines*, 26-222 (Ottawa: Statistics Canada, annual).

24. Details of the agreement are contained in a confidential letter from Thatcher to the presidents of three Japanese fertilizer corporations: Thatcher to M. Mihashi et al., personal files, June 18, 1970.

25. "Saskatchewan Past and Present Potash Picture," briefing material for incoming NDP Minister of Mineral Resources, ca. July 1971.

26. Saskatchewan Government Information Services (SGIS), 71-743, December 10, 1971.

27. Due to fears that the U.S. Antitrust Division would interpret Canpotex to be a combination in restraint of trade, many American producers were reluctant to join. In the wake of the antitrust case launched in 1976 several withdrew. Having agreed not to increase royalties before 1981, the government rationalized this new tax as a fee for the government's services as administrator of prorationing. Originally set in 1972 at a level of approximately $1.00/ton ($K_2O$ equivalent) it was doubled in 1973. See *Financial Post*, July 24, 1976, and "Potash Proration Fee Regulations," o.c. 825/72 and 1270/73.

28. J.T. Cawley (deputy minister DMR) to M.J. Sychuk, personal files, May 29, 1970.

29. The Mineral Resources Act, RSS (1965), chap. 50, s. 9.

30. "Potash Prorationing," Minister's Directive PCD-1, DMR, June 23, 1972; *Leader-Post*, July 19, 1972.

31. "Potash Production Summary 1971-72 Fertilizer Year" and "Summary of Potash Production Allowables Fertilizer Year 1972-73," DMR.

32. For reports of these events see *Leader-Post*: July 19, 1972, August 12, 1972, October 5, 1972, November 8, 1972; *Star-Phoenix*: December 12, 1972, February 7, 1973, October 26, 1973; *Globe and Mail*: August 22, 1972; SGIS: 72-842, October 12, 1972.

33. For reports of arguments in this case see numerous stories in *Star-Phoenix*: October 28, 1974 to November 20, 1974.

34. *Star-Phoenix*, November 15, 1974.

35. An Act to Amend the Minerals Resources Act (1976), s. 2.

36. *CCP v. Government of Saskatchewan*, SCA, (1977) 1 WWR, 525.

37. *CCP v. Government of Saskatchewan*, SCC, (1978) 6 WWR, 427.

38. *Ibid.*, 428.

39. On the potentially tenuous constitutionality of Alberta's regulatory system see A. Thompson, "Implications of Constitutional Change for the Oil and Gas Industry," *Alberta Law Review*, VII, 3 (1969), 370.

40. *Harmony in Diversity: A New Federalism for Canada*, Alberta Government Position Paper on Constitutional Change (Edmonton: Government of Alberta, 1978).

CHAPTER 12
Staples, Power, and Rent

A nation is made up of groups and classes with conflicting interests.
The only example of a human society without internal conflicts was
Robinson Crusoe, and even he may have suffered from ambivalence.
An economy is an entity consisting of groups with conflicting interests
held together by rules of the game. When the conflicts become so acute
that the rules are unplayable, the economy ceases to be viable, and
explodes or changes into a different entity. ... When we are talking
about the consuming power of a family, a class, or a nation, as though of
an individual, we must never forget to pose at the same time the
detective-story question, *cui bono?* which is often mistranslated: What's
the use? but properly means, Who gets the swag?

> Joan Robinson
> *The Accumulation of Capital*
> 16-17

While this book has been primarily an historical study of the role of
the provincial state in regional economic development, it is useful to
conduct a somewhat more analytic probing of the economic entrepreneurship that has been exercised at various stages by the governments of Saskatchewan and Alberta. A serious response requires that
we undertake at least a summary discussion of the staple tradition in
Canadian historical writing and of the theory of economic rent, and
that we examine the bargaining inevitably surrounding the allocation
of economic rent and linkages from staple industries.

The Staple Tradition
From the fur trade beginning in the eighteenth century, through the
wheat boom in the early years of this century, to contemporary developments of oil, gas, potash, nickel, uranium and coal, the prairie economy has been highly dependent on the export of staples to the rest of

Canada and beyond. Not only have successive staple industries been the driving force behind the economic fate of the prairies – both the booms and the depressions – but each staple has in complex ways affected the political and social character of the region.

Following Gordon Bertram, let us define staple industries as those "based on agriculture and extractive resources, not requiring elaborate processing and finding a large portion of their market in international trade."[1] Bertram extends the concept of staples beyond agriculture, forestry, fishing, and mining to include primary manufacturing. Primary, as opposed to secondary, manufacturing comprises activities (such as flour milling) in which the value added[2] by manufacturing is low relative to the value of the staple input, or highly capital intensive activities (such as the production of simple petrochemicals) upgrading the staple into some standardized intermediate product. By contrast, secondary manufacturing activities (the textile industry is a classic example) involve more processing of the primary inputs and therefore often generate more employment per unit of capital invested, tend to produce finished goods, and typically depend to a larger degree than primary manufacturing on domestic markets. (In this discussion "domestic" refers to the regional market. Analogously "export" and "import" refer to goods or services that cross the regional border without reference to whether they also cross the national border.) The development of precise definitions of staple industries, of primary and secondary manufacturing, is an exercise for statistically minded economists. However, with much imprecision, these concepts have been central to both academic and political debates over economic development – in the prairies and elsewhere.

As a point of reference we begin by elaborating a naive staple model for the prairies. Assume that (1) the region initially possesses an abundant supply of land and other natural resources relative to capital and labour, thereby providing it with a significant comparative cost advantage in certain staple industries, (2) a strong export demand exists for the output of such staple industries, (3) significant economies of scale exist in most secondary manufacturing activities, and (4) the region faces high costs of transport to major export markets. What do these assumptions imply for a rational economic development policy for the prairies? The high transport costs provide a degree of natural protection against manufactured imports and permit the emergence of a small amount of prairie manufacturing activity (such as food processing) to supply the domestic market, but simultaneously high transport costs effectively deny the ability of most prairie manufacturers to compete in export markets. With only the small domestic market, prairie manufacturing plants cannot expect to realize the scale economies of manufacturers located in more densely populated regions; hence the prairies are at a comparative cost disadvantage in most manufacturing industries. Conversely, despite the necessity of prairie producers to absorb transport costs to export markets, the comparative cost advantage in certain staple industries is sufficient to generate not only normal returns to capital and labour thus employed, but a residual income, defined as economic rent, which we may originally conceive as accruing to the owners of the land or other resources utilized. To maximize the productivity of domestic labour, capital, and natural resources, the prairies should specialize initially in staple exports, importing their requirements of most manufactured goods.

To this naive model now add the concepts of "linkages" and "leakages," thereby introducing a rudimentary dynamic analysis.[3] Provided the development of a new staple industry does not merely reallocate capital and labour from one industry to another and does in fact increase aggregate regional income then, as the recipients of this new income spend it (as workers spend their wages, capitalists their interest and profits, and resource owners their rents – in the case of farmers their income can analytically be divided among wages, profits and rents), they create a second round of new income amplifying the increase due to the staple industry itself. This multiplier effect, or "final demand" linkage, proceeds indefinitely, with income recipients at each round in turn spending their incremental income. Much as optimistic proponents of new potash mines, pulp mills and petrochemical plants may expansively describe the potential of final demand linkages, they are severely limited by leakages out of the regional economy – expenditures on imported goods, savings, and taxes imposed by the federal government, for which there are no exactly balancing expenditures. If capital invested in a new staple industry is owned by capitalists residing outside the region, there is also an immediate leakage of the interest and profits they withdraw from the region.

In addition to final demand linkages, new staple industries may over time generate additional income via "backward" and "forward" linkages. The former refer to additional income created in industries that expand to provide inputs to the staple sector; the latter to additional income in industries that, using the region's staples as inputs, transform them further. The implication of the naive staple model is that the focus for entrepreneurial initiatives – whether by the state or private capitalists – should be on the development of export staples and closely linked industries for which the region enjoys a comparative cost advantage due to the existence of the staple sector. The regional economy will diversify into secondary manufacturing, to the extent warranted, via one of the three linkage processes, but only in the wake of the successful implantation of the staple export sector.

Those familiar with the simple Keynesian model of income determination in an economy encompassing foreign trade will recognize that the above discussion can easily be cast in Keynesian terms. The level of the export demand for the regional staples is established by forces external to the model. The regional income consistent with any level of staple exports can be expressed as the product of an "export base multiplier" times the exogenously determined level of export demand. The value of the multiplier will be larger, the more significant the linkages; smaller, the more extensive the leakages. Alternatively the naive staple model can be considered an application to the Canadian experience of the classical economic theory of comparative advantage in international trade. The conclusion of this theory, which originated with the British economist David Ricardo in the early nineteenth century, is that a country can maximize the national income (which ignores problems associated with the distribution of that income) by specializing in those sectors in which it has a comparative cost advantage (i.e. those sectors in which it is relatively more efficient than other countries, even if in absolute terms other countries are more efficient in all sectors), and by using its export earnings to import its requirements of goods emanating from sectors in which it has a comparative cost disadvantage.

Manufacturing v. Staples: The Canadian Debate

Without venturing into the epistemological question of the possibility of objective knowledge free of a priori assumptions and moral judgments, we can safely observe that the founders of the staple tradition in Canadian historical writing attached a prescriptive as well as descriptive significance to staples. The major exponents of the staple tradition, such as W.A. Mackintosh and Harold Innis, were well aware that "incomes derived from the export of raw materials are notoriously variable," and that prolonged periods of depressed demand could engender serious crises when, as frequently occurred, fixed investments in staple industries were based on overly optimistic demand expectations. They were also aware of the potential for unequal political and market power in determining the terms of trade between staple exporting "hinterlands" and "metropoli" which furnished manufactured goods in exchange. Despite such caveats, the exploitation of Canada's comparative advantage in successive staples was assumed to be a rational policy for development. "There are certain generalizations concerning the development of new countries which must be borne in mind in interpreting the economic history of Canada," wrote Mackintosh in 1939.

In the first place, rapid progress in such new countries is dependent upon the discovery and development of cheap supplies of raw materials by the export of which to the markets of the world the new country may purchase the products it cannot produce economically at that stage of its development. Such supplies are invariably obtained by the exploitation of natural resources. In the second place, rapid development is further dependent on the ability of a new country to borrow capital abroad and to adopt also technical knowledge and equipment developed in older countries. Without such borrowings and adoptions, progress is inevitably reduced to the slow pace of domestic accumulation of savings and the development of local inventions.[4]

Since the 1960s, however, the Canadian staple tradition has become an arena for the international political and academic debates of development economics.[5] A recurrent debate in the latter literature is the extent to which a country should specialize in industries for which its available supplies of resources, labour, and capital provide it a comparative advantage or, alternatively, should minimize its external trade and attempt to develop indigenous industries capable of supplying the maximum range of goods and services. Implicit in the latter position is a critique of static comparative advantage and defence of the potential over time to "learn by doing." As opposed to the staple tradition which emphasizes the successful development of the staple export sector as a necessary preliminary to linked manufacturing development, the primary goal of most (but not all) advocates of more autarkic development has been the immediate implantation of a secondary manufacturing sector. Since such manufacturing industries will initially at least display a cost disadvantage relative to foreign competitors, they obviously cannot secure significant export markets, and can only secure the domestic market if protected by tariffs and quotas against imports, or if favoured with subsidies. Proponents of development via import substitution respond by enumerating the problems posed by economic specialization: instability of export earnings, potential secular erosion of terms of trade between exports and imports, and the risk of creating structural rigidities within the economy that forestall further economic development or generate serious wealth and income inequalities, or both. Let us take each of these arguments in turn.

Relative to the norm for manufacturing there exists for staple industries an undeniably larger variability – on the demand side, of export prices and volumes and, on the supply side, of the output of many agricultural industries. Provided the problem is variability and not long-term secular decline, and provided investment in the industry is based upon some measure of central tendency and not the peaks of the cycle, this argument should not per se militate against staple developments. Faced with the choice of developing two industries – an unstable staple industry or a stable manufacturing industry – each displaying the same expected cost benefit ratios before allowance for variability, a "risk-averse" country would choose the latter. But if the comparative advantage in the former is substantial, the question becomes – stability at what price?

Despite the growth of technologically simple labour-intensive manufacturing exports by certain developing nations, the majority of exports by such countries are staples, and a majority of their imports are manufactured goods from developed countries. Thus changes in the price ratio of primary to secondary goods can be expected to affect the aggregate balance of payments between developing and developed countries. That there exists a secular erosion in the price of staples relative to manufactured goods in foreign trade is a thesis associated with Raoul Prebisch, a prominent Latin American economist and former director of the United Nations Committee on Trade and Development (UNCTAD).[6] The thesis has been extensively employed to justify import substitution manufacturing investment, but it is not at all clear that it is an empirically valid generalization. While the thesis is true for particular commodities and countries, and true for indices of all staple commodities during specific periods, the evidence of any overall secular trend is far from established. Obviously, during the 1970s, price indices of the staples relevant to the Canadian prairies – energy commodities, cereals, and fertilizers – have increased relative to price indices for manufactured goods.

The third critique of staple development – the risk of structural rigidities – amounts essentially to a discussion of the differential effects of the technologies of different industries upon the potential for future development, and upon the distribution of income and of entrepreneurship. It is the most complex and most valid component of the critique. Mining technologies, for example, typically display important scale economies and require large indivisible investments. Given political pressures for rapid development of reserves, the capital requirements far exceed the savings potential of an undeveloped region or country, and thereby necessitate recourse to foreign debt or equity capital. The early staple scholars were too sanguine concerning the consequences of foreign borrowing. They underestimated the price frequently paid in economic rents lost to foreign firms, or the effects of foreign firms in channeling linked developments into the home as opposed to host country.

The capital intensive nature of mining (including petroleum) technology creates few direct jobs. Those created often require skills initially unavailable within the region, implying the need to import skilled and professional labour as well as capital. There is thus a danger that a foreign enclave will monopolize entrepreneurship and not transmit specialized skills to the local labour force. The host government may procure sufficient rental income from the staple to create a well-paid public bureaucracy capable of providing social services but incapable of playing an entrepreneurial role in the economy. The demonstration effects of the small well-paid labour force within the staple sector and the civil service may create pressures for an artificially high wage rate throughout the economy. Workers outside the staple sector seek parity with those within it. If they succeed in raising their money wages, capitalists raise prices and a wage-price spiral may well ensue, with workers in the staple sector exacerbating the spiral by attempting to maintain traditional wage differentials between themselves and other less skilled workers. Inflation will adversely affect the trade balance between exports and imports, and may force recurrent devaluations of the local currency. The protracted 1973 strike for higher wages by relatively well-paid Chilean copper miners, for example, in a staple industry providing the majority of that country's export earnings, posed a serious crisis to the development policies of the contemporary Unidad Popular government. Inasmuch as the miners' union belonged to the governing coalition, the crisis was self-inflicted and not the product of foreign or domestic opposition.

The critique of economic specialization and of its corollary, heavy dependence upon foreign trade, has now entered into the Canadian staple tradition. Of the more scholarly applications of the critique to Canadian experience with staples an important example is Tom Naylor's revisionist history of Canadian economic development from Confederation to World War I, a period traditionally viewed as encompassing a classic case study of successful industrialization via staples and linkages therefrom. According to the traditional view the prairie wheat boom constituted the leading staple which in turn generated substantial linkages—final demand linkages to protected domestic consumer goods industries, forward linkages to railroads and hence to iron and steel, backward linkages to industries such as farm implement manufacturing. Most of this linked industrial investment located, of course, in central Canada.

Naylor begins his critique by posing the staples versus secondary manufacturing distinction: "Canada's commercial and financial system grew up geared to the international movement of staples rather than to abetting secondary processing for domestic markets." "Canada's social structure, and therefore the proclivities of its entrepreneurial class, reflected and reinforced its innate colonialism. The political and economic elite were men associated with the staple trades, with the international flow of commodities and of the capital that complemented the commodity movements. They were wholesale dealers and bankers in Montreal in particular, and to a lesser extent in Toronto and Halifax." During this period, the Canadian economy "had only begun to make the difficult transition from a mercantile-agrarian base to an industrial one. Wealth was accumulated in commercial activities and tended to remain locked up in commerce. Funds for industrial capital formation were in short supply. Commercial capital resisted the transformation into industrial capital except under specific conditions in certain industries, in favour of remaining invested in traditional staple-oriented activities."[7] Naylor's conclusion is that financial and commercial interests, both indigenous and foreign, twisted capital markets in favour of staples (wheat in particular) and immediately linked industries (railroads, iron and steel, farm implements) and away from the broad range of secondary manufacturing activities required to reduce Canadian dependence on manufactured imports and to generate a more innovative entrepreneurial elite: "The strength of commercial capitalism in Canada was the result of the British colonial connection, and together they served to lock the Canadian economy into the staple trap."[8] Although American direct investment has replaced British portfolio investment as Canada's dominant external source of finance, the pattern of overinvestment in a succession of staples – pulp and paper, minerals, oil and gas – at the expense of secondary manufacturing has allegedly been repeated throughout the century. Because of this bias in favour of staples Canada has developed, such critics conclude, a "dependent" economy.

Naylor is concerned with the allocation of capital by the central Canadian elite and the extent of foreign control over the ensuing pattern of industrial investment; only within that context is he concerned with prairie development. He presumably would not deny the overwhelming comparative advantage of the early prairie economy in staples, wheat in particular, although he rightly criticizes the irrational overinvestment in the wheat economy. Large areas were ploughed and seeded that later proved too arid to support grain farming, and the construction of a second and third transcontinental railroad was a folly largely prompted by grossly overoptimistic expectations generated by the wheat boom. However, there is a non sequitur in much of the critique of staple development. One cannot conclude from the undeniable problems posed by staples that an autarkic strategy with priority on secondary manufacturing will necessarily do better. Despite examples of successful autarkic development, industrialization of the Soviet Union being the most important, the economic development literature is now replete with case studies to demonstrate the failure of many national development strategies (socialist as well as capitalist) heavily biased towards secondary manufacturing and economic autarky.

The extent of secondary manufacturing and the quality of domestic Canadian entrepreneurship engendered by the prairie wheat boom may have been imperfect, but would the results of the proposed alternative path have been superior? That, in a different methodological context, is the question posed by Professors Chambers and Gordon in a controversial article on the significance of the wheat boom. "[W]hat would have happened," they asked, "if all the [prairie] land that was brought under cultivation between 1901 and 1911 had been impenetrable rock?"[9]

By way of answer Chambers and Gordon constructed a model, having in its simplest version two sectors, to test whether the wheat boom, even at its height during the first decade of this century, contributed significantly to rising per capita incomes. On the assumption of equal rewards to labour in the two sectors, the wage rate in the manufacturing sector determines the level of rents land owners receive in the staple wheat sector. Rents are such that the tenant farmer receives a net income for his labour equal to the manufacturing wage. Were it higher, labour would migrate from manufacturing to farming bidding down tenant farmer incomes and bidding up rents; were it lower, a reverse process would ensue. In the case of homesteaders owning their own land, their income analytically can be disaggregated into a rental and wage component. In Chambers and Gordon's simple formulation of a "counterfactual alternative" Canada could, over a wide range, expand at constant prices its domestic sales of manufactured goods and, because it contributed only a small fraction of manufactured goods in international trade, its exports of such goods. Thus any number of prairie farmers could have been absorbed as workers in the manufacturing sector at the going wage (although those drawn to Canada by the prospect of rental income from cheap land might not have migrated under the counterfactual scenario). All that would be lost in terms of per capita income is the rental income on land in wheat. By their calculations that amounted at most to 8.4 per cent of the observed per capita increase in Canadian incomes from 1901 to 1911.

Despite ideological and methodological differences Naylor, Chambers and Gordon are all arguing that the Canadian comparative advantage in staples over manufacturing has been exaggerated and that it has always been economically feasible to divert capital and labour from the former to the latter with little sacrifice of aggregate or per capita income. On the evidence available, however, it would be unwise to dismiss the value to Canada of its staple industries. While an extensive manufacturing sector may or may not be a desirable ultimate goal of development policy, the early staple writers were, in broad terms, probably correct to have viewed manufacturing investment as complementary to, and not competitive with, staples. In other words, the successful implantation of a staple sector, implying the need to capture rent by domestic as opposed to external interests and the efficient pursuit of linkages (both in terms of location and rate of investment), may, within Canada at least, be the appropriate strategy for initial development. It is worth exploring these issues somewhat further. Of course, Canada now faces acute problems, which we are not here addressing, of reforming the manufacturing sector of previously industrialized regions.

The critics of Chambers and Gordon have ranged over many empirical and theoretical issues. Certain alternate estimates of prairie agricultural rents are much higher and place the contribution of the wheat boom to increased Canadian per capita income above 20 per cent.[10] Some agricultural rent was expropriated by the CPR in above-normal returns on the transportation services it provided. Rents realized by farmers were also reduced by the costs, reflected in high freight rates, of construction of excess railroad capacity prior to World War I. Railroads enjoyed substantial subsidies from both federal and provincial governments however, and to the extent these reduced freight rates, they served to increase realized agricultural rents. The cost of such subsidies must be subtracted from realized rents to ascertain the net rent to include in any national income reckoning. Analysis of these and other such niceties has served to sustain a lively academic debate over the actual magnitude of agricultural rents.[11]

An early rejoinder to Chambers and Gordon, among other criticisms, insisted that staple theory has primarily been concerned with aggregate, not per capita, income.[12] As a descriptive statement of the early staple writings this argument is accurate, but one cannot dismiss by fiat the importance of increased per capita income as a development goal. Most individual workers, farmers and capitalists obviously seek to maximize (their own) per capita incomes. Those presiding over large institutions, both private and public, may be intent upon "empire building," i.e. the growth of aggregate income, but even here the goal will always be subject to some lower constraint on wage rates and rate of return to capital, i.e. some lower constraint on per capita incomes. However a concern for aggregate income is relevant. Increases in *per capita* income may well be dependent upon increases in *aggregate* income. For example, to the extent scale economies in manufacturing have been significant and Canadian manufactured goods could initially find few export markets (due to high production costs and trade barriers), policies designed to expand aggregate domestic income, employment and population displayed external benefits – by augmenting the market for Canadian manufactures and lowering unit manufacturing costs. In other words the contribution to per capita income of the wheat boom cannot be measured solely in terms of the size of agricultural rents.

There can be little doubt that, without the prairie wheat economy, the aggregate income of the country would have been lower. The most important reason is simply the implausibility of Chambers and Gordon's assumption that, without major price adjustments, the manufacturing sector could have absorbed the 1901 to 1911 influx of prairie farmers.[13] Most Canadian manufacturing depended (and still does depend) upon the protected domestic market, but to have absorbed the hypothetically displaced farmers, Canada would have had to increase manufacturing exports which, in a world of trade barriers, could only have been realized by lowering the price of such goods – and hence manufacturing wages. Within Canada lower manufacturing prices and wages imply a transfer of income from workers to consumers (not mutually exclusive groups) but no net loss in real income. In export markets, however, lower manufacturing prices imply a net transfer out of the country to foreign customers and this loss must be considered in assessing the impact of the "counterfactual." Of course, if we are concerned solely with per capita income and ignore the issue of economies of scale in manufacturing, then we could imagine a scenario in which, without the prairie economy, Canadian manufacturing employment expands at constant wages and prices, but only to the point where all manufactured imports are displaced. Total employment in this scenario is lower than it actually was in 1911 (i.e. fewer immigrants come to the country) but we revert to Chambers and Gordon's model in which the only loss is agricultural rent.

In conclusion, export demand for wheat provided the sustained level of demand – via linkages channeled to a protected Canadian manufacturing sector – without which the Canadian economy would almost certainly have operated at a lower level of aggregate income, and probably at a lower level of per capita income. From the perspective of maximizing the potential to accumulate wealth and power by a nascent Canadian bourgeoisie, the components of John A. Macdonald's National Policy – settlement of the prairies, an all-Canadian railroad, high protective tariffs on manufactured goods – were probably rational (which is not to deny that particular decisions, such as investment prior to World War I in a second and third transcontinental railroad, were definitely irrational).

Manufacturing versus Staples: The Prairie Dilemma

What should we make of the anti-staple critique in the context of the prairie economy? Within the agricultural sector there is scant evidence of any staple-induced structural rigidities that have prevented investment in new farming techniques, in agricultural diversification, or in development of closely linked industries where profitable. However the evolution of farm technology has created social rigidities — slowly eroding the relative equality of income and wealth distribution that characterized dry land grain farming by the initial homesteaders. There are, of course, important technological differences between dry land grain farming which, displaying fewer scale economies, has permitted many individual family farms to survive, and ranching which, enjoying more scale economies, tended from the beginning to fewer and larger units. Grain farming created a relatively homogeneous class structure of family farmers employing little farm labour and it dispersed entrepreneurship widely. Ranching concentrated entrepreneurship among ranch owners, a proportionately smaller group, and divided the rural community more sharply between those who owned land and accumulated capital, and the hired help who did not. The prominence of ranching in southern Alberta and grain farming in Saskatchewan constitutes a partial explanation of the more substantial regional bourgeoisie in the former province prior to the depression of the 1930s.

Agriculture remained subject to acute booms and busts until implementation since the depression, in Ottawa and the provincial capitals, of various price support and supply control programs. These reforms were very much a response to the demands of populist organizations, and they have lessened the variation and raised the mean of net farm incomes. But by increasing the certainty of positive returns on capital invested, such reforms accelerated the adoption of technological innovations embodied in expensive machinery and equipment requiring long payback periods to justify acquisition. A general feature of nearly all new agricultural technology has been its labour saving bias. Its adoption has increased average farm size, decreased the agricultural labour force and contributed to rural depopulation.

Prior to World War II most investment in agriculture or closely linked industries was, of course, private, undertaken by individual farmers or, in the case of the grain handling system, by large corporations. However, there existed significant exceptions (such as the co-operatively owned grain marketing system) which proved the feasibility of successful collective non-private entrepreneurship. While co-operatives and numerous government-run marketing agencies have survived and continue to enjoy substantial political support among farmers, collective entrepreneurship has not proved significant in most new farm technologies. There exist examples (such as co-operative farms promoted by the CCF during the 1940s, and Hutterite communal farms) of attempts to adapt modern farm technology to collective institutions or to regulate its adoption (untried proposals to legislate a maximum farm size; actual limits to the substitution of a few large inland grain terminals, to which grain is trucked, for the many small country elevators served by railroad branch lines). However, the technology itself has militated against collective entrepreneurship or creation of a rural consensus on policies to regulate. Collective institutions are placed under great stress when required consciously to jettison certain of their members in order that the rest prosper, and for the rural economy that has been precisely the decision posed by the labour saving bias of new agricultural technology. Those farmers in a position to benefit from any technological innovation have naturally opposed any government restriction on its adoption. Not surprisingly, therefore, the increased capitalization of postwar farming has virtually all been undertaken by individual farmers or private corporations (often albeit with funds provided by government). Accompanying the shift to farming as "agribusiness" has been a corresponding shift in political ideology among farmers. Most well-capitalized farmers have abandoned definitively the radical populist heritage in favour of a somewhat contradictory ethos that simultaneously extols private over public enterprise while favouring considerable government regulation to avoid the rigours of competitive markets with their low margins and unstable prices.[14]

Investment in new farm technologies has not been uniform across the prairies, and the increase in average net farm income has been won at the expense of increased rural stratification. Small family farmers, who remain poor relative to urban wage levels, still constitute a sizeable fraction of the total, but they have progressively less in common with the successful farmer turned businessman. To the extent left populism continues to enjoy significant support in the Canadian prairies (as measured, for example, by continued support for the New Democratic Party), it is increasingly concentrated among smaller and poorer farmers.

Should, since World War II, the prairies have given greater priority to the implantation of secondary manufacturing and less to the development of new mineral staples? Prior to the 1970s the history of oil and potash does afford evidence to support the critique of staple-led development: asymmetrical bargaining permitting resource corporations to capture economic rent, failure to pursue feasible linked developments, dissipation of potential rents by an excessive rate of resource development relative to the available market, and the inability to generate significant regional entrepreneurship (public or private) in the resource sector. But the history of the 1970s illustrates that these phenomena need not be permanent aspects of staple-led development. Via social democratic and dirigiste capitalist strategies respectively, Saskatchewan and Alberta have developed the requisite entrepreneurship to overcome past rentier traditions. The comparative advantage of the prairies during this period has overwhelmingly lain in mineral staples, and the central economic problem has not been manufacturing versus staples, but whether the region could assemble sufficient entrepreneurial ability and political power to capture the potential benefits — first in terms of rents and then in terms of linked industries — from resource development.

Were it needed, the CCF experiments during the 1940s in import substitution secondary manufacturing furnish further evidence that the immediate pursuit of manufacturing was probably a poor strategy. Although the financial capital invested in them was small, the CCF government dissipated much of the scarce entrepreneurial capacity it possessed in the launching, rationalization, and political justification of its small manufacturing corporations. "Human capital" thus expended was unavailable for the development of the newly discovered mineral staples. Furthermore there was a political price to pay for the failure of the woollen mill, shoe factory/tannery and other manufacturing ventures. The failures adversely affected public support for further public entrepreneurship and when, for example, the Planning Board did, after 1948, attempt to develop a public entrepreneurial role in oil, there was little public support and, under the joint attack of the oil industry, financial institutions and the media, the cabinet capitulated.

The failure, by both the CCF post-1948 and the Liberals, to accord a high priority to public collection of resource rents and a public entrepreneurial role in the resource sector, has doubtless lost Saskatchewan considerable income and linked development. Arguably, however, the province's comparative disadvantage in most manufacturing industries has been overwhelming, and even the most efficient rent collection and public investment program could have had little effect on the provincial industrial structure. Alberta is a different case.

There are parallels between John A. Macdonald's National Policy and the emerging Alberta industrial strategy discussed in Chapter Nine: oil replaces wheat; pipelines replace railroads; Alberta Gas

317

Trunk Line replaces the CPR. The Alberta government hopes, with its petroleum rents and via linkages from the oil and gas industry, that it can engender substantial industrial development. Will it succeed? It faces serious problems. The capital intensive nature of closely linked industries (such as petrochemicals) does little to increase direct employment and thus creates few final demand linkages for local manufacturers of consumer goods. The high transport costs to major external markets are both a blessing and a curse. On the assumption Alberta manufacturers must sell at predetermined prices in export markets they will have to absorb the transport costs. Conversely, on the assumption that external manufacturers pass on the transport costs of goods imported into the province, such costs provide some natural protection for local manufacturers. Of course, to a degree, the provincial government is prepared to overcome cost disadvantages by subsidies, paid for by petroleum and natural gas rents. Indifference to the province's development goals by the foreign-based companies controlling the majority of assets in the oil and gas industry is a third problem. The provincial response has been the growth of hybrid corporate entities (such as Alberta Gas Trunk Line and the Alberta Energy Company) enjoying favoured government treatment but operating with largely autonomous management.

Whether Alberta's current strategy of staple-led growth will procure for the province an industrial economy can only be answered after the passage of another generation. The employment data for the 1970s, however, are impressive. From 1969 to 1977 the total provincial non-agricultural labour force grew at a compounded annual rate of 5.6 per cent. The fastest growing sectors have been commercial services, finance and real estate, mines (including petroleum), and construction, but manufacturing employment has realized a 3.7 per cent average annual growth, the second highest of any province this decade. (Ironically, Newfoundland's manufacturing employment, which only grew by 4,400 – from 12,000 to 16,400 – during the eight-year period, experienced a higher rate of growth, 4.0 per cent annually, than Alberta's.) It is worth mentioning that combined public and para-public employment grew over this period at a rate (3.7 per cent annually) below that of the overall labour force. Although it has provided one of six new jobs, public employment financed by resource rents has not been the major source of new employment. Industrial growth is obviously occurring, but the provincial manufacturing base is small (72,400 manufacturing jobs in 1977). Profiting as it has from oil and gas exports, Alberta growth has in part been at the expense of oil-importing provinces. To that extent Canada has merely redistributed economic activity without solving any of its chronic economic problems of high unemployment and regional inequality of income distribution. However, the entrepreneurial dynamism of the arriviste Alberta bourgeoisie suggests that, in one region at least, Canadian capitalism is less moribund than many, on the left in particular, have concluded.[15]

At this stage in history, when the prairies have opted for a variant of political conservatism, it becomes a mere "counterfactual alternative," but what if Saskatchewan and Alberta had been organized as one politically powerful province (as many in the old Northwest Territories desired prior to 1905), and what if the CCF had constituted the government of such a province in the decade following World War II, and what if the CCF's left populist and Fabian entrepreneurs had successfully diversified their activities and maintained public provincial ownership of the principal mineral resource industries? The economic history of postwar Canada would be substantially different. Or would it? Therein lie several potential exercises in the new quantitative economic history.

Economic Rent – Scarcity and Power

Economic rent – a fundamental concept of economic theory that we treated in a cavalier manner in our initial naive staple model – is central to an understanding of entrepreneurship by provincial governments. Economic rent can be defined as an excess income arising in any industry above that necessary to generate a normal return to the man-made capital and labour employed. Initially, let us distinguish between economic rent, on the one hand, and a normal return to capital and labour. It is beyond our scope to enter into the theory of capital and of the determination of the wage level, but it is worth culling two central ideas from the economic theory. The first is a pervasive theme of orthodox economics — declining marginal productivity. Since society has not reached a point of economic satiation (i.e. people want more than they have), all productive factors – labour, man-made capital goods, and natural resources – are scarce. To say the same thing another way, an additional unit of any factor will produce something of value and can command a positive price. However as any one factor becomes more abundant relative to all others, the marginal productivity of each additional unit of the factor in question must at some point decline. If, further, we assume the price paid per unit of each factor – wage rate per hour of labour, rate of profit per unit of capital – varies proportionately to the productivity of the marginal unit, then the factor price falls as it becomes relatively more abundant, rises as it becomes relatively more scarce. There are many problems with this intuitively appealing idea (especially in defining what is meant by a unit of capital), and while it may, if properly qualified, serve as a partial explanation, it must always be used in conjunction with the second idea – wage and profit levels vary as a function of the relative power of those classes owning capital and those classes selling their labour. The two ideas are not independent. For example, if the owners of capital have power, they will restrict entry into an industry creating a scarcity of capital and raising the rate of profit earned. A powerful union can have the same effect on wage rates.

Although the institutional details of each industry differ from every other, it is useful to consider as a benchmark a "normal" industry – with an average distribution of power between owners of capital and labour – and to consider the returns generated in such an hypothetical industry, as "normal" returns. In any industry in which the returns significantly exceed the normal, we shall refer to the excess as economic rent. Economic rent may accrue in industries which use essentially only labour and man-made capital goods, but it has a particular significance for staple industries based on the application of labour and capital to the exploitation of natural resources. In such industries the limits to the supply of a natural resource impose a further constraint – beyond that of the available supplies of capital and labour. The natural resource constraint may take the form of an immutably fixed God-given supply, as is more or less the case for agricultural land, or of a rising unit cost of additions to the resource supply.[16]

Like the theory of comparative advantage, the theory of economic rent applied to natural resources originated with Ricardo. Rent arises, argued Ricardo, "because land is not unlimited in quantity and uniform in quality. ... When in the progress of society, land of the second degree of fertility is taken into cultivation, rent immediately commences on that of the first quality, and the amount of that rent will depend on the difference in the quality of these two portions of land."[17]

The actual rent generated by a resource depends upon the goals of those with power under the existing institutional arrangements, a truth of which Ricardo was quite conscious. A major motivation in his advancing a theory of rent was to attack the political power of rural landlords who had succeeded in maintaining import restrictions on foreign grain.[18] On marginal land landlords can extract no rent, for implicit in the idea of the margin is that the productivity of such land is just sufficient to generate normal returns to capital and labour and any attempt to impose a rent would render it uneconomic to cultivate. On intramarginal land landlords can extract a rent equal to the difference between its productivity (in terms of output per unit of land to which is applied a fixed quantity of farm labour) and that of land on the margin. Import restrictions, Ricardo argued, increased the demand for domestic cereals, called into production land of ever lower productivity and thereby increased rents extracted on intramarginal land by those he described as "country gentlemen." In this theory landlords serve no useful purpose whatever. It is the tenant farmers who hire farm labour and organize production. The farmer's profit is the residual after paying all costs, plus rent. Since most costs – subsistence wages, seed, etc. – are assumed to rise proportionately to the rise of grain prices, farmers do not benefit from higher cereal prices, but instead find their profits squeezed by higher rents. Lower profits among farmers are transmitted throughout the economy via higher food prices and hence higher wage costs to manufacturers. The end result is the strangulation of Britain's dynamic manufacturing classes by parasitic "country gentlemen." The solution was to remove the barrier to foreign grain, thereby lowering demand for domestic cereals, lowering cereal prices and denying country gentlemen their ability to extract exorbitant rents. Ricardo's theory of rent was a central intellectual component to nineteenth century British free trade doctrines, and in particular to the Anti-Corn Law League which, in 1846, finally achieved total repeal of the Corn Laws.

Although they can be exhausted by improper use, fish from the sea, forests, and agricultural land are resources that can provide an indefinite flow of services. Other resources, such as oil, constitute stocks that are used up in the course of providing their services. The utilization of both "flow" and "stock" resources, but particularly the latter, entails expectations about the future. The margin which governs the potential of stock resources to generate rent is not the costs associated with the most expensive (i.e. least productive) reserves currently in use, but the costs of unused reserves that can reasonably be expected to be drawn into use in the future. Since we are discussing a hypothetical margin, the level of rent on currently exploited reserves will change as a function of expectations. If society optimistically expects that future technological progress and new discoveries will relieve the constraints posed by the known commercially exploitable reserves of key economic resources, the potential to command rent will remain low. Conversely if society subscribes to a neo-Malthusian theory that is a good deal less sanguine about the consequences of exponentially growing demand and a finite world, the level of resource rent will be much higher. As we discussed in Chapter Nine, the combination of lowered estimates of yet-to-be-discovered conventional oil reserves and higher estimates of the real costs of alternative energy sources is a necessary, although not sufficient, component in explaining oil price increases in the 1970s.

Where economic rent arises purely due to an artificial scarcity imposed by some powerful group within society, it is economically efficient to remove the restriction so that prices reflect only normal returns to capital and labour. That, it could be argued, is the appropriate policy for Saskatchewan potash where rent has arisen due to barriers to entry to a cartelized industry, not due to any scarcity of potash reserves. After 1972 fertilizer companies, acting as a cartel, used their market power to increase fertilizer prices and share in the rents accruing to farmers, or more generally to agribusiness, as a consequence of a strong international demand for cereals.

Economic efficiency should not, however, be analysed independently of income distribution and the relative power of different agents in the industry. By imposition of new taxes in 1974 and by nationalization since 1975 of one half of the productive capacity within the province, the Saskatchewan government moved in its turn to capture much of the rent that the fertilizer companies had captured from potash customers – farmers, most of them in the United States. Having become a major member and beneficiary of the North American potash cartel, the Saskatchewan government now has a large financial interest in sustaining the current potash price level, as opposed to expanding production to the point where rents vanish. To the extent the Saskatchewan government has transferred rent from excess profits in a producers' cartel to the provincial treasury, the income redistribution in the industry since 1974 has been in the direction of greater equality. To the extent high potash prices transfer income from American farmers to Saskatchewan, the equity implications are less clear, but inasmuch as the average Saskatchewan income is below that of the average fertilizer-buying American farmer again the redistribution is in the direction of equality.

While potash prices are unjustifiably high in terms of economic efficiency, there is a valid distribution argument, in the context of the North American market, that the ensuing rents are justified as a transfer to a region whose per capita income has traditionally been below the North American average. In overseas markets, however, customers are typically poorer than in Saskatchewan. Given the potential of intermediaries to garner any rent Saskatchewan sacrificed, it would be difficult for the province to conduct price discrimination in favour of overseas customers, but as it stands our argument serves as a rationale for Saskatchewan to avoid all responsibility for the negative income distribution effects of high fertilizer prices and yet reap very handsome rents. There are overseas markets in particular countries where, in conjunction with the United Nations Food and Agriculture Organization, the province could sell potash below current market prices with the assurance it was thereby transferring income to the ultimate consumer of cereals and not merely providing the potential for rents to be taken by intermediaries.

In the two examples discussed – Ricardo's "country gentlemen" and the potash cartel – scarcity is a function of market barriers reinforced by political power. However, where a resource scarcity is imposed by nature and not by man, efficient allocation of the scarce resource implies that its price include a rent component. The rent arising from optimal resource pricing has on occasion been called "user cost"[19] to suggest the opportunity cost in using today what cannot then be available tomorrow. In general, efficient resource utilization entails choosing, among the infinite available options, the optimal rate(s) of utilization over time that, subject to constraints such as size of reserves, maximize(s) some measure of net benefits. The appropriate technique for making such a choice is the calculus of variations which, unfortunately, can transform relatively simple expectations about the future into very complicated mathematics.

To illustrate the use of rent to determine the efficient intertemporal allocation of a scarce resource, consider the case of conventional oil. To date the world has consumed approximately 350 billion barrels. Known world conventional oil reserves and annual consumption are approximately 650 billion and 22 billion barrels respectively.[20] The estimation of reserves yet to be discovered is a particularly hazardous exercise. Most current estimates are in the order of one trillion barrels – implying ultimate recoverable world conventional oil reserves (past consumption, known reserves, plus yet undiscovered reserves) to be in the order of two trillion barrels. If annual growth of demand continued at the 6 per cent rate experienced in the 1960s, the ultimate recoverable reserves would be exhausted in thirty years. It appears, however, that slower economic growth, new higher oil prices, and conservation programs will at least halve the growth rate, to 3 per cent annually, in which case oil will be available for forty years. Some experts would challenge the above ultimate recoverable reserve estimate as too conservative. But even if we double it, to four trillion barrels, all conventional oil reserves will, with 3 per cent annual demand growth, still be exhausted in sixty years.[21] Given the uncertainty associated with all such calculations, society can no longer ignore the "margin" – the point of exhaustion of low-cost conventional oil and the cost of alternative energy sources, all of which are vastly more expensive.

The Organization of Petroleum Exporting Countries has restricted its production to force price to a level more or less equal to the costs (defined to include normal returns to capital and labour) of alternative energy sources. Such a policy is the solution to the monopolists' relatively simple goal of maximizing rents accruing from the resource. Since quantity demanded is relatively insensitive to price (i.e. a rise in price brings about a less than proportionate fall in demand), OPEC can increase total oil revenues and hence total rents by raising its per barrel take. The cost of energy alternatives imposes an upper limit on oil prices and per barrel taxes, for above that limit the demand for OPEC oil obviously vanishes. A monopolist's solution is not socially optimal but nor, we shall show, is a policy that prices oil on the basis of historical costs net of all rent. To the extent society uses price as a means of determining the efficient intertemporal allocation of remaining oil reserves, what is an optimal pricing policy?

Let us make a number of simplifying assumptions – willingness to pay is an adequate if imperfect measure of social benefits, the production costs of all conventional oil are equal and in real terms constant over time, social costs and benefits in different years can be compared by use of a time discount factor. Provided the price constraint imposed by the cost of alternative energy sources is not binding, an optimal pricing mechanism would, via the demand function for oil, allocate such that in all years during which conventional reserves last, the discounted net benefit of an additional barrel – price paid less production costs – is equal. A positive rate of time discount implies that society, in comparing net benefits accruing in different years, discounts them more heavily the later they accrue. Thus to satisfy the basic optimality condition that the *discounted* net benefit per additional barrel be equal for all years, it is necessary that the *undiscounted* net benefit, and hence price, rise over time. To price oil otherwise must be suboptimal because total welfare could be increased by adjusting prices to decrease consumption in years of low discounted net benefits and to increase it in years of high net benefits. Optimal pricing lowers consumption in the near future relative to what it would be under a regime of historical cost of production prices. Any barrel diverted from earlier to later use prolongs the period over which the conventional reserves are consumed, and postpones the need for expensive alternatives. To sell conventional oil at a cost of production price fails to give adequate weight to the interest of future consumers who are thereby forced to resort to expensive alternatives earlier than is optimal.

In our example there is an upper constraint on price (equivalent to a lower constraint on conventional oil production) set by the cost of alternatives, say $15 (in 1977 dollars) for the amount of energy contained in a barrel of oil. The optimal solution entails rents being charged in all years, the price of conventional oil rising over a number of years to $15 per barrel, and after the constraint becomes binding, the last remaining reserves being sold at that price. The optimal price and its rate of increase at any time depend upon the cost of alternatives, the rate of discount, the nature of the demand function, the quantity of remaining conventional reserves and associated production costs.

Changed expectations with respect to the size of conventional reserves yet to be discovered and with respect to costs of alternative energy sources have both served to increase the optimal level of rents and prices required to assure efficient intertemporal allocation of remaining conventional oil. The higher is estimated to be the cost of alternative energy sources, the more valuable are the remaining low-cost reserves that delay the need to incur the costs of alternatives, and the higher should be the price charged per barrel. The lower are estimated to be the ultimate recoverable conventional reserves, the sooner the date of switchover to alternatives and the higher should be the current price to assure optimal allocation. Only if conventional reserves are considered inexhaustible are no rents warranted and price should equal cost of production. Unfortunately such expectations are completely unrealistic.

As with the discussion of potash, the issue of efficient pricing should not be divorced from that of income distribution. Let us restrict ourselves to the issues posed within Canada. Although Canada has become a net importer since 1975, the country enjoys a high degree of self-sufficiency in oil and therefore most income redistribution effects of higher prices post-1973 are transfers within the country. (In addition to the international transfer via higher prices on net oil imports, the high degree of foreign ownership in the oil industry creates potentially sizeable international income transfers via repatriated dividends.) Opponents of higher prices have argued that any conservation benefits, in terms of a more efficient intertemporal allocation of domestic reserves and reduced imports, are more than offset by regressive distribution effects. How valid is such a critique? Initially it is worth noting that Canadian oil prices have rarely risen, from 1973 to 1979, above three quarters of the world level.[22]

On the supply side higher prices increase the income of those engaged in the industry, including the governments of producing provinces as landlords collecting royalties on the oil in place. Implicit in the critique is that higher prices are a cause of excessive increases in profits within the industry, but the power of the oil industry to earn excess profits is only related to oil prices to the extent that prices determine industry profitability independently of the tax and royalty structure. While the Canadian oil industry has increased its after-tax rate of return on capital since 1972,[23] there is little reason to believe that in the current political environment a regime of lower prices would have sufficed to prevent the industry from realizing an increase. The major income transfer attributable to higher domestic prices has been a regional transfer from consumers in oil-importing provinces to the treasuries of the oil-exporting provinces and, to a lesser extent, to Ottawa. Consumers in the oil-exporting provinces (Saskatchewan and Alberta) have been largely compensated for the effects of higher prices by a combination of lower taxes and increased provincial government services. Since per capita income in the oil-exporting provinces is above the national average in the case of Alberta and close to it for Saskatchewan, the regional transfer has augmented the regional inequality of income distribution. The distribution effects within the oil-exporting provinces have not of course been particularly egalitarian, but there is no reason to suggest it is worse than the internal distribution effects that would obtain within the oil-importing provinces were the price now to be lowered. Furthermore, provincial ownership of resources and the rights of the provinces to the royalties therefrom are sufficiently important constitutional provisions that most provincial governments are not prepared to advocate lower prices, which could only come into effect by federal fiat, because such an exercise of federal power entails too serious an erosion of provincial jurisdiction. Thus on the supply side there exists a distribution argument against higher prices, but it is not compellng.

On the demand side higher prices affect income distribution if the proportion of income spent by individuals on energy varies significantly with the level of income. It does, and in such a fashion that the poor spend proportionately more on energy than do the rich. In conclusion, higher oil prices have increased the inequality of income distribution within Canada. However, rather than subsidize energy-intensive industry and consumption by inefficiently low prices, it is more rational to exploit the conservation effect of higher prices and insist that part of the rent garnered, both by the provinces and Ottawa, be used to offset the regressive distribution effects.

Conclusion

The aggregate level of rents in a staple industry depends first upon the extent of the natural resources provided by nature, second upon the institutional arrangements under which the staple is developed, third upon the goals pursued and expectations made by the claimants with power under the given institutional arrangements, and finally upon the outcome of bargaining. Power to determine the rate of development, or whether it occurs at all, is divided among the claimants over rent. Even if all agree that one particular sequence of development will maximize expected aggregate rents (which abstracts from problems of divergent expectations among claimants) there is no reason that sequence of development will necessarily be chosen. There is a potential for mutually advantageous bargaining but also, as the history of the prairies has demonstrated, a potential for much conflict. Originally we assumed that economic rent in a staple industry accrues to the owners of natural resources employed, but in practice the claimants also comprise those who possess necessary capital and technology, those who work in the industry, and consumers of the staple with an interest in reducing rent by lowering price.

Having come this far, we must leave economics for politics if we are to say anything about the outcome of bargaining. A sine qua non for a government to capture rent and other benefits is that its leaders be ideologically oriented to take entrepreneurial risk – be prepared to reject a low level of rent available with certainty and bargain for a higher level that may prompt prospective investors to retaliate, be prepared to invest public funds if the price of private investment is too high, be prepared to sacrifice immediate for probable but uncertain future benefits. The ideological proscription against public entrepreneurship by the Alberta government under Social Credit, and the Saskatchewan government under the later CCF and the Liberals, limited the ability of those governments to garner economic rent or linked developments from their respective mineral staples.

If the will to bargain is necessary, equally important to the success of any government strategy are the decisions of relevant classes and interest groups to grant or withhold support. In the 1960s the federal claim to increased resource rents via the Carter Commission tax reform proposals failed due to the diffuse nature of support for reform and the well-focused lobbying of the mining lobby, abetted by provincial governments of the day. The entrenched opposition of the Saskatchewan business community to the CCF-NDP, and its willingness at various stages to ally itself with external capitalists, have vitiated the ability of successive CCF and NDP governments to capture resource rents or to invest publicly in the provincial resource sector. Conversely the quasi-corporatist unanimity of support by indigenous classes given to the Alberta Conservatives has certainly contributed to the latter's success.

In conclusion, the broad pattern of development in postwar Saskatchewan and Alberta traced in the pages of this book can be summarized as a movement away from dependent regional capitalism. The transition from the passive rentier phase of development in the 1940s and 1950s to the interventionist developmental strategies of the 1970s has not however occurred via a shift in the regional economic base from primary staple industries to secondary manufacturing activities. Rather, the break with rentier traditions has occurred when provincial governments have determined to exploit the region's comparative advantage in mineral staples, and have mobilized the requisite domestic entrepreneurial skills to capture the potential benefits from oil, gas and potash development. Where prairie governments diverted their scarce entrepreneurial abilities into the chimerical strategy of implanting secondary manufacturing, they failed and paid a political price for failure; by contrast, they have succeeded by and large in the 1970s where they have exploited favourable market conditions in their resource industries and have concentrated their bargaining power in order to maximize the provincial share of rents and of closely linked industries. While we advance no claims of universality for our conclusions, our study of prairie oil, gas and potash suggests that the initial asymmetries and disadvantages which are so often a feature of resource development can, given time and under certain conditions, be overcome. Any a priori presumption against staples is suspect. Within the traditions and norms of North American capitalism, the choice of a staple-led strategy of development may well be the most rational course – always provided (and it is admittedly no small proviso) local entrepreneurial initiative and skills are available to exploit changing markets and to maximize the potential benefits that inhere in such development.

If the hard choices of prairie development necessarily occur within the limits of a staple-dependent region, then the strength of regional entrepreneurship and the distribution of political power have been the decisive factors in determining how – and for whose benefit – the staples are developed. The source of such entrepreneurship and power thus cannot be a matter for indifference. As in so many other periods of Canadian history, in the postwar development of the prairies it has been the state which has assumed the leading role in charting and implementing economic strategy: more specifically, the provincial state. Since the Second World War the central problem of development in Saskatchewan and Alberta has been whether or not the governments of these provinces could, with the passage of years and the appearance of a favourable political climate, mobilize the requisite will, expertise, and power to break with their inglorious rentier traditions. In turn, their ability to do this has depended crucially upon the outcome of political debates and conflicts. If the economics of the prairie region determined the boundaries of such debates, politics nonetheless mattered. The primary source of the entrepreneurial initiative and of the changes which have overtaken prairie capitalism since the opening of the new postwar mineral staples has been public, not private. In the final analysis it has been the ideas of politicians and the actions of governments that mattered most of all.

Notes

1. G.W. Bertram, "Economic Growth in Canadian Industry, 1870-1915: The Staple Model," reprinted in W.T. Easterbrook and M.H. Watkins (eds.), *Approaches to Canadian Economic History* (Toronto: McClelland and Stewart, 1967), 75.
2. "Value added" in any industry refers to the difference between the value of goods and services produced and the cost of intermediate goods and services purchased from other industries. It provides a measure of the returns to resources, labour and capital engaged in the industry, net of income accruing to intermediate industries.
3. See A.O. Hirschman, *The Strategy of Economic Development* (New Haven: Yale University Press, 1958), esp. chap. 6.
4. W.A. Mackintosh, *The Economic Background of Dominion-Provincial Relations*, Appendix III of the *Royal Commission Report on Dominion-Provincial Relations*, edited by J.H. Dales (Toronto: McClelland and Stewart, 1964), 13.
5. Good examples of the merging of the staple tradition with development economics are M.H. Watkins, "A Staple Theory of Economic Growth," reprinted in Easterbrook and Watkins, *op. cit.*, 49-73; G.K. Helleiner, *International Trade and Economic Development* (London: Penguin, 1972). In recent years Watkins has become increasingly critical of the consequences of staple development. Cf. M.H. Watkins, "The Staple Theory Revisited," *Journal of Canadian Studies*, XII, 5 (1977), 83-95.
6. See W. Elkan, *An Introduction to Development Economics* (London: Penguin, 1973), 45 ff.
7. R.T. Naylor, *The History of Canadian Business 1867-1914* (Toronto: James Lorimer, 1975), I, 3-4.
8. *Ibid.*, II, 283.
9. E.J. Chambers and D.F. Gordon, "Primary Products and Economic Growth: An Empirical Measurement," *Journal of Political Economy*, LXXIV, 4 (1966), 317.
10. See G.W. Bertram, "The Relevance of the Wheat Boom in Canadian Economic Growth," *Canadian Journal of Economics*, VI, 4 (1973), 545-66. Bertram calculates similar estimates, in the order of 20 per cent, for the contribution of the wheat boom to per capita income growth, for the two decades—1901-11 and 1911-21.
11. For a good discussion of the conceptual problems in assessing the impact of freight rates see K.H. Norrie, "The National Policy and Prairie Economic Discrimination, 1870-1930," *op. cit.*
12. J.H. Dales, et al., "Primary Products and Economic Growth: A Com-

ment," *Journal of Political Economy*, LXXV, 6 (1967), 876-80.

13. F. Lewis, "The Canadian Wheat Boom and Per Capita Income: New Estimates," *Journal of Political Economy*, LXXXIII, 6 (1975), 1249-57.

14. For a good discussion of the evolution of prairie farming practices, entrepreneurial strategies, and political attitudes see J.W. Bennett, *Northern Plainsmen: Adaptive Strategy and Prairie Life* (Chicago: Aldine Publishing Company, 1969).

15. Growth rates are calculated from data in *Estimates of Employment by Province and Industry*, 72-008 (Ottawa: Statistics Canada), January 1971, 26; April 1978, 22.

16. For an introduction to the subject of resource economics see A. Scott, *Natural Resources: The Economics of Conservation* (Toronto: McClelland and Stewart, 1973), esp. chap. 1. For a more advanced treatment see O.C. Herfindahl and A.K. Kneese, *Economic Theory of Natural Resources* (Columbus: Charles Merrill, 1974), esp. chap. 4.

17. D. Ricardo, *Principles of Political Economy and Taxation*, edited by R.M. Hartwell (London: Penguin, 1971), 93-94.

18. *Ibid.*, chap. 22.

19. Scott, *Natural Resources, op. cit.*, 7 ff.

20. Figures cited are drawn from A.R. Flower, "World Oil Production," *Scientific American*, CCXXXVIII, 3 (March 1978), 42-49; G. Foley, *The Energy Question* (London: Penguin, 1976), 132-46; *World Oil*, August 15, 1977, 43-48.

21. Under these simple assumptions, the number of years to exhaust oil reserves is implicitly defined by the equation giving the sum of terms of a geometric series.

22. Our discussion of the income distribution consequences of oil price increases draws considerably upon E.R. Berndt, "Canadian Energy Demand and Economic Growth," in G.C. Watkins and M. Walker (eds.), *Oil in the Seventies* (Vancouver: The Fraser Institute, 1977), 72-80.

23. According to Statistics Canada data the after-tax rate of return in the Canadian mineral fuels industry (after-tax income plus deferred taxes and long term interest, the sum divided by invested capital) increased from 8.2 per cent in 1972 to 14.9 per cent in 1975. Data reproduced in G.D. Quirin and B.A. Kalymon, "The Financial Position of the Petroleum Industry," in Watkins and Walker, *ibid.*, Table 1, 217. Quirin and Kalymon, it should be noted, argue that the rate of return is insufficient to justify the risks inherent in new energy projects, and urge reductions in tax and royalty levels.

Index

107; gasoline outlets and refinery, 75; and populism, 22, 23, 196; *see also* Wheat Pools

Co-optation of populist governments by business elites, 251

Cowley, Elwood, 259

CPR v. Attorney General for Saskatchewan, 285

Cripps, Sir Stafford, 137, 138

Crown Corporation Act (Saskatchewan, 1945), 117

Crown corporations: Alberta's policy towards, 216; CCF position on (1944), 103; for oil development, 90, 181, 183-84, 238-39; Manning's opposition to, 67, 68; Thatcher's criticisms of, 198, 199; *see also* Business ventures of CCF government; Potash Corporation of Saskatchewan

Crown reserves (Alberta), 89-90

Crown reserves (Saskatchewan); farm-out agreements for, 184-86; Oil Policy Committee recommendations on, 183-83, 184; Planning Board recommendations, 179-82, 186, 187

Debt, provincial (Alberta), 18-19, 78

Debt, provincial (Saskatchewan), 128

Demand cycle for potash, 203, 204, 259

Democracy in Alberta, 149-53 *passim*

Demographic impact of petroleum development in Alberta, 162

Dependency and foreign investment in staples, viii, 8-9, 10, 11, 172; *see also* Bargaining cycle between governments and foreign resource companies

Depression, 32, 99, 155

Deterding, Sir Henri, 52

Development strategies for natural resources, 10, 11, 72, 89-90

Dinning Natural Gas Commission, 63

Diversification, economic: in Alberta, 151-52, 155, 156, 159-62, 166, 168, 169, 215, 224, 233, 235-37, 241, 242, 246; and development of new staples, 104-6, 196; prairie need for, 9, 10, 11, 99; in Saskatchewan, 99-100, 101-6, 132, 133; and social ownership, 101-4

Dome Petroleum, 244, 245

Dominion-Provincial Relations, Royal Commission on (Rowell-Sirois), 6, 19

Douglas, Major C.H., 32-33

Douglas, T.C., ix, 140, 251; creates Economic Advisory and Planning Board, 129, 130; oratorical style, 98-99, 198; as Premier, 106, 109, 132; and resource development, 137, 177, 185, 193

Dow Chemical of Canada, 244

East-west transfer of wealth and power, 11, 173-74, 216, 222-23, 234, 237, 243, 247

Economic Advisory and Planning Board (Saskatchewan), 10, 129-33, 135, 138-42 *passim*, 192; campaign over disposition of crown reserves, 178-82, 186, 187

Economic Advisory Committee, Saskatchewan (1944-45), 108-9

Economic development strategy, Alberta, 216, 217, 230-47

Economic diversification, *see* Diversification, economic

Economic hinterland, prairies as, 15

Economic planning: emphasis in Regina Manifesto, 94; *see also* Economic Advisory and Planning Board (Saskatchewan)

Economic waste, 296, 297, 298

Elections, Alberta: 1935, 33; 1940, 34; 1944, 35, 81; 1948, 82; 1952, 63, 66; 1967, 165; 1971, 148, 165-66; 1975, 166

Elections, federal: 1911, 17; 1921, 30; 1945, 36; 1949, 144; 1958, 37; 1963, 200

Elections, Saskatchewan: 1921, 30-

entrepreneurship, 28

Independent Association of Alberta, 234

Independent oil companies (Alberta), 157, 158, 159, 224; and conservation efforts in Turner Valley, 56-57

Indians, 20

Industrial democracy, 142

Industrialization, petroleum-linked, *see* Petroleum-linked industrialization

International Minerals and Chemical (IMC), 192-93, 197, 201, 271, 272

Interstate Oil Compact (U.S.), 51, 53

Johnson, Al, 143

Keynes, J.M., 33

Khaddafi, Colonel, 218, 221

Kierans, Eric, 260-61

King, Carlyle, 131

King, Mackenzie, 30, 35, 36

Land Bank Commission, advocated by Saskatchewan NDP, 253

Lang, Otto, 271

Laskin, Bora, 4, 298, 299, 300

Laxer, James, 254

League for Social Reconstruction, 94-97, 100, 109

"Leakages," 306, 307

Leduc oil discovery (1947), 19, 35, 43-45, 58

Left, Anglo-Canadian: centralism of, 5, 6, 7

Left, Francophone: attitude to federalism, 7

Left populism, 22, 23

Leitch, Merv, 238

Levitt, Kari, 4

Lewis, David, 36

Liberal Party of Alberta, 18

Liberal Party of Saskatchewan, 199

Libya, 218

Linkages, 306, 307; effects of oil and gas development, 160-61; and

wheat, 310

Lipset, S.M., 21

Lloyd, Woodrow, 251, 252, 254, 255

Loram Company Ltd., 163

Lougheed, Edgar, 155, 162

Lougheed, Senator Sir James A., 17, 46, 152, 153-54

Lougheed, Peter, 61, 197, 216, 231, 250, 301; early career, 162-63; election victory (1971), 148-49, 165-66; family background, 153-155; re--election (1975), 166; reorganizes party, 164-65; wins provincial Conservative leadership, 164; work with Mannix group, 163-64

Macdonald, Sir John A., 5, 15, 281, 314

McGillivray Commission (1938), 56, 76-78, 80

Mackintosh, W.A., 307-8

Macpherson, C.B., 149-53 *passim*

Manitoba Grain Growers' Association, 29, 30

Manning, Ernest, 35, 100, 164, 165, 167; attitude to foreign investment, 84, 171; becomes Premier of Alberta, 34; natural resource policies, 57-59, 62, 64, 65-68 *passim*, 87; opposition to public ownership, 67, 82

Mannix group, 115, 163, 167

Mannix, Frederick C., 163-64

Manufacturing: in Alberta, 161, 233, 237; prairie cost disadvantages, 273, 306; primary *vs.* secondary, 305; *vs.* staple industries, 104-6, 307-19; ventures of CCF government in Saskatchewan, 105-6, 112, 116-17, 119, 120, 132, 133, 139-43 *passim*

Market demand prorationing, 50-51, 52, 158, 159, 239, 285; Alberta's system, 58, 59, 60; allocative process in, 51, 59, 60, 158; and economic rent, 59-60; inefficiency for managing scarce resources, 60; major oil companies and, 59, 60;

and oil prices, 59; opposition of independent oil companies to, 56; for potash, 204-5, 207-10 *passim*, 265; steps in, 51, 59; U.S. antitrust case against, 266-67

Martin, W.M., 30-31

Mathias, Philip, 4

Maximum permissible rate (MPR) of production, 51, 58, 60

Medicare, 109, 200

Mill, John Stuart, 285

Mineral Resources, Department of (Saskatchewan), 186, 192

Mineral Resources Act (Saskatchewan), 296, 298

Mineral rights, 156-57; alienation of, 110-11

Mineral tax (Alberta), 224

Mineral Taxation Act (Saskatchewan, 1944), 110-11, 285

Mines and Minerals Act (Alberta), 238

Mowat, Sir Oliver, 281-82

Multiplier effect, 306

National Energy Board, 228, 229, 235

Nationalization of potash resources (Saskatchewan), 263, 267-74, 294, 322

National Oil Policy (NOP), 168-69

National Policy, 9, 15, 281, 314, 317

National Progressive Party, 30, 31

Natural gas, 10, 11, 45; pricing policy in Alberta, 228-30; question of exporting from Alberta, 61-68, 82, 158, 228, 229, 246; state monopoly in distribution of (Saskatchewan), 114-15

Natural Resource Revenue Plan (Alberta), 224, 225

Naylor, Tom, 310-11

Nelles, H.V., 3-4

Net royalty lease, 186

New Democratic Party (NDP): founded (1961), 37; policies as government of Saskatchewan since 1971, 252, 255-75

New Mexico potash lobby, 205-7 *passim*, 209, 295

Nickle, Carl, 185

Non-agricultural staples, 132, 133

Nonpartisan League, 25-28, 196, 198

Noranda Mines Ltd., 195, 295, 297

North, development of, 18, 118-21, 133

Oil, 10, 11, 19; boom, Alberta, 44-45; exploration for, in Saskatchewan, 135-36, 178; fugacity of, 48, 49; impact on economic diversification and urbanization in Alberta, 159-62, 166; physical properties necessitate state intervention, 47, 48; regulatory structure for, *see* Regulation, governmental; rule of capture for, 49

Oil and Gas Conservation Act (Saskatchewan, 1952), 182

Oil and Gas Conservation Board (Alberta), 55-58 *passim*, 65, 78; functions of, 60-61; *see also* Energy Resources Conservation Board (Alberta)

Oil companies, 45, 52, 216, 219, 220, 224, 264; return to Saskatchewan in 1949, 178; strike (1974), 227

Oil crisis, 172, 217-23, 237

Oil export tax, federal, 225, 226, 239

Oil fields (Alberta), 45

Oil industry, 134, 156; *see also* Oil regulation

Oil Policy Committee (Saskatchewan), 182-83

Oil policy in Alberta, 78-91, 156-59, 168-74 *passim*, 223-28, 230-47

Oil policy in Saskatchewan, 10, 134-36, 177-87, 196, 258, 259; Planning Board report on (1949), 179-82, 186, 187

Oil prices, 102, 239, 323-26; Canadian government freeze on, 225, 288-89; and prorationing, 59; Texas Gulf pricing structure, 76-78

Prudhoe Bay oil field, 169, 221, 223, 231
Public investment, 73; *vs.* private investment, 100, 177-86 *passim*, 201; *see also* Crown corporations; Entrepreneurship, provincial
Public lands and resources: provincial ownership of, 15-16, 17, 18, 111, 156-57, 284; provincial control over, 282-87
Public ownership of the means of production, 100
Pulp mill (crown venture, Saskatchewan), 119-20

Rate of development, 87, 88, 89
Regina Manifesto, 6, 37, 93-94, 100
Regional economic development, *see* Development strategies
Regionalism: of Alberta, 173-74, 216, 232-34; constitutional basis of, 280-81; insensitivity of Anglo-Canadian left to, viii, 5, 6, 7
Regulation, governmental, of natural resources, 10, 38, 46-49; in Alberta (oil), 45-47, 54-61, 78-91, 224-26, 238-39; (gas), 61-68, 82; by Canadian government, 226, 239; and constitutional issues, *see* Constitutional position of provincial natural resources legislation; in Saskatchewan, 110-11, 190-92, 225, 259, 260, 287-90; in the U.S., 50-54, 85
Rent, economic: analysis of the concept, 319-26; bargaining surrounding distribution of, 73, 76, 77, 288, 326, 327; and CCF policies in Saskatchewan, 144, 177, 179-81 *passim*, 183, 184, 188, 317; defined, 20, 290, 306, 319; federal claim to, 261-62; and Lougheed government in Alberta, 223, 227, 239, 240-41; and NDP policies in Saskatchewan, 259, 261, 272, 273; and prorationing, 59-60; and provincial entrepreneurship, 159, 250, 260, 261, 286; and provincial resources ownership, 102, 261-62, 263, 267; and Social Credit policies in Alberta, 59-60, 80, 87-90 *passim*, 223; and "sowing the oil," 230, 231
Rentier approach to resource development, 11, 197, 327-28; of Alberta Social Credit government, 72, 91, 158, 159, 167, 170-71; costs of, 73-74; of Ottawa, 246; of Saskatchewan CCF government, 177, 209
Resource companies and governments, bargaining cycle between, 8-9, 10-11, 45, 72-75
Resource industry lobby, 262
Resources: provincial control of (Alberta), 237-38; constitutional division of powers over, 293
Ricardo, David, 320, 321
Right-of-Entry Act (Alberta), 157
Right populism, 22, 23, 80
Risk-aversion, governmental: 74, 89, 158; *see also* Rentier approach to resource development
Roosevelt, Franklin, 53
Roper, Elmer, 63
Rotstein, Abraham, 4
Royalite Oil Company, 47, 54, 57
Royalties: petroleum, *see* Oil royalty legislation overriding royalty system, 87, 90, 180, 181, 184; potash, 190-93
Royalties, provincial: eliminated as allowable income tax deduction, 226, 289
"Rule of capture," 49
Rupert's Land Act (1868), 14-15

Sarnia, 244, 245
Saskatchewan Government Insurance Office, 113
Saskatchewan Government Telephones, 113
Saskatchewan Grain Growers' Association, 31

338